Also in the Variorum Collected Studies Series:

HARRY A. MISKIMIN
Cash, Credit and Crisis in Europe, 1300–1600

ROBERT-HENRI BAUTIER
Sur l'histoire économique de la France médiévale: la route, le fleuve, la foire

ELIYAHU ASHTOR
East-West Trade in the Medieval Mediterranean

ELIYAHU ASHTOR
Studies on the Levantine Trade in the Middle Ages

PHILIP GRIERSON
Later Medieval Numismatics (11th–16th Centuries)

ROBERT S. LOPEZ
The Shape of Medieval Monetary History

FREDERIC C. LANE
Studies in Venetian Social and Economic History

JACQUES HEERS
Société et économie à Gênes (XIVe–XVe siècles)

ANGUS MACKAY
Society, Economy and Religion in Late Medieval Castile

C.R. BOXER
Dutch Merchants and Mariners in Asia, 1602–1795

C.R. BOXER
Portuguese Conquest and Commerce in Southern Asia, 1500–1750

C.R. BOXER
Portuguese Merchants and Missionaries in Feudal Japan, 1543–1640

Bullion Flows and Monetary Policies in England and the Low Countries, 1350–1500

Professor John H. Munro

John H. Munro

Bullion Flows and Monetary Policies in England and the Low Countries, 1350–1500

VARIORUM

Published by VARIORUM
Ashgate Publishing Limited
Gower House, Croft Road,
Hampshire GU11 3HR
Great Britain

Ashgate Publishing Company
Old Post Road
Brookfield, Vermont 05036
U S A

ISBN 0–86078–312–X

A CIP catalogue record for this book is available
from the British Library and the US Library of Congress.

Printed by Galliard (Printers) Ltd
Great Yarmouth, Norfolk
Great Britain

COLLECTED STUDIES SERIES CS355

1970-81

CONTENTS

This volume contains xvi + 312 pages

1984 also [illegible] vol. which has

PUBLISHER'S NOTE

The articles in this volume, as in all others in the Collected Studies Series, have not been given a new, continuous pagination. In order to avoid confusion, and to facilitate their use where these same studies have been referred to elsewhere, the original pagination has been maintained wherever possible.

Each article has been given a Roman number in order of appearance, as listed in the Contents. This number is repeated on each page and quoted in the index entries.

For my family

Jeanette, Robert and Valerie

INTRODUCTION

Anyone publishing essays in monetary history risks being called a monetarist. It has become unnecessarily a pejorative label that is hardly justified by an interest in the historical role of monetary changes and a belief that "money matters" in the economy. Furthermore, no modern "monetarist", economist or historian, would ignore real factors and make the money supply the sole determinant of long-term changes in price levels and economic activity. But one does not have to be a monetarist to challenge the predominant view that demographic forces, unaided by money, were responsible for price movements in medieval and early-modern Europe.

Most demographic models seeking to explain these secular price trends contain two serious and related fallacies. First, the most popular model confuses changes in relative prices with changes in the price level. With micro-economic analysis, it can readily explain why, with population growth and diminishing returns to agriculture, grain prices rose more than most other prices during these eras, but not why a composite index of all prices would rise. Second, even those models using price-indices neglect to observe that prices were then expressed in silver-based moneys-of-account that were tied to the currently circulating silver penny. Money may be ignored in a micro-economic model concerning a narrow segment of the economy, but not in a macro-economic model. Thus, one might unwisely seek to show, in a macro-economic model using these micro-economic techniques, that population growth shifted the aggregate-demand schedule up an increasingly inelastic aggregate-supply schedule, supposedly resulting in both increased total output Q_2 and a higher price level P_2. But this $P_2.Q_2$ would have meant a large increase in the silver-money value of that output and in the total money spent. Such models thus fail to explain these increases in money expenditures.[1]

If economic historians cannot ignore the role of money, some might still be considered monetarists when they resort to the Fisher Identity in the form $M.V \equiv P.T$, which lies behind the classical Quantity Theory of Money. By this theory, an exogenous increase in the stock of Money (M), wholly spent on Transactions (T), would ultimately lead to a proportional rise in the price-level P, if the transactions Velocity of money (V) and the volume of Transactions (T) were constants, with the economy at Full Employment, or if changes in V and T were proportional and independent of changes in M. But no economist or historian would accept all these rigid assumptions in analyzing any long-term changes in the economy.

Furthermore, even though $M.V \equiv P.T$ is still widely used, historians would profit from using one of its more modern, revised forms. Most economists prefer the equation $M = k.P.y$, based upon the Cambridge Cash Balances function about the demand for money, which differs from the classic Fisher Identity in two respects. First, while M and P retain their original meanings, unmeasurable T has been replaced with quantifiable y, which represents *real* Net National Income (NNI), in constant prices, so that $P.y =$ the value of NNI in nominal or current money-of-account prices. Secondly, the term k represents the proportion of NNI (P.y) that the public desires to hold in cash balances (M), with a composite demand for money in terms of transactions, precautionary, and speculative motives, involving some inverse relationship to real interest rates. More simply, Cambridge k is the ratio of money stock to national income (NNI); and it is also mathematically the reciprocal of V (1/V) as the income-velocity of money. Thus we may rewrite the Fisher Identity as the equation $M.V = P.y$: conceptually less satisfactory, but, for many, more readily understandable than the Cambridge equation $M = k.P.y$.

These new equations provide historians with very valuable tools in demonstrating the importance of monetary factors and their symbiotic relationships with real factors in explaining both secular price trends and economic development. Neither has to be taken strictly as a quantity theory of money nor is either unicausal or unilinear in any causation. Thus, supposing that the money supply was essentially endogenous, one may argue that the various economic processes increasing y (NNI) – e.g. population growth, technological changes, and investment – induced the requisite monetary expansion: in M or in V or in both together. If, however, inflation also occurred, historians must then explain why the monetary expansion was greater than the rise in real output and real incomes: why, with ΔP, $\Delta(M.V) > \Delta y$. Conversely, with both depopulation and deflation, they must explain why the contraction in M.V – in M or V or both – was evidently greater than the fall in y (NNI).

What roles did demographic, institutional, technological and other real factors play in altering both these variables, M and V, in late-medieval and early-modern Europe? Were there any autonomous or exogenous changes in M that contributed to changes in y (NNI), V (k), and ultimately, by some combination of these variables, in P? Did changes in P then induce further changes in y and in the other variables? How did coinage debasements and credit innovations affect these monetary changes? What were the economic and social consequences of both monetary changes and changes in the price level: of inflation and deflation?

Answers to some of these questions may be found in this collection of essays on the monetary history of England and the Low Countries during the fourteenth and fifteenth centuries. This was an era of severe depopulations, of drastic price swings, and ultimately of monetary contraction with pronounced deflationary trends, whose features are especially well documented in these two regions, which boast an unusually complete series of mint, monetary, and price data. But if questions of monetary contraction and deflation have become major concerns in my later writings, the contrary was true of my earliest publications: those on coinage debasements, in which I rejected views that they were undertaken to remedy any perceived scarcity of money. Focusing on the Burgundian Low Countries from 1384 to 1477, I argued instead that the real motives for aggressive debasements (as opposed to purely defensive reactions) were fiscal rather than monetary: to acquire greater seignorage revenues from the mints in financing warfare. Furthermore, captivated by the writings of Michael Postan, I could not then believe that later-medieval Europe, so heavily depopulated, with a much reduced demand for money, would have suffered from a relative scarcity of money, especially with periodic infusions of new money from both coin debasements and credit innovations.

Subsequent research from archival and printed sources, however, led me to collect and process mint-output, monetary, price and wage data over a far broader time-span: in England, from 1235 to 1600; and in the Low Countries, from 1334 also to 1600. While my views on mint policies, debasements, and population remain basically the same, those concerning broader questions of monetary history have quite markedly changed. The evidence convinced me that England, the Low Countries, and possibly other parts of western Europe did suffer a century of monetary contraction, from about the 1370s to the 1470s, with prolonged periods of deflation, spasmodically interrupted by bouts of war- and debasement-induced inflations, often providing a cure worse than the disease.

Although I believe that monetary contraction ultimately became greater than the extent of depopulation, I must still plead agnosticism about the causes. Any explanation must still involve the traditional arguments concerning a diminishing stock of precious metals and thus a reduction in M: from circulation losses, depletions of European mines, and balance of payments deficits with the East. The evidence, however, does not convince me that Europe experienced a constantly growing bullion outflow. It leads me to a supplementary explanation: changes in the income-velocity of money and thus in propensities to hoard, including a greater diversion of precious metals into artistic uses.

In a somewhat similar vein, Harry Miskimin, Jack Goldstone, and Peter Lindert have recently produced demographically-based Velocity models to explain inflation in the sixteenth-century Price Revolution: involving greater population densities, more rapid urbanization, more complicated financial and commercial networks, expansions in credit, and diminished cash balances with higher living costs and a changing ratio between producers and dependents.[2] Although many might consider these models to be anti-monetarist, Velocity, despite the importance of such real factors, remains a monetary variable. Furthermore, since the money supply clearly did expand during the Price Revolution, and since both nominal and real interest rates evidently fell, these models implicitly contradict some traditional Keynesian assumptions: that Velocity varies inversely with the money supply and directly with interest rates.

Their models also suggest that a demographically-induced fall in Velocity was similarly responsible for the prolonged deflation that followed the Price Revolution, from the 1650s to the 1740s. The specific mechanics of this "demographic-deflation" model remain unclear, and are even less clear if applied to the convulsive fourteenth century. In fact, with the Black Death and catastrophic depopulation, by perhaps 40% from 1348 to the 1370s, western Europe experienced not deflation but soaring inflation: because y contracted so much more rapidly than M.V; and very likely also because V increased as so many fortunate survivors rapidly exhausted inherited cash balances in hedonistic spending sprees. In the ensuing sharp deflation from the 1370s, when livestock and industrial prices fell with grain prices, if not proportionately, Velocity evidently did decline for reasons suggested in my essays: especially those concerning hoarding. But those reasons do not include any de-urbanization or retrogression in commercial networks and credit institutions.

Regrettably this collection cannot include an earlier but too lengthy and statistically complex essay on price changes from 1300 to 1500; nor does it contain recent essays on monetary and price changes and the role of credit extended into the 1550s.[3] Subsequent publications will elaborate arguments in the final essay VIII concerning the vital question: why did money and deflation matter for the real economy? My brief answer now is that various institutional impediments and binding contracts prevented a fall or proportional decline in interest rates and many nominal wages, so that deflation increased these real cost burdens in the late-medieval economy, over surprisingly long periods of time.

Finally, a few words about the mint-accounts, which constitute such an important source of evidence for the essays in this volume. I have taken some pains, especially in articles VI and VIII, to explain why mint-outputs cannot be used as short-term proxies for the money-supply; and, furthermore, why the effects of debasement upon both money stocks and prices cannot be precisely determined. But, even as Platonic shadows of reality, the mint-accounts can serve as important indicators of the direction, nature, and longer-term extent of monetary changes. The mint accounts given in article I are based upon my doctoral research; and subsequent research produced a broader range of accounts, both spatially and temporally. Mr. T. H. Lloyd also discovered and published some new Calais mint data for 1387–1403, which were incorporated into essay IV; but a subsequent examination of his source revealed errors that were corrected in V and subsequent essays, which made some further changes and reduced the hypothetical range of missing accounts. As noted in VIII, I had been incorrectly accused of missing a few fifteenth-century Burgundian mint accounts, which, in fact, had always been included in my coinage statistics. There do remain, however, some missing accounts for both countries: but more of them are from the fourteenth-century than the fifteenth; and if ever found they may possibly widen, not narrow, the disparity between these two centuries' monetary histories.

JOHN H. MUNRO

Toronto,
15 July, 1991

NOTES

[1] If there had been no change in monetary circulation – in the stock and/or flow of money – a demographically-produced growth in total output would have depressed the price level, i.e. resulted in deflation. Furthermore, if the numeraire or money-of-account was expressed instead in bushels of wheat, whose relative and real price indisputably rose with population during these eras, then the wheat-based price-index P would also have fallen – since most commodities would have been exchanged for fewer bushels of wheat; the result again would have been deflation. Money does matter.

[2] Harry Miskimin, "Population Growth and the Price Revolution in England," *Journal of European Economic History*, 4 (1975), 179–85; Jack A. Goldstone, "Urbanization and Inflation: Lessons from the English Price Revolution of the Sixteenth and Seventeenth Centuries," *American Journal of Sociology*, 89 (1984), 1122–60; and Peter Lindert, "English Population, Wages, and Prices: 1541–1913," *Journal of Interdisciplinary History*, 15 (Spring 1985), 609–34, especially pp.618–29. But see also criticisms in Michael Bordo, "Explorations in Monetary History: A Survey of the Literature," *Explorations in Economic History*, 23 (1986), pp.373–74.

[3] John H. Munro, "Mint Outputs, Money, and Prices in Late-Medieval England and the Low Countries," in Eddy Van Cauwenberghe and Franz Irsigler, eds., *Münzprägung, Geldumlauf und Wechselkurse/Minting, Monetary Circulation and Exchange Rates: Akten des 8th International Economic History Congress (Trierer Historische Forschungen*, Vol. 7), Trier: University Press, 1984, pp.31–122; J. H. Munro, "Die Anfänge der Übertragbarkeit: einige Kreditinnovationen im englisch-flämischen Handel des Spätmittelalters (1360–1540)," in Michael North, ed., *Kredit im spätmittelalterlichen und frühneuzeitlichen Europa* (*Quellen und Darstellungen zur Hansischen Geschichte*, vol. 37), Cologne-Vienna: Böhlau Verlag, 1991, pp.39–69; J. H. Munro, "The International Law Merchant and the Evolution of Negotiable Credit in Late-Medieval England and the Low Countries," in Dino Puncuh and Giuseppe Felloni, eds., *Banchi pubblici, banchi privati e monti di pietà nell'Europa preindustriale: amministrazione, tecniche operative e ruoli economici*, Genoa: Società Ligure di Storia Patria, 1991, pp.29–62; and J. H. Munro, "The Central European Mining Boom, Mint Outputs, and Prices in the Low Countries and England, 1450–1550," in Eddy Van Cauwenberghe, ed., *Money, Coins, and Commerce: Essays in the Monetary History of Asia and Europe from Antiquity to Modern Times*, Leuven: Leuven University Press, forthcoming.

ACKNOWLEDGEMENTS

I would like to express my sincere gratitude to all of the following: the editors of *The English Historical Review* and the Longman Group UK Ltd for their gracious permission to reproduce Article I; the editors of *Revue belge du numismatique et de sigillographie* and the Société Royale de Numismatique de Belgique for similar permission to reproduce Article II; the editors of *Revue belge de philologie et d'histoire/Belgisch tijdschrift voor filologie en geschiedenis* for like permission to reproduce Article III; Yale University Press for its kind permission to reproduce Essay IV; the editors of *The Numismatic Chronicle* and the Royal Numismatic Society of Great Britain for their courtesy in permitting reproduction of Article V; Carolina Academic Press for its gracious permission to reproduce Essay VI; Presses Universitaires de Lille, France, for similar permission to reproduce Essay VII; and finally the editors of *Explorations in Economic History* and Academic Press (Orlando, Florida) for their courtesy in permitting reproduction of Article VIII.

I

An economic aspect of the collapse of the Anglo-Burgundian alliance, 1428-1442[1]

THE duke of Burgundy's *volte-face* by the Treaty of Arras (1435), which shattered his alliance with England, has rightly been considered one of the most decisive events of fifteenth-century European history. The consequences of that treaty fostered a more clearly separate and national development of England, the Low Countries, and France: it helped to doom the English to defeat in the Hundred Years' War and to the almost total loss of their French territories, which had engaged their energies for so long; it encouraged a virtually independent Burgundy to concentrate its growing power in the Low Countries; and thus it freed the French to develop a more unified, viable national monarchy. Not surprisingly, many historians have closely examined the military and political circumstances that encouraged Duke Philip the Good of Burgundy to desert the English at Arras and make his peace with Charles VII of France.[2] But no one has yet devoted as much attention to the economic conflicts between England and Burgundy, which also helped to undermine their fourteen-year-old alliance.

Economic discord resulted in part from Burgundy's territorial expansion in the Low Countries, an area long commercially vital to England. Already possessing Flanders, the richest of the principalities, Duke Philip the Good in the 1420s acquired the neighbouring counties of Namur, Holland, Zealand, Hainault, and finally the duchy of Brabant-Limburg. In uniting these lands under his rule, Philip the Good had to face a growing problem of conflicting economic interests in their commercial ties with England. The urban draperies, the most important industry in the Burgundian Lowlands, were then experiencing a crisis from their almost total dependence upon English wools, which were Europe's finest. Because of the industry's 'inelastic' demand, the wool export trade had become

1. I wish to thank Professor Harvey Dyck (University of Toronto) and Professor Peter Krosby (S.U.N.Y. at Albany) for their generous assistance and advice in the revision of this article.

2. Paul Bonenfant, *Philippe le Bon* (Brussels, 1944), pp. 33–70; J. G. Dickinson, *The Congress of Arras, 1435: a Study in Medieval Diplomacy* (Oxford, 1955), pp. 163 ff.; E. F. Jacob, *The Fifteenth Century, 1399–1485* (Oxford, 1961), pp. 260–4; C. A. J. Armstrong, 'La double monarchie France-Angleterre et la maison de Bourgogne, 1420–1435: le déclin d'une alliance', *Annales de Bourgogne*, xxxvii (1965), 81–112; Marie-Rose Thielemans, *Bourgogne et Angleterre: relations politiques et économiques entre les Pays-Bas Bourguignons et l'Angleterre, 1435–1467* (Brussels, 1966), pp. 49–61.

burdened with increasingly heavy taxes, which furnished the English crown with its major source of revenue.[1] By the late fourteenth century, the wool customs had risen to about 35 per cent *ad valorem* and so raised the production costs of the Lowlands' cloth industry that its sales dropped sharply in the depressed European markets of this period.[2] Moreover, the Lowlands' draperies suffered further losses of long-held markets to England's rapidly expanding cloth industry; for English cloth enjoyed a significant advantage in being produced from the same fine wools tax-free, while bearing only a minimal 2 per cent export duty. Worst of all, many towns and mercantile groups in the Lowlands welcomed this growing flood of English woollens.

This ruinous English competition in the cloth trade was a problem not easily resolved. To be sure, the powerful Flemish drapery towns of Ypres, Ghent and Bruges had succeeded in having English cloth permanently banned from their county by the mid-fourteenth century.[3] But denying this cloth the great emporium of Bruges served only to divert the growing English cloth trade to various Dutch and Brabantine ports, chiefly Middelburg and later Antwerp. By the late 1420s, the Dutch and Brabantine drapery towns had become so concerned about the volume of English cloth imports that they demanded for themselves the same protection as the Flemish had long enjoyed.[4] In July 1428, Philip the Good granted the Dutch leaders' demands in an ordinance prohibiting English cloth imports into Holland and Zealand[5]; the next month, his cousin Duke Philip of St. Pol imposed a similar ban for Brabant.[6] This protectionist policy soon, however, encountered bitter opposition: the non-drapery towns of Middelburg and Antwerp and also the large Dutch mercantile marine found English cloth essential for their commerce. Antwerp and various Dutch towns, moreover, were then building an important industry in dyeing and finishing English 'white' cloths for re-export to Germany, the Baltic lands and central Europe; and, finally, the powerful Cologne Hanse had invested

1. Eileen Power, *The Wool Trade in English Medieval History* (London, 1941), pp. 77–90.

2. Hans Van Werveke, 'De Omvang van de Ieperse Lakenproductie in de veertiende eeuw', *Mededelingen van de Koninklijke Vlaamse Akademie voor Wetenschappen, Letteren, en Schone Kunsten*, ix: 2 (1947), 20–25; R. S. Lopez and H. A. Miskimin, 'The Economic Depression of the Renaissance', *Econ. Hist. Rev.* 2nd series, xiv (1962), 408–26.

3. J. H. Munro, 'Bruges and the Abortive Staple in English Cloth', *Revue Belge de Philologie et d'Histoire,* xliv (1966), 1145–6.

4. Total English cloth exports had risen from an annual average of 28,800 cloths in 1415–19 to one of 41,500 cloths in 1425–9 (estimated from E. Carus-Wilson, *England's Export Trade, 1275–1547* (Oxford, 1963), pp. 91–93). During 1427, Dutch and Brabantine town delegates met at Malines, Haarlem, and Leyden to discuss a ban on English cloth imports. N. W. Posthumus (ed.), *Bronnen tot de Geschiedenis van de Leidsche Textielnijverheid, 1333–1795*, i (The Hague, 1910), 116–18, no. 102.

5. Frans van Mieris (ed.), *Groot Charterboek der Graaven van Holland en van Zeeland,* iv (Leyden, 1756), 923–4.

6. E. Van Even (ed.), *Inventaire des chartes et autres documents appartenant aux archives de la ville de Louvain, 1125–1793* (Louvain, 1873), p. 125, no. 174.

heavily in exporting English cloth from London to the Antwerp Fairs.[1] The combination of a threatened Hanse boycott of these fairs and the pressures of English and Dutch cloth merchants soon forced the removal of the Brabantine ban.[2] At the same time, the defiance of Middelburg and other Dutch towns rendered the Holland-Zealand ban ineffectual.[3]

While there is no evidence that Philip the Good himself had seriously sought to impose a protectionist policy upon the Lowlands, he ought to have drawn two important conclusions from the fate of these cloth bans. First, the Dutch and Brabantine drapery towns did not possess the economic and political dominance of their Flemish counterparts, who faced no serious local resistance in maintaining their cloth ban. Second, Philip's rule of the Burgundian Lowlands was far from being strong and centralized, because most of the principalities were too recently acquired and all had enjoyed a long tradition of municipal independence – and internal bickering. Nevertheless, Philip would again employ general cloth bans in an economic war with England.

Even before the 1428 cloth ban quarrel had been settled, a more explosive conflict with England had erupted over the vital wool trade. In 1429, the English parliament enacted for three years a series of laws known as the Calais Staple Partition and Bullion Ordinances, which were designed to make the wool staple the crown's chief bullion-supplier. The Stapler merchants, virtually the sole wool-sellers to the Lowlands, were required: to 'putte to more encrese and avauntage' the prices of wool; to sell only for ready cash 'in hand', permitting no credit; and, most important, to deliver one-third of the wool price in bullion to the Calais mint. The statute also required pledges from the Staplers to take all the coined money directly into England.[4]

Similar bullionist measures had been imposed on the wool trade in the later fourteenth century and all had failed dismally through opposition from the Staplers themselves, who found that foreign resistance to the bullion exactions seriously injured their sales.[5] To

1. N. J. M. Kerling, *Commercial Relations of Holland and Zealand with England* (Leyden, 1954), pp. 72–86; Hermann Van der Wee, *Growth of the Antwerp Market and the European Economy*, ii (The Hague, 1963), 10–25; Thielemans, pp. 331–3.

2. The ban was officially repealed in Mar. 1431, but was allowed to lapse before that. See K. Koppman (ed.), *Die Recesse und Andere Akten der Hansetage von 1236 bis 1430*, viii (Leipzig, 1897), 365–6, no. 558; E. R. Daenell, *Die Blütezeit der Deutschen Hanse*, i (Berlin, 1905), 389; *C[alendar of] P[atent]* R[*olls*], *1429–1436*, p. 26.

3. H. J. Smit (ed.), *Bronnen tot de Geschiedenis van den Handel met Engeland, Schotland, en Ireland, 1150–1485*, i (The Hague, 1928), 625–7, no. 1012; 635, no. 1024.

4. *Rot*[*uli*] *Parl*[*iamentorum*], iv. 359–61, nos. 60–66; *S*[*tatutes of the*] R[*ealm*], ii. 253–6 (8 Hen. VI, c. 17–20). Approximately one-third of the price in bullion: £6 for a wool-sarpler worth £18 to £20; £5 for a sarpler worth £16. The pledges required that no merchant 'n'apprestera derere à nulle marchaunt nulle maniere de money par luy resceu'.

5. Similar laws were enacted in 1340, 1364, 1379, 1391, and 1397. See J. H. Munro, 'Wool, Cloth, and Gold: Bullionism in Anglo-Burgundian Commercial Relations,

obtain better results this time, the King's Council enlisted the support of a small group of wealthy Staplers by agreeing not to sell any further wool-export licences and by giving this group control of the Staple government and wool trade. The chief mechanism for granting these monopoly powers was the Partition Ordinance, which required merchants to make 'true and even partition' of all receipts, not according to their individual sales but to the amount of wool each had brought to the Staple. As this measure worked in practice, it forced out of business those lesser merchants who depended upon a rapid turnover of small stocks: first, they received proportionately less for their sales in the initial partition of receipts than did merchants with large stocks; second, they lacked sufficient working-capital to maintain their trade over the long period of the several successive 'partitions' required to produce the last of their receipts. Consequently, the few surviving large merchants – later estimated to be twenty or thirty in number – were able to monopolize the trade, fix prices and enforce the bullion laws.[1]

While this bullionist scheme may seem foolish, it should be understood in the context of current concepts and fiscal problems. Almost all then accepted as an article of faith the notion that a country's commercial prosperity and wealth depended strictly upon its supply of gold and silver. More directly responsible for the Calais ordinances, however, was the current crisis in the French war, in which the English for the first time suffered both major military defeats and serious treasury deficits.[2] Worst of all, the Crown badly needed ready cash to pay the wages and ensure the loyalty of the recently-enlarged Calais garrison.[3] This garrison had long been a costly burden, but its preservation was vital in maintaining the important Staple trade and in keeping open the gateway to France.

The Calais ordinances were probably also a retaliatory measure of the Crown against the monetary policies of Philip the Good, who was as ardent a bullionist as the English. Since November 1425, he had been financing his wars in Holland and France by heavily debasing his coinage, especially gold.[4] That he thereby succeeded in

1384–1478' (unpub. doctoral dissertation, Yale University, 1965; Ann Arbor microfilm), pp. 66–93).

1. For a fuller analysis of the partition system, see Eileen Power, 'The Wool Trade in the Fifteenth Century', Power and Postan (eds.), *Studies in English Trade in the Fifteenth Century* (London, 1933), pp. 87–90. A detailed contemporary Dutch description may be found in Smit, *Bronnen*, ii. 697–9, nos. 1126–8.

2. Jacob, p. 255; Anthony Steele, *Receipt of the Exchequer, 1377–1485* (Cambridge, 1954), pp. 430–1.

3. Since July 1426, parliament had assigned one-third of the wool customs for Calais; the same 1429 parliament granted a special subsidy of £6,667 for the enlargement of the Calais garrison. *Rot. Parl.* iv. 340–1, no. 24; and P[ublic] R[ecord] O[ffice], C76/112, m. 24. The Crown's resort to 'tallies' or promissory notes for wages seems to justify its concern.

4. See Munro, pp. 108–15, 342–7. In November 1425, Duke Philip began striking at the mints of Dordrecht and then of Namur inferior gold coins (17 carats) that were

attracting large amounts of bullion to his mints and in increasing his mint seignorage profits more than proportionately is clear from Tables I and II. Although the source of this bullion cannot be determined, the success of Philip's mints might explain why the English coinage output fared so badly between 1425 and 1429: it then suffered a drop of 45 per cent, while the (real) value of Burgundian coinage increased more than fivefold. Particularly striking is the catastrophic fall in English gold minting and the correspondingly impressive surge in Burgundian gold coinage.[1] In view of these circumstances, the Crown undoubtedly believed itself justified in demanding from its Burgundian ally the bullion 'robbed' from England at this critical time.[2] But in any event, the King's Council could not have responded by debasing English coinage because of a long tradition of domestic hostility to any alterations of the coinage. Since the 1350s, when parliament had forbidden debasement without its consent,[3] the Crown had been forced to adopt the alternative method of extracting required bullion from the export trade; to resort once more to this policy seemed the Council's only recourse. But the Council needed more than just gold to meet the ever more serious French challenge after 1429 – it needed the Burgundians.

Opposition to the Calais ordinances, implemented in February 1430, united the duke and his drapery towns as no previous issue had. Philip the Good understandably felt threatened by this assault upon his mints, his seignorage revenues, and the 'wealth' of his

---

debased 37 per cent from the standard set in his monetary ordinance of June 1418; then in June 1428 and again in Jan. 1429, he reduced the gold content of the coins by a total of 1½ carats, for a further debasement of 6·25 per cent. Between July 1426 and June 1429, Philip also debased his silver coinage (at Namur) by 26 per cent. Throughout this time, England's coinage remained unaltered; and the most significant feature of Philip's debasements is that he altered the Burgundian mint-ratio to make it progressively more favourable to gold than England's. Thus, before the Burgundian debasements, the Burgundian and English mint-ratios were, respectively, 10·16:1 and 10·73:1, so that the English ratio 'favoured' gold. By 1429, the ratio of the Namur mint, where most of the Burgundian gold coinage of this period was struck, was 12·01:1 – considerably more favourable to gold than the English ratio. So was the Flemish mint-ratio (Ghent), then 11·16:1.

1. Philip may have chosen to attract gold, by debasing it, because gold coinage was traditionally the more accepted medium of the two in financing international transactions, such as warfare. But gold coinage was the more acceptable because it was generally less likely to be debased than was silver. See Marc Bloch, 'Le problème de l'or au moyen age', *Annales d'Histoire Economique et Sociale,* xix (1933), 1–34.

2. It is also quite possible that the bullion laws were designed in part to prevent the passing of Philip's debased gold coins, especially those minted at Ghent in imitation of the English noble. Parliament in 1429 had complained that foreign merchants were demanding payment in gold nobles alone, which they exported and had 'forged into oyer coygnes, so that yai wynne in ye aloy of ech noble xx d'. (*Rot. Parl.* iv. 360–1). In 1428–9, the Ghent mint had coined 4,460 gold *marcs de Troyes* into imitation nobles. See Table I and n. 1, p. 237.

3. Edward III's drastic debasements of the late 1340s and the consequent inflation had provoked the parliamentary ban of 1352. See the 'Statute of Purveyors', 25 Ed. iii, stat. 5 c. 13, in *S.R.* i. 322; also, Albert Feavearyear, *The Pound Sterling* (rev. ed., Oxford, 1953), pp. 18–20, 31–32.

TABLE I

Combined value of gold and silver minting and of mint seignorages, in pounds sterling, for England and the Burgundian Lowlands, 1420–1440

	ENGLISH MINTS London and Calais		BURGUNDIAN MINTS Ghent, Namur, Dordrecht, Louvain, and Brussels		
Michaelmas Years	Total value of coinage in £ st.	Total seign. in £ st.	Total value of coinage in £ st.*	Total seign. in £ st.*	Total value of seign. in £ *gros* Flemish
1419–20	£45,533	£473	£62,944	£925	£965
1420–1	67,865	708	60,681	890	928
1421–2	110,930	1,155	77,490	1,126	1,173
1422–3	182,196	1,889	54,991	817	850
1423–4	179,671	1,832	53,785	800	831
1424–5	102,580	1,012	30,057	427	457
1425–6	67,196	649	69,039	1,924	2,383
1426–7	59,244	571	69,484	2,915	3,809
1427–8	58,335	552	24,235	648	815
1428–9	57,398	519	157,175	2,937	3,582
1429–30	60,261	540	123,135	1,223	1,523
1430–1	65,292	580	94,042	1,218	1,620
1431–2	57,898	506	114,197	3,162	4,641
1432–3	50,462	438	58,075	3,521	5,252
1433–4	38,553	344	121,494	779	879
1434–5	27,160	241	132,127	897	1,018
1435–6	17,495	157	124,493	815	928
1436–7	6,478	66	61,587	444	502
1437–8	7,467	74	32,210	216	327
1438–9	13,342	127	24,843	157	177
1439–40	7,869	78	7,367	59	66

Sources:

Calais Mint: Public Record Office, (L.T.R.) E 364/49, 61–63, 65–66, 69, 72; (K.R.) E 101/192–93; and *C.P.R. 1422–1429*, pp. 337–8, 520; *C.P.R. 1429–1436*, pp. 256–7, 259.

London Mint: Sir John Craig, *The Mint: a History of the London Mint* (Cambridge, 1953), appendix II; and G. C. Brooke, E. Stokes, 'Tables of Bullion Coined, 1337–1550', *Numismatic Chronicle*, ix (1929), 27–69.

Ghent Mint: Archives Générales du Royaume, Acquits de Lille, liasses 936–7.

Namur Mint: A.G.R., Chambre de Comptes, no. 18,203; Acquits de Lille, liasse 1933.

Louvain Mint: A.G.R., C.C., nos. 18,065–068.

Brussels Mint: A.G.R., C.C., nos. 17,986–989.

Dordrecht Mint: accounts printed in P.O. Van der Chijs, *De Munten der Voormalige Graafschappen Holland en Zeeland* (Haarlem, 1858), pp. 373–7, 399, 402, 404, 413, 429.

* The Burgundian statistics for estimated values in pounds sterling English were calculated by multiplying the *marcs de Troyes* of the mint outputs and the seignorages by the following: £11·6582 sterling per *marc* for gold and £1·087 sterling per *marc* for silver. Since the value of English gold and silver coinage was constant in pounds sterling from 1411 to 1464, these statistics provide a valid comparison between English and Burgundian mintings in this period. The final column provides the actual seignorage receipts in pounds *gros* of Flanders, as recorded in the mintmasters' reports to Duke Philip the Good.

lands, at a time when he himself was actively seeking bullion. The gravity of this threat was emphasized in 1430 and 1431 when, as Table II shows, his mint output fell sharply. For his cloth-making subjects and drapery merchants of Flanders, Brabant and Holland,

TABLE II

The coinage of pure gold and silver marcs de Troyes *in the mints of England and the Burgundian Lowlands 1420–1440*

	ENGLISH MINTS London and Calais*		BURGUNDIAN MINTS Ghent, Namur, Dordrecht, Louvain, and Brussels	
Michaelmas Years	Gold *Marcs de Troyes*	Silver *Marcs de Troyes*	Gold *Marcs de Troyes*	Silver *Marcs de Troyes*
1419–20	3,715·3	2,042·3	—	57,905·9
1420–1	5,631·2	2,039·5	42·1	55,372·3
1421–2	9,118·7	4,254·4	368·3	67,338·0
1422–3	14,664·8	10,335·6	14·4	50,434·8
1423–4	13,254·7	23,135·5	160·0	47,764·1
1424–5	6,216·9	27,693·7	571·4	21,522·9
1425–6	3,534·2	23,913·8	4,585·0	14,338·3
1426–7	3,048·1	21,811·3	5,797·3	1,746·4
1427–8	2,609·4	25,679·4	1,489·2	6,323·2
1428–9	1,605·2	35,586·7	6,061·4	79,585·8
1429–30	1,513·0	39,210·1	4,533·1	64,661·8
1430–1	1,413·0	44,910·8	6,964·4	11,821·1
1431–2	934·1	43,217·2	9,616·7	1,917·7
1432–3	700·2	38,912·5	4,969·7	125·9
1433–4	907·1	25,738·2	4,285·6	66,096·2
1434–5	575·7	18,812·1	6,804·6	48,571·7
1435–6	575·7	9,547·9	6,939·5	40,101·8
1436–7	485·3	754·4	3,007·5	24,401·7
1437–8	450·4	2,038·6	1,236·1	16,374·3
1438–9	640·9	5,401·5	934·7	12,829·4
1439–40	490·1	1,983·4	371·8	2,790·1

Sources: See Table I, for the mint accounts of Ghent, Namur, Dordrecht, Louvain, Brussels, London, and Calais.

* The English mint outputs, as recorded in Tower Pounds, were converted into *marcs de Troyes* at a ratio of 1·429 *marcs* to the Tower Pound. The *marc de Troyes* weighed 244·753 grams, or roughly 8 ounces.

the Calais ordinances meant disaster. Their wool was already so expensive that further price increases might leave the market fully to the English cloth trade. But even more serious was the ordinances' disruption of the credit-financing system upon which the wool trade, cloth manufacturing and marketing so vitally depended.[1] Most

1. For an analysis of the credit system and its significance in the wool trade, see M. Postan, 'Credit in Medieval Trade', *Economic History Review*, 1st ser., i (1928), 240–4, and Power, 'Wool Trade', pp. 65–66. In general, the buyer paid one-third 'down' in cash and arranged credit for the remainder in two 'bills' over a year. For a contemporary description of the importance of credit in the wool trade, see L. Gilliodts-van Severen and M. E. Scott (eds.), *Le Cotton Manuscrit Galba* (Brussels, 1896), no. 135, pp. 310–11, in which a Stapler memorandum states that 'les leins ne purront estre deliverez à nulle value sans estre *apprestez*'.

drapers lacked sufficient working-capital to make the whole payment in cash at the time of purchase and they would have found it prohibitive to borrow the necessary funds, if available. Meeting the bullion requirement itself would also have been expensive: in evading the traditional ban on bullion exports – soon to be rigidly enforced – in bidding up the market price of metals and in paying the Calais mintage fees.[1] Thus the traditionally independent drapery towns looked to Duke Philip for leadership in ending these injurious ordinances.

Initially, the Burgundians relied on negotiations with the English to settle their grievances. In December 1430 Philip sent his first Flemish mission to Calais, where it held several inconclusive meetings with the Staplers and Henry Cardinal Beaufort, the probable author of the decrees.[2] Six months later, in June 1431, Philip's councillors convoked a formal conference of the Flemish towns and the Staplers at Bruges. The duke's officials apparently hoped that this meeting would resolve the problem of wool purchases 'without being required to furnish gold and silver bullion', but the English were obdurate.[3] They also refused the representations of a subsequent Flemish delegation to Calais, sent to protest against the damages inflicted upon their drapery industry.[4]

Rebuffed, Duke Philip then appealed to the estates of his realms to devise 'remedies against these prejudicial ordinances'.[5] On 14 September 1431, an historic assembly met at Antwerp, the first 'Estates-General' or parliament of the Burgundian Lowlands, with deputies from Flanders, Holland, Zealand and Brabant, under the direction of Philip and his councillors.[6] During October and November Philip summoned two further such Estates-General at Malines and Brussels. They apparently explored the possibility of a general retaliatory ban on English cloth, a proposal further discussed by the Flemish towns in December.[7] This flurry of anti-Calais activity then ceased and was not resumed for another eighteen months.

1. The bullion requirement would prove costly if ingots were supplied and the demand raised the price of the metal above the official price; or, if coins were supplied as bullion for reminting at Calais, thus necessitating a double mintage-fee.

2. A[rchives] G[énérales du] R[oyaume de Belgique], C[hambre des] C[omptes], no. 32,485 (Bruges account), fo. 57. Subsequent meetings with Cardinal Beaufort, to May 1431, are noted in N. H. Nicolas (ed.), *P[roceedings and Ordinances of the] P[rivy] C[ouncil of England]*, iv (London, 1837), 18.

3. A.G.R., C.C., no. 42,549 (Franc de Bruges account), fo. 28^{v}: 'omme weghen te vindene daer bi dat men Inghelsche wulle zoude moghen ghecrighen zonder *billoen* van goude of van zelver daer over te moeten leverne . . .'

4. A.G.R., C.C., no. 32,485 (Bruges), fo. 63^{v}.

5. A.G.R., C.C., no. 42,549 (Franc de Bruges), fo. 45^{v}.

6. A.G.R., C.C., *ubi supra;* other texts in Joseph Cuvelier (ed.), *Actes des Etats Généraux des anciens Pays-Bas, 1427–1477* (Brussels, 1948), pp. 8–11. A prior assembly of May 1427 involved only Flanders and Hainault on the governance of the latter county.

7. *Ibid.,* and A.G.R., C.C., no. 32,486 (Bruges), fo. 57^{v}, 58, 58^{v}.

The possible reasons for Philip's delay in directly retaliating against the Calais ordinances are worth examining, if only to understand the full dimensions of the problems he faced. First, in view of later developments, the proposal to ban English cloth probably encountered strong opposition, especially since the 1428 cloth bans

TABLE III

Wool and coinage at Calais: English woolsacks shipped to Calais, and the output of the Calais mint 1420–1440

		THE CALAIS MINT		
Michaelmas Years	Woolsacks shipped to Calais	Silver *marcs* coined	Gold *marcs* coined	Total value of coinage in £ st.
1419–20	11,384	—	—	—
1420–1	11,832	—	—	—
1421–2	13,402	1,323·4	656·9	£9,098
1422–3	14,476	6,513·3	3,372·6	46,398
1423–4	15,913	19,314·1	1,962·5	43,874
1424–5	11,195	25,469·3	1,262·3	42,402
1425–6	12,247	21,514·6	702·3	31,575
1426–7	16,083	19,655·0	389·2	25,903
1427–8	15,351	24,074·1	191·2	28,398
1428–9	11,398	32,923·5	148·1	37,516
1429–30	7,066	36,584·6	164·6	41,687
1430–1	10,433	42,321·2	173·2	48,023
1431–2	10,540	41,193·3	—	44,778
1432–3	8,663	37,724·0	—	41,007
1433–4	838	24,951·7	—	27,123
1434–5	12,923	18,199·5	—	19,783
1435–6	2,531	8,936·2	—	10,119
1436–7	66	—	—	—
1437–8	156	—	—	—
1438–9	505	537·7	—	584
1439–40	17,731	—	—	—

Sources: E. Carus-Wilson and O. Coleman, *England's Export Trade, 1275–1547* (Oxford, 1963), calculated from tables in pp. 57–65.
P.R.O. (L.T.R.), E 364/59, 61–63, 65–66, 69, 72; (K.R.) E 101/192–93; *C.P.R. 1422–1429*, pp. 337–8, 520; *C.P.R. 1429–1436*, pp. 256–7, 259.

had just recently been lifted. Second, one might argue that the Calais ordinances were impossible to enforce fully for long,[1] and thus that the Burgundians no longer considered the Staple issue to be as critical as it had first appeared. Table III suggests, however, that these ordinances were probably effective in acquiring bullion for the Calais mint – and also in damaging the wool trade: for the years 1430–3, following the enactment of the laws, the annual average of the Calais mint output was 42 per cent *above* that of 1426–9, while the annual average of wool shipments to Calais was 32 per cent *below* the 1426–9 average. Moreover, for the corresponding periods, the annual average number of drapers renting stalls in the Ypres

1. Eileen Power ('Wool Trade', pp. 84, 86–87) doubts that the regulations were rigidly enforced and notes several instances of evasion of the Calais ordinances.

Lakenhalle fell from 215 to 166, a sizeable drop that probably reflects the inability of smaller Flemish drapers to survive the costs of the Staple ordinances.[1] Nevertheless, Duke Philip still needed the English to maintain his French conquests and for him the bullion problem was apparently not yet serious enough to rupture the alliance. For, as Tables I and II demonstrate, his Burgundian mints were prospering once more: further and more drastic debasements had increased the mint output 20 per cent in 1432, with the greatest amount of gold yet coined – more than ten times the English gold coinage output. This was also the largest amount of gold that Philip's mints would ever strike.

In the following year, 1433, both the Staple and monetary issues forced a decision upon the Burgundians. First, the Partition and Bullion laws, which were supposed to lapse that year, were instead re-enacted in July for an indefinite term. At the same time, parliament strengthened the Staplers' monopoly powers to ensure better enforcement of the payment laws.[2] Undoubtedly the mounting costs of the Calais garrison, and then a bloody mutiny in April over unpaid wages, had stiffened the Council's determination to maintain the bullion policy.[3] Second, this extension of the Calais ordinances was singularly inopportune for Duke Philip, because by mid-summer, at a time of rising military expenditures, his debasements were no longer attracting much bullion to his mints.[4] Most likely, the excessive degree of debasement and consequent inflation had caused a ruinous distrust of his coinage. Philip's only solution for reviving his mints was a strengthening and deflation of the coinage, a step which would also be necessary to protect his revenues against inflation.[5] Moreover, he apparently decided that a more orderly coinage should be imposed upon the monetary chaos of his recently-acquired territories. The resulting monetary reform of October 1433 provided the Burgundian Lowlands with its first common coinage and one that was virtually pure in gold and silver. By this reform, Philip had considerably deflated the value of his new coinage and subsequently promised to maintain its stability for at least twenty

1. A.G.R., C.C., no. 38,651–7 (Ypres accounts).

2. *Rot. Parl.* iv. 454, no. 63; and *S.R.* ii. 287.

3. *Rot. Parl.* iv. 473, no. 20; and P.R.O. C76/115, m. 10: 'certes dissensiones et discordie inter locumtenentem . . . et soldarios eiusdem ville'. In Dec. 1432, the Council had urgently requested funds for the Calais garrison, 'for asmuche the Kyng considereth well the greete povertee and indigence that the souldeours have long sufferede . . .' Nicolas, *P.P.C.* iv. 139. On the April revolt, see J. H. Ramsay, *Lancaster and York*, i (Oxford, 1892), 449–50.

4. See Tables II and III. From 1429 to mid-1433, Philip debased gold by a further 21 per cent and silver by 15 per cent. By mid-1433, only the Namur mint was in operation and most of its coinage had been struck by 30 May (A.G.R., C.C., nos. 18,202–03). On Philip's financial problems at this time, see Bonenfant, pp. 58–59.

5. For an explanation of the economics of strengthening or *renforcement* of the coinage, see Marc Bloch, *Esquisse d'une histoire monétaire de l'Europe* (Paris, 1954), pp. 63 ff.

years.[1] This monetary reform, however, presented a problem. Obviously it would be easier to attract bullion to the mints by debasing coinage than by strengthening it – despite forced recoinages, minimal seignorage fees, and the inducement of stable values. Philip the Good therefore set about ensuring that no bullion should leave his lands, especially for Calais.[2]

Simultaneously, Philip renewed his attack on the Calais ordinances by requesting general consent to a retaliatory ban on English cloth. His councillors met first with Flemish and Brabantine delegates, then with leaders of the Holland-Zealand towns. But, with strong objections to the ban from all except the Flemish, 'no conclusion was reached'.[3] The fact that between October 1433 and May 1434 Philip had to convoke no less than seven further conferences and sessions of the Estates-General on the proposed ban demonstrates how determined and strong was the opposition of the Dutch and Brabantine cloth-importing interests.[4]

Meanwhile, in co-operation with the duke, the Flemish drapery towns embarked on diplomatic negotiations abroad. In late 1433, a Flemish mission headed by Philip's personal envoy met with the King's Council at Westminster 'to beseech for annulment or some moderation of the ordinances imposed on the wool trade at Calais'.[5] The protracted discussions, from December to March, only proved the futility of such diplomacy and the duke's need for more positive action. More promising were Flemish negotiations with the Hanseatic League, then the largest dealers in both English and Flemish cloth. The Flemish secured the full support of the Hanse *kontor* at Bruges and, in late October, both sent letters to the Hanse Diet at Lübeck to solicit its aid. They explained that Hanse merchants now had to pay far higher prices for Flemish cloth because of the English Staple ordinances, 'which they further stiffen from year to year, so that wool can only be obtained at great and heavy cost'.[6] The *kontor* mayor maintained, furthermore, that 'by the costliness

1. The gold coinage was strengthened by 28 per cent and the silver by 23 per cent. Complete ordinance in L. Deschamps de Pas, 'Essai sur l'histoire monétaire des comtes de Flandre', *Revue Numismatique,* 2nd ser. vi (1881), 471–2. For the rest of the Burgundian Lowlands, see H. E. Van Gelder and M. Hoc, *Les monnaies des Pays-Bas Bourguignons* (Amsterdam, 1960), pp. 9–11.

2. In Nov. 1435, Duke Philip strictly enforced a ban on bullion exports. Deschamps de Pas, 'Histoire monétaire', *Revue Numismatique,* 2nd ser. vii (1882), 117. On the problem of obtaining sufficient bullion for the mints, see A.G.R., C.C., no. 32,488 (Bruges account), fo. 65.

3. R. Van Marle (ed.), *Le comté de Holland sous Philippe le Bon* (The Hague, 1908), no. 7, pp. viii-ix; and Smit, *Bronnen,* i. 654, no. 1054.

4. Between 29 Oct. and 15 Nov. 1433, meetings were held at Ghent, Antwerp, Malines, Lier, and Brussels 'van den Inghelschen lakene te verdrivene ute ons gheduchts heeren lande' (A.G.R., C.C., no. 42,552, fo. 28; no. 32,488, fo. 64^{v}). Between 14 Jan. and 15 May 1434, further meetings were held at Ghent (twice) and Bruges (A.G.R., C.C., no. 32,488, fo. 67^{v}, 69, 83; no. 42,452, fo. 22, 31^{v}; Cuvelier, pp. 12–16).

5. A.G.R., C.C., no. 32,488, fo. 64, 65 (Bruges); no. 42,552, fo. 29 (Franc de Bruges).

6. G. von der Ropp (ed.), *Hanserecesse 1431–1476,* i (Leipzig, 1876), 131–4, no. 191.

I

of wool more than half the drapery industry has perished'. They then announced – prematurely – the agreement of the duke and the Estates of Flanders, Brabant, Holland-Zealand, and Hainault to ban all English cloth 'as a remedy so that the English might be pressured into revoking these unreasonable ordinances and selling wool as they used to do'. Finally, the *kontor* mayor argued that if the proposed ban proved successful 'we might again purchase more [Flemish] cloth at better prices', and thus that the League should co-operate in the ban by temporarily forgoing its commercial privileges in the Low Countries.[1]

Although the Hanseatic League might normally have objected to such restrictions on its commerce, its own current conflict with England over the Baltic trade assisted the Burgundian cause.[2] Thus in February 1434 the League Diet at Elbing made no objections to the temporary loss of trading privileges involved in the proposed cloth ban.[3] The Anglo-Hanseatic dispute subsequently became so inflamed that on 5 June the League Diet at Lübeck imposed its own ban on the English cloth trade.[4] At that time, Philip had just prorogued a session of the Estates-General at Bruges, which had made no definite resolution on banning English cloth.[5] But, with the League's closure of England's alternative market, he now rushed to force through his own long-sought ban.

On 15 June Philip's councillors met at Ghent to obtain formal consent for the ban from the Flemish, Brabantine, and Hollander delegates. Only the Zealanders, dominated by the shipping towns, refused by their pointed absence.[6] Nevertheless, the decree that Philip signed on 19 June 1434 affected all the Burgundian Lowlands and all foreign merchants trading there. The long text leaves no doubt about Philip's motives and should end the common argument that this ban (and succeeding ones) was only 'protectionist'.[7] The introduction, to be sure, maintains that the large increase in English cloth imports had injured and 'seriously diminished' the drapery industries in the Low Countries. Yet the real culprits are clearly

1. G. von der Ropp (ed.), *Hanserecesse 1431–1476*, i. 135–6, no. 192.

2. See Michael Postan, 'Economic and Political Relations of England with the Hanse, 1400–1475', *Studies in English Trade*, pp. 116–22.

3. *Hanserecesse*, i. 173, no. 268.

4. *Ibid.* i. 202, no. 321.

5. Cuvelier, pp. 15–16; H. Vander Linden (ed.), *Itineraire de Philippe le Bon* (Brussels, 1940), pp. 121–2.

6. A.G.R., C.C., no. 32,488 (Bruges), fo. 71^{v}; Smit, *Bronnen*, i. 661–2.

7. See Henri Pirenne, *Histoire de Belgique*, ii (Brussels, 1908), 417–18; Hans Van Werveke, 'The Low Countries', in M. Postan (ed.), *Cambridge Economic History*, iii (Cambridge, 1962), 325–6; Van der Wee, ii. 45–49; J. A. Van Houtte, 'La genèse du grand marché international d'Anvers à la fin du moyen age', *Revue Belge de Philologie et d'Histoire*, xix (1940), 109–14; Kerling, pp. 76–78. But, see also Georg Schanz, *Englische Handelspolitik gegen Ende des Mittelalters*, i (Leipzig, 1881), 442–3; Power, 'Wool Trade', p. 84; and Thielemans, pp. 60–61, who link the 1434 cloth ban to the Staple question, yet stress only the protectionist aspect, from the increased costs of wool.

identified as the Staplers who had 'greatly raised their wool prices, and fixed them at excessive levels'. With some exaggeration, the text then maintains that the Staplers 'furthermore will sell wool only for gold and silver bullion and will not accept current coin, so that all the bullion of our lands is being taken to England, leaving our lands hardly any and thereby causing them great damage and injuries'.[1] The bullionist emphasis of the decree, however, does not render the protectionist issue irrelevant. One cannot dismiss the role of the drapery towns in advocating this ban, since the increased wool costs resulting from the Calais ordinances did place them at a serious competitive disadvantage. At the same time, the standard interpretation of the duke's role in the cloth ban – that he merely acceded to the drapers' demand for protection – is misleading. One must also recognize the vital importance of the duke's own bullionist concern about the Calais payment laws. It is quite clear that Philip himself supervised most of the diplomatic missions and the sessions of the Estates, and that he personally sought the cloth ban as a retaliatory measure for forcing revocation of the English laws.

The Burgundian ban did not, however, hurt England enough to achieve this aim. Thus, while English *denizen* cloth exports fell 22 per cent in the Michaelmas year 1434–5, exports by alien merchants increased, so that the total decline was only 9 per cent.[2] The Hanse were obviously not adhering to their own ban, as the English customs accounts show. Moreover, in open defiance of Philip's ban, the Cologne Hanse were shipping English cloth through the Lowlands, and Zealanders were marketing it in Middelburg.[3] Similarly, as Table III shows, an apparent boycott of Calais wool during 1434 was also a failure; for, despite the harshness of the payment regulations, the Flemish, Dutch and Brabantine drapers could not long forgo English wool. Thus the chief result of the Staple conflict and cloth ban was to create new tensions between England and Burgundy, and further the disintegration of their alliance.

The precise date when Philip the Good resolved to desert the alliance is not certain. He had not done so in 1431 by his truce with Charles VII, forced upon him after several defeats in France – defeats he attributed to the English failure to send him the promised funds and troops.[4] Nor had he sought to withdraw from the war when the

1. Charles Piot (ed.), *Inventaire des chartes de la ville de Léau* (Brussels, 1879), no. 8, pp. 26–28 (full text): '. . . en willen sy die selven wolle onsen ondersaten niet vercoepen, ten sy by billoen van goude of van silvere, sonder te willen ontfangen gancbair munte, dair by dat alle 't billoen van onsen voirsc. landen . . . getogen wordt in 't voirs. ryke van Engelant'. For Hanse complaints about Philip's rigorously-enforced ban on bullion exports, see *Hanserecesse,* i. 233, no. 357 (July 1434); see also n. 2, p. 235.

2. Estimated from tables in Carus-Wilson, *Export Trade,* pp. 93–94.

3. *Ibid.,* and K. Höhlbaum (ed.), *Hansisches Urkundenbuch,* vii (Leipzig, 1907), 48–52, nos. 95, 96, and 103.

4. Joseph Stevenson (ed.), *Letters and Papers Illustrative of the Wars of the English in France During the Reign of Henry VI,* ii (London, 1864), 196.

victorious King Charles resumed his attacks in 1433. Apparently, the crucial decision came only in mid-1434, when the Calais bullion problem, then clearly requiring retaliation, sufficiently demonstrated to Philip the 'perfidy' of his English ally. At the same time, the restoration of the pro-Burgundian count of Richemont in Charles' government made a separate peace with the French king seem propitious.[1] Some months later, in January 1435, Philip met with the count of Richemont and French ambassadors at Nevers to negotiate the basic terms of the subsequent peace treaty.[2] After concluding the negotiations on 6 February, they invited English and papal representatives to attend a general peace conference at Arras in the late summer.

Although the English were apparently unaware of Duke Philip's decision for a separate peace with the French, the King's Council was sufficiently alarmed by the Nevers conference to authorize, for the first time, negotiations for the 'modification and moderation' of the Calais ordinances. The Council's instructions to its ambassadorial mission admitted that the Burgundians had found these laws 'highly prejudical, excessive, and oppressive' and had 'on many occasions begged for the complete repeal or modification of the ordinances, to permit an increase in trade'.[3] But the negotiations of this English mission in February and also of a subsequent mission in July were failures.[4] The July mission was headed by England's staunchest advocate of the bullionist policy, Cardinal Beaufort; evidently his proposals for moderation of the laws were unacceptable to Duke Philip and his Flemish ambassadors. Nor were the prospects for a general peace any more promising. English ambassadors, again headed by Cardinal Beaufort, did attend the Congress of Arras in August. But they refused to consider the rigid French terms and angrily quit the conference on 6 September. The rest was anti-climax. On 21 September Duke Philip and King Charles signed the Treaty of Arras, rightly described by Miss Dickinson as 'a triumph for Burgundy, a disaster for England, and a humiliation for France'.[5] Philip kept most of his conquests and obtained from Charles the Somme towns, exemption from homage and military obligations – virtual recognition of independence, and promises of aid should the English attack 'because of this present agreement'.

1. Bonenfant, p. 59. Known to the French as the 'comte de Richemont', he was Arthur, earl of Richmond, brother of the duke of Brittany and brother-in-law of Duke Philip the Good. He had originally served the English but deserted to Charles VII in 1424, serving him as Constable until 1427. E. Perroy, *Hundred Years War* (trans. Douglas, London, 1959), pp. 268–70, 273–4, 292–5.

2. Dickinson, *Congress of Arras,* pp. 163–5.

3. P.R.O., C76/117, m. 7; Thomas Rymer (ed.), *Foedera*, x. 605–6. The ambassadors included Richard Bokeland, treasurer of Calais, and Hamo Sutton, the Staple Mayor.

4. P.R.O., C76/117, m. 3; *Foedera*, x. 619–20.

5. Dickinson, p. 197; see also, pp. 160–98; Bonenfant, pp. 58–65 and Thielemans, pp. 66–72.

The English reaction to this Burgundian desertion, which made defeat in the Anglo-French war almost inevitable, was predictable. Immediately the faction-riven Council united in rebuffing Philip's peace overtures. It publicly berated him as a traitorous villain and so roused the London mobs that they massacred numerous Flemish merchants.[1] As the new military commander, the duke of Gloucester went to Calais to prepare an invasion of Flanders and to direct piracy attacks along the Flemish coast. Shortly after, in December, the King's Council sent letters of 'friendship' to the Holland-Zealand towns in a heavy-handed and unsuccessful attempt to win them away from Philip's cause.[2] The Dutch turned these letters over to Philip, who, roused to fury and swayed by his Francophile councillors, responded in February with a virtual declaration of war against England.[3] The Burgundian war-council then made plans for laying siege to Calais.

The decision to attack Calais proved to be rash, but seemed logical at the time. Seizure of Calais would remove a serious threat to Philip's southern flank and might cripple, if not destroy, the English supply-line to France. Moreover, the duke evidently hoped that gaining control of the Staple would finally force the English to abolish the hated Calais ordinances, which parliament had pointedly re-affirmed the previous October, following '*le jour d'Arras*'.[4] Thus in March, when Philip and his councillors assembled at Ghent to enlist Flemish support for the war, they bitterly assailed the Staple's pricing system and bullion regulations, 'for they threaten to deprive the duke's lands of all money and livelihood'.[5] Undeniably, their long harangues were successful in gaining the duke Flemish funds and troops.[6] But Philip received no such aid from the Dutch and Brabantines, who were not enthusiastic about his war and opposed the general ban on English trade that he had issued in May.[7] Only the Flemish participated, and they paid a heavy price.

The July siege of Calais produced the most ignominious defeat of Philip's reign. His fleet and French auxiliaries failed to arrive on

1. Thielemans, pp. 66–67.

2. Gilliodts-van Severen, *Cotton Manuscrit Galba,* no. 177, p. 429.

3. Thielemans, p. 79; Bonenfant, pp. 64–67. For Henry VI's reply, protesting his desire for peace, see *Cotton Manuscrit Galba,* no. 178, p. 431.

4. 14 Hen. VI, c. 2 and 5 in *S.R.* ii. 289–91; and *Rot. Parl.* iv. 490, no. 19.

5. The speeches are recorded in both L. Douet-D'arcq (ed.), *Chronique d'Enguerran De Monstrelet,* v (Paris, 1861), 212; and F. Morand (ed.), *Chronique de Jean Le Fevre de St. Remy,* ii (Paris, 1876), 378. According to the latter, the Sovereign Bailiff of Flanders stated that 'la laine d'Angleterre est mise si hault que les marchans n'y pevent prouffiter, et que, plus estre, il fault payer ung tiers de buillon, et baillier deux phelippes [Burgundian gold coin] pour ung noble; par lesquelles institucions et ordonnances, la monnoie de nostre tres redoubté seigneur seroit en voye de aller à néant et sons pays estre sans gaignage'.

6. J. J. De Smedt (ed.), 'Kronyk van Jan van Dixmude', in *Corpus Chronicorum Flandriae,* iii (Brussels, 1856), 45–46; A.G.R., C.C., no. 32,490 (Bruges), fo. 45, 46^{v}.

7. Smit, *Bronnen,* ii. 672, 678–80, nos. 1084, 1095–6.

I

time; worse, the badly-organized Flemish militias could not defend themselves against English forays from Calais; they mutinied and fled. Gloucester pursued them and laid waste to south-west Flanders, while his fleet ravaged the coast unopposed up to Bruges.[1] Though Philip had lost the war in less than a week, he refused to recognize reality, and let the hostilities, in the form of piracy, drag on for almost three years. Nor was he willing to recognize the damage inflicted upon the Burgundian economy[2]; for the war had caused the most serious interruption in the history of the English wool trade, a mere 66 sacks being shipped to Calais in 1436–7.[3] That year the Flemish drapery towns suffered mass unemployment and famine, which provoked several insurrections. But in vain did the Flemish town councils beg the duke for a truce.[4]

Dutch opposition to Duke Philip was even stronger and more exasperating. Encouraged by the King's Council, the Holland-Zealand towns continued their English trade[5]; and, in August 1436, when the duke's officials tried to confiscate English cloth found in Middelburg, the citizenry murdered them.[6] Philip's anger mounted. In March 1437, his *stadhouder* convoked an assembly of the Holland-Zealand towns and harshly condemned them for giving the duke virtually no aid in the war and for trading with England, despite the repeated bans. The Dutch replied by pleading poverty from war-damages to their commerce, especially to their cloth industry.[7] In reality, the Dutch leaders were then preparing to fight not their English friends but their Hanseatic competitiors in the Baltic trade, and a year later they unilaterally deserted Philip to make war upon the Hanse.[8] In these circumstances, Philip had no alternative but to permit the Dutch, in May 1438, to begin negotiations with the English on a peace and trade treaty.[9]

By that time, Duke Philip had received from the foreign merchant community in Bruges an ultimatum to make peace with England. The foreign merchants, having suffered commercial losses by the

1. Thielemans, pp. 80–107.

2. *Ibid.* pp. 11–14, for a discussion of a memorandum, presented by the councillor Hugues de Lannoy, which analysed Flanders' current economic plight and recommended peace with England.

3. See Table III. The war almost immediately shut down the Calais mint. P.R.O. (L.T.R.), E364/72, m. 49. Also, cloth exports by the London Merchants Adventurers fell from 8,700 pieces in 1434–5 to only 2,084 pieces in 1435–6. Carus-Wilson, *Export Trade,* p. 94.

4. Bruges had already revolted in 1436, following the Calais débâcle. See *Chronique de Monstrelet*, v. 321–3.

5. Smit, *Bronnen,* ii. 678, 680, nos. 1092–3, 1097; *Foedera*, x. 654–5.

6. Smit. *Bronnen,* ii. 674–5, 677, nos. 1089, 1095; Kerling, p. 76.

7. Van Marle, no. 9, pp. x-xiv. See also Smit, *Bronnen*, ii. 686, no. 1110, on the Dutch complaints.

8. Van Marle, nos. 13–14, pp. xxv-xxxiii (20 Apr. 1438). See also T. J. Jansma, 'Philippe le Bon et le guerre hollando-wende', *Revue du Nord*, xlii (1960), 5–18.

9. Smit, *Bronnen,* ii. 691, 694, nos. 1118, 1125; Nicolas, *P.P.C.* v. 95.

war, bluntly warned the duke that they would otherwise quit Flanders and boycott its trade.[1] Following urgent appeals for peace from the Flemish and Brabantine towns, Philip finally agreed to negotiations in June.[2] In the King's Council, however, hatred of the 'so-called duke of Burgundy' was so intense that not until November did the peace faction (under, ironically, Cardinal Beaufort) prevail. Even so, the Council would agree to treat only with Philip's wife, the Duchess Isabella.[3] A long series of Anglo-Burgundian treaty conferences began the next month. Fairly quickly, both sides agreed upon a military truce, but negotiations over reparations and the commercial disputes proved difficult. Again the English rejected all requests for moderation of the Staple ordinances and retorted with the demand that Philip remove his rigid prohibition on the shipping of foreign bullion through the Lowlands.[4] Finally, on 29 September 1439, Duchess Isabella and delegates from Flanders, Brabant and Malines agreed to sign a peace and commercial treaty with England.[5]

The English had clearly won, for the Flemish had to pay heavy reparations and the treaty nowhere refers to the Calais ordinances and bullion problems. Philip the Good was also forced to admit the failure of his retaliatory cloth ban and permit the legal resumption of the English cloth trade in its former Burgundian markets. To be sure, he subsequently re-affirmed the century-old Flemish prohibition on English cloth,[6] but the English had not contested this Flemish ban for years; Philip made no mention of a ban for the rest of the Low Countries, and the treaty itself specified restoration of 'free trade'. As a result of trade restoration, both wool and cloth exports jumped significantly after 1439; and, while the average of wool exports never again approached the pre-1430 level, English cloth exports during the early 1440s reached their highest volume thus far.[7] Meanwhile the Dutch, who had been conducting separate negotiations with the English since mid-1438, were stubbornly

1. L. Gilliodts-van Severen (ed.), *Inventaire des Archives de la Ville de Bruges,* v (Bruges, 1877), 199; *Cotton Manuscrit Galba,* 440.

2. A.G.R., C.C., no. 32,491 (Bruges), fo. 102 (Mar. 1438), fo. 105^{v} (June 1438). For a different view, see Thielemans, pp. 116–18.

3. Smit, *Bronnen,* ii. 710–11, nos. 1142–44; P.R.O., C76/121, m. 17; Gilliodts-van Severen, *Cotton Manuscrit Galba,* pp. 440–1. The English ambassadors, headed by Cardinal Beaufort, also included the Staple Mayor, John Reynewell.

4. In Mar. and Apr. 1439. See F. Priem (ed.), *Précis analytique des documents des archives de la Flandre-Occidentale à Bruges: Comptes du Franc,* ii (Bruges, 1844), 53; and Gilliodts-van Severen, *Cotton Manuscrit Galba,* pp. 440–1. For the negotiations in general, see Thielemans, pp. 119–30.

5. Gilliodts-van Severen, *Cotton Manuscrit Galba,* pp. 445–6; *Foedera,* x. 791–3. Full text in Emile Varenbergh, *Histoire des relations diplomatiques entre le comté de Flandre et l'Angleterre au moyen age* (Brussels, 1874), no. 7, pp. 579–95. The treaty, to last until 1 Nov. 1447, was subsequently renewed many times.

6. On 1 Dec. 1439. Text in Gilliodts-van Severen, *Archives de Bruges,* v. 189–90, no. 1015. See also n. 3, p. 226.

7. Average annual cloth exports in 1440–4 were 57,000 pieces. Carus-Wilson, *Export Trade,* from tables pp. 60–61, 94–96.

resisting reparations-claims for alleged piracy and did not sign a similar commercial treaty until April 1445.[1] The lack of a formal treaty, however, did not prevent them from partaking fully in the English cloth trade boom after 1439.

Between the enactment of the Calais ordinances and the signing of the Anglo-Burgundian treaty there had passed a full decade of mutual disaster. It seems incredible that the bullionist conflict, after having disrupted the vital commerce of two interdependent countries and contributed to the collapse of their alliance, should still be unresolved. While there are many possible explanations for both English and Burgundian bullionism – the traditional concepts of wealth, the seignorage profits from minting, the urgent needs for ready cash in financing warfare – the results hardly appear to have justified maintaining these monetary policies so tenaciously. Indeed both English and Burgundian merchants had fully informed the King's Council that its Calais ordinances were costing England considerably more revenue than could ever be gained in bullion exactions from the wool trade. It was the growing strength of mercantile opposition that finally, though only temporarily, checked the English bullion laws. A Commons petition of 1437 provided the first major domestic attack by charging that the 'streitnes of an Ordenance as touching receit of Billion' had discouraged Dutch trade with the Staple. The Crown, however, rejected the plea to let merchants 'receyve alle maner payement' for the 'redyer utterance' of wool.[2] The following May, Dutch ambassadors, trying vainly to convince the King's Council of the folly of its Calais ordinances, presented a detailed, vivid contrast between the current Staple operations and those under the former 'free' system of credit-payments and much lower, competitive pricing. Noting that Calais wool purchases had fallen by more than one-half, the Dutch concluded sarcastically: 'We think that the King of England must be extremely disturbed to know that merchants no longer respect the Staple . . . whereby the King is losing his customs revenues.'[3]

The combined domestic and foreign resistance did not prove sufficient to thwart the Crown's bullionist policy until 1442, three years after the Anglo-Burgundian treaty. In February, an angry group of small wool-merchants, 'enforcid to leve their merchaundises of Woll be cause they may not be rulers of their owen goodes', succeeded in having parliament repeal the Partition Ordinance.

1. Smit, *Bronnen*, ii. 832–8, nos. 1295–6. See Thielemans, pp. 143–5.

2. *Rot. Parl.* iv. 508–9, no. 37.

3. Smit, *Bronnen*, ii. 697–9, nos. 1126–8. The Dutch demanded that the Staple commerce be as 'vry' as it was in the past, 'na ouder custumen . . . te betalen mit reden gelde'; wool then cost 'den derden of den vierden penninc min' than at present; merchants used to pay no more than £10 a sarpler, 'ende 't ander *up lange dage*'. The Dutch also wanted resolution of the problems 'van den belliene ende payement, dair die voirnoemde coopluyde menichwerff gemoeyt hebben geweest'.

While they now convinced the Crown that the partition system was partly responsible for the serious decline in customs, 'as it apperith sufficiently of record in your Escheqier', their attack on the bullion law itself was not so successful. The only concession that parliament would grant was deletion of the requirement for the 'whole payment in ready money' at the time of sale, thus implicitly permitting credit on two-thirds of the wool price.[1] Nevertheless, the statute repealing the Partition Ordinance was itself sufficient to undermine the rest of the Crown's bullionist policy, for the new law permitted freer elections for the Staple government. Shortly after, the lesser wool-merchants overthrew the monopolist faction which had alone supported the payment laws. In October, the new Staple mayor shocked the Council by refusing to grant the king a badly-needed loan unless the bullion law was fully annulled. Cardinal Beaufort again stubbornly refused, saying that if the Burgundians 'coude feel that the Kyng for this his necessitee sholde thus dispense with th'estatut of bringing in of bullion, he shulde never hereafter by constreint make hem bringe in any bullion'. The Staple mayor sharply retorted that 'it is impossible, it can not be done to bringe in the iiide part in bullione', because the duke of Burgundy had rigorously prevented compliance by searching merchants for gold on the way to Calais. Finally, he pointed out to the Council that 'there is nothing wherof monnoie sholde grow for the said necessitees but by shipping of wolles' and now threatened to embargo wool exports unless the 'estatut be dispensede wit'.[2] Henry VI and his Council had no choice but to agree, yet the king gave his consent 'only for this tyme' and begged the Staplers to bring in 'as moche bullyone as ye shall mowe godely get'.[3]

Thus Philip the Good appeared to have won after all. But Philip, despite his stringent ban on bullion exports, was not as responsible for this victory as was the inherent vulnerability of the English bullion laws themselves. Enforcement of the laws had depended upon the support of the leading Staplers, who had demanded in return the Partition Ordinance, and this monopoly-privilege so antagonized the other merchants that they ultimately overthrew the whole system. Most of these merchants saw that the bullion requirements were injurious to their trade and would produce strong resistance abroad. That domestic English opposition counted most is

1. *Rot. Parl.* v. 64, no. 38; and *S.R.* ii. 324–5 (20 Hen. VI, c. 12). In attacking the bullion regulations, the petitioner argued that the 'seide streite rule hath caused Merchantz Estraungers to labour unto their Lordes of their partie, to make so grevous and streite serch uppon Bullion comyng unto your Mynt at Caleys, so that men of divers Countries in conveyeng of Bullion hath bene gretely hyndered aswell in their persones as in theire goodes, so that the seide Mynt is fallen into grete decay'. See also Table III.

2. Nicolas, *P.P.C.* v. 216–19.

3. *Ibid.* p. 222 (letter of Henry VI, 18 Oct. 1442).

clear, if only because Philip proved unable to unite his lands in retaliation. The Burgundian victory of 1442, it should be added, was short-lived. Henry VI had never promised surrender in the Crown's bullionist policy. Eventually the 'partitionists' of the Staple regained control and re-imposed the old ordinances, again provoking Burgundian bans on English cloth in 1447–52 and once more in 1464–7.[1] Not until parliament finally and fully repealed the Calais ordinances in 1473 did the issues of wool, cloth, and gold cease to dominate Anglo-Burgundian relations.

1. Both Michael Postan in 'Credit in Medieval Trade' (p. 242) and Eileen Power in 'Wool Trade' (p. 89) stated that the Staple ordinances were inoperative after 1442. The texts cited in the two previous notes suggest that this view is mistaken. I intend to publish evidence on the continuation of this bullionist conflict to the 1470s.

II

AN ASPECT OF MEDIEVAL PUBLIC FINANCE: THE PROFITS OF COUNTERFEITING IN THE FIFTEENTH-CENTURY LOW COUNTRIES

The fine art of counterfeiting, today a crime most usually committed by private individuals against the state, was in late-medieval Europe much more commonly the special prerogative of princes, especially those with less affluent domains, who frequently employed it as one of their more important fiscal measures. Under such circumstances a private crime could thus become a state virtue, but the effect was still the same : to defraud the public, though more particularly the subjects — and rulers — of neighbouring principalities, where the counterfeit coins were usually intended to circulate. One should realize at once, however, that the most prevalent « monetary » policies of this era, characterized by coinage debasements and mint-ratio alterations, were designed more to raise revenues than to influence the aggregate money supply [1]. Counterfeiting was in fact only a variation of such coinage policies, whose objective was to attract as much bullion (*billon*), domestic and foreign, as possible to the prince's mint,

(1) The theory of debasement, its fiscal and monetary aspects, is discussed at greater length in John H. MUNRO, *Wool, Cloth, and Gold: The Struggle for Bullion in Anglo-Burgundian Trade, c. 1340-1478* (Brussels and Toronto, Éditions de l'Institut de Sociologie de l'U.L.B. and University of Toronto Press), to be released shortly. This study contains the documentary and statistical evidence to support the unfootnoted assertions made in the first part of this article ; and we therefore saw no need to repeat the citations here.

and to permit him to extract the maximum amount of *seignorage*, the feudal tax on minting, from the metal so coined (2). The very fact that princes, in seeking to lure foreign bullion to their mints, fully expected, permitted, and indeed intended that some of their coinage issues should leave their lands serves to demonstrate the essentially fiscal nature of their debasement policies.

How the prince, whether operating a « legitimate » or counterfeiting mint, sought to maximize a bullion influx and his mint profits can best be understood by examining the particular mechanics of medieval minting and debasement. First, the monetary systems of this era operated primarily upon a silver standard, which was supplemented by gold coinage for high-value transactions, in foreign trade and warfare in particular. Second, and consequently, the local money-of-account systems for recording payments, reckoned in pounds, shillings, and pence (1 lb. = 20s. = 240d.), were tied directly to the silver coinage, so that, for example, one *livre gros*, *tournois*, or *sterling* always represented 240 of the country's *current* penny coins (3). To represent the values of the various subdivisions of the *denier gros*, the Low Countries employed the following money-of-account units : 1 denier = 3 esterlins = 24 mites. Third, within the various coinage systems, the relative values of the coins themselves were, of course, essentially determined by their intrinsic metal contents (4). In view of the sub-

---

(2) As Nicolas Oresme acidly remarked : « Videtur michi quod principalis et finalis causa propter quam princeps sibi vult assumere potestatem mutandi monetas est emolumentum vel lucrum quod inde potest habere. » Charles Johnson (ed.), *The « De Moneta » of Nicholas Oresme and English Mint Documents*, London, 1956, p. 24.

(3) It should be noted, however, that the Low Countries, amongst others, employed several other monies-of-account that did not themselves represent existing silver coins, or no longer did so. Nevertheless, they were still tied to the current silver coinage, because each maintained a fixed relationship to the *livre gros*. Thus : £40 old Flemish « *pond paymente* » = £24 of the *livre* of 40 *gros* = £12 parisis (or *livre* of 20 *gros*) = £1 *gros*. For a discussion of the money-of-account (and the debate over its functions) see : Hans Van Werveke, *Monnaie de compte et monnaie réelle*, in *Revue belge de philologie et d'histoire*, XIII, 1934, p. 123-152 ; and Peter Spufford, *Monetary Problems and Policies in the Burgundian Netherlands, 1433-1496*, Leiden, 1970, p. 13-28, 166-169.

(4) As the Burgundian mint accounts demonstrate, this statement is true, but true only for coins above the value of a *demi-gros*. The smaller coins, the *mites*, called « *monnoie noire* », contained proportionately less silver than the

sequent documents on counterfeiting, it would be helpful to understand the two following measures employed in the Low Countries and France to specify these metal contents (5) :

A. *Fineness* (*aloi*)

1. For commercially « fine » silver, equal to 23/24ths (95.83 per cent) pure silver, the standard was 12 *deniers argent-le-roy*, with 24 *grains* to the *denier*.

2. For gold, as currently, the standard was 24 *carats* ; but in fact, the effective mint-standard of this period was that of the English gold *noble* : 23 7/8 carats.

B. *Weight* (*taille*)

The standard mint-weight was the *marc de Troyes*, containing 8 Paris *onces*, with 24 *deniers* to the *once*, and 24 *grains* to the *denier*, and weighing 244.753 grams. The prescribed weight of the coin was not, however, expressed in *deniers* and *grains* but in fractions of the *marc* : by the *taille* or number to be cut from the *marc* of the *aloi* specified.

If weight and fineness necessarily determined the hierarchy of coinage values, the prince himself assigned the coins their money-of-account values by specifying how many were to be cut from the *marc* of pure metal. The total money-of-account value of the coins so struck from the *marc* was called the *traite*, which can be readily calculated by the following formula :

$$\text{traite} = \frac{\text{price of the coin} \times \text{taille to the marc}}{\text{fineness (in deniers or carats)}}$$

Thus the traite of a *marc argent-le-roy* struck into double *gros*, having a *taille* of 50 to the marc and a fineness of 6 *deniers* would be : $\frac{2\text{d.} \times 50}{6/12} = \frac{100 \times 12}{6} = 200\text{d.}$ or 16s. 8d. *gros*. From this *traite* the mint-master deducted the prince's *seignorage* and also the *brassage*, which comprised both the actual costs of minting

others, in relation to their money-of-account values, because their minting costs (*brassage*) were proportionately higher : so much more alloy had to be added, and so many more had to be struck per unit of precious metal.

(5) For the following statistics, see : A. Engel and R. Serrure, *Traité de numismatique du moyen âge*, I, Paris, 1915, p. 4-7 ; A. Dieudonné, *Manuel des poids monétaires*, Paris, 1925, p. 32-35 ; and F. von Schrötter, *Wörterbuch der Münzkunde*, Berlin, 1930, *passim* (alphabetically by item).

and his own fee [6] : the remainder was thus the money-of-account price at which the mint purchased bullion. To the merchant, the minted coins had to be worth more than the equivalent bullion in order to cover at the very least these charges, and often also his sundry « costs » should he have to wait in receiving these coins. Normally coins did command such a « premium » because trading by bullion was technically illegal, and, more important, because coins were so much more portable and convenient to use than bullion [7].

In essence, a debasement of any kind encouraged merchants to supply the mint with more bullion by augmenting this « premium » on coinage, its exchange-value to the merchants. In order for the debasement to prove fully successful, both the prince and the merchants supplying bullion had to profit equitably, and such a division of the spoils demanded that three conditions be met. First, these merchants had to receive more coins of the same nominal or face value for their bullion than they would have obtained before the debasement ; and they had to be able to buy more goods than before, often with a lesser amount of actual gold or silver, and before the consequent inflation consumed these gains. Second, they obviously had to receive a better « price » for their bullion, in relation to both goods and the other metal, than was being offered elsewhere, on the market or at foreign mints. Since by definition a debasement meant an increase in the *traite* value of the coined metal, the prince therefore met these two conditions by raising the mint's money-of-account price for bullion to the required level. But third the prince ought to obtain the equivalent of more pure metal in his seignorage revenues, similarly to avoid loss from the ensuing debasement-induced inflation. On the other hand, he dared not be too excessive in his

(6) On *brassage* and *seignorage*, see Pierre Cockshaw, *Le fonctionnement des ateliers monétaires sous Philippe le Hardi*, in *Bulletin du Cercle d'études numismatiques*, VII, 1970, p. 24-36 ; and J. H. Munro, *Wool, Cloth, and Gold*, ch. 1. The brassage included the costs of the alloys, labour, tools, and the like, but *not all* the true costs of minting. As subsequently to be noted the prince himself had to pay (generally out of the seignorage) the salaries of his own staff of monetary officials (*garde de la monnaie, maître-général des monnaies, essayeurs*, etc.) and also meet the capital costs of the mint. See also P. Cockshaw, *o. c.*, p. 27-32 ; P. Spufford, *o. c.*, p. 130-3.

(7) For a discussion of the concept of coinage « premium », see Sir Albert Feavearyear, *The Pound Sterling: a History of English Money*, 2nd ed., revised by E. V. Morgan, Oxford, 1963, p. 10-36.

seignorage charges: for the higher the seignorage (and brassage) fees, the lower would be the mint-price for bullion. The mint accounts do in fact show that those greedy princes who at first failed to respect the first two conditions discussed were generally forced, if reluctantly, to reduce their seignorage charges in order to secure a continued influx of bullion.

The following table demonstrates the division of gains offered by the Flemish debasement of April 1387, by which Duke Philip the Bold of Burgundy reduced the silver content of the double gros by 21 per cent:

TABLE I

Debasement of the Flemish Double Gros: 3 April 1387

	Double Gros of 29 October 1386			*Double Gros of 3 April 1387*		
Fineness	6 deniers			5 deniers 4 grains		
Weight	57 to the marc			$59\frac{1}{2}$ to the marc		
			Per Cent of the Traite			Per Cent of the Traite
Traite		19s. 0d.	100.0		23s. 0d. 12m.	100.0
Brassage	1s. 1d. 12m.		5.2	1s. 7d.		6.9
Seignorage	2d. 12m.		1.1	8d. 12m.		3.0
Total Charges		1s. 4d.	6.3		2s. 3d. 12m.	9.9
Mint Price		17s. 8d. = 106 double gros	93.7		20s. 9d. = $124\frac{1}{2}$ double gros	90.1

Source: John Bartier and Andrée Van Nieuwenhuysen (eds.), *Les ordonnances de Philippe le Hardi et de Marguerite de Maele*, I (Brussels, 1965), p. 188-190, no. 128; p. 229-231, no. 146.

It will be noted that Duke Philip raised his seignorage fees to a far higher extent than he did the brassage, whose slight increase would probably have covered little more than the increased expenditures for alloy and labour in minting these debased coins. The following example, which will figure prominently in the subsequent discussion, suggests even more strongly that the initiative for debasement (and counterfeiting) came from the prince himself and not from the mint-master, as some historians are wont to maintain. By this debasement of November 1428, Philip the Good, third duke of Burgundy, increased not only the money-of-account price but also the percentage of the *traite* for *both* his seignorage and the mint price for bullion, at the direct expense of the mint-master's brassage fee.

TABLE II

Debasement of the Flemish Double Gros: November 1428

	Double Gros of June 1418		Per Cent of the Traite	*Double Gros of November 1428*		Per Cent of the Traite
Fineness	6 deniers			5 deniers 8 grains		
Weight	68 to the marc			$68\frac{1}{2}$ to the marc		
Traite		22s. 8d.	100.00		25s. 8d. 4m.	100.00
Brassage	1s. 2d.		5.13	1s. 2d. 4m.		4.55
Seignorage	4d.		1.47	6d.		1.95
Total Charges		1s. 6d.	6.60		1s. 8d. 4m.	6.50
Mint-Price		21s. 2d.	93.40		24s. 0d.	93.50
		= 127 double gros			= 144 double gros	

Source: Louis Deschamps de Pas, *Essai sur l'histoire monétaire des comtes de Flandre de la maison de Bourgogne*, in *Revue numismatique*, 2nd ser., 6, 1861, p. 458-478; 7, 1862, p. 117-143.

The ultimate test, the « touchstone » one might say, of a debasement's profitability was, of course, the degree of success in circulating the coins above their intrinsic worth. This was the more difficult to achieve with gold coins, first because their considerably higher value obviously led merchants, especially those engaged in foreign trade, to inspect them more closely; and if merchants who detected the debasement chose to accept them, they would do so only at commensurately lower money-of-account (silver) prices, probably at little more than their bullion values.

Second, although the prince might try to impose a money-of-account value upon gold coins, their effective exchange value was instead usually determined by the market, as influenced by the current gold to silver ratio in international trade and by foreign mints. Only so long as the market price for gold coins remained the same as that assigned by the prince could his gold debasements hope to succeed (8).

(8) If the official money-of-account or silver-exchange value of the debased gold coin was set higher than that permitted by the market, merchants who had converted their bullion into such coins would lose anticipated profits or even suffer a net loss in spending them; consequently, they would deliver less bullion to the mint once this happened. But if, on the other hand, the official

For these reasons, amongst others, the silver coinage was conversely the one more likely to undergo debasement (9). Even so, the effectiveness of silver debasements could be somewhat limited if they were too widely advertised, for the mercantile community would then again quickly react by « discounting » the silver coinage to secure the same amount of precious metal for their goods as before. It would do so, however, by discounting *all* silver coins, good and bad alike, not by reducing the coins' money-of-account values — consider the difficulty of commensurately reducing the penny's value to convenient fractions — but by raising prices of goods in general (10). Those merchants distributing the debased silver coins would thus still make at least a *relative* gain under such circumstances, which would consequently also force good silver coins to the mint. It should further be realized that the degree of price increases would not necessarily correspond exactly to the degree of debasement, since price levels would depend upon two other factors : the net increase in coinage units *left* in circulation ; and the individual elasticities of demand for and supply of the various commodities (11). Finally, and most obviously,

---

rate of the coin, *traite* value, and mint-price for gold bullion were all set lower than the corresponding market prices, then merchants would obviously sell their bullion « on the market » rather than to the mint (or official money-changers).

(9) Another reason may be cited : since silver coinage was largely the medium of local, domestic trade, while gold served the needs of international trade, a silver debasement would prove, *ceteris paribus*, less damaging to the prince's international relations and thus to his prestige. But this article is concerned with those princes who were willing to assume these risks in their debasement policies.

(10) See A. Feavearyear, *Pound Sterling*, p. 11, 16-36. Flemish monetary and financial documents of the fourteenth and fifteenth centuries also show that this form of « discounting » consistently prevailed.

(11) Three other factors, accompanying debasement, would also influence the degree of inflation : (a) a further increase in the money supply from influxes of foreign bullion, which the debasement would likely attract — though by no means all would be retained ; (b) an increased *velocity* of circulation [by the Fisher Identity, $M.V = P.T$], if the populace anticipated further debasements and thus sought to spend their (silver) coins quickly, before they suffered further depreciation ; and (c) an increase in exports and a decrease in imports [by the Keynsian equation, $Y = C+I+G+(X-M)$] that might well result from the coinage devaluation — that is, the fall in its foreign-exchange rates.

merchants would also gain from such debasements by using inferior coin to repay debts previously fixed in money-of-account prices.

Of all forms of debasement, by far the most effective and thus the most common was counterfeiting. Sometimes a prince's counterfeiting consisted only of issuing inferior imitations of his earlier, better coins; and this policy could prove to be quite profitable if he undertook the debasements in a series of alterations so rapid and individually so minor that the mercantile community could not react quickly enough to « discount » the coinage. But even simpler to achieve, more profitable for the prince, and in the short-run less damaging to his economic interests was issuing counterfeits of popular, widely-distributed foreign coins. Merchants domestic and foreign required little sophistication to appreciate the gains to be made by receiving for their bullion more coins from the counterfeiter than from the legitimate mint. Often the gains were quite large enough to warrant the costs of shipping and of reminting the good foreign coins themselves into the imitations [12] and also the risks of confiscation should they be detected when circulated abroad. Certainly counterfeiting was the most promising method of conducting gold debasements, and all the more profitable in view of the coins' high unit values. At the same time, it was also the most successful method of attracting foreign bullion to the prince's mint.

Nevertheless, one may well wonder how long counterfeits or debased coins in general could continue to circulate successfully abroad, before detection, confiscation, and other counter-measures managed to curb their distribution. Such coins, however, were in fact not so easily detected, chiefly because of the very inaccuracy

(12) Debasement or counterfeiting, it must be noted, did not automatically make it worthwhile to remint good (foreign) coins into bad, because in so doing merchants would lose, first, the « premium » on the good coins, representing their seignorage and brassage charges; and then they would have to pay these same charges again when having such coins reminted. Consequently, it should also be noted, the operative gold to silver exchange ratio for bullion was not that of the respective coinage values or *traites*, but rather *two* other ratios: the ratio of the gold *traite* to the mint-price for silver bullion; and conversely the ratio of the silver *traite* to the mint-price for gold bullion. The Flemish mint ratios of Nov. 1428 (Table II) for example were: 11.16:1 for the *traites*, 10.92:1 for gold bullion, and 1:11.94 for silver bullion. The difference between the two « bullion » ratios was thus a measure of protection that mint charges provided the prince against the export of his coins to foreign mints.

of medieval minting techniques. Indeed, the impossibility of making each and every coin of an issue identical and exact in weight explains why the mint indentures specified coinage weights by the number to be cut from the *marc*, rather than by the *denier* and *grain* units ; and why they also had to permit some margin of error — tolerance or *remède* — even in the *taille*. Furthermore, once in circulation, virtually all coins lost some weight from normal « wear and tear » ; and the purer the coin, the softer and more susceptible it was to such weight losses — not to mention the loss from clipping and « sweating » or rubbing, which the absence of milling-marks made irresistible. Hence, a significant percentage of « good » coins from each issue would likely weigh as little as their imitations, so that weighing individual fraudulent coins would not itself necessarily reveal the deception. Only by testing an unbiased random sample of, say, at least 50 pieces could one produce definite proof. In fineness, on the other hand, a coinage issue would likely have demonstrated a greater uniformity than in weight. But testing fineness, by the touchstone, was a rather more exacting and sophisticated technique for the average merchant than was weighing. Indeed for the vast majority of merchants, the retail merchants especially, coin-testing was far too difficult, time-consuming, and expensive to be worthwhile. When discernible weight variations in particular were to be expected, moreover, merchants perforce had to accept coins by *tale* or number, at face value, so long as the prince's stamp on the coin still commanded confidence.

One must readily admit, to be sure, that the large-scale foreign merchants, money-changers, bankers, and mint-officials were all fairly quick to test coins for fraud. The prince was also equally quick to issue proclamations sternly condemning and banning fraudulent foreign coins — sometimes, for good measure, banning all foreign coins. But in reading both the monetary ordinances and the Flemish town accounts, one is struck by how often and by how long after the initial detection of the fraud were these proclamations issued, with apparently no more effect than King Canute's command to halt the tides. Quite evidently, counterfeiters were blessed in their nefarious activities by the still primitive state of communications, literacy, and law-enforcement — by public ignorance, in brief. At the same time, their success did depend also upon observing some simple, sensible precautions : not to adulterate the coins with so much base alloy that, like Henry VIII's debased silver *testons*, « they blush for shame » [13] ; and not to make a clumsy forgery of the victimized coin's stamp. But so confident were many proud counterfeiters that their coins would receive little inspection by the populace that they inserted their own signature into the stamp's design [14].

Perhaps no region of northern Europe in the fifteenth century was more frequently subjected to having its coins counterfeited than were the Burgundian Low Countries. First, as the decisively dominant commercial and industrial centre of northern Europe, and more particularly as the international entrepôt *par excellence* their economies required a large volume of coinage and so necessarily received a large influx of foreign coins. Second, the esteem which Burgundian coins normally commanded invited counterfeiting. Third, the Burgundian realm unfortunately had, as its neighbours on the eastern frontier, a host of petty Rhenish principalities whose fiscal solvency often depended upon an unscrupulous manipulation of the mint [15] ; and to the south lay France, with whose impecunious King Charles VII the duke of Burgundy was at war between 1419 and 1435. King Charles, bereft of most of his domain and of France's tax resources for much of this period, was unmatched anywhere else in Europe for the drastic extent of his coinage debasements [16]. But Duke Philip the Good himself, during the years of serious warfare in Holland and France,

---

(13) Cited in Feavearyear, *The Pound Sterling*, p. 63.

(14) See the numismatic analysis by M. Pierre Cockshaw in Part II of this article. Evidently, counterfeiting princes inserted their own « signature » into the stamp precisely to exonerate themselves from the charge of counterfeiting.

(15) For a further discussion of monetary relations between the Burgundian Low Countries and the Rhenish principalities, see P. Spufford, *Monetary Problems*, p. 106-129 (for the years 1433-196) ; and a recent paper of Pierre Cockshaw, delivered.

(16) See in particular Jean Lafaurie, *Les monnaies des rois de France* : *Hughes Capet à Louis XII*, Paris, 1951, p. 68-102. In the Dauphin's first round of silver debasements, between 1417 and 1422, the *traite* of the *blanc* was increased from £10 *tournois* to £370 t., leaving the *blanc* only 2.7 % of its original silver content. He then returned to a « strong » coinage. For the second and third rounds of debasement, see *infra*, n. 24.

1425 to 1433, was far from being loath to utilize his mints in similarly augmenting his treasury (17).

At the same time, Duke Philip had sought to justify his debasements as purely defensive retaliations against his neighbours' monetary policies — against the operation of Gresham's Law, which were inundating his lands with fraudulent foreign coins and so denying his mints bullion (18). There was indeed some justice to his contentions ; and no more vivid illustration of the threat posed by neighbouring counterfeiters, and of the large profits to be reaped from their debased imitations of Burgundian and Imperial coins, can be presented than the following mint-assay report. The assay, conducted at the Louvain mint on 21 December 1430, three months after Philip had inherited the duchy of Brabant and this mint, was considered to be of such importance that it required the presence of Philip's councillors, the burgermaster and échevins of Louvain, and deputies from Brussels and Antwerp (19). After

---

(17) See *infra*, p. 140, and Tables IV-VI. As Philip later commented upon this period of warfare : « this burdensome and murderous war [in Holland]... had cost me, besides all the heavy expenses that I incurred throughout this period on the French war, over a million gold *saluts*, which at first I was extremely ill-prepared to find ». *Dagboek van Gent*, I, 57-8, as cited in Richard VAUGHAN, *Philip the Good: Apogee of Burgundy*, London, 1970, p. 307-308.

(18) See for example Philip's ordinance of 25 May 1433, ordering a debasement of the Namur coinage : « Pour obvier aux cours de plusieurs estranges monnoies d'or et d'argent de divers seigneurs d'Alemaigne et autres forgées à Tournay, en fortresses et ailleurs, lesquelles ont eu cours et esté de petite valeur et non suffisant, apportées, mises et haulcés à plus grant pris que ne valent en nos dits pais ; et encore sont les dictz monnoies estraignes journellement empirées, et soubs umbre de ce que les plusieurs d'icelles sont faictes et forgées à la facon des nostres si près que la difference ne s'en peut bonnement congnoistre si non par les gens qui se meslent de fait de monnoies, elles sont journelement princes et receus en nos dits pais, dont plusieurs fraudes et inconveniens sur le fait de la marchandise se committent de jour en jour ». Renier CHALON, *Recherches sur les monnaies des comtes de Hainaut*, Brussels, 1848, p. 208-211, doc. no. 15. Philip of St. Pol, Philip the Good's predecessor as duke of Brabant, similarly justified his debasement of Sept. 1429 by maintaining that : « overmits alrehande vremde munten, die in onse voirscr. lande zeer hoege boven hoere werde gegaen hebben, metten welcken *t'gout ende t'selver uten selven lande zeer getogen* [zijn] ». ARCHIVES GÉNÉRALES DU ROYAUME, *Chambre des Comptes*, no. 131, f°. 85ro-vo.

(19) A.G.R., *Chambre des Comptes*, carton 65/2. « Assaye fais en la ville de Louvain le 21e jour de décembre mil 430 en la presence d'aucuns du conseil de monseigneur le duc, du bourgmaistre et echevins de la dite ville de Lou-

analyzing the weight and fineness of eleven foreign coins, eight of them unabashed counterfeits, and noting the current rates at which they were being accepted, the assayors then calculated the « surplus » per *marc de Troyes* of fine metal to be made in striking and distributing each of them. The report can best be summarized by the following table, whose figures, except for the ones enclosed in square-brackets, are those of the mint-assayors themselves.

TABLE III

Burgundian Assay of Foreign Coins Struck at the Mints of Wezemaal-Rummen, Reckheim, Liège, Arnhem, and Tournay, conducted at Louvain, 21 December 1430.

A. SILVER COINS

Those struck in Imitation of the Burgundian *cromstaert* [Burgundian *cromstaert* as struck at the mints of Louvain, Ghent, and Dordrecht]

[a. fineness :	5 deniers 8 grains *argent-le-roy*
b. taille :	$68\frac{1}{2}$ to the marc]
c. rate :	8 esterlins of Brabant [= $2\frac{2}{3}$d. gros of Brabant = 2d. gros of Flanders]
d. traite of the silver marc :	34s. 2d. gros of Brabant = 25s. 8d. 4 mites gros Flemish

1. *Cromstaert of Rumène* [*Rummen*] : by *Jean de Wesemal* [Wezemaal]

a. fineness :	4 deniers 18 grains
b. taille :	72 to the marc
c. current rate :	8 esterlins [= $2\frac{2}{3}$d. gros of Brab.]
d. traite of the marc :	40s. 6d. gros of Brabant
e. surplus per marc :	76 placques of Brabant [= 6s. 4d. gros Brabant]
[f. percentage gross profit :	18,54 %]

2. *Cromstaert of Reyckem* [*Reckheim*] by Guillaume de Sombrecht [sic : Sombreffe]

a. fineness :	4 deniers 3 grains
b. taille :	72 to the marc
c. current rate :	8 esterlins [= $2\frac{2}{3}$d. gros of Brab.]
d. traite of the marc :	46s. 11d. gros of Brabant
e. surplus per marc :	155 placques [sic : should be 153 pl.] = 12s. 9d. gros of Brabant
[f. percentage gross profit :	37,32 %]

---

vain, et des deputéz des villes de Brouxelles et d'Anvers, pour le bien, utilité et prouffit de mondit seigneur le duc et de son pays de Brabant, des estranges monnoyes d'argent [et d'or] cy-apres declairés.... On a enchargié au maistre de la monnoye dudit Louvain de assembler de chacune desdictes monnoyes pour par l'assayeurs dicelle monnoye en faire les assays afin de plus a(m)pplamente congnoistre de la dicte perte ».

3. *Cromstaert* [*or Placque*] *of Tournay* [of King Charles VII of France] « le denier d'argent que aussi len forge presentement audit Tournay sur le cromstert de monseigneur, dont au lieu du lyon a trois fleurs de lys. »

a. fineness :	5 deniers
b. taille :	69 to the marc
c. current rate :	1 cromstaert [= 8 esterlins of Brab. = 2d. gros Flemish]
d. traite of the marc :	27s. 7d. 18 mites gros Flemish [= 36s. 9d. 9 mites gros of Brabant]
e. surplus per marc :	23½d. gros Flemish [= 1s. 11d. 12 mites gros. Flem. = 2s. 7d. 9m. gros of Brab.]
[f. percentage gross profit :	7,65 %]

The last two silver coins, as the subsequent numismatic analysis will verify, were not actually counterfeits of the *cromstaert*, though their issuers may have hoped that they might be accepted as such. They circulated in fact at a rate of 2 esterlins less than the various *cromstaerts* ; but even so they were, according to the assay, considerably overvalued :

4. *Gryffon of Liège*

a. fineness :	4 deniers
b. taille :	72 to the marc
c. current rate :	2 placques [= 2d. gros of Brabant]
d. traite of the marc :	36s. 0d. gros of Brabant
e. surplus per marc :	22 placques of Brab. [= 1s. 10d. gros of Brabant
[f. percentage gross profit :	5,37 %]

5. *Staende Mannekens of Guillaume de Sombrecht* [sic : Sombreffe-Reckheim]

a. fineness :	4 deniers
b. taille :	109 to the marc
c. current rate :	2 placques [= 2d. gros of Brabant]
d. traite of the marc :	54s. 6d. gros of Brabant
e. surplus per marc :	244 placques = 20s. 4d. gros of Brabant
[f. percentage gross profit :	59,51 %]

B. GOLD COINS : « Et quant aux estranges monnoyes d'or qui ont cours audit pays on a plus grant perte pour le peuple que en la monnoye blanche cy-dessus. »

	Counterfeits	*Coin Imitated*
1. *Gryffon or Florin of Liège*, and *Ecu of Liège*, « que`en forge presentement audit Liège contrefais apres ceulx de monseigneur. » (N.B. : two coins)		*Louvain Schild* (*Écu*)
a. fineness :	14½ carats	[16 carats
b. taille :	69½ to the marc	68 to the marc]
c. current rate :	37½d. gros Flem. [= 4s. 2d. gros of Brab.]	37½d. gros Flem. = 4s. 2d. gros of Brab.

d. traite of the marc :	£17. 11s. 6d. gros Flem.	£15. 18s. 9d. gros. Flem.
e. surplus per marc :	32s. 9d. gros Flem. = 43s. 8d. gros of Brab.	
[f. percentage gross profit :	13,70 %]	
2. *Ecu of Rumène* [*Rummen*] struck by Jean de Wezemaal		*Louvain Schild* (*Écu*)
a. fineness :	$13\frac{1}{2}$ carats	[16 carats
b. taille :	$69\frac{1}{2}$ to the marc	68 to the marc]
c. current rate :	$37\frac{1}{2}$d. gros. Flem.	$37\frac{1}{2}$d. gros Flem.
d. traite of the marc :	£18. 18s. 1d. gros Flem.	£15. 18s. 9d. gros Flem.
e. surplus per marc :	£2. 19s. 4d. gros Flem [£3. 19s. 4d. 13m. gros of Brab.]	
[f. percentage gross profit :	18,61 %]	
3. *Couronne of Tournay* [of Charles VII] ([20])		*Louvain Pieter*
a. fineness :	$20\frac{1}{2}$ carats	[21 carats
b. taille :	$68\frac{1}{2}$ to the marc	68 to the marc]
c. current rate :	49d. gros Flem.	49d. gros Flem.
d. traite of the marc :	£16. 5s. 1d. gros Flem.	£15. 10s. 10d. gros Flem.
e. surplus per marc :	14s. 3d. gros Flem. [= 18s. $11\frac{1}{2}$d. gros of Brab.]	
[f. percentage gross profit :	4,58 %]	
4. *Mailles of the Rhine* [*Rummen-Wezemaal*] : « contrefaites après celles de l'empereur que fait forgier ledit [demoiseau de] Wesemale audit lieu de Rumène. »		*Imperial Florin*
a. fineness :	$14\frac{1}{2}$ carats	[19 carats
b. taille :	74 to the marc	72 to the marc
c. current rate :	43d. gros Flem.	42d. or 43d. gros Flem. ?*]

* If the Imperial florin's current rate was 43d. gros, the same as that of the *maille of the Rhine* of Rummen, the *traite* of the gold marc would have been £16. 3s. 0d. gros ; if 42d. gros, then £15. 18s. 4d., which is very close to the *traite* of the florin's gold *marc* given in the report. Nevertheless, it seems more likely that the rate was indeed 43d. gros, and that the florin was thus overvalued by 1d. gros.

(20) It appears, however, that the Louvain *pieter* was originally itself a counterfeit of the Tournay *couronne* : for the latter was first struck by Charles VII in May 1427, while the former was first struck, by Philip of St. Pol, in May 1430. See Marcel Hoc, *Histoire monétaire de Tournai*, Brussels, 1970, p. 95 sq ; A.G.R., *Chambre des Comptes*, no. 18.065.

d. traite of the marc :	£21. 9s. 8d. gros Flem.	£15. 18s. 9d. gros Flem.
e. surplus per marc :	£5. 10s. 11d. gros Flem. [= £7. 7s. 6d. 10m. gros of Brab.]	
[f. percentage gross profit :	34,80 %]	
5. *Mailles of Arnhem* [or *Arnoldus*] of the Duke of Guelders		
a. fineness :	12½ carats	
b. taille :	77 to the marc	
c. current rate :	28d. gros Flem.	
d. traite of the marc :	144 mailles and 20d. gros Flem [sic] = £16. 17s. 0d. gros Flem. [sic : should be £17. 5s. 0d. gros.**]	£15. 18s. 9d. gros Flem.
e. surplus per marc :	18s. 3d. gros Flem [sic] = 24s. 4d. gros of Brab. [should be : £1. 6s. 3d. gros Flem.**]	
[f. percentage gross profit :	8,24 %]	

Sources : Archives Générales du Royaume, *Chambre des Comptes*, carton 65:2 (unsorted and uncatalogued). An eighteenth century copy of a Flemish-language version of this mint-assay (with some errors) may be found in A.G.R., *C. des C.*, reg. no. 580, fo. 90ro-93vo. The fineness and taille of the Louvain mint's silver and gold coins (in square brackets in the table) were taken from the Louvain mint account of 4 October 1430 - 19 March 1431, in A.G.R., *C. des C.*, reg. no. 18,067. The mint-assay also did not provide the fineness and taille of the Imperial florin ; but these figures were obtained from another contemporary manuscript in A.G.R., *C. des C.*, carton 65 : bis 1 (also uncatalogued).

** The mint-assayors, or the scribe, evidently made an error in calculating the traite of the gold marc for the Arnhem *maille* or *Arnoldus*, because a gold marc should have yielded $\frac{(77 \times 24)\ 147.84}{12.5}$ *mailles*, or 147 mailles and 23½d. gros Flem., not 144 mailles 20d. The traite, at 28d. gros Flem. per *maille*, would then have been £17. 5s. 0d. gros (per marc of 24 carats). The eighteenth-century Flemish copy in fact does give a traite value of £17. 4s. 10½d. gros Flem. ; and thus a « surplus » of £1. 6s. 1½d. gros.

The one gold coin in this report not specifically accused of being a counterfeit was the worst one, the Guelders *maille* or *Arnoldus*.

According to another contemporary mint-report in the same collection, the fineness of this coin, originally 18 carats, had in recent years deteriorated from 14 carats, descending to just 11½ carats by the mid-1430s ([21]). Evidently the *Arnoldus* had originally been struck in imitation of the Imperial florin ; the several series of eventually drastic debasements, however, no longer permitted it to pass for a florin, so that its market rate fell to 28d. gros. Flemish. Yet that price was clearly still well « above its true worth », in the language of the documents, and thus the *Arnoldus* was in effect circulating as a counterfeit of its more recent issues. The Guelders *Arnoldus* and the Rummen *maille* were by no means the only counterfeit florins that had recently undergone considerable debasement. That other mint-report also contends that, recently, the *florin* or « *postulaat* » of neighbouring Utrecht had been reduced from 17 to 15 carats ; the Jülich *florin*, from 19 to 18 5/12ths carats ; and the German *Fredericus*, from 16 to 14 carats ([22]).

Of all Philip's inconsiderate neighbours, undoubtedly Charles VII, then his inveterate foe, provided the gravest challenge to the Burgundian mints. With the renewal of heavy fighting in France, culminating in the siege of Orléans, Charles launched his mints in Aug. 1427 on a series of debasements, unparalleled for their drastic extent, that reduced the silver content of his *blanc* 70 per cent by June 1429 ([23]). For Duke Philip, the most injurious of the French debasements were probably those conducted at the mint of Tournay, a Dauphinist enclave within the Burgundian Lowlands, that permitted an easy distribution of fraudulent coins ([24]). First utilizing the Tournay mint in May 1427 to strike the *couronne*, at a respectable 23 carats and a taille of 67 to the marc, Charles steadily reduced its gold content to just 16 carats and a

---

(21) A.G.R., *Chambre des Comptes*, carton 65bis/1.

(22) A.G.R., *Chambre des Comptes*, carton 65bis 1.

(23) Lafaurie, *Monnaies des rois de France*, p. 97-102. After another series of debasements in 1426, Charles had once more returned to a stronger coinage in December of that year, with a silver *traite* of £ 8.0.0. *tournois*. His third round of debasements raised the *traite* of the marc to £28.0.0. t. : far from being so miserably debased as the *blanc* of 1422, but for two years an even more rapid change.

(24) See M. Hoc, *Histoire monétaire de Tournai*, p. 95-116.

taille of 67 by December 1432 ([25]). Nevertheless, Duke Philip, who had himself earlier adopted, in November 1425 (Dordrecht mint), a policy of « favouring » gold over silver, and of heavily debasing the former, eventually succeeded quite effectively and most profitably in meeting all foreign mint competition for that metal, as the following table suggests ([26]) :

Impressive as the later mint outputs may be, one can well appreciate why Philip, after the deep slump in gold minting during 1429-30, should have commanded that assay of foreign counterfeits in December 1430, and why he then responded to the challenge with further and even more drastic debasements of his gold coinage ([27]).

Duke Philip's silver coinage, as one might expect, fared rather less well. To be sure, his Flemish silver debasement and recoinage of November 1428, the first in ten years (Table II), produced the quite astounding total of 72,460.7 silver marcs by September 1429. But thereafter, until the Burgundian monetary reform of October

---

(25) *Ibid.*, and J. LAFAURIE, *o. c.*, p. 97-102.

(26) In Nov. 1425 at the Dordrecht mint (Holland), and the following year at the Ghent and Namur mints, Philip commenced striking the gold *clinquaerts*, with 17 carats, a *taille* of 67 to the *marc*, and a *traite* of £15. 15s. 3d. *gros*. By December 1431 (chiefly at Namur), he had debased this coin to 15 carats and a *taille* of 68 to the *marc*, thus raising its traite to £17. 17s. 10d. *gros*. In that same month of December, he then began debasing the Brabantine *pieter* (at Namur as well as at Louvain) ; by May 1433 the *pieter* had been reduced from 21 carats (and a taille of 68½) to 18 carats, and its traite was correspondingly raised from the original £15. 10s. 10d. to £18. 17s. 10d gros. A.G.R., *Chambre des Comptes* no. 580, f° 94ro-vo ; no 18. 203, and nos 18.065-8. At the same time the hypocritical Duke Philip was himself counterfeiting the prized English gold *noble*. His first imitations were struck at Ghent and Namur in June 1425, with 23¼ carats and a taille of 35½ to the *marc*, compared to the English *noble*'s 23⅞ carats and *taille* of 35 to the *marc*. But few of these were struck, apparently because they were too inferior to pass successfully. Then in Sept. 1427 the Ghent mint issued a much stronger *noble* of 23⅞ carats also, and a taille of 35¼. But these coins on the other hand offered merchants too small an advantage to attract much bullion to Philip's mints. The third, and finally successful *noble*, of Nov. 1428, had the same *taille* of 35¼ to the *marc*, but a reduced fineness of 23½ carats. Between 10 Nov. 1428 and 25 Feb. 1430, the Ghent mint struck 4,577 *marcs* of pure gold into these counterfeit *nobles*. A.G.R., *Acquits de Lille*, liasse 937 ; and for the ordinances, L. DESCHAMPS DE PAS, *Histoire monétaire des comtes de Flandres*, in *Revue numismatique*, 2nd ser., 6, 1861, 462-5, 468-71.

(27) See the preceding note, for debasements at the mints of Louvain and Namur.

TABLE IV

Coinage of pure gold marcs de Troyes, and the Seignorage Receipts of the Burgundian Mints at : Dordrecht, Namur, Ghent, and Louvain 1424-5 to 1432-3

Michael-mas Years : 1 Oct. - 30 Sept.	Gold marcs coined	Seignorage in pure gold marcs	Seignorage Receipts on gold coinage in £ gros	Total Seignorage on Gold and Silver minting in £ gros
1424-5	571.4	7.5	£103.2	£456.5
1425-6	4,585.0	146.1	2,156.2	2,382.7
1426-7	5,797.3	245.9	3,761.3	3,808.9
1427-8	1,489.2	45.6	691.5	814.4
1428-9	6,061.4	104.0	1,547.3	3,582.1
1429-30	1,368.1*	21.4	351.5	1,667.6
1430-1	8,178.0	103.9	1,656.1	1,939.2
1431-2	11,901.4	298.6	5,087.5	5,142.3
1432-3	6,065.8	314.5	5,459.2	5,473.3

* In 1429-30, the Louvain mint coined 3,347.0 gold marcs for the then duke of Brabant, Philip of St. Pol ; after 30 Sept. 1430, the duchy and the Louvain mint both passed into the hands of Duke Philip the Good.

Sources : A.G.R., *Acquits de Lille*, liasse no. 937 (Ghent) ; *Chambre des Comptes*, no. 18,203 (Namur) and 18.065-8 (Louvain) ; ALGEMEEN RIJKSARCHIEF (Nederland), *Rekeningen van de Grafelijkheidsrekenkamer te 's-Gravenhage*, nos. 4937 : I-III (Dordrecht and Zevenbergen).

1433, Philip left his silver coinage, except at his Namur mint, stable, untouched — and a fit prey for all his predatory neighbours. The following Tables V and VI record the alterations of the silver coinages at Charles VII's Tournay mint and at Philip's Namur mint ; and demonstrate the catastrophic effect that the issues of counterfeit *cromstaerts*, from not only the Tournay but those other neighbouring mints as well, had upon the Burgundian silver minting (28) :

---

(28) The English were also partly responsible for denying silver bullion to the Burgundian mints. Though long maintaining a strong, stable coinage, the English mints then conversely « favoured » silver over the Burgundian mints ; and, more important, the 1429 Parliament, in evident retaliation against Philip's debasements and counterfeiting of the *nobles*, required the Calais wool staple, selling chiefly to his subjects, to exact full payment in ready cash, one third of it in « bullion ». From 1428-9 to 1431-2, the silver coinage output of the Calais mint rose from 32,923 *marcs* to 42,321 *marcs*. See J. H. MUNRO, *An Economic Aspect of the Collapse of the Anglo-Burgundian Alliance, 1428-1442*, in *English Historical Review*, 85, 1970, p. 225-244 (and especially Table III, p. 233).

TABLE V

Debasements of the Silver *Cromstaerts* and *Double Gros*
at the mints of Charles VII and of Duke Philip the Good
December 1427 - October 1433

	Charles VII Tournay *Cromstaert*		Duke Philip the Good *Cromstaerts* of Ghent, Louvain, and Dordrecht		Duke Philip the Good *Double Gros* of Namur	
Date of Alter-ation	Silver Content	Traite in £ gros	Silver Content	Traite in £ gros	Silver Content	Traite in £ gros
Dec. 1427	6 den. 1 gr. 67 taille	£8.0.0. t. =£1.2.5.gr.	[6 den. 68 taille]	[£1.2.8d.]	[4 den. 23 gr. 54 taille]	[£1.1.7¼d.]
July 1428					4 den. 12 gr. 54 taille	£1.4.0d.
Nov. 1428			5 den. 8 gr. 68½ taille	£1.5.8.4m.		
Jan. 1429					4 den. 4 gr. 54 taille	£1.6.0d.
April 1429	5 den. 8 gr. 68 taille	£1.5.6d.				
June 1429					4 den. 54 taille	£1.7.0d.
Sept. 1430	5 den. 4 gr. 68 taille	£1.6.4d.				
June 1431	5 den. 68 taille	£1.7.2d.				
Aug. 1431	4 den. 20 gr. 68 taille	£1.8.1½d.				
Dec. 1431					3 den. 18 gr. 54 taille	£1.8.9.14m.
Jan. 1432	4 den. 18 gr. 68 taille	£1.8.7½d.				
Sept. 1432	4 den. 16 gr. 68 taille	£1.9.2d.				

May 1433					6 den. 70 taille (8 est.)	£1.11.1.7m.
Aug. 1433					6 den. 70 taille (2d. gr.)	£1.3.4d.
Oct. 1433			6 den. 72 taille	£1.4.0d.		

TABLE VI

Output of Silver *marcs de Troyes, argent-le-roy,* by the mints of Tournay (Charles VII), Ghent, Dordrecht, Louvain, and Namur: 1 October 1428 to 25 October 1433

Michaelmas Years	Charles VII: Tournay	Duke Philip the Good of Burgundy: Ghent	Louvain	Dordrecht	Namur	Burgundian Total
1428-9		72,461	—	—	7,125	79,586
1429-30	13,527	34,992	[19,468*]	4,051	10,202	49,245
1430-1	12,824	5,585	2,728	1,607	3,507	13,428
1431-2	15,948	111	360	844	1,446	2,761
1432-3	17,668	-nil-	-nil-	318	126	444
1-25 Oct. 1433	1,237	-nil-	-nil-	-nil-	-nil-	-nil-

* coined for the then duke of Brabant, Duke Philip of St. Pol; not included in the total Burgundian silver coinage.

Sources for Tables V and VI:

a. Tournay: Comte DE CASTELLONE, *Les monnaies d'argent du système flamand frappées à Tournai au nom de Charles VII,* in *Revue numismatique,* 2nd ser., 4, 2, 1898, p. 103-15.

b. Ghent: A.G.R., *Acquits de Lille,* liasse no. 937.

c. Louvain: A.G.R., *Chambre des Comptes,* no. 18.065-8.

d. Namur: A.G.R. *Chambre des Comptes,* no 18.203; and *Acquits de Lille,* liasse 1933.

e. Dordrecht: A.R.A. (Nederland), Rekenkamer no. 4937: II (account of 12 Dec. 1429 - 20 Feb. 1433, probably also including the coinage of the Zevenbergen mint. No silver was struck before this account: see no. 4937: I).

Since, as previously argued, banning fraudulent coins was almost always a fruitless measure, the prince had only one recourse for the protection of his mints: to alter his own coinage. That generally meant debasing his coinage to the same, or — just to be certain, and to gain an extra dividend — even greater degree, and offering merchants at least an equivalent price for their bullion. It was in this fashion that counterfeiting inflicted its most ruinous damages upon the economy: by provoking a spiralling series of debasements that inevitably produced a runaway inflation, from both mercantile « discounting » of the coinage and from the increased number of circulating coins. But even for debasements, the law of diminishing returns eventually sets in, as merchants withold bullion in expectation of yet further price increases, as the populace loses confidence in coinage and takes refuge in bullion or other real assets, as the prince finds that his sources of credit are evaporating and that his revenues are being sapped by inflation. Finally, therefore, the prince is compelled to return to a strong coinage, to institute a *renforcement*, as Duke Philip the Good did by his monetary reform and unification of October 1433 - June 1434 [29]. At the same time, by issuing a common coinage for all of the Burgundian Lowlands, and one quite distinctly different in design, weight, and alloy, he did manage — for a few years at least — to foil the counterfeiters. Thus, on 25 October 1433 the Tournay mint ceased issuing its imitation *cromstaerts* — though Philip also influenced it to do so by some unfriendly persuasion, at the point of a sword [30].

The profits of both counterfeiting and of debasements in general, therefore, were ultimately subject to the strict limitations imposed by cutthroat competition, retaliations, and reprisals. At the same time, in trying to estimate real profits, one must remember that the figures for the « surpluses per marc » cited in Table III represent only the gross returns, and that these gains had to be shared amongst the bullion supplier, the prince, and usually also

(29) See P. SPUFFORD, *Monetary Problems*, pp. 4-6, 30-1 ; and J. H. MUNRO, *Wool, Cloth, and Gold*, chapter 4.

(30) See M. HOC, *Histoire monétaire de Tournai*, p. 97-101 ; and P. SPUFFORD, *Monetary Problems*, p. 93-5. The Tournay mint ceased coining the debased *cromstaerts* on 25 Oct. 1433 ; and although it did mint some *patards* as imitations of the new Burgundian *double gros*, between Nov. 1433 and June 1434, it did not debase them. On 10 Feb. 1434, Philip forced the Tournay échevins to agree to cease all minting for six years in return for his promise to « respect » the town's neutrality. (A.G.R., *Trésor de Flandres*, I, nº 2368). The Tournay mint formally closed on 21 Sept. 1435, and did not re-open until June 1440, henceforth minting only coins of the French royal type.

his mint-master. Furthermore, the statistics conceal a number of costs for the prince : apart from the cost of the alloy (included in the brassage, and born by the mint-master), the salaries for his *garde de la monnaie*, the *essayeurs*, and various other monetary officials that he may have retained, and the capital expenditures on the mint itself [31]. But clearly some sizeable pure profits did remain for the counterfeiters ; and if these profits would eventually be eradicated by inflation, they were nevertheless a clear net gain for the short-run. Medieval public finance was in essence largely a matter of constantly recurring short term considerations, requiring scarce ready money. That fact of life explains why most princes « farmed » their tax revenues and tolls for immediate cash, rather than wait for these receipts slowly to dribble into their treasuries over the year. Few were the princes, in an age when credit and banking institutions were still rudimentary, when normal revenues depended so much on relatively fixed feudal and domain dues, when new taxes were so difficult to impose and even more difficult to collect, who could thus always afford to ignore the quickly-realisable cash profits of counterfeiting and debasement.

---

(31) See n. 6, *supra*. Although seignorage was thus not a pure profit, the prince also gained other revenues from his mint : the *remèdes*, or surplus metal resulting from any minting deficient in weight or fineness ; confiscations of « illegal » coins as *billon* ; and the « farms » of the mint, or the sale of the *brassage* rights in minting (that is, the portion of the *brassage* representing the mint-master's own fees).

III

BILLON — BILLOEN — BILLIO

FROM BULLION TO BASE COINAGE (AN ESSAY IN NUMISMATIC PHILOLOGY)

As a graduate student at a North American university several years ago, I was strictly warned to beware the seductive *faux pas* of confusing the French word *billon* with the English *bullion*. To be sure, I found this caveat to be well directed for the translation of the terms in contemporary languages. Indeed, the modern French term, in meaning solely petty coin heavily alloyed with some base metal, usually copper, or just plain copper coinage (1), is virtually the antonym of *bullion*, as unminted gold or silver in the mass, most commonly represented in the form of unadulterated bars or ingots. The cognates of *billon* in other modern Romance languages, such as *biglione* or *viglione* in Italian and *vellon* in Spanish, similarly mean petty, base, cupric coin (2).

Yet my researches into fourteenth- and fifteenth-century monetary history and numismatics soon convinced me that the late-medieval French *billon* (occasionally also *buillon, boillon*), the Netherlandish *billoen* (very often also *billioen*; or *bolioen*, *belgioen*, *bulgioene*, and several other variants (3)), and the continental late-Latin *billio* (sometimes *billo, billona* (4)) were all most commonly used, approximately if not always

(1) E. g. "monnaie d'argent contenant une grande quantité de cuivre, ou de cuivre contenant un peu d'argent". P. LAROUSSE, *Grand dictionnaire universel du* XIXe *siècle*, II (Paris, 1865), 750, col. 4; "monnaie de cuivre mêlée ou non d'argent". P. ROBERT, *Dictionnaire alphabetique et analogique de la langue française*, I (Paris, 1960), 480, col. 1. For the English definition, see n. 11 *infra*.

(2) "*Biglione* (*viglione*): argento di bassa lega; fr. *billon* ... La variante *viglione* per il tramite dello spagn. *vellon*". C. BATTISTI and G. ALESSO, *Dizionario etimologico italiano*, I (Florence, 1968), 517. "*Vellon*: moneda de cobre que se uso en lugar de la fabricada con liga de plata". *Diccionario de la lengua espãnola* (Real Academia Espanola, Madrid, 1970), p. 1328, col. 2.

(3) *Infra*, p. 302 and n. 32.

(4) For the variants of the Latin term used in medieval England, see *infra*, p. 302 and n. 33.

precisely, in the sense of the contemporary English *bullion*. I further noticed that quite a few French and Belgian numismatists and monetary historians casually accepted or used the word *billon* in its medieval context as though it meant *bullion*. Irritatingly enough, however, they were also wont to use this term in its modern sense, without bothering to explain or note this significant difference in usage.

Even more disconcerting was the discovery that various historical dictionaries provided no solution for this conundrum of conflicting meanings ; that indeed they seemed to verify my professor's caveat for the medieval period as well. Thus the *Dictionnaire historique de l'ancien langage français* of La Curne de Sainte-Palaye states that the term *billon* "est spécialement affecté aux monnaies, et on s'en sert pour désigner toute sorte de matière qui est alliée, c'est-à-dire mêlée au-dessous du degré fixé pour la fabrication des monnaies" ; and after providing numerous examples, it concludes that "de là, ce mot se prenait pour toute monnaie decriée, légère, ou défectueuse" ([5]). The more widely known *Dictionnaire de l'ancienne langue française* of Fréderic Godefroy, while curiously omitting the monetary meanings of *billon* in its first edition (stating only "jeu de billes, morceau, débris") ([6]), provided the following definition of *billonneur* in its supplementary Vol. VIII : "celui qui allie un métal précieux avec d'autres métaux qui sont en proportion plus considérables" ([7]). The esteemed *Middelnederlandsch Woordenboek* of E. Verwijs and J. Verdam similarly defines the Flemish-Low German word *billioen* as "goud en zilver, met andere metalen vermengd, en minder karaten edel metaal bevattende dan bij de ordonnantiën was voorgeschreven" ([8]). Further devaluing the term, so to speak, directing us all the more away from the sense of *bullion*, the famous ***Glossarium Mediae et Infimae Latinitatis*** by Charles du Fresne, Sieur du Cange, defines the medieval continental-Latin *billio* (and also the French

(5) III (Paris, 1877), 12.

(6) I (Paris, 1881), 651.

(7) *Ibid.*, VIII (Paris, 1893), 326. See also *infra*, pp. 303-304 and n. 36 for the definitions of *billon* in *Dictionnaire de la langue française du seizième siècle*.

(8) I (The Hague, 1885), 1257 ; and similarly in J. VERDAM, *Middelnederlandsch Handwoordenboek* (The Hague, 1964), p. 98, col. 2. Cf. Edward GAILLARD, *Glossaire flamand (de l'Inventaire des archives de la ville de Bruges*, de L. GILLIODTS-VAN SEVEREN) (Bruges, 1882), pp. 256-7 : "*billoen* : monnaie decriée ; ... matières d'or ou d'argent dont l'alliage est au-dessous de taux normal".

billon, the Spanish *vellon*) in precisely its modern sense as just a copper, or heavily alloyed silver coin : "nummus aereus, vel ex aere et argento conflatus" (9).

Finally the unquestionably authoritative *New English Dictionary on Historical Principles (The Oxford English Dictionary)* stoutly denies any real connection between *billon* and *bullion*, and instead offers a distinctly different origin for the English term. Noting that *bullion* (also *bullioun*, *bolion*, *bolyon*, *bullyon*, *bulloyn*, *bulloin*, *bulloigne*, *bullen*, *billion*, *bulline*) first appears as such in fourteenth-century Anglo-Norman, with the apparent meaning of "mint or melting-house" (10), the *N.E.D.* suggests that the word is cognate to *bouillon*, and thus derived from either the Old French or Latin verb to boil (11). To be sure, many late-medieval English texts do employ the term *bullion* to mean the royal mints or royal coinage exchanges — if not precisely "melting-houses" — as well as uncoined gold and silver ; but the *N.E.D.* yet does not manage to explain convincingly how the French or Latin verb "to boil" should come to mean, specifically, "to melt down precious metals for minting", and thus evolve into *bullion*.

But that possibly minor cavil aside, how can one effectively explain away the definitions cited in all these highly respected historical dictionaries, for the medieval as well as the modern periods, and then justify equating *billon* — *billoen* — *billio* with *bullion* ? The answer and justification can be found in hundreds (if not thousands) of French, Flemish, and Latin texts of the fourteenth- and fifteenth-century Low Countries : texts of ordinances, proclamations, and edicts that prohibit the export of *billon* or *billoen* (or *billionem* in the Latin accusative case) (12). Quite obviously there would have been very little if any logic in prohibiting, and prohibiting solely, the

(9) New edition by Léopold Favre, I (Niort, 1883), 660, col. 2-3. However, see also *infra*, p. 303 and n. 34.

(10) Ed. James A. H. Murray, I (Oxford, 1888), citing *statute* 9 Edward III, c. 2, 1336 : "... puissent sauvement porter a les eschanges ou *bullion* ... argent en plate, vessel d'argent ... ".

(11) *Ibid.* : "Of obscure etymology ... the form appears to point to identity with F. *bouillon* med. L. *bullio* ... If this etymology be correct the sense of "boiling" must have undergone a purely English development into those of "melting", "melted mass of metal". ... The Fr. *billon*, base metal, is unconnected in origin ...". Cf. *The Concise Oxford Dictionary of Current English* (ed. H. W. and F. G. Fowler, 4th edition, Oxford, 1951), p. 155 : "*bullion* : n. & a. Gold or silver before (or as valued apart from) coining or manufacture ... A. F. prob. = F. *bouillon* soup, f. med. L. *bullionem* ... (L. *bullire* BOIL + -ION) ; but the meanings are E. only".

(12) See *infra*, p. 300 and notes 27, 28, 33, for the Latin variants.

export of copper coins, of what was called *monnaie noire*, or of heavily debased gold and silver coins as such. One can understand bans on their importation, most certainly, but not those on their export, nor the apparent absence of bans on exporting good coins and precious metals in general, especially in view of the bullionist-mercantilist temper of these times. For a resolution of those questions, a close analysis of the various texts will reveal that the term *billon* — *billoen* — *billio* then had two quite closely related meanings — neither of which was that found in modern Romance languages. The first, general, in fact all-encompassing definition, and the one most closely matching the sense of the English *bullion*, was in essence : all such precious metals (gold and silver) that were legally required to be taken to the ruler's mint for coinage. As the following examples indicate, that normally meant *all* forms of precious metals except those formally exempted by edict. Such exemptions obviously included the ruler's own current coins, and also certain favoured foreign gold coins, especially those acting as international mediums of exchange in this era, gold and silver jewelry, and intact plate or artifacts.

(1) Monetary ordinance, issued for the duchy of Brabant, June 1434, by Duke Philip the Good of Burgundy [13] :
... gereckent zijn over *billoen* als dat niet te moeghen draghen of vueren uten Brabant *alle* manieren van goude ende van zilver *uutgeschiedene alleen* den Saluyt van Francrijke, den Nobels [English and Burgundian], Florijns [Italian and Imperial], Ducaten [and other legal-tender coins so listed, including the domestic Burgundian] ... ende oic gelijk vessele ende juwelen van goude ende van zilver.

(2) Monetary ordinance issued for the Burgundian Low Countries, 14 June 1466, by Duke Philip the Good [14] :
Item, seront reputés pour *billon* quant à le non pouvoir vuyder hors de nosdis pays *toutes* manières dor et dargent excepté seulement ceulx qui cy après sensuivent [list of legal-tender gold and silver coins] ... en oultre declairont que vaiselle dor et dargent *entière* ne sera pas reputée pour *billon*, ne semblement joyaulx dor et dargent que chascun selon son estat

(13) Algemeen Rijksarchief (België), Rekenkamer, karton 65 : 1 (unsorted).

(14) A. R. A., Rekenkamer, no. 133, fo. 175 vo.-179 ro. ; cf. the text of Duke Charles' monetary ordinance issued for the Burgundian Low Countries, 13 October 1467, as published in L. Gilliodts-van Severen (ed.), *Inventaire des archives de la villes de Bruges*, V, 537-54.

> et aussi orfevriers et merciers pourront mener dehors non rompuz sans fraude ... n'estoit quilz les menassent hors en entencion de les vendre pour estoffe et matière, laquelle vaisselle et joyaux dor et dargent en ce cas fourfaiz ...
> Item, que aucun ne pourra achater *billon* en nosdis pays se ce nest pour delivrer en nosdis Monnoies sur le ban de trois ans, excepté les orfevriers lesquelz en pourront achater pour ouvrier de leurs mestres jusques à vingt *marcs* dargent à une fois sans fraude ([15]).

The second and more narrowly defined meaning of *billon* — *billoen* — *billio*, and one that La Curne de Sainte-Palaye did suggest in part, is "decried" coinage ([16]) : coins, most commonly foreign coins, whose circulation and even possession were forbidden, for whatever reason the prince might declare, as indicated by the following text from the "Tractatus Nove Monete" (1280) ([17]) :

> Dicitur autem *bilho* moneta *defensa* qui videlicet *cursu caret.*

This definition was quite consistent with and in fact subsumed within the first ; for, in the first place, such demonetized coins then had value only for their bullion contents ; and in the second because all edicts declaring such coins to be *billon* (*billoen, billio*) at the same time similarly ordered them to be sold to the official money-changers or the mints, on pain of confiscation and fines. For instance, in October 1397 Duke Philip the Bold of Burgundy, as Count of Flanders, banned the widely used English *nobles*, virtually pure gold coins at 23 7/8 carats fine, ordering their confiscation as *billon*, in retaliation against the English Crown's quite justifiable confiscation of all imported Flemish nobles, counterfeit imitations that Philip had been striking at Ghent and Bruges since 1388 ([18]). The Bruges mint ac-

(15) The term *marc* as used here is a mint weight, the *marc de Troyes* = 8 Paris *onces* = 244.753 grams. It is not be confused with the English *mark* which = 2/3 *pound sterling* (13s. 4d.), as on p. 299 (However note that the *marc* also equals 2/3 *livre de Troyes*).

(16) *Supra*, n. 5.

(17) In C. J. Johnson (ed.), *The 'De Moneta' of Nicholas Oresme and English Mint Documents* (Edinburgh, 1956), p. 71.

(18) Louis Deschamps de Pas, *Essai sur l'histoire monétaire des comtes de Flandre de la maison de Bourgogne* (Paris, 1863), doc. no. 78, p. xvi. For a discussion of this episode, see J. H. Munro, *Wool, Cloth, and Gold : the struggle for bullion in Anglo-Burgundian trade, c. 1340-1478* (Brussels and Toronto, 1972), chapter 2. The English statute of Jan. 1397 was entitled "Ordinance de la Bullion". *Rotuli Parliamentorum*, III, 340 : no. 19 ; Public Record Office, C 76/84; m. 16.

counts for the period 1397-1400 record several seizures and reminting of English nobles as *billon*, for example (19):

> Autre recepte de *billon* dor et dargent livré en ladite Monnoie par aucune des officiers de mons ... De Godefroy le Heilt pour xii nobles Dengleterre livréz par Beirut de Herweiden le xxie jour davril lan mccc iiii[xx] et ix, qui poisent iii onces dor, valent iii li. ix s. ix d. gros.

The English term *bullion* lacks, however, this particular signification of "decried" coinage (though implicitly assuming it); and perhaps one reason for this is that the medieval English Crown and Parliament never permitted either the circulation of *any* foreign coins, or the export of specie in any form at all, especially including English coin, except on special licence (20). Thus the need to distinguish between current, legal-tender and demonetized coin did not arise in the same fashion as on the continent. This rather sharp difference between English and Burgundian monetary policies was acidly commented upon in the following report to Henry VII during the Anglo-Burgundian commercial negotiations of 1499 (21):

> They sayne, that hit cannot be showne by eny tretes made with any of your noble progenitors to eny of your subiectes to convey *billion* oute of the archdukis [Philip the Fair's] landes. They thynk that theye do very moche for your

(19) A. R. A., "Comptes en rouleaux", no. 786. See also nos. 783: b (1397), 785 (1398), and Rekenkamer, reg. no. 13, 925, fo. 4-5 vo. In November 1399, the Flemish towns sent a delegation to Duke Philip "omme hem to versoukene ende te supplyerne dat de *noble* van Inghelant cours mochte hebben ghelijc den sinen, ende dat menne mochte ute voeren zonder ghereckent te sine *billon*...". W. PREVENIER (ed), *Handelingen van de Leden en van de Staten van Vlaanderen, 1384-1405* (Brussels, 1959), p. 182, no. 467. Duke Philip refused their request, replying: "Mais quant les Angloiz voulient consenter que les *nobles de Flandres* aient cours en Angleterre et à Calais et *ne soient pas reputés billon*, mons [eigneur] aura volentiers adviz sur la requeste dessuz dicte". Archives département du Nord (France), B. 630/14.238. The ban was officially rescinded on 31 July 1400.

(20) The first recorded ban (though one evidently repeating earlier edicts) was Edward I's Statute of Stepney, of 1299: "Qe nule bone moneye de argent en plate ne en áutre manere ne isse ne soit hors de nostre Roiaume". 27 Edwardi I, *Statutes of the Realm*, I, 131-5. See also statutes 9 Ed. III, c. 1; 38 Ed. III, stat. 1, c. 2; 5 Ric. II, stat. 1, c. 2; 2 Hen. IV, c. 5; 4 Hen. IV, c. 15-6; 5 Hen. IV, c. 9; 9 Hen. IV, c. 8; 1 Hen. V, c. 7, etc. in *S.R.*, I-II, *passim*. In actual practice licences for the export of English coin were fairly readily granted and sold; but the total ban on specie exports remained on the statute books until 1663, when the re-export of foreign coins and bullion was finally permitted. Full freedom to export specie in general was not granted until "Peel's Law" of 1819. See Albert FEAVEARYEAR, *The Pound Sterling: a History of English Money* (2nd. ed., rev. E. V. MORGAN, Oxford, 1963), pp. 3-4.

(21) Georg SCHANZ, *Englische Handelspolitik gegen Endes des Mittelalters*, II (*Zoll- und Handelsstatistik, Urkunden, Beilagen*, Leipzig, 1881), 196, no. 8.

subjectes to graunt them to conveigh oute of the archdukis landis all money current in thoos parties and also all manere of plate wrought and brought to eny man certen forme and fasshion [i.e. unbroken]. For the archdukis subjectes may not have like pryvylage to convey money nether plate oute of your realme of England into the archdukis parties, [nor] all manere of cune ...

A few more examples will suffice to demonstrate fully that the late-medieval *billon* — *billoen* — *billio* was used to mean in essence *bullion*. In 1429, the English Parliament, partly in retaliation against the successful bullionist-monetary policies of Duke Philip the Good (22), required merchants of the Calais Staple, whose customers were very largely the duke's subjects, to exact about one-third of the sales price in bullion for each wool-sack sold, as follows (23) :

That ye *Bullyon* be brought into ye mynte at Caleys ... for ech sarpler [= 2.25 sacks] of Wolle, of which the sak weyght is sold for xii marcs [1 *mark* = 13s. 4d. sterling], vi *li.* ; x marcs, v *li* ... to be forged into the Kynges coigne.

After various futile attempts and prolonged negotiations to have the Calais Staple Bullion ordinances revoked, "daer bi dat men Inghelsche wulle zoude moghen ghecrighen zonder *billoen van goude of van zilver* daer over te moeten leverne" (24), Duke Philip finally retaliated against the English in June 1434 by banning all imports of their woollen cloths, maintaining as his chief justification :

dair toe en willen sy [the Calais Staplers] die selven wolle onsen onderseten niet vercoepen, *ten sy by billoen van goude of van silvere sonder te willen ontfangen gancbair munte*, dair by dat alle 't *billoen* van onsen voirsc. landen van Brabant, Vlaenderen, Hollant ende anderen getogen wordt in 't voirsc. ryke van Engelant ... (25).

(22) See Munro, *Wool, Cloth, and Gold*, ch. 3-5 and *An Economic Aspect of the Collapse of the Anglo-Burgundian Alliance, 1428-1442*, in *English Historical Review*, LXXXV (1970), 225-44.

(23) *Rotuli Parliamentorum*, IV, 359 : no. 60 ; The Anglo-Norman text of stat. 8 Henrici VI, c. 17-8 is : "Item que la *Bullion* soit porte a le mynte a Caleys ..." *S.R.*, II, 253-4.

(24) A.R.A., Rekenkamer, no. 42, 549, fo. 28 vo.

(25) Charles Piot (ed.), *Inventaire des chartes, cartulaires, et comptes en rouleaux de la ville de Léau* (Brussels, 1879), pp. 26-8, no. 8. Two years later, on the eve of Duke Philip's siege of Calais, his Sovereign Bailiff of Flanders, Collard de Malines, remonstrated against these Calais Ordinances before the Ghent populace, saying in part : '... plus estre, il fault payer ung tiers de *buillon* et baillier deux *Phelippes* [or *rijders*, a Burgundian gold coin], pour ung *noble*". F. Morand (ed.), *Chronique de Jean le Fèvre de St. Remy*, II (Paris, 1876), 378.

Though these Calais Ordinances were finally suspended as unenforceable (in the 1440s), subsequently Edward IV reimposed a modified version in 1463, requiring that in payment for each wool-sack sold "la demy part soit en loialle money Dengelterre, plate, ou *bullion d'argent ou d'or*, et tout mesme la money et cest Roialme duement amesne" ([26]). Again the Burgundian ambassadors to London vigorously protested that the Calais Staplers

> ordonnent aussi, quand il leur plaist, sur la maniere des payemens des laynes que partie du pris sera *billon*, et se l'acheteur ne peult finer de *billon*, ilz se recompensent et prendent de l'acheteur, au lieu de tel *billon*, quelque somme environ d'un *noble* pour chaque sarplier ([27]).

Finally, perhaps the most conclusive evidence for the true meaning of the term in the late Middle Ages is the following text from the Anglo-Burgundian trade treaty of 1478 :

> poterunt mercatores et subditi Regie Anglie deinceps *quascumque massas auri vel argenti, vocatas Billionem*, extra Patrias ... Domini Ducis Karoli, noviter defuncti ... proviso quod huius modi *Billonam* [sic] per se aut factores suas emptam ([28]).

If one thus accepts as proved that in this era *billon* — *billoen* — *billio* meant *bullion*, in all its various forms, including demonetized coinage, and *not* petty, base, copper coin, one is naturally led to wonder how the latter sense nevertheless did evolve to become the contemporary definition in Romance languages. A reasonable hypothesis, and possibly the only valid one, is that it evolved from the more specific medieval definition of the term as "decried" or demonetized coinage, as the following may demonstrate.

Much as princes might have wished to exclude all foreign coins from their realms, only those ruling insular, marginally commercial countries like

(26) Statute 3 Edwardi IV, c. 1, in *S.R.*, II, 392-4 ; *Rot. Parl.*, IV, 503 : no. 18.

(27) M. R. Thielemans, *Bourgogne et Angleterre : relations politiques et économiques entre les Pays-Bas bourguignons et l'Angleterre, 1435-1467* (Brussels, 1966), pp. 470-1, doc. no. 8 : 8. This conflict was finally settled in the early 1470s, and resolved *pro forma* by the Anglo-Burgundian trade treaty of 1478, an article of which stated : "Concordatum est quod, si haberi non possit *Billona*, ad quam tamen habendam mercatores instare poterunt, nichil in recompensam exigetur, et si quid exactum sit restituetur". Thomas Rymer (ed.), *Foedera, Conventiones, Literae et Acta Publica*, XII, 77-8.

(28) *Ibid.*, XII, 74-5. Repeated in the treaty renewal of 3 April 1489, in Gilliodts-van Severen (ed.) *Inventaire des archives de la ville de Bruges*, VI, 325, no. 1234.

England (and Scotland) could have done so effectively. Conversely the princes of the Low Countries, whose economies then provided the fulcrum for northern European commerce and depended on the continual influx and efflux of a multitude of foreign coinages, perforce had to accept at least the better (gold) ones as legal tender. At the same time, both to protect their mercantile communities and themselves against fraud, and above all their mints (and mint-*seignorages*) from the deleterious operation of Gresham's Law ([29]), the princes of the Low Countries, as indeed everywhere, were quick to ban and, so far as possible, to confiscate all foreign counterfeit or fraudulently debased coins as bullion for their mints. Indeed the Burgundian mint accounts do show that, with the exception of the previously cited *guerre des "nobles"* between Philip the Bold and Richard II, virtually all foreign coins confiscated or purchased as *billon* were of this fraudulent type — or of dubious quality ; and such coins on the average contained a very high percentage of base alloy. The only legal-tender coins that normally contained similar proportions of base metal were the petty, small denomination coins : in the Low Countries, the half- and quarter-*groots* and *mites*, as fractions of the penny (*denier*) that were then, as noted earlier, commonly called *monnoie noire* (*zwarte geld*) as an indication of their high alloy content. At the same time, as the final and indeed most important consideration, the mint accounts also suggest that the major source of bullion for coinage was often such fraudulent foreign coins confiscated or purchased from money-changers as *billon* ; and their importance as a mint supply seems to accord with the relative scarcity of freshly-mined gold and silver bullion in Europe, particularly during the century ca. 1350-ca. 1450 ([30]).

(29) See J. H. MUNRO, *An Aspect of Medieval Public Finance : The Profits of Counterfeiting in the Fifteenth-Century Low Countries*, and the accompanying article of Pierre COCKSHAW, *De quelques imitations de monnaies au XVe siècle*, in *Revue belge de numismatique*, CXVIII (1972), 127-63. «Gresham's Law», stating that «bad coin drives out the good», had already been clearly enunciated by Copernicus and Oresme, and was well known at the Burgundian court, appearing virtually without fail in its monetary ordinances from the late-fourteenth century — almost two centuries before the Elizabethan official Thomas Gresham wrote on such matters.

(30) See MUNRO, *Wool, Cloth, and Gold*, ch. I and 6 ; FEAVEARYEAR, *Pound Sterling*, pp. 43-5 ; J. U. NEF, *Mining and Metallurgy in Medieval Civilization*, in POSTAN and RICH (eds.), *Cambridge Economic History*, II, 456-8 ; Harry MISKIMIN, *Economy of Early Renaissance Europe*, 1300-1460 (Englewood Cliffs, N. J., 1969), pp. 138-58 ; and with some qualifications F. GRAUS, *La crise monétaire du XIVe siècle* in *Revue belge de philologie et d'histoire*, XXIX (1951), 445-54 ; and Andrew WATSON, *Back to Gold — and Silver*, in *Economic History Review*, 2nd ser., XX (1967), 1-34.

Together these reasons would thus justify postulating that the medieval term *billon* — *billoen* — *billio*, though originally signifying *bullion* in general, came to be more and more restricted in application to just those coins that had been so "decried" as the most prominent form of "mint-metal", and thus evolved to mean debased coins in general, and by erroneous association the legal-tender petty coins as well, because of their high cupric or other base-metal alloys. In more modern times, such coins came to be made almost entirely of copper. Since the time that *billon* lost its original meaning, the French language has found no effective substitute to translate the term *bullion* other than the clumsy and not completely accurate *or ou argent en lingots*. The Dutch language has permitted the term *billoen* to disappear in fact entirely, similarly without providing a single substitute, though its usual translation of bullion as *ongemunt goud of zilver* has at least greater precision (31).

One final problem remains: the true origin of the English, originally Anglo-Norman, word *bullion*. The "boiling cauldron" approach may safely be eliminated as lacking any real substance. Instead, employing Ockham's Razor, one may reasonably conjecture that the word *bullion* was borrowed directly from the Flemish *billoen*, and most likely from a variant also cited in the Verwijs and Verdam *Middelnederlandsch Woordenboek : bulioen* (or *boelioen, bolioen*), which, spoken quickly, is certainly very close in sound to the English *bullion* (32). The Flemish term was in turn most likely derived from the French (or neighbouring Walloon) *billon*, if not directly from the Latin *billio*. Conversely however, citing more recent etymological research on the medieval Latin used in England, one might maintain that *bullion* was instead derived directly from the domestic variants *bullio, bulliona*. But the earliest of the citations for these spellings is dated 1465 (33), well more

(31) Even simpler and more precise is the German *der Münzbarren*, or *ungemünztes Edelmetall*. (All references from the *Cassell French-English, Dutch-English*, and *German-English* dictionaries, respectively).

(32) I, 1257. See also PREVENIER, *Handelingen van de Leden van Vlaanderen*, p. 152, no. 409 (May 1398) : "raed ende avys te hebben ... upten Inghelschen noble ende 't *bullioen*" ; and various other citations *Ibid., passim*. See also *infra*, Appendix, no. 4.

(33) R. E. LATHAM (ed.), *Revised Medieval Latin Word-List from British and Irish Sources* (London, 1965), p. 59. The more common variants are also cited : *bilo* (1282), *billio* (1369), *billonus* (c. 1300), *bilho* (1289), *bilium* (1254), *billona* (1496), *billiona, billionia* (1506).

than a century after the first recorded Anglo-Norman use of *bullion*, so that one may just as well assert that the latter term was responsible for these Latin variants. The Flemish primacy over either the French or the Latin in influencing the English term may be advanced on two further grounds : that England's most important commercial and thus monetary relations by far, overwhelmingly so in wool and textiles, were with the cross-Channel, Netherlandish-speaking Low Countries ; and that *Nederlands*, because of this region's economic paramountcy, was then the *lingua franca* of northern European commerce, from the Straits of Dover to Novgorod.

*

* *

That some relationship may have existed between *billon* and *bullion* did not, however, entirely escape the attention of all historical lexicographers. The earliest of those cited, the Sieur du Cange (1610-1688), though giving "nummus aereus" as the first definition of *billio* — *billon* — *vellon*, noted that this did not entirely correspond with the reading of some documents, and so suggested that the term might "occasionally" mean "a mass of money" (*interdum massa monetaria*) ; and at the end of the reference he (or a later editor) added "aurum vel argentum in massam, seu *Billam*, i.e. baculum, conflatum, *necdum purgatum* ; vide *billus*" ; he also noted the similarity to the French word for stick *bille* and the English word *billet* [= "small bar of metal". *Concise Oxford Dictionary*] (34). Such now logically appears to have been the true origin of the Latin *billio* as a monetary term. Subsequently (1877) La Curne de Sainte-Palaye, in his own supplementary comments on the French *billon*, directly quoted du Cange's latter observation, citing another, rather ambivalent text in support of the possible alternative definition of the term as "lingot" — including in translation du Cange's quite gratuitous qualification "qui n'est point affiné" (35). The only other lexical reference suggesting such a relationship of these terms, though one for the subsequent period, that has come to my attention is Edmond Huguet's *Dictionnaire de la langue française du seizième siècle*, which (citing a text of Calvin !) similarly suggests "lingot" as an alternative to the favoured "mélange d'or ou d'argent et d'un métal de valeur

(34) *Glossarium Mediae et Infimae Latinitatis*, I (1883 ed.), 660, col. 2-3.

(35) *Dictionnaire historique de l'ancien langage français*, III, 12.

moindre ; alliage" ([36]). But what is above all surprising is that no one has yet thought to pursue, to explain and to resolve this apparent paradox in meanings, to show how the contemporary definition in Romance languages has evolved. Hopefully this present exercise in historical numismatic philology, if not necessarily furnishing the final explanation for these changes, has at least made a contribution to that resolution, by posing the question correctly.

Appendix

Additional texts concerning bans on the export of *billon — billoen.*

(1) 1343-4 : Bruges Municipal Accounts : Dat hi bulgioene ute voerde jeghen tverbod van der stede [van Brugge] cxx lb. L. Gilliodts-van Severen (ed.), *Inventaire des archives de la ville de Bruges*, IV, 153.

(2) 1 June 1349 : Edict of Count Louis de Male of Flanders : ... que toutes personnes qui seront trouvées emportans malicieusement ou en quelconques manière que se soit hors de nostre pays aucun *billon dor ou dargent* soient arrestés et detenus pour dou tout à nostre volenté et le *billon* forfait ... à nous. Th. De Limburg-Stirum (ed.), *Cartulaire de Louis de Male. 1348-1358*, I (Bruges, 1898), 125, no. 123.

(3) 19 August 1357 : Letter of Count Louis de Male : ... car ainsi le voulons pour lavanchement de nos monnoies et remedijer au dit *buillon de fin or*, qui va hors de nostre dit pays, mais ceste chose tenés en secré sur le serement que fait nous avés. Limburg-Stirum, *Cartulaire de Louis de Male*, II, 194-5, no. 929.

(4) 1365-6 : Bruges Municipal Accounts : Van dat hi *bulioen* vercochte ende uten lande voerde, [fine of] xii lb. Gilliodts-van Severen, *Archives de Bruges*, IV, 153.

(5) 25 September 1386 : Ordinance of Duke Philip the Bold : Item, entant quil touche ceulx qui porteroient *buillon* hors du dit pais de Flandres, ou qui fondroient *buillon*, ou qui allouroient ou recevroient monnoies deffendues et tout ce qui s'en despent ... mondit seigneur a ordéné quil en usera raisonablement en la forme et manière que ses prédécesseurs en ont joy et usé ou temps passé. Laurent (Henri), *La loi de Gresham au moyen âge : essai sur la circulation monétaire entre la Flandre et le Brabant à la fin du* XIVe *siècle* (Brussels, 1933), pp. 151-2, doc. no. 11.

(36) I (Paris, 1925), 583.

(6) 1396-7 : Bruges Mint Account : Autre recept de *billon dor et dargent* livré à ladite Monnoie y aucuns des officiers de mondit seigneur lesquelz ont commisionné diceluy seigneur de garder que aucun ne porte le dit *billon* hors du pays de Flandres au contraire des ordenances des monnoies de mondit seigneur sur peine diceluy *billon* estre forfait à lui. A.R.A., Comptes en Rouleaux, no. 783 (b).

(7) 1398 : Bruges magistrate's sentence : De Ferrier de Comilles de Maillorque, marchant demourant à Bruges, lequelz avoit nagaires chargié à ung nomme Alain Termaieur porteur de lettres, certaine quantité de *boillon dargent*, pesant xxviii marcs et v onches de Troyes, pour porter à Paris ... laquelle chose est contre lordonnance faicte par mondit seigneur ... sur le fait de ses monnoyes, dont lamende et punition est ledit *boillon* estre fourfait à monseigneur et ceulx qui le portent ou font porter estre bannys certains terme hors du pays de Flandres ... L. Gilliodts-van Severen (ed.), *Cartulaire de l'ancienne estaple de Bruges*, I, 403, no. 482.

(8) 1454 : Monetary ordinance for Flanders : Dat zy negheen *belgioen* ute den lande en voeren ... teenigher munten dan in de munte ten Brugghe. Gilliodts-van Severen, *Archives de Bruges*, V, 385.

(9) 1458 : Monetary edict of Duke Philip the Good : Complaining that many money-changers and merchants "ont leur dit *billon dor* livré en autres monnoies estranges, comme à Tournay et ailleurs, ou autrement distribué à leur prouffit", the duke ordered that a fine of 8 s. *gros* be imposed on money-changers "pour chascun marc dor quilz deffauldront à deliverer". A. R. A., Acquits de Lille, no. 931 : 3.

(10) 13 October 1467 : Monetary Ordinance of Duke Charles the Rash : Item, et quiconque de quelque estat ou condicion quil soit que en nos pays, seignouries et villes dessusdiz ou en aucun diceulx sera trouvé avoir *billon dor ou dargent fondu ou non fondu* pour y cellui porter ou faire porter hors de yceulx nos pays et seignouries en pays estranges ou de lun de nozdis pays ouquel naurons monnoye ouverte fourfera ledit *billon* et avecq ce fourfera pour chascun marc de Troyes, assavoir pour lor xii lb. gros, et pour largent xiii lb. par. monnoyes de Flandres. Gilliodts-van Severen, *Archives de Bruges*, V, 540-1.

IV

Bullionism and the Bill of Exchange in England, 1272–1663: A Study in Monetary Management and Popular Prejudice

NO SCHOLAR HAS DONE MORE to elucidate the functions, nature, and history of the medieval bill of exchange than Raymond de Roover. For de Roover, the great contribution of the bill of exchange was to provide a simple, effective loan contract that fully circumvented the ecclesiastical and civil bans on usury without any taint of fraud. It did so, he argued, by "cleverly concealing" the rate of interest within the exchange rates on bills.[1] Since canon and civil law defined usury

1. See the following by Raymond de Roover: "What is Dry Exchange? A Contribution to the Study of English Mercantilism," *Journal of Political Economy* 52 (1944) 250–66; "New Interpretations of the History of Banking," *Journal of World History* 2 (1954) 38–76; "Cambium ad Venetias: Contribution to the History of Foreign Exchange," *Studi in onore di Armando Sapori* (2 vols. Milan 1957) 1.629–48 (all reprinted in *Business, Banking, and Economic Thought in Late Medieval and Early Modern Europe: Selected Studies of Raymond de Roover,* ed. Julius Kirshner [Chicago and London 1974] 183–259); "Early Accounting Prob-

specifically and exclusively as a fixed, predetermined, certain return on a loan (*mutuum*), any uncertain return was considered to be a legitimate profit, a reward for risk.[2] The return on a bill of exchange was uncertain and therefore licit because the rate of exchange might rise or fall before the *recambium* or return bill was drawn. Any number or combination of factors could produce such fluctuations: a change in either country's mint par by debasement or reinforcement, a change in the official or market evaluations of gold and silver, changes in either country's trade and balance of payments, speculative buying and selling of bills in the money markets—or indeed changes in the market rate of interest.

De Roover nevertheless criticized the canonists for their "fallacious reasoning" in defending the bill: for not seeing, as many secular writers did, "that interest was being charged under the cloak of exchange," that "the market favored the lender," and that the banker "rarely lost." The very fact that the spread of exchange rates on bills between two cities varied with their usance, the length of time until the bill's maturity, was for him conclusive proof of an interest charge for the

lems of Foreign Exchange," *Accounting Review* 19 (1944) 381–407; "Le contrat de change depuis la fin du treizième siècle jusqu'au début du dix-septième," *Revue belge de philologie et d'histoire* 25 (1946–47) 111–28; *Money, Banking and Credit in Mediaeval Bruges* (Cambridge, Mass. 1948); *Gresham on Foreign Exchange: An Essay on Early English Mercantilism* (Cambridge, Mass. 1949); *L'évolution de la lettre de change, XIVe–XVIIIe siècles* (Paris 1953); *The Rise and Decline of the Medici Bank, 1397–1494* (Cambridge, Mass. 1963); "Le marché monétaire au moyen age et au début des temps modernes: Problèmes et méthodes," *Revue historique* 244 (1970) 5–40.

2. John T. Noonan, *The Scholastic Analysis of Usury* (Cambridge, Mass. 1957) 38–81, 89–99, 133–53, 175–95; T. P. McLaughlin, "The Teaching of the Canonists on Usury (XII, XIII and XIV Centuries)," *Mediaeval Studies* 1 (1939) 81–147; 2 (1940) 1–22; Raymond de Roover, "Scholastic Economics," *Quarterly Journal of Economics* 69 (1955) 161–90; and his "The Scholastic Attitude Toward Trade and Entrepreneurship," *Explorations in Entrepreneurial History* 2nd ser. 1 (1963) 76–87 (both reprinted in *Business, Banking, and Economic Thought* [n. 1 above] 306–45).

"sale of time," an oft-cited canonical criterion for usury. The return on a bill of exchange was, therefore, interest plus handling charges plus a speculative gain or loss.

De Roover was undoubtedly correct in contending that the usury ban was almost universally applied and that it had a profound influence upon medieval investment and banking. At the very least, interest-bearing contracts could not be enforced at law. For the bill of exchange and credit instruments in general, the usury ban effectively precluded open discounting and thus prevented them from becoming fully negotiable devices until more modern times.[3]

One may, however, still challenge de Roover's thesis that the usury ban was the cardinal force in making the bill of exchange such a popular and widespread investment contract. In the first place, lenders had simpler and equally effective means of evading the usury ban. In particular, they could include the interest charges in the amount of principal stated in the contract (and thus deduct interest in advance). They could also charge *poena* or penalty for "late" payment, prearranged. Whether any feelings of guilt about such elements of fraud dissuaded many from engaging in these subterfuges is certainly a moot question.[4]

Secondly, de Roover is not entirely fair to the canonists, who were quick and astute enough to condemn as usurious *cambio fittizio*—fictitious or, popularly, "dry" exchange. These were straight loan contracts, involving no foreign transactions, in which *cambium* and *recambium* were drawn simultaneously with predetermined exchange rates.[5] In discussing true mercantile bills, the canonists correctly contended, I believe, that the return was profit and not usury. What de Roover calls interest might better be termed the banker's op-

3. See the sources cited in n. 1 above and n. 125 below.

4. See Michael M. Postan, "Private Financial Instruments in Medieval England," *Vierteljahrschrift für Sozial- und Wirtschaftsgeschichte* 23 (1930), reprinted in his *Medieval Trade and Finance* (Cambridge 1973) 29–31; Noonan (n. 2 above) 100–32, 249–68.

5. See de Roover, "What is Dry Exchange?" and "Cambium ad Venetias" (n. 1 above); Noonan (n. 2 above) 175–92.

portunity cost: a return equivalent to the yield on other, foregone investment opportunities of similar risk and duration. The merchant buying a bill might, for example, have chosen instead to invest his funds in a *commenda-* or *collegantia-*type of limited liability trade contract. From these he could expect to earn profits that no one would contend were usurious; but they were not fundamentally different from the yield on bills.[6] Even if the "cards were stacked" in favor of the deliverer—who would not otherwise furnish funds to buy bills—the average rate of return did not have to be zero to be regarded as profit rather than interest. The fact remains, as de Roover's own evidence from the Datini and Medici archives shows, that some bills were not redeemed, that losses did occur, and that the yields varied with continuously oscillating exchange rates.[7] This is not a mere legalistic quibble, for the very uncertainty of returns on bills undoubtedly discouraged some conservative investors from purchasing such bills. On the other hand, the limitation of liability that bills of exchange provided the purchaser made them a more attractive investment than a profit- and loss-sharing *compagnia* contract. That may have been as important a consideration for the investor-lender as avoiding the usury ban.

Thirdly, many bills of exchange transactions indicate that lending or borrowing was often of lesser concern than transferring funds between countries, or making various international payments without having to ship precious metals. As de Roover's examples from the Datini archives show, even trilateral bills of exchange, to settle country A's deficits with B by drawing on credits in C, required only local currency payments in the three countries involved (often *in banco*, by

6. Noonan (n. 2 above) 133–53, 175–92, 249–68; *Medieval Trade in the Mediterranean World: Illustrative Documents,* ed. Robert S. Lopez and Irving W. Raymond (New York 1955) 157–235; Abraham L. Udovitch, "At the Origins of the Western *Commenda:* Islam, Israel, Byzantium?" *Speculum* 37 (1962) 198–207.

7. De Roover: *Medieval Bruges* 62–63, 353; *Gresham* 144–46; *Medici* 115–21; "Cambium ad Venetias" 243–50 (all in n. 1 above); and his *The Bruges Money Market Around 1400* (Brussels 1968).

bank-account transfers).[8] The attractions of the bill of exchange as a transfer instrument were far greater in the Middle Ages than now, first of all because the transport of precious metals was exposed to much greater risks of shipwreck, piracy, and brigandage. Even if safe delivery could be assured, transportation costs, relative to other prices, were then far higher. Finally, except for those few gold coins that enjoyed international acceptance, most of the metals would have had to be minted on arrival. Thus the merchant had more costs to pay in seignorage taxes, mintage charges, and exchange fees. Consequently, the "specie points" were much more widely separated than today. Only when foreign exchange rates fell well below or rose high above mint par, to cover all these costs, was it more economical to export or import bullion than to use bills of exchange.[9] Normally the exchange rates would rise or fall in this fashion to produce bullion movements only when a country had an overall surplus or deficit in its balance of payments.

Of all the risks facing the bullion exporter possibly the greatest was official brigandage: the confiscation of his metals by frontier officials on departure. Perhaps an adviser to Elizabeth I was unhistorical in declaring (ca. 1570) that "marchauntes naturall exchaunge . . . was first diuised and used by the trewe dealinge marchauntes immediately after that princes did inhibit the cariadge of gould and silver out of their Realmes."[10] But certainly the almost universally imposed ban on bullion exports deserves as much credit as the

8. De Roover: *Lettre de change* 64–65; *Medieval Bruges* 65–66; "New Interpretations" 206–07 (all in n. 1 above); and his "La balance commerciale entre les Pays-Bas et l'Italie au quinzième siècle," *Revue belge de philologie et d'histoire* 37 (1959) 374–86. Flanders then usually had a trade surplus with Spain but a deficit with Italy.

9. De Roover, *Gresham* 77–83, 138–40, 150–54 and *Lettre de change* 57–58 (both in n. 1 above). See also John H. Munro, *Wool, Cloth, and Gold: The Struggle for Bullion in Anglo-Burgundian Trade, 1340–1478* (Brussels and Toronto 1973) 29–31.

10. *Tudor Economic Documents,* ed. Richard H. Tawney and Eileen E. Power (3 vols. London and New York 1924) 3.362, no. iii.5 (Taverner to Elizabeth I's government, ca. 1570).

usury ban for fostering the use of the bill of exchange, from the early fourteenth to seventeenth centuries. One may contend, however, that some rulers applied the export ban to bullion alone, not to legal tender coins. That is quite true, but their coins were rarely accepted as anything but bullion in another country. Even the widely accepted Italian florins and ducats were generally undervalued abroad, since rulers naturally gave preference to their own coins in setting official rates.[11] Exports of specie would therefore lose the premium or *agio* that coins normally commanded over bullion in domestic payments by virtue of their greater portability and convenience. That agio, normally equivalent to the cost of seignorage and mintage, thus afforded the ruler some protection against the export of his coins.[12] Finally, while it is also true that no export ban on precious metals could ever be fully enforced, the risk of confiscation and fines remained for the merchant a cost that made bills of exchange more attractive.

Can any rational justification be found for late medieval bullionism—those policies designed both to induce an influx of precious metals and to prevent their efflux? Was bullionism merely a "phobia"? Did pre-Enlightenment Europe suffer from the delusion that money—gold and silver—was in itself wealth or the sole form of wealth? Certainly some such identification is evident, for example, in the Tudor tracts "A Treatise Concerninge the Staple" and "Howe to Reforme the Realme" by Clement Armstrong (ca. 1530):[13]

> The holl welthe of the reame is for all our riche commodites to gete owt of all other reamys therfore redy money; and after the money is brought into the holl reame, so shall all

11. See the monetary ordinances of the Burgundian Low Countries cited in Munro (n. 9 above) 46, 101–02, 150, 169, 198–99; and also Denis Richet, "Le cours officiel des monnaies étrangères circulant en France au XVIe siècle," *Revue historique* 225 (1961) 359–96.

12. De Roover, *Gresham* (n. 1 above) 77–83; Munro (n. 9 above) 25–30.

13. *Tudor Economic Documents* (n. 10 above) 3.105, 124.

peple in the reame be made riche therwith. And after it is in the reame, better it were to pay 6d. for any thyng made in the reame than to pay but 4d. for a thyng made owt of the reame, for that 6d. is owres so spent in the reame and the 4d. spent owt of the reame is lost and not ours.

Condemning the loss of money spent on "wynes and silkes, [the] ones every yere piste agenste the walles and [the other] torne to ragges," he concludes that it is "better to have plentie of gold and silver in the realm than plentie of merchauntes and merchandizes." His hostility to the bill of exchange will be cited later. Similar if more poetic sentiments can be found a full century earlier in the famous *Libelle of Englyshe Polycye* (1436), which spewed venom at Italian merchants especially. By importing "thynges of complacence, . . . nifles, trifles, that litell have availed,"

> . . . they bere the golde oute of thys londe
> And souke the thryfte awey oute of oure honde;
> As the waffore [wasp] soukethe honye fro the bee,
> So mynúceth [diminishes] oure commodite.[14]

In that same era (1435) even the commercially sophisticated Flemish—so dependent upon foreign trade, so liberal generally in their monetary policies—evinced considerable passion in denouncing a Hanseatic request for permission to take with them any gold or silver that they themselves had brought to Flanders or had earned from their trade there: "for it would be the ruination of the land of Flanders and its entire commerce; and we hope that the aforesaid [Hanse] delegates would not desire that."[15] European documents of the fourteenth and fifteenth centuries are filled with similar state-

14. *The Libelle of Englyshe Polycye: A Poem on the Use of Sea-Power, 1436,* ed. Sir George F. Warner (Oxford 1926) 21–22. See also G. A. Holmes, "The 'Libel of English Policy,'" *English Historical Review* 76 (1961) 193–216.

15. *Hanserecesse von 1431–1476,* ed. Goswin von der Ropp (7 vols. Leipzig 1876–92) 1.332–33, no. 398:4 (3 June 1435). See also nos. 357, 397.

ments that the export of precious metals would lead to a country's impoverishment.[16]

In economies without fully developed credit institutions, central banks, and fiat moneys, however, concern about a country's coinage supply was hardly irrational. Furthermore, many historians contend that late medieval Europe experienced a veritable *famine monétaire,* chiefly from a well-documented slump in silver mining but perhaps also from chronic trade deficits with Asia that produced a drainage of precious metals. For some scholars, that monetary contraction was a major cause of that era's "great depression"; for others, it was at least a secondary factor aggravating the depression from the later fourteenth century.[17] Some historians, on the other hand, deny the existence of any serious monetary

16. See Eli F. Heckscher, *Mercantilism,* trans. Mendel Shapiro, rev. ed. E. F. Söderlund (2 vols. London and New York 1955) 2.175–216; Jacob Viner, "Power versus Plenty as Objectives of Foreign Policy in the Seventeenth and Eighteenth Centuries," *World Politics* 1 (1948–49) 1–29, reprinted in *Revisions in Mercantilism,* ed. Donald C. Coleman (London 1969) 61–91; Jacob Viner, *Studies in the Theory of International Trade* (London 1955) 1–57.

17. See, in particular, W. C. Robinson, "Money, Population and Economic Change in Late-Medieval Europe," *Economic History Review* 2nd ser. 12 (1959) 63–76; Johan Schreiner, "Wages and Prices in the Later Middle Ages," *Scandinavian Economic History Review* 2 (1954) 61–73; Robert S. Lopez and Harry A. Miskimin, "The Economic Depression of the Renaissance," *Economic History Review* 2nd ser. 14 (1962) 408–26; Harry A. Miskimin, "Monetary Movements and Market Structure: Forces for Contraction in Fourteenth- and Fifteenth-Century England," *Journal of Economic History* 24 (1964) 470–90; idem, *The Economy of Early Renaissance Europe, 1300–1460* (Englewood Cliffs 1969) 25–31, 132–58; N. J. Mayhew, "Numismatic Evidence and Falling Prices in the Fourteenth Century," *Economic History Review* 2nd ser. 27 (1974) 1–15. On monetary problems in general, see especially William A. Shaw, *The History of Currency, 1252–1894* (London and New York 1896) 1–60; Marc Bloch, *Esquisse d'une histoire monétaire de l'Europe* (Paris 1954) 35–77; Henri Laurent, "Crise monétaire et difficultés économiques: En Flandre, aux XIVe et XVe siècles," *Annales d'histoire économique et sociale* 5 (1933) 156–60; F. Graus, "La crise monétaire du 14e siècle," *Revue belge de philologie et d'histoire* 29 (1951) 445–54; Sir Albert E. Feavearyear, *The Pound Sterling: A History of English Money,* 2nd ed. rev. E. Victor Morgan (Oxford 1963) 10–15; Carlo Cipolla, "Currency

problems in this era; many others reject the entire thesis of a late medieval depression. Although I myself have long defended the depression thesis, I had adhered essentially to the Postan school, which emphasizes demographic decline, the various disruptions of the European economy by plague and warfare, and other "real" factors as the primary causes of that depression.

According to the Postan school, and its most recent, most able proponent John Hatcher, the accumulated silver stocks were so large by 1300 that no contraction in mining could possibly have reduced the money supply to match the great fall in Europe's population, by a third or more.[18] "Men were dying," writes David Herlihy, "but coins were not."[19] The very serious inflations that swept most of Europe from the late 1340s to the late 1370s certainly indicate that per capita spending had risen rapidly; or, conversely, in terms of the Fisher Identity ($MV = PT$), that T had obviously contracted much more than had M and V.[20] From the late 1370s,

---

Depreciation in Medieval Europe," *Economic History Review* 2nd ser. 15 (1963) 413–22; Andrew M. Watson, "Back to Gold—and Silver," *Economic History Review* 2nd ser. 20 (1967) 1–34; John U. Nef, "Mining and Metallurgy in Medieval Civilisation," *Cambridge Economic History of Europe*, ed. Michael M. Postan et al., 2 (Cambridge 1952) 430–93; Etienne Fournial, *Histoire monétaire de l'occident médiéval* (Paris 1970).

18. Michael M. Postan, "Some Economic Evidence of Declining Population in the Later Middle Ages," *Economic History Review*, 2nd ser. 2 (1950) 221–46, reprinted in his *Essays on Medieval Agriculture and General Problems of the Medieval Economy* (Cambridge 1973) 186–213; idem, "Moyen âge: Rapport," *IXe Congrès international des sciences historiques* (2 vols. Paris 1950) 1: *Rapports* 225–41, revised and republished as "The Economic Foundations of Medieval Society," in his *Essays on Medieval Agriculture* (1973) 3–27; idem, "Medieval Agrarian Society in Its Prime: England," *Cambridge Economic History* 1 (2nd ed. 1966) 560–70; idem, *The Medieval Economy and Society: An Economic History of Britain, 1100–1500* (London and Berkeley 1972) 27–40, 224–46; John Hatcher, *Plague, Population, and the English Economy, 1348–1530* (London 1977) 31–62; Munro (n. 9 above) 2–3, 14–25.

19. David Herlihy, *Medieval and Renaissance Pistoia: The Social History of an Italian Town, 1200–1430* (New Haven 1967) 125.

20. Ibid. 122–47; E. H. Phelps Brown and S. V. Hopkins, "Seven Centuries of the Prices of Consumables," *Essays in Economic History*, ed.

to be sure, prices did fall, in some places sharply. But I had attributed that deflation to severe hoarding and reductions in coinage velocity, in response to the economic and social crises, rather than to any reduction in M. I am no longer willing, however, to defend the position that changes in M were inconsequential for the late medieval European economy. For recently C. C. Patterson and N. J. Mayhew have published impressive articles demonstrating that a country's coinage can diminish drastically unless it is frequently and substantially replenished with fresh mintings.[21] Coins do die. Furthermore, my own recent investigations of mint outputs and prices in England (1235–1500) and the Low Countries (1334–1500), summarized in tables 1 and 2, also lend support to Harry Miskimin's famous but often challenged thesis that, relative to the transactions demand for money, northern Europe's coinage supplies seriously contracted during the late Middle Ages.[22]

How then, and to where, did a country like medieval England lose its precious metals? At the outset one must dis-

---

Eleanora M. Carus-Wilson (3 vols. London 1954–62) 2.183, 193–94; Harry A. Miskimin, *Money, Prices, and Foreign Exchange in Fourteenth-Century France* (New Haven 1963) 53–71; Earl J. Hamilton, *Money, Prices, and Wages in Valencia, Aragon, and Navarre, 1351–1500* (Cambridge, Mass. 1936) appendixes; Léopold Génicot, "Crisis: From the Middle Ages to Modern Times," *Cambridge Economic History* 1 (2nd ed. 1966) 677–94.

21. C. C. Patterson, "Silver Stocks and Losses in Ancient and Medieval Times," *Economic History Review* 2nd ser. 25 (1972) 205–35; Mayhew (n. 17 above). See also Marion M. Archibald, "Wastage from Currency: Long-Cross and the Recoinage of 1279," *Edwardian Monetary Affairs, 1279–1344*, ed. N. J. Mayhew (Oxford 1977) 167–86.

22. In *Economy of Early Renaissance Europe* (n. 17 above) 132–58, Miskimin has argued that chronic trade deficits drained precious metals from northwestern Europe to the Mediterranean basin and from there to Asia. For a contrary view, that England's balance of payments remained positive in the late Middle Ages (possibly with a diminishing surplus), see Terence H. Lloyd, "Overseas Trade and the English Money Supply in the Fourteenth Century," *Edwardian Monetary Affairs* (n. 21 above) 96–124. I myself am not so confident that accurate estimates of balance of payments may be made from medieval English or other customs accounts.

tinguish clearly between (1) the disappearance of coins and bullion from the country's money supply, and (2) a loss of metal from the coins themselves, for the consequences might differ. One should also consider whether the losses of metal were temporary or permanent. The most obvious and possibly the most important reason for the first type of loss was a deficit in the balance of payments. That might have been caused by one or more of the following: a trade deficit, military expenditures abroad, loans and subsidies to foreign allies, remittances of ecclesiastical taxes and revenues. If this type of loss was often temporary and reversible, obviously losses from shipwrecks, burials, and unrecovered hoards were permanent. The second type of loss was caused chiefly by wear and tear in normal circulation, and by fraudulent clipping and "sweating" of coins. The latter was only a temporary loss in that the clippings or metal rubbings would usually reappear as reminted coins in that country's or another's circulation. Loss from wear and tear was, of course, permanent and may have amounted to as much as 1% per annum. Mayhew, adopting a much more conservative loss rate (0.2%), estimated that in fourteenth century England "seven tons of silver vanished into thin air through wear alone every decade."[23]

Even though the coins themselves would disappear much more slowly than that, such a deterioration of the coinage could have very serious consequences for minting and the money supply. It could bring mint production to a halt and encourage the export of precious metals through the operation of Gresham's Law. Thus, so long as large numbers of underweight or fraudulent coins circulated at their decreed

23. Mayhew (n. 17 above) 3: from 1279 to 1334 a hypothetical million pounds of freshly minted pence would have contained 352.389 tons of fine silver. A loss of 2% over ten years would thus have amounted to 7.048 tons. He has evidently employed an estimate of weight loss of 0.2% per annum given in Sir John Craig, *The Mint: A History of the London Mint from A.D. 287 to 1948* (Cambridge 1953) xvi, 60. If so, that would amount to 1.83% in the first decade, not 2.0%; and to 3.32% in the second decade, not 4.0%; etc. Patterson (n. 21 above, 220–21), however, offers a much higher estimate of per annum loss: 1.0%.

TABLE 1. Decennial Averages of English Mint Outputs in Kilograms of Fine Metal and Current Pounds Sterling, 1250–1259 to 1530–1539

Decade	*Silver Coinage Output in Kilograms (Fine metal)*	*Gold Coinage Output in Kilograms (Fine metal)*	*Total Value of Coinage Output in £ sterling*	*Index of Value of Coinage Output (1275–99 = 100)*
1250–59	21,156.5		65,909.0	161.3
1260–69	12,116.6		37,746.8	92.4
1270–79	6,532.5		20,380.9	49.9
1280–89	26,182.7		81,904.0	200.4
1290–99	2,088.2		6,532.0	16.0
1300–09	29,300.8		91,658.0	224.3
1310–19	9,275.8		29,016.3	71.0
1320–29	1,802.1		5,637.2	13.8
1330–39	341.1		1,176.6	2.9
1340–49[1]	3,370.9	397.2	27,709.8	67.8
1350–59	10,991.9	1,759.3	117,505.9	287.5
1360–69	1,071.1	2,121.9	95,098.1	232.7
1370–79	354.7	606.0	27,347.4	66.9
1380–89	257.0	313.9	14,450.4	35.4
1390–99	233.9	539.8	24,042.5	58.8
1400–09	48.6	149.1	6,579.7	16.1
1410–19[2]	870.0	1,404.8	70,894.2	173.5
1420–29	4,136.0	1,610.4	95,868.7	234.6
1430–39	5,360.8	200.7	34,401.6	84.2
1440–49	250.7	79.2	4,930.5	12.1
1450–59	1,360.5	54.1	8,879.4	21.7
1460–69	4,389.9	854.1	78,778.6	192.8
1470–79	1,905.4	515.7	44,198.9	108.1
1480–89	926.4	207.9	18,731.9	45.8
1490–99[3]	2,034.2	291.8	30,545.0	74.7
1500–09	4,306.0	948.9	85,962.8	210.3
1510–19	945.7	778.7	55,549.3	135.9
1520–29[4]	5,111.1	447.4	63,741.3	156.0
1530–39[5]	6,886.4	398.8	74,018.9	181.1

TABLE 1.—*Continued*

[1] The decennial mean of the gold coinage is the amount struck from 20 January 1344, when gold minting commenced, to 29 September 1349, thus 5.69 years, divided by 10.

[2] The mint accounts are missing from Michaelmas 1408 to 29 November 1411, when a debasement and general recoinage commenced. The coinage for the missing years has been estimated by averaging the preceding three years.

[3] Average of 1495–99 only; accounts for 1490–94 are missing.

[4] Average of 1520–23 and 1527–29 only (7 years).

[5] Average of 1530, 1534, and 1537–39 only (5 years).

SOURCES: C. E. Blunt and J. D. Brand, "Mint Output of Henry III," *British Numismatic Journal* 39 (1970) 61–66; C. G. Crump and C. Johnson, "Tables of Bullion Coined under Edward I, II, and III," *Numismatic Chronicle* 4th ser. 13 (1913) 200–45; G. C. Brooke and E. Stokes, "Tables of Bullion Coined from 1377 to 1550," *Numismatic Chronicle* 5th ser. 9 (1929) 27–69; Frederick A. Walters, "The Stamford Find and Supplementary Notes on the Coinage of Henry VI," *Numismatic Chronicle* 4th ser. 11 (1911) 171–72 (for York in 1423–24; Calais in 1436, 1439–40); Public Record Office, L.T.R. Exchequer E.364/59, 61–63, 65–66, 69, 72; K. R. Exchequer E.101/192–93 (Calais 1422–40); *Calendar of the Patent Rolls, 1422–1429* (Norwich 1901) 337–38, 502; *Calendar of the Patent Rolls, 1429–1436* (London 1907) 256–57, 259 (Calais 1422–40); Terence H. Lloyd, *The English Wool Trade in the Middle Ages* (Cambridge 1977) 241 (Table 15: Calais, 1384–1404). The London statistics for 1432–33, 1510–11, and 1537–39 have been corrected from information in Sir John Craig, *The Mint: A History of the London Mint from A.D. 287 to 1948* (Cambridge 1953) 408, 412–14.

TABLE 2. A Comparison of Long-Term Averages of the English and Flemish-Burgundian Mint Outputs, 1235–1499

Period of the Per Annum Mean	Value in Current Pounds Sterling	Value in Constant Pounds Sterling*	Pure Silver Struck in Kilograms	Pure Gold Struck in Kilograms
ENGLAND				
A. 1270–1369	47,661.88	53,467.21	9,095.69	427.83 [1,645.51][1]
B. 1370–1469	36,617.30	31,580.61	1,726.19	581.20
B as % of A	76.8	59.1	19.0	135.8 [35.3][1]
C. 1235–1299	44,998.63	55,708.28	14,424.92	—
D. 1300–1399	43,364.22	46,610.40	5,699.92	573.80 [1,024.65][2]
E. 1400–1499	39,845.89	31,800.17	2,133.18	549.64
C as % of D	103.8	119.5	253.1	—
E as % of D	91.9	68.2	37.4	95.8 [53.6][2]
FLANDERS–BURGUNDIAN LOW COUNTRIES				
A. 1335–1369		86,561.14	6,262.60	1,455.07
B. 1370–1469		33,654.51	3,440.32	475.14
B as % of A		38.9	54.9	32.7
C. 1335–1399		67,767.38	5,247.32	1,108.12
D. 1400–1499		28,514.42	4,077.49	297.83
D as % of C		42.1	77.7	26.9

* Constant pounds sterling = values of English coinage, 1351–1411
1 kg fine gold = £42.8676; 1 kg fine silver = £3.8619.

[1] Average of 1344–69 (26 years).

[2] Average of 1344–99 (56 years).

TABLE 2.—*Continued*

SOURCES: *Recherches sur les monnaies des comtes de Flandre,* ed. Victor Gaillard (2 vols. Ghent 1852–56) 2: *Sous les règnes de Louis de Crécy et de Louis de Mäle;* Hans van Werveke, *De muntslag in Vlaanderen onder Lodewijk van Male,* Mededelingen van de koninklijke Vlaamse Academie voor Wetenschappen, Letteren en Schone Kunsten van België; Klasse der Letteren 11 no. 5 (Brussels 1949) appendix II (20–21); archival sources cited in John H. Munro, *Wool, Cloth and Gold: The Struggle for Bullion in Anglo-Burgundian Trade, 1340–1478* (Brussels and Toronto 1973) 187–97; and in Peter Spufford, *Monetary Problems and Policies in the Burgundian Netherlands, 1433–1496* (Leiden 1970) 176–93; and the mint accounts published in the appendices of Pieter O. van der Chijs, *De munten der voormalige hertogdommen Brabant en Limburg* (Haarlem 1851); Pieter O. van der Chijs, *De Munten der voormalige graafschappen Holland en Zeeland* (Haarlem 1858); and Algemeen Rijksarchief (België), Rekenkamer nos. 18,121–28 (Bruges); 18,204–08 (Namur); 17,880–82 (Antwerp [not listed in the above]. For the English mints, see the sources cited in table 1 above.

values—as halfpence, pence, groats (4d.)—merchants would eventually respond to the metal loss by discounting the entire coinage, good and bad coins alike. They would thus bid up the market price of bullion in money-of-account terms and thereby reduce or eliminate the premium on coinage. Unless the premium was high enough to cover the costs of minting, merchants obviously would not willingly supply bullion to the domestic mint, but would take it, and heavy good coins, to foreign mints; or they would utilize good coins and plate in foreign trade, reserving the worn, inferior coins for domestic commerce, further reducing the standard. Unless the prince could compel merchants to furnish bullion or foreign coins, he could reactivate his mints only by a debasement that would match the current inferior standard and so restore the premium on coinage.[24]

24. Feavearyear (n. 17 above) 10–15; Munro (n. 9 above) 25–30. For an analysis of such discounting and consequent price increases, see Mavis Mate, "Monetary Policies in England, 1272–1307," *British Numismatic Journal* 41 (1972) 37–45.

Thus a type 2 coinage loss could generate a type 1 loss: in particular the export of precious metals to foreign mints striking debased coins, often counterfeits of another country's good coins. The attractions of counterfeiting, a private vice that became in some princes' fiscal arsenal a public virtue, are obvious. In return for their bullion, merchants received from the counterfeiting mint a greater number of imitation coins than of the good coins offered by the honest mint. The risks of detection were fairly small, because the very inaccuracy of medieval minting techniques, as well as normal wear and tear, meant that a fair proportion of honest coins would also be underweight. When some weight variations were normal, merchants perforce had to accept coins by tale or face value. The more standard types of coinage debasement may be best understood as a counterfeiting of the ruler's own previous coinage that similarly augmented the coin's premium over bullion. For again, the mint offered merchants more coins of the same face value, in money-of-account terms, but with reduced precious metal contents. So long as the merchants supplying the bullion spent the debased coins quickly enough, before the almost inevitable inflation ensued from the augmented money supply, they stood to gain.[25]

The prince who engaged in counterfeiting or debasement of course also profited. The late medieval Flemish and Burgundian mint accounts demonstrate that debasements normally produced very substantial seignorage revenues: not just in money-of-account terms but in the amounts of fine metal sequestered as a tax from the incoming bullion. Such mint profits must be considered a prime motivation for "aggressive" debasements. In an age of steadily mounting fiscal pressures but relatively fixed feudal incomes, seignorage constituted one of the few independent and elastic revenue sources at a

25. See John H. Munro, "An Aspect of Medieval Public Finance: The Profits of Counterfeiting in the Fifteenth-Century Low Countries," and Pierre Cockshaw, "De quelques imitations de monnaies au XVe siècle," both in *Revue belge de numismatique* 118 (1972) 127–48 and 149–63; Munro (n. 9 above) 25–34, 47–53, 70–72, 75–83, 87–88, 187–214; Bloch (n. 17 above) 40–70.

prince's command.[26] For the prince, therefore, such mint policies and bullionism in general often had perfectly rational fiscal ends, however injurious they might be to the community at large in the long run.

But not all mint and bullionist policies were so profit-inspired and rapaciously aggressive. Princes were naturally concerned to protect the integrity of their mints, their coinage, and their country's "stock of treasure." Their honor and sovereignty were at stake, as well as their purse. Thus many mint alterations were legitimately defensive responses to foreign debasements or to any physical deterioration of the coinage. Certainly an influx of foreign debased or counterfeit coins depreciated the current standard of circulation more rapidly than did wear and tear, and thus encouraged an outflow of precious metals, usually to the offending mints. That manifestation of Gresham's Law is plaintively described in thousands of medieval monetary ordinances, frequently as the justification for the debasement.[27]

There remains one element of medieval mint policies that has particular significance for England: bimetallic ratios, or the relative prices offered for gold and silver bullion. The reintroduction of gold coinage in Western Europe in 1252, by Genoa and Florence, was a mixed blessing. On the one hand, it provided Europe with a much more suitable medium

26. Munro (n. 9 above) 52, 83, 198–211. See also Hans van Werveke, "Currency Manipulation in the Middle Ages: The Case of Louis de Mäle, Count of Flanders," *Transactions of the Royal Historical Society* 4th ser. 31 (1949) 115–27; and Peter Spufford, *Monetary Problems and Policies in the Burgundian Netherlands, 1433–1496* (Leiden 1970) 130–46.

27. See the documents and ordinances cited in Munro (n. 9 above) 33, 87, 101, 150, 157, 161, 169, 170; Munro (n. 25 above) 137–48; and also the ordinances cited in Appendixes A, B, and E below). A contemporary expression of Gresham's Law can be found in the later editions of *De Moneta* by Nicholas Oresme (1320–84); but the particular passages are a subsequent addition, possibly by Flemish mint officials: *The De Moneta of Nicholas Oresme, and English Mint Documents*, ed. Charles Johnson (London and New York 1956) xii, 32–33. See also Henri Laurent, *La loi de Gresham au moyen âge: essai sur la circulation monétaire entre la Flandre et le Brabant à la fin du XIVe siècle* (Brussels 1933).

for international trade that was cheaper to ship, relative to its purchasing power, and more trustworthy generally than silver coinages. Since the high value of gold coins made them unsuitable for most domestic trade, and since merchants in international trade were more likely to test coins, gold was much less subject to debasement. But gold was acquired at the expense of silver: if not purchased with silver, received in lieu of silver. A. M. Watson has indeed argued convincingly that Western Europe's adoption of gold coinages with high exchange values produced large outflows of silver, particularly in the later fourteenth and fifteenth centuries, to the Islamic world and Asia, which placed correspondingly higher values on that metal.[28] Since most European domestic economies were based upon silver, with moneys-of-account pricing systems tied directly to the current silver penny, their gold coinages may have become agents of deflation and contraction, unless counteracted by silver debasements.[29]

Late medieval complaints about the "scarcity of white money," therefore, must be considered in terms of coinage deterioration, foreign mint competition, and the country's own mint policies, especially concerning gold. In England, an effective gold coinage was not established until the noble of July 1344.[30] From that time the crown consistently maintained

28. Watson (n. 17 above). See also Robert S. Lopez, "Back to Gold, 1252," *Economic History Review* 2nd ser. 9 (1956) 219–40; and the very perceptive comments in Mate (n. 24 above) 34–35. The alteration of mint ratios (gold bullion price to silver coin, silver bullion price to gold coin values) to attract one or the other metal is too complicated to discuss here, except to note that the alteration had to be large enough to surmount the costs of seignorage, brassage, exchange, and transport. See Munro (n. 9 above) 29–32.

29. I have elaborated this further in "Bullion Movements and Monetary Contraction in Late-Medieval England and the Low Countries, 1235–1500," *International Conference on Pre-Modern Monetary History 1200–1750* (University of Wisconsin 28 August–2 September 1978), whose proceedings are to be published shortly. See also Shaw (n. 17 above) 1–60.

30. Henry III's gold penny of 1257 was ultimately a failure, as was Edward III's gold florin of December 1343. The gold noble, from July 1344, was worth 6s. 8d. or half a mark sterling. Feavearyear (n. 17 above) 24–32; Craig (n. 23 above) 36, 59–75.

mint ratios favoring gold over silver. With no silver debasements from 1351 to 1411, and not another until 1464, silver output declined sharply while gold output values remained generally much higher until the late fifteenth century. Flanders, England's chief trading partner, also pursued pro-gold policies with similar results until 1384, when the count reversed the mint ratio to favor silver. From then until 1425, when the mint ratio was altered to favor gold once more, the Flemish (and Burgundian) mints coined correspondingly more silver than the English; from 1425 to the next mint ratio alteration in 1466, correspondingly more gold.[31]

For medieval England, this analysis provides only a partial explanation of her bullionist policies, which were the most severe of any in Western Europe. English bullionism, and its role in shaping public attitudes toward credit, can be understood properly only if the case histories of the following six monetary policies are considered together: (1) bans on the importation of foreign coins; (2) bans on the export of bullion and coin; (3) parliamentary opposition to coinage debasement, forcing the crown to pursue "sound money" policies; (4) laws requiring exporters to supply bullion to the mints; (5) "employment" laws obligating importers to export English goods of equivalent value; and (6) attempts to control foreign exchange transactions and to limit the use of credit. Only broad, general analyses can be given here; but all the official ordinances (1275–1663) for each of these categories are listed in the Appendixes.

Early bans on coin imports and the export of plate and specie

As Appendixes A and B suggest, the predominant reason for the earlier bans on bullion exports was to support prohibitions against the import and circulation of counterfeit, debased, and

31. Munro (n. 9 above) 74–89, 100–03, 149–50, 168–71, 187–210; Munro, (n. 29 above) table 9. For prices, see Herman van der Wee, *The Growth of the Antwerp Market and the European Economy (Fourteenth to Sixteenth Centuries)* (3 vols. The Hague 1963) 1.173–331, 3 (graphs).

clipped coin: to check the operations of Gresham's Law. But the very first (extant) ban, issued on 7 December 1278, was prompted more by domestic causes of a deteriorating coinage standard. There had been no general recoinage since 1247, and clipping had recently become rampant. Edward I's decree, specifically prohibiting the export of "silver plate, clipped, and broken coins [to foreign mints]," was then followed in 1279 by a successful recoinage that necessitated only a minor reduction in weight (0.41%).[32] The newly restored "sterlings," however, now became an especially tempting target for continental counterfeiters. Sterlings had long been imitated in northern Europe because their unique reputation for both fineness (92.5% silver) and historic stability let them circulate as an international medium, before gold coinages became prevalent in northern Europe. Some imitations were faithful to the sterling; but from the early 1280s various princes in the Low Countries struck decidedly debased counterfeits that came to be known as pollards and crockards.[33] Edward I launched his first attack on counterfeits in the *Statutum de Moneta Magnum* of 1284: it prohibited the importation and circulation of all continental coins; and, for those apprehended with "counterfeited or strange coins," it prescribed "grievous forfeiture." On 21 June 1291 he reissued that prohibition in the *Statutum de Moneta Parvum* with more ex-

32. *Foedera, conventiones, litterae, et . . . acta publica, 1066–1383,* ed. Thomas Rymer et al. (Record Commission edition, 4 vols. London 1816–69) 1.ii.564; *Calendar of Close Rolls 1272–1279* (hereafter *CCR*) (London 1900) 518. For the recoinage and subsequent problems, see the excellent complementary articles by Mate (n. 24 above) 41–54, 75–79, and Michael Prestwich, "Edward I's Monetary Policies and Their Consequences," *Economic History Review* 2nd ser. 22 (1969) 406–07; *Mint Documents* (n. 27 above) xxii–xxx.

33. Jules Chautard, *Imitations des monnaies au type esterlin frappées en Europe pendant le XIIIe et le XIVe siècle* (Nancy 1871); S. E. Rigold, "The Trail of the Easterlings," *British Numismatic Journal* 26 (1949–51) 31–55; N. J. Mayhew and D. R. Walker, "Crockards and Pollards: Imitation and the Problem of Fineness in a Silver Coinage," *Edwardian Monetary Affairs* (n. 21 above) 125–46.

plicit penalties: confiscation of the metals on the first offense; of accompanying goods on the second; and of all goods, chattels, and "their bodies" on the third, presumably final, offense.[34]

Such draconian penalties, however, did not prevent an apparent inundation of crockards and pollards during the 1290s, at the time of Edward I's French war and Flemish alliance. In 1295, moreover, Philip IV ended almost a century of French monetary stability and inaugurated two centuries of periodic but often drastic coinage alterations that in turn provoked and responded to veritable *guerres monétaires* across Europe. The Low Countries retaliated against Philip's debasements in kind, especially by issuing more inferior crockards.[35] As table 1 shows, English mint outputs plummeted during the 1290s. Finally, in May 1299, Edward I responded by having Parliament enact the famous *Statutum de Falsa Moneta*. Reiterating the ban on all foreign coin imports, especially counterfeit sterlings, the act also prohibited the export of all silver coin, plate, and bullion. Unlike the ad hoc ban of 1278 (which had not included good coin), this one was intended to be permanent. It also prescribed far more severe penalties: forfeiture of life and goods.[36] But the only effective if short-term remedy was to demonetize and then forcibly recoin the counterfeits. Such a reminting was successfully achieved between Easter 1300 and late 1302; that was followed by re-

34. *Statutes of the Realm* (hereafter *SR)* (11 vols. London 1810–28) 1.219–21. On 20 October 1283, Edward I had ordered his searchers to seize any clipped or false coin brought into the kingdom. *Calendar of Patent Rolls 1281–1292* (hereafter *CPR)* (London 1893) 86. See Mate (n. 24 above) 54–61; Prestwich (n. 32 above) 408–09.

35. See Adrien Blanchet and A. Dieudonné, *Manuel de numismatique française* (4 vols. Paris 1912–36) 2.203–34; A. Grunzweig, "Les incidences internationales des mutations monétaires de Philippe le Bel," *Le moyen âge* 59 (1953) 117–72; Hans van Werveke, "Munt en politiek: de Frans-Vlaamse verhoudigen voor en na 1300," *Miscellanea Mediaevalia* (Ghent 1968) 209–26; Rigold (n. 33 above); Prestwich (n. 32 above) 409–12; Mate (n. 24 above) 57–66.

36. *SR* (n. 34 above) 1.131–35 (27 Ed I).

markably high mint outputs at London and Canterbury until 1309.[37]

As table 1 also indicates, coinage outputs then fell sharply. By the early 1330s the fall had become a disastrous slump that marks the nadir of medieval English minting. Counterfeiting and various debasements in France and the Low Countries undoubtedly contributed to this slump, for the crown issued numerous proclamations (listed in Appendixes A and B) commanding strict enforcement of the bans against both foreign coin imports and the export of precious metals. Frequently the two bans were combined into one ordinance aimed specifically at counterfeits, as in the Statute of York of 1335. Not surprisingly, complaints about the scarcity of money became more frequent in the parliaments of the 1330s.[38]

Debasements of the coinage

In the same year as the Statute of York, Edward III responded more decisively with the first significant debasement of the coinage since the chaotic reign of Stephen (1135–54), reducing the silver fineness and weight by 13.1%.[39] Although forced by

37. *Foedera* (n. 32 above) 1.ii.919 (26 March 1300); Mate (n. 24 above) 63–79; Prestwich (n. 32 above) 411–16; C. G. Crump and C. Johnson, "Tables of Bullion Coined Under Edward I, II, and III," *Numismatic Chronicle* 4th ser. 13 (1913) 208–15 (London), 228–32 (Canterbury). See also table 1 above; and Mavis Mate, "High Prices in Early Fourteenth-Century England: Causes and Consequences," *Economic History Review* 2nd ser. 28 (1975) 1–16.

38. See table 1, and Appendixes A and B below; Crump and Johnson (n. 37 above) 214–17, 232–33; *Rotuli Parliamentorum* (hereafter *Rot Parl*) (6 vols. London 1767–77) 2.62: no. 14 (1331), 377: no. 15 (1334); *Foedera* (n. 32 above) 2.ii.814 (3 April 1331); *SR* 1.273–74 (9 Ed III stat 2 c. 1–11 [1335]); R. Cazelles, "Quelques réflexions à própos des mutations de la monnaie royale française (1295–1360)," *Le moyen âge* 72 (1966) 83–105, 251–78; Joseph Ghyssens, "Le monnayage d'argent en Flandre, Hainaut et Brabant au début de la guerre de Cent Ans," *Revue belge de numismatique* 120 (1974) 109–91; Michael Prestwich, "Currency and the Economy of Early Fourteenth Century England," *Edwardian Monetary Affairs* (n. 21 above) 45–58.

39. Crump and Johnson (n. 37 above) 216–17; Prestwich (n. 32 above) 410; Prestwich (n. 38 above) 45–46.

Parliament to restore at least the old sterling fineness in January 1344, Edward reduced the penny's weight four more times, for an overall loss of 19% by June 1351.[40] If the initial debasement was certainly defensive, the subsequent ones were more likely aggressive measures related to the fiscal demands of his French war. These debasements, as a form of disguised taxation, provoked strong public hostility, as debasements certainly did elsewhere in medieval Europe. England was unique, however, in having a parliament that could express such opposition effectively. In January 1352, by the Statute of Purveyors, Parliament exacted the king's promise never again to "impair" the current gold and silver coinages in weight or fineness, but to restore them to their "ancient state."[41] Several succeeding parliaments exhorted Edward III to restore the coinage as promised, but had to be content with royal renunciations of debasements.[42] When another debasement was finally undertaken sixty years later (1411–12), after serious coinage deterioration and foreign counterfeits called galley-halfpence had certainly contributed to a "graunde Escarcete" of money, the crown first had to obtain Parliament's consent.[43] The next two debasements (1464, 1526) were also more than a half century apart, and were probably justifiable for the same reasons.[44] No other West European nation even approached such conservatism in its mint policies.

40. *Rot Parl* 2.138: no. 15; *SR* 1.299 (17 Ed III c. 1 [December 1343]); Crump and Johnson (n. 37 above) 216–21.

41. *Rot Parl* 2.240: no. 32; *SR* 1.322 (25 Ed III stat 5 c. 13). Earlier, in March 1348, a Commons petition had requested that "la bone Monoye ne soit en nule manere chaunge," *Rot Parl* 2.201: no. 6. For complaints of monetary scarcity and of counterfeits in circulation, see also ibid. 2.160: nos. 15–16 (1346), 167: no. 19 (1347); *SR* 1.320 (25 Ed III stat 5 c. 2 [1352]); Edward Ames, "The Sterling Crisis of 1337–1339," *Journal of Economic History* 25 (1965) 496–522; Feavearyear (n. 17 above) 15–20.

42. *Rot Parl* 2.253: no. 37 (1353), 260: no. 33 (1354), 276: no. 12 (1363); 3.64: no. 39 (1379).

43. *Rot Parl* 3.658–59: no. 28. See also ibid. 3.470: no. 61 (1401); *SR* 2.122 (1401), 163 (1410), 168 (1411), 191 (1415), 195 (1416).

44. Munro (n. 9 above) 161–62; Feavearyear (n. 17 above) 37–45, 48–49; Craig (n. 23 above) 72–75. In debasing the coinage in 1464, however, Edward IV appears to have had strong fiscal motives as well.

Bans on the export of all forms of precious metals

Having thus lost ready access to debasement as a weapon to protect their mints and coinages, what recourse did English kings have? Obviously they sought to enforce more stringently their bans on exports of precious metals. Appendix B shows an interesting historical progression of such bans. The first (1278) applied to silver bullion alone; the second added silver coin, domestic and foreign. Gold in plate or as bullion was periodically included in export bans from 1307, and permanently from 1344, when English gold coins were first struck.[45] For the next twenty years English gold nobles could be freely exported; evidently the crown viewed this new gold coinage as a supplementary medium whose use in foreign trade might thus keep silver within England. A surprisingly liberal monetary ordinance was included in the Statute of the Staple of September 1353: foreign merchants were permitted to reexport good foreign coin; and all merchants, to export current English gold and silver coins. But that concession was a temporary expedient necessitated by Edward III's scheme to let only foreign merchants export wools, so that he might tax exports at the higher alien rate.[46] This monetary liberalism came to an abrupt end ten years later when, in 1363, Edward organized a group of English merchants as the Calais Staple Company to control the wool trade. Thereafter, from 20 January 1364 to 1 August 1663, the export of gold and silver in any form was strictly forbidden except, as in the past (Appendix B), by royal licenses, which were generally restricted to the military and aristocracy.

Laws requiring wool exporters to supply bullion to the mints

Bans on the export of precious metals were not, of course, seen as a sufficient remedy for England's monetary problems;

45. See n. 30 above.

46. *Rot Parl* 2.249: no. 18; *SR* 1.338 (27 Ed III stat 2 c. 14). On the Staple policy, see Terence H. Lloyd, *The English Wool Trade in the Middle Ages* (Cambridge 1977) 204–12.

and the crown then resorted to various measures imposed on the export and import trades to conserve and augment the bullion supply. The export trade was the first to suffer, in March 1340, when Parliament responded to complaints about the "great dearth of money" by requiring merchants to supply the mint with two marks (26s. 8d.) in silver plate for each woolsack exported.[47] The crown had to admit defeat in 1348 when merchants complained in Parliament that the count of Flanders, Louis de Mäle, had made compliance impossible by rigorously enforcing his own ban on bullion exports.[48] Nevertheless, as Appendix C shows, English monarchs resurrected variations of this bullionist policy ten more times before finally renouncing it in the 1470s. With one exception (1379), these ordinances required only the wool trade to supply bullion because it was by far the major export trade, until the mid-fifteenth century, and because it had an apparently captive market, chiefly in the Low Countries. Although the Low Countries rightly considered themselves victimized, they had certainly provoked most of the ordinances themselves by their coinage debasements, especially counterfeiting.

The connections between such debasements, English bullionism, and a consequent hostility to credit can best be seen in the ordinance imposed at the Calais Staple in March 1364, a year after its establishment. The crown, justifiably concerned "que les monoies que feurent receux pur leines . . . estoient si febles que les dites leines et marchandises ne poent estre venduz au pris convenable," required that only English coin be received for wool sales, and thus set up a mint at Calais. Merchants evaded this regulation, however, by credit transactions—"par voi d'apprest sanz rien paiere d'or ou d'argent." Moreover, they continued to export good English

47. *Rot Parl* 2.105: no. 14 (petition of October 1339 requesting that 40s. in silver plate be supplied for each sack exported); *SR* 1.289 (14 Ed III stat 1 c. 21), 291 (14 Ed III stat 2 c. 4); *Rot Parl* 2.137–38: no. 16 (1343).

48. *Rot Parl* 2.202: no. 15 (referring to the reissue of the ordinance by the crown in January 1348). Cf. Munro (n. 9 above) 35–37; Lloyd (n. 46 above) 183–84, 196–97.

coin to the offending foreign mints. Expressing dire fears that consequently "notre dit roialme serra destitut deinz breve des monoies," the crown then demanded that merchants buying wool bring 5s. weight (3 oz.) fine gold for each sack to the mint.[49] No further mention is made of this onerous bullion regulation, but the Calais mint itself was very successful in coining gold until the early 1380s.[50] Then, from October 1388, the Flemish sought to lure English gold by counterfeiting the prized English noble.[51] Richard II responded first by banning the Flemish noble and then in 1391–92, and more forcefully in 1397–99, by requiring merchants to bring one ounce in foreign gold—bullion or Flemish nobles—to the mint for each woolsack exported. The bullion laws themselves provoked so much hostile opposition from both English and Flemish merchants that they were allowed to lapse.[52] But the crown did finally eliminate the counterfeits, reputedly a quarter of the English gold circulation, by ordering a general recoinage of all suspect nobles in January 1401. The Flemish mint ceased issuing its nobles in June 1402;[53] and for the next twenty years the Low Countries posed no serious monetary threat to England.

From 1425 on, the Burgundian Low Countries, responding to French and German debasements, again engaged in a series

49. *Foedera* (n. 32 above) 3.ii.725 (1 March 1364). For other payment regulations at Calais, see ibid. 3.ii.699 (10 May 1363), 724 (22 February 1364), 727 (16 March 1364), 773 (26 July 1365). See also Louis Deschamps de Pas, "Etude sur les monnaies de Calais," *Revue belge de numismatique* 39 (1883) 185–86; A. Stanley Walker, "The Calais Mint, 1347–1470," *British Numismatic Journal* 2nd ser. 6 (1931–32) 107–08.

50. Crump and Johnson (n. 37 above) 234–35, 242–45; Lloyd (n. 46 above) 241.

51. Munro (n. 9 above) 46–58.

52. *CCR 1385–1389* (London 1921) 647 (12 February 1389: ban on Flemish nobles); *CCR 1392–1396* (London 1925) 110 (28 December 1392: ban on Flemish nobles); *Rot Parl* 3.285: no. 7 (bullion law of November 1391); 340: no. 19 (Ordenance de la Bullion of January 1397); 369–70: no. 80 (late 1397); 429: no. 86 (October 1399). See Munro (n. 9 above) 53–57; Lloyd (n. 46 above) 243–47.

53. *Rot Parl* 3.470: no. 61 (1400); *SR* 2.122 (2 Hen IV c. 6); Munro (n. 9 above) 243–47; Lloyd (n. 46 above) 245.

of drastic mint manipulations, with further counterfeiting of the gold noble as well, which produced the very epitome of English bullionist retaliation: the Calais Staple Bullion Ordinances of 1429.[54] That legislation required the Staplers to raise wool prices; to exact the "hool paiement" in ready money, to be received as English coin; and to bring one third of the sales price in bullion to the Calais mint.[55] These requirements brutally disrupted the traditional credit system upon which the wool trade and the Low Countries' drapery industries had long depended. In buying wools, drapers from the Low Countries had normally paid one third down in cash and provided two bills or letters obligatory for the remainder, payable in six and twelve months following at one of the Low Countries' fairs. Only when the drapers had sold their textiles, usually at these fairs, could they afford to redeem their bills with the Staplers.

When the Staplers, and also the Merchants Adventurers in the cloth trade, collected these bills, they did not send the money home in specie. Instead they remitted their funds by buying bills of exchange drawn upon London by the Mercers: that is, they advanced Flemish money to the Mercers, who bought goods at these fairs, shipped them to England, and then used the sterling proceeds to redeem their bills. In England, the Staplers themselves similarly bought wool from the growers by this tripartite credit system, sometimes selling foreign bills to the Mercers to obtain the cash for their down payments.[56] Obviously this interlocking credit system with

54. For the background to this, see Eileen E. Power, "The Wool Trade in the Fifteenth Century," *Studies in English Trade in the Fifteenth Century,* ed. Eileen E. Power and Michael M. Postan (London 1933) 82–90; Munro (n. 9 above) 82–126; Lloyd (n. 46 above) 257–62.

55. *Rot Parl* 4.359: no. 60; *SR* 2.254–55 (8 Hen VI c. 18).

56. For analyses of fifteenth century credit operations, see H. L. Gray, "English Foreign Trade from 1446 to 1482," and Eileen E. Power, "Wool Trade in the Fifteenth Century" (n. 54 above) 16–18, 54–58, 62–70; Eileen E. Power, "The English Wool Trade in the Reign of Edward IV," *Cambridge Historical Journal* 2 (1926–28) 24–35; Michael M. Postan, "Private Financial Instruments" (n. 4 above) and his "Credit in Medieval Trade," *Economic History Review* 1st ser. 1 (1928) 234–56;

bills of exchange would thwart the crown's whole bullionist policy. To ensure that no such transactions took place, the 1429 statute obligated the Staplers to sign declarations that "no Merchaunt seller, sal not leen agayn to no Merchant, no manere money of hym receyved, noyr of Wolle ne [Wolle] Felle."[57] The result was a bitter Anglo-Burgundian conflict, and bitter strife within the Staple itself, that raged sporadically until the 1470s, as the English crown reasserted, revised, and withdrew these laws, later reissuing modified versions, all summarized in Appendix C. Since I have analyzed this bullionist conflict extensively elsewhere, suffice it to say that both sides lost the war.[58] Irreparable damage was done to both the English wool trade and the draperies of the Low Countries, except for those that switched to Spanish wools. The English crown had veritably killed the goose that laid the golden eggs, at least for royal finance.[59]

Employment Laws

Although the crown required *importers* to deliver bullion to the mint only once, in 1379–80,[60] from the late fourteenth century it subjected the import trades to complementary bullionist measures known as the Employment Acts. They

M. R. Thielemans, *Bourgogne et Angleterre: Relations politiques et économiques entre les Pays-Bas bourguignons et l'Angleterre, 1435–1467* (Brussels 1966) 356–61; *The Cely Papers . . . 1475–1488,* ed. Henry E. Malden, Camden Third Series 1 (London 1900) introduction.

57. *Rot Parl* 4.359: no. 60. Very likely this ordinance refers as much to the Staplers' buying bills of exchange from the Mercers-Adventurers in the Low Countries as it does to their extending sales credit to the Flemish and Dutch wool buyers at Calais. See Munro (n. 9 above) 86.

58. Munro (n. 9 above) chaps. 3–6; idem, "An Economic Aspect of the Collapse of the Anglo-Burgundian Alliance, 1428–1442," *English Historical Review* 85 (1970) 225–44.

59. Although the English cloth trade undoubtedly benefited greatly from the damage inflicted upon the English wool trade and the Low Countries' draperies, the English crown itself did not gain because the rate of duty on cloth exports was so low: about 2% vs. about 35% for wool.

60. *Rot Parl* 2.66: no. 54; *CCR 1377–1381* (London 1914) 193.

were designed, in essence, to prevent a supposed outflow of precious metals by forcing importers to export their net earnings in English goods alone. The initial statute of November 1390 was quite modest in its aims: only alien importers were affected, and they were obligated to "employ" just half of their net receipts on English merchandise.[61] The same act removed the Staple to English home ports and revived Edward III's alien wool cartel, with the obvious intent of having such merchants "employ" their proceeds on wool exports. But strong domestic opposition forced Richard II to restore the English wool trade and the Calais Staple in 1392.[62] That left as a viable export for aliens just woolen cloth, then still quite secondary to wool.

Furthermore, the 1390 statute seemed to legitimize the export of the other half of the import receipts in precious metals. Indeed, when Henry IV reiterated the ban on precious metal exports in January 1401, his statute permitted aliens complying with the Employment Law to export on license the rest of their earnings in coin.[63] That evidently produced vigorous protests in both this and the following parliament, of September 1402. The latter enacted a far more severe Employment Law requiring all importing merchants, domestic and foreign, to employ the full value of their imports upon English export goods, "without carrying any Gold or Silver in Coin, Plate, or Mass."[64] The following Parliament of January 1404 confirmed this statute and enacted enforcement mechanisms obligating alien importers to furnish surety for equivalent exports to the royal Customers, to sell all imports and to employ the receipts within three months, and to register with English "hosts," who were to record all such transactions

61. *Rot Parl* 3.278: no. 6; *SR* 2.76 (14 Ric II c. 1); see also *CCR 1389–1392* (London 1922) 184 (ban on the export of precious metals of June 1390).

62. *Rot Parl* 3.285: no. 7 (also containing the 1391 bullion law); *SR* 2.76 (14 Ric II c. 5); De Roover, *Gresham* (n. 1 above) 38–42, 45–46; Lloyd (n. 46 above) 243.

63. *Rot Parl* 3.468: no. 53; *SR* 2.122 (2 Hen IV c. 5).

64. *Rot Parl* 3.468: no. 53; 510: nos. 104–05 (1402); *SR* 2.138 (4 Hen IV c. 16).

and ensure compliance with the law.[65] These Employment and Hosting Laws were reenacted, with some refinements and new penalties summarized in Appendix D, over the following eighty years. The final statute, of November 1487, affirming a penalty of one year's imprisonment, was made "perpetual."[66]

Royal and public hostility to bills of exchange transactions

Even if these statutes were but rarely enforced, they are nevertheless significant as manifestations of a bullionist mentality that helps to explain both royal and public hostility to the bill of exchange. Indeed, from first to last, these statutes contained similar "employment" provisions for bills of exchange transactions, restrictions that the crown took much more seriously than the rest of the legislation. Such hostility to the bill of exchange has puzzled some historians, since the bill was designed to obviate bullion exports.[67] But, as the history of the Staple bullion laws has demonstrated, the crown was well aware that in this respect the bill of exchange was a two-edged sword that hampered its policies to secure foreign bullion. This very reason is cited in the first extant proclamation concerning the bill of exchange, issued by Edward I on 14 October 1283. He thus forbade anyone "to make exchange of the King's money in parts beyond [the] sea by receiving there money or silver on condition that they by themselves, their friends or fellows, shall pay in England the sum of such money or the price of such silver, whereby the money or silver

65. *Rot Parl* 3.543: no. 80 (1404); *SR* 2.145–46 (5 Hen IV c. 9). For petitions demanding enforcement of the hosting laws, see *Rot Parl* 3.661–62: no. 35 (1411); 4.104: no. 29 (1416); 126–27: no. 21 (1420); 276: no. 17 (1425); 328–29: no. 31 (1427); 402: no. 32 (1432); 453–54: no. 62 (1443); 5.24–25: no. 38b (1439); 155: no. 4 (1449). Only the 1439 hosting law (*SR* 2.303–05, 18 Hen VI c. 4) seems to have been enforced, and then just in the 1440s. See Public Record Office (London), K. R. Exchequer Accounts Various E. 101/128/30–31 (March 1440–April 1444); Alwyn A. Ruddock, "Alien Hosting in Southampton in the Fifteenth Century," *Economic History Review* 1st ser. 16 (1946) 30–37.

66. *SR* 2.517–18 (3 Hen VII c. 9).

67. See de Roover, *Gresham* (n. 1 above) 41.

that ought to come to the realm may not come as it was wont to do."[68] Certainly by this time, indeed by at least the 1260s, Italian banking firms had brought the bill of exchange to England, especially in their role as papal tax collectors.[69]

A second reason for royal opposition to bills of exchange transactions is that they were regarded as infringements of the royal prerogative to establish exchange rates, asserted at least as early as 1100.[70] Exchange rates—foreign coin or bullion for domestic coin, gold for silver—were clearly seen to have an effect upon the mint's ability to attract bullion. Private money changers were also suspected of purchasing bullion or heavy coins above the official rates and of exporting those metals instead of delivering them to the king's mint or Exchange. Thus, in June 1351, Edward III complained in an edict that "because our gold and silver coins are so much stronger and lower priced than coins of other kingdoms, merchants have been taking our said coins to foreign mints for their own gain, so that little coin remains in our kingdom." He blamed foreign counterfeiters especially for causing this export of metals. Therefore he proclaimed that "no exchange nor sale of any manner of gold or silver money shall be made anywhere except by those to whom we assign [the Exchange] to be held in our name."[71] The following January 1352

68. *CCR 1279–1288* (London 1902) 244.

69. Richard W. Kaeuper, *Bankers to the Crown: The Riccardi of Lucca and Edward I* (Princeton 1973) 3–6, 20–24, 27–48. The device then used may still have been the *instrumentum ex causa cambii* rather than the fully developed bill of exchange: a notarized promise to pay rather than an informal command. But in de Roover's view, "this distinction, being purely formal, is more superficial than real." See his "New Interpretations" 203, *Medieval Bruges* 49–51, *Lettre de change* 29–31 (all in n. 1 above).

70. Craig (n. 23 above) 29. See also *Foedera* (n. 32 above) 1.i.207 (28 September 1232).

71. *Foedera* (n. 32 above) 3.i.223–24 (21 June 1351: "que nul eschaunge ne vente de nule manere de monoie, d'or ne d'argent, soit fait en citee . . . forsque par celui ou par ceux, que nous a ceo assigneroms a tenir en nostre noun, ou par lour deputees, es lieux ou ils serront ordenez par nous.").

Parliament enacted 25 Edwardi III stat. 5 c. 12, which forbade anyone but the King's Exchanger to exchange money for profit.[72] This was the first of two key statutes cited until the seventeenth century in asserting royal control over all foreign exchange transactions.

A third reason for general hostility to bills of exchange was the belief that they were used to cloak surreptitious exports of precious metals, especially ecclesiastical taxes and revenues. As early as 1307 Parliament forbade religious houses to send money to their superiors or to Rome by exchange: "sub nomine redditus, tallagi, aposti, seu impositionis cujuscumque alias nomine escambii, vendicionis, mutui, vel alterius contractus quocumque."[73] Possibly the major role of the bill of exchange in fourteenth century English finance was to remit ecclesiastical payments of various kinds abroad. A deep and growing resentment at the amounts of such remittances, especially revenues from benefices, was thus bound to arouse public hostility against bills of exchange transactions.[74] The

72. *SR* 1.322; *Rot Parl* 2.241: no. 38. See also *CCR 1354–1360* (London 1908) 222 (June 1355). Mavis Mate, in commenting on an earlier version of this paper, suggested that the original intent of this legislation may merely have been to protect those merchants to whom the crown had farmed the Exchange. But subsequent parliaments did not place such an interpretation upon the 1352 statute.

73. *Rot Parl* 1.217 (Carlisle Parliament of March 1307). This parliamentary ordinance was undoubtedly instigated by a decree of Pope Clement V, dated 1 February 1306, that required holders of new ecclesiastical benefices in England to remit the "first fruits," the first year's net income, to the papal treasury—the famous papal annates that subsequently, in the 1530s, played a significant role in the Henrician Reformation (William E. Lunt, *Financial Relations of the Papacy with England to 1327* [Cambridge, Mass. 1939] 487–90). But the 1307 ordinance was evidently also partly in response to a Commons petition of 1305 demanding that the Cistercians be prevented from sending any money abroad (*Rot Parl* 1.178: no. 11). The prohibition was soon relaxed. In April 1307, Parliament permitted papal agents to send "reasonable amounts" of money to Rome "per viam cambii" on condition that they first obtain royal licenses to do so (ibid. 1.222b). See also n. 106 below.

74. See G. A. Holmes, "Florentine Merchants in England 1346–1436," *Economic History Review* 2nd ser. 13 (1960) 193–98, 203–08. See also *Rot Parl* 4.626: no. 27 (1410).

Italians, of course, managed all these transactions, secular and ecclesiastical; and the nature of their commercial activities, their role as papal agents, and their obvious wealth and power invited envious suspicions. They were observed to import much costly merchandise, to collect papal taxes in large sums of cash, but to export fewer and fewer English goods, especially as their share of the wool trade fell sharply after the 1350s.[75] When Italian merchants explained that they remitted their earnings not in specie but "by making money over by exchange," by buying bills of exchange from other merchants, they were often misunderstood and generally disbelieved.

A strong parliamentary movement to suppress the bill of exchange developed during the 1370s, when exports were depressed and the mint outputs had fallen to very low levels.[76] In the aggressive Good Parliament of 1376, during Edward III's final year, a petitioner demanded that no one be permitted to send money abroad "par lettre de Lumbard" and that no Lombard be allowed "to make such letters" on pain of forfeiture and imprisonment.[77] Richard II in effect granted this petition when renewing the ban on the export of precious

75. Lloyd (n. 46 above) 99–224; Munro (n. 9 above) 37–39; Holmes (n. 74 above) 198–204; Eleanora M. Carus-Wilson and Olive Coleman, *England's Export Trade, 1275–1547* (Oxford 1963) 43–57. By the late 1360s, alien wool exports had fallen to 29% of the total; by 1400, to less than 10%.

76. Craig (n. 23 above) 411–12 (app. 1); Carus-Wilson and Coleman (n. 75 above) 49–51, 78–81; Eleanora M. Carus-Wilson, "Trends in the Export of English Woollens in the Fourteenth Century," *Economic History Review* 2nd ser. 3 (1950), reprinted in her *Medieval Merchant Venturers* (London 1954) 252–55; George A. Holmes, *The Estates of the Higher Nobility in Fourteenth-Century England* (Cambridge 1957) 115–20. See table 1 above.

77. *Rot Parl* 2.338: no. 103 (April 1376). See a previous petition, of January 1365, against the export of money "en autri Court hors du Realme par instrumentz . . . en asseurtee de paiement faire as creansours," ibid. 2.286: no. 16. In the Good Parliament (1376), another petitioner complained about Florentines and Lombards who, in buying wools, "preignent les dites marchandies a creance." Ibid. 2.350: no. 160.

metals in October 1377.[78] With Richard's full support, the parliament of January 1380 strengthened the long-standing ban on aliens' holding ecclesiastical benefices by forbidding anyone acting as agent or attorney for such benefices to send money abroad "par lettre d'eschange," merchandise, treasure, or otherwise without the king's special license.[79]

The following year a committee of mint officials presented reports to explain why "no gold or silver comes into England" but was instead exported. While all were agreed that foreign, especially Flemish, debasements were a major reason, several also blamed an excess of imports over exports and "Exchanges made to the Court of Rome" and elsewhere. As remedies they all opposed any alteration of the English coinage "for the universal damage it would cause." Instead they recommended in particular: (1) that "each merchant importing merchandise into the kingdom be required to export domestic goods of the same value"; (2) that no exchanges to the Court of Rome be allowed; (3) that "no exchanges nor other payments by letter be made outside of Flanders for payment in England on account of any merchandise."[80] This committee was thus responsible for enunciating a balance of trade theory whose principles would subsequently be enacted in the Employment Laws. The committee was also responsible for the enactment of 5 Ricardi II stat. 1 c. 2 later that year, in November 1381. This was the other law upon which the crown based its authority to regulate bills of exchange until 1661.[81]

78. *Rot Parl* 3.22–23: no. 91 (October 1377). See Appendixes B and E below.

79. *SR* 2.14–15 (3 Ric II c. 3); *Rot Parl* 3.82–83: no. 37 (January 1380).

80. *Rot Parl* 3.126–27: nos. 1–2. In 1379 a Commons petitioner had complained that "pur defaute de bone ordinance, nul or, n'argent n'en vient en Engleterre, mais de ce q'est en Engleterre grande partie ad este, et de jour en autre est, emporté hors de la terre." But he agreed with Mint officials "qe la Monoie ne soit chaungé en aucun poynt." Ibid. 3.64: no. 39. See Feavearyear (n. 17 above) 33–36.

81. *SR* 2.17–18; *Rot Parl* 3.119–21: no. 107. The petition inspiring the statute had made no provision for prelates and peers; that exemption was the crown's amendment.

In its first provision the statute forbade the export of all precious metals except for military payments, "by Exchanges made in England or elsewhere to be received abroad." But the second provision exempted prelates and peers of the realm on condition "that, of the same Payments only, they make Exchanges in England by good and sufficient Merchants to pay beyond the Sea, and first special Leave and Licence [be] had of the King, as well for the Exchangers as for the Person which ought to make the Payments, containing expressly the Sum which shall be so exchanged." To obtain such special licenses, merchants were to swear "that they shall not send beyond the See any Manner of Gold or Silver under the Colour of the same Exchange." The very next year a group of English and Italian merchants presented a joint petition in the Commons pleading for repeal of this statute "because wools and other English merchandise are not being sold as they used to be, nor can they be without exchange between merchant and merchant, as practiced in all the good cities of the world." Richard II advised the merchants to request special exemptions from the Chancellor.[82] The records subsequently show several licenses for bills of exchange granted to various Italian merchants; and also several cancellations of licenses.[83]

While the statute itself remained unamended, the subsequent enactment of the 1390 Employment Laws included a compromise that both legitimized the mercantile bill of exchange and more firmly regulated its use: to ensure that exports at least matched imports and that alien importers did not export specie. Thus, while only half of alien import receipts had to be "employed" (until 1402), the *full* value of any sum they remitted abroad had to be spent on English export merchandise within three months of making that ex-

82. *Rot Parl* 3.138: no. 36.

83. *CCR 1389–1392* (n. 61 above) 106, 341; *CCR 1392–1396* (n. 52 above) 518–48; *CCR 1399–1402* (London 1927) 199; *CCR 1405–1409* (London 1931) 395; *CCR 1409–1413* (London 1932) 439–45; Rogers Ruding, *Annals of the Coinage of Great Britain and Its Dependencies* (3rd ed. 3 vols. London 1840) 2.142; Holmes (n. 74 above) 195–96, 204, 207.

change, which still required a royal license.[84] One modern economist has applauded this statute for its wisdom in requiring merchants to produce export earnings that would counterbalance the purchase of foreign currency in bills, and thus avoid a specie outflow.[85] But it was hardly necessary to make the same aliens who remitted funds make the exports themselves. Furthermore, the use of such bills of exchange would produce a specie ouflow only if: (1) the purchases of bills drawn on places abroad were not matched in value by bills drawn on London, so that foreign exchange rates were rising against sterling (pence per florin); that would be the case when England was experiencing a balance of payments deficit; (2) the foreign exchange rate rose above the specie export point. In any event, it is doubtful that the framers of this statute really understood the relationships between bills, exchange rates, and specie movements.

Certainly such laws and controls did nothing to abate public suspicions, frequently voiced in Parliament, that importers were using these bills to disguise bullion exports. Italian pleas for repeal because "Merchandise ne purra estre faite sanz Eschaunge entre Merchant et Merchant" only served to invite new controls.[86] In 1402 Parliament required merchants to provide surety for the "employment" of all funds exchanged abroad;[87] and in 1410, another statute stipulated that estreats of "briefs d'Eschange" were to be deposited with the Exchequer every fifteen days.[88] The only concession that the aliens won was an amendment, enacted in 1421, to extend

84. *Rot Parl* 3.278: no. 7; *SR* 2.76 (14 Ric II c. 2).

85. Paul Einzig, *The History of Foreign Exchange* (2nd ed. London and New York 1970) 95–96.

86. See *Rot Parl* 3.553: no. 38 (1404).

87. *Rot Parl* 3.510: nos. 105, 107 (Michaelmas 1402); *CCR 1399–1402* (n. 83 above) 596 (September 1402). See also a petition in the 1407 parliament complaining about the use of bills to remit money to Rome; it requested that all ecclesiastical elections should be free: *Rot Parl* 3.621: no. 56. This was a period of very low mint output and one that experienced a flurry of monetary legislation (1397–1411). See Craig (n. 23 above) 412; and table 1 above, Appendixes A–E below.

88. *Rot Parl* 3.626: no. 27; *SR* 2.165 (11 Hen IV c. 8).

the time within which "employment" of funds had to be made: from three to nine months after the bill was drawn.[89]

Bans and restrictions upon the use of credit in foreign trade

The major feature of fifteenth century commercial legislation was a general assault upon the use of credit in foreign trade, including bills of exchange. The most striking example was, of course, the Calais Staple bullion laws of 1429, reenacted for the last time, in modified form, in 1463.[90] When Edward IV finally renounced this policy and reorganized the Staple by the Act of Retainer in February 1473, he granted the Staplers special exemption from other exchange restrictions as well. The statute noted that since wools were sold for foreign moneys, "which hath no cours within this Reame," the Staplers could not receive payment "withoute eschaunge made in the Landes beyond the See, which eschaunge, if they any make, shuld be unto theym by dyvers other Statutes to excessively grevous and penall."[91] The Staplers' right to make such exchange transactions abroad "contrarie to thoo Estatutes" was reconfirmed by Parliament in 1487, 1503, and 1515. It was never challenged thereafter.[92]

89. *Rot Parl* 4.155–56: no. 24; *SR* 2.210–11 (9 Hen V stat 2 c. 9). The aliens (evidently Italians) also pointed out that "pur defaute de tielx chaungeours" they would indeed have to export specie "& tielx Merchandises . . . ne fuissent achatiez par tielx Merchants chaungeours, a graunde damage du Roi." The next year, when they boldly requested that the period of grace be extended to one year, the crown curtly refused them. *Rot Parl* 4.178: no. 37 (1422).

90. *Rot Parl* 5.503: no. 18; *SR* 2.393–94 (3 Ed IV c. 1 [April 1463]). The Staplers were to take "redy payment and contentation for the same Wolle, Wolfell, . . . wherof the half part be in lawfull money of Englond, Plate or Bullion of Sylver or Gold." See Munro (n. 9 above) 155–79; Lloyd (n. 46 above) 278–81. *Pace* Lloyd, who argues that no credit at all was permitted, I interpret "contentation" from many contemporary documents to mean agreement to pay, i.e. credit sales.

91. *Rot Parl* 6.60: no. 59. For the crown's final renunciation of the policy, by the Anglo-Burgundian treaty of 12 July 1478, see *Foedera*, ed. Thomas Rymer et al. (2nd ed. 20 vols. London 1726–35) 12.77–86.

92. *Rot Parl* 6.395–97: no. 14; 525: no. 3. See Lloyd (n. 46 above) 279–81; Munro (n. 9 above) 176–78.

Thus the wool trade had not been alone in suffering such credit restrictions. In fact, the same bullionist parliament of September 1429 had forbidden any English merchant to sell any kind of merchandise to any foreign merchants on credit, "but oonely for redy money, or Merchandis' for Merchandis'."[93] In the next parliament, however, held in January 1431, some merchants loudly complained that this ordinance had prevented them from selling woolen cloths abroad. Parliament therefore reluctantly permitted cloths to be sold "upon Loan of Payment, to be made in Money or in Merchandise, from Six Months to Six Months next"—in two bills over one year. But the credit ban was reaffirmed for the sales of all other merchandise to aliens.[94]

The reasons given for the 1429 credit ban are very illuminating about public attitudes toward alien merchants. The petitioner complained that foreigners used credit to exploit the English, "consideryng, that thorowe the grete apprestes that has been made [t]hem in this Roiaume, thai have ful gretely encreased and avaunced [t]her Merchandises, and broght doune to noght the pris of the commodite of this Roiaume, makyng [t]hem riche and us pouere, that is shame and abusion."[95] Such attitudes were very common in the 1430s, an era of economic dislocation and depression.[96] Other condemnations of credit combine bullionist fears, a devout loathing of usury, and envious hatred especially of the Italians, whose international banking networks undoubtedly gave them enormous commercial advantages. Thus a petition in the July 1433 parliament charged that alien "broccours" were making "many bargeins and chevysaunces of usurie, grevous, horrible, and dishonest," and that they generally "sende [t]her money

93. *Rot Parl* 4.360–61: no. 66; *SR* 2.257 (8 Hen VI c. 24).

94. *Rot Parl* 4.377: no. 31; *SR* 2.263–64 (9 Hen VI c. 2).

95. *Rot Parl* 4.361: no. 66.

96. See Munro (n. 9 above) 106–26; Holmes (n. 74 above) 197–202; Ralph Flenley, "London and Foreign Merchants in the Reign of Henry VI," *English Historical Review* 25 (1910) 644–47; Carus-Wilson and Coleman (n. 75 above) 58–61, 93–96.

overe the See by soche eschaunges . . . betwene merchaunt and merchaunt," without exporting any English goods.[97] The Italians were singled out for especially abusive attack in the 1437 parliament and in the famous *Libelle of Englyshe Polycye,* written the previous year.[98] The latter accused the Italians of buying English wool on long-term credit, selling the wool in Venice or Bruges for ready money, and then lending that money to English merchants, giving "it oute by eschaunge to be paide ageyne . . . here in Englonde." If the bill is paid "at the receyvyng and sighte of a letter," the English merchant loses 12d. on the pound; if the usance is one month, he loses 24d. Thus the Italians "gayne ageyn in exchaunge makyng, full lyke usurie," "bere there golde sone overe the see into Flaundres ageyne" when the bills are collected, and live comfortably there while letting the English wool dealers wait for their money.

The next assault upon the bill of exchange came in the 1480s, a period of international economic disruptions and considerable inflation.[99] In response to renewed charges that the Italians were "empoverysyng" the realm, Richard III's one parliament of January 1484 forbade them "to make any money over the See by exchange."[100] Although Henry VII granted the Italians' petition to repeal this statute in November 1485, shortly after his victory at Bosworth, he too sought to restrict their credit dealings in the "Acte Agaynst Exchaunge and Rechaunge without the Kynges Lycence" of November 1487.[101] Another statute of the same parliament outlawed "drye exchaunge" and other "dampnable bargaynes groundyt in

97. *Rot Parl* 4.449: no. 51; 453–54: no. 62.

98. *Rot Parl* 4.509: no. 37 (". . . thurgh whiche apprestes thai have been and yet beth daily gretly enriched, thair Merchaundis' double avanced"); *Libelle* (n. 14 above) xxvi–xxviii, 21–24. See also Power, "Wool Trade in the Fifteenth Century" (n. 54 above) 64–65.

99. Phelps Brown and Hopkins (n. 20 above) 183, 194; van der Wee (n. 31 above) 2.89–112; 3. graphs 2–4, 6–7, 16–17, 44–50.

100. *Rot Parl* 6.263: no. 27; *SR* 2.489–93 (1 Ric III c. 9).

101. *Rot Parl* 6.289–90: no. 20; *SR* 2.507–08 (1 Hen VII c. 10); 2.515 (3 Hen VII c. 7).

usurye."[102] Genuine "merchant's exchange" escaped this fate; but a statute of the 1489 parliament, in renewing for twenty years the ban on the export of precious metals, also forbade anyone to "paye or delyver wyttyngly be way of exchaunge" any precious metals to any aliens for any merchandise, on pain of double forfeiture.[103] That provision does not seem to have been enforced; and there were no further restrictions on exchanges in the following forty years of general prosperity and monetary stability. Indeed, toward the end of that period, in May 1522, the crown for the first time formally authorized the circulation of certain foreign gold coins.[104]

Abortive foreign exchange controls, 1531–1663

Although the exchange laws evidently lay dormant for four decades, popular attitudes certainly do not seem to have changed in Tudor times. Thus Clement Armstrong, writing in the 1530s, lamented the revocation of the Calais bullion laws, asserting that since then

> the staplers . . . covenauntid with the adventurers in London [the Merchants Adventurers and Mercers] to delyver ther money, that rose of ther wolle sales, to theym by exchaunge. So begane the staplers and the adventurers for ther own singler profite to make ther exchaunge to geders in kepyng owt of the reame all such money as yerly shuld be brought into the reame for our riche comodites. . . . Which money the adventurers of London, receyvyng it at the marte of the

102. *SR* 2.514 (3 Hen VII c. 6). See also *Tudor Economic Documents* (n. 10 above) 3.363 (ca. 1570); de Roover, *Gresham* (n. 1 above) 181; and n. 5 above.

103. *SR* 2.546 (4 Hen VII c. 23 [January 1489]).

104. *A Bibliography of Royal Proclamations of the Tudor and Stuart Sovereigns, 1485–1714*, ed. Robert Steele (4 vols. London 1910) 1.9: nos. 82, 88 (May and November 1522): legal circulation and official rates for Italian ducats and florins, French écus, and then Imperial caroli. See also ibid. 1.12: no. 105 (November 1526); 20: no. 1792 (March 1539); and *SR* 3.949 (34–35 Hen VIII c. 27 [January 1543]); 1030–31 (37 Hen VIII c. 25 [November 1545]).

staplers [in the Low Countries], bestowith it ther upon all
straunge merchaundise and bryngith it over into England,
wher before that tyme the staplers for ther wolle
broughte ther money into England.[105]

A renewal of accusations that aliens did not "employ" their import receipts upon exports but "delivered the money to merchants in exchange" led Henry VIII, in July 1531, to issue a proclamation resurrecting 5 Ricardi II stat. 1 c. 2.[106] That licensing of exchange contracts proved so vexing that the Merchants Adventurers asked the mayor of London, Richard Gresham, to intercede on their behalf. In July 1538, he duly informed the king that his new regulations were causing the cloth trade great harm, "for the merchaunts can no more be wythoute exchaunges an[d] rechaunges, than the shyppes in the see to be why[th]oute wattyr." He also argued "th[at these] exchaunges and rechaunges doo moche to the stey of [the said] golde in Englaunde, wych wolld ellse be conveyde [over]."[107] Whether convinced or not, Henry VIII restored full freedom of "exchaunges and rechaunges by marchaunts" on 6 August 1538.[108]

Despite the wisdom of Gresham's arguments, the govern-

105. *Tudor Economic Documents* (n. 10 above) 3.94 ("Treatise Concerninge the Staple").

106. *Royal Proclamations* (n. 104 above) 1.14: no. 127; Ruding (n. 83 above) 1.307 (with a date of 29 September 1530). In July 1530 the council had advised Henry VIII "that all the statuttes sholde be inserchyd" to find a solution for the increasing "conveyaunce of coyne out of the realme." Georg Schanz, *Englische Handelspolitik gegen Ende des Mittelalters* (2 vols. Leipzig 1881) 2. *Urkunden* 631–32: no. 155. Obviously the exchange laws had long lain dormant. In January 1532, Parliament banned the payment of annates to Rome to prevent the "impoverisshement" of the realm: *SR* 3.385–88 (23 Hen VIII c. 20).

107. Schanz (n. 106 above) 2.632–33: no. 156. See also 2.635: no. 158 (Chancellor Thomas Audley's letter of ca. 1538).

108. Schanz (n. 106 above) 2.634: no. 157 (30 July); *Royal Proclamations* (n. 104 above) 1.19: nos. 172 (30 July), 173 (6 August). See analyses of this policy in de Roover, *Gresham* (n. 1 above) 182–83 and Richard H. Tawney, "Introduction" to Thomas Wilson, *A Discourse Upon Usury* [1572] (New York 1925) 143–44.

ment, especially under Elizabeth I, increasingly entertained the belief that foreign bankers in the Low Countries were acting in concert to drive down the exchange rate on sterling (Flemish groots per pound sterling) in order to cause an outflow of precious metals to Antwerp.[109] To be sure, a royal commission on the exchanges set up in response to the cloth trade crisis of 1564 correctly explained that such a trade deficit would produce the fall in exchanges and specie outflow. Nevertheless, the report also maintained that "the Rysynge and Fallynge of the Exchange by Cunynge handlyng dothe spessyally Consyste in the Conspyrasye of the greate Bankers [in Antwerp]" in the absence of such crises. It thus recommended inter alia that the crown establish some banking agency to regulate exchange rates.[110] But not until another commercial crisis in the mid-1570s produced another report reciting the same conspiracy theory to explain the exodus of specie did Elizabeth experiment with such a policy to "peg the pound."[111] In September 1576 she appointed her chief minister William Cecil (Lord Burghley) Royal Exchanger; and, citing "abuses of merchants and brokers upon bargains of exchange," she forbade any bills of exchange transactions that were not licensed and endorsed by one of three deputy exchangers. They, in turn, were forbidden to authorize any

109. Thus, in January 1551, William Lane advised the crown that the "fall off the exchange . . . ys the only cawse that all we the merchants . . . Robbe ynglonde and cary a waye all the golde in the land in to forin Remes." *Tudor Economic Documents* (n. 10 above) 2.182–84. In June 1551, Warwick (later duke of Northumberland) forbade "eschaunge and reeschaunge" in the hope of preventing specie outflows; but he had to withdraw this proclamation in March 1552, after vigorous merchant protests. *Royal Proclamations* (n. 104 above) 1.42: no. 398; *SR* 3.154 (5–6 Ed VI c. 19); Ruding (n. 83 above) 1.320; de Roover, *Gresham* (n. 1 above) 183; Tawney (n. 108 above) 145–46.

110. *Tudor Economic Documents* (n. 10 above) 3.346–59: no. iii.4 (quotation on 352). See de Roover, *Gresham* (n. 1 above) 184–93; Tawney (n. 108 above) 147–48.

111. De Roover, *Gresham* (n. 1 above) 193–94. See also Taverner's recommendations to the crown (ca. 1570–75) in *Tudor Economic Documents* (n. 10 above) 3.359–63; no. iii.5.

bills by unknown merchants or any bills in which "the moneys of this Realme [are] deliuered vnder the iust values of their standerd." Finally, the deliverer and taker were to be taxed 1½d. in the pound on both *cambium* and *recambium*.[112] A storm of protest from English and Italian merchants ensued. Politely but firmly, the Italians rejected charges of manipulating the exchange rates, explaining "that the abondaunce of the deliverers or of the takers make thexchaunge rise or fall [in Antwerp]." Again they denied exporting their receipts in specie, patiently reiterating that "we deliver it by exchaunge unto your Englishe merchaunts, that may better traffique outwardelye" than they could. It is doubtful that, after several centuries of antialien prejudice, many Englishmen would admit that the Italian import and banking trades helped finance the English export trades. Finally, the Italians argued that the tax on bills of exchange was likely to bring about the very thing that the new system was designed to prevent: the export of specie to make payments abroad.[113] That may have been the most convincing argument. The licensing scheme was evidently allowed to expire by July 1577.[114]

Apart from various royal proclamations to reassert the old statutes on exchanges, summarized in Appendix E, the final serious attempt to assert the royal prerogative in exchange was Charles I's appointment of Henry Earl of Holland as

112. *Tudor Economic Documents* (n. 10 above) 2.167–69: no. iii.15; *Royal Proclamations* (n. 104 above) 1.76: nos. 706–07; Ruding (n. 83 above) 2.148. See analyses in de Roover, *Gresham* (n. 1 above) 193–94, 210–18; Tawney (n. 108 above) 149–53.

113. Schanz (n. 106 above) 2.642–46: no. 163 (Italian merchants' petition), 646–47: no. 164 (English merchants' petition); *Tudor Economic Documents* (n. 10 above) 2.169–73: no. iii.16.

114. According to de Roover, the Exchanger's accounts terminate on 11 July 1577: *Gresham* (n. 1 above) 217–18. For subsequent attempts to license the exchanges until the 1620s, for further royal commissions on exchanges (1586, 1600, 1621–22), and for the Misselden–Malynes debate on this issue, see de Roover, *Gresham* (n. 1 above) 193–210; Tawney (n. 108 above) 153–54; Heckscher (n. 16 above) 2.243–52; and Appendix E below.

Royal Exchanger, in May 1627, with exclusive powers over the exchange of money and precious metals. This measure was actually directed not against bills of exchange but against the activities of the London goldsmiths, who, as money changers and bullion dealers, were accused of exporting precious metals.[115] The following June a House of Commons committee condemned Charles's measure for its "inconvenience." As Tawney remarks, "the Royal Exchanger seems after 1628 to vanish from history."[116] Nevertheless, in June 1661 Charles II issued a proclamation for the enforcement of those two old statutes of Edward III and Richard II that had been so often used to license bills of exchange.[117]

An end to assertions of royal prerogative in exchange dealing necessarily had to await the crown's final rejection of medieval bullionism. The end came just two years later in statute 15 Caroli II c. 7. Clearly reflecting Thomas Mun's now famous concept of the "overall balance" in foreign trade, the preamble affirmed that "several considerable and advantageous trades cannot be conveniently driven and carried on without the species of money or bullion." Therefore, from 1 August 1663, the export of "all sortes of Forreigne Coyne or Bullion of Gold or Silver" was declared lawful.[118] Mun argued that, by exporting silver for the purchase of goods in the Baltic and Asia, England gained far more treasure in return from the sale of such goods in Western Europe.[119] Whether or not England did then enjoy an overall "favorable balance," the bill of exchange also played an important role in these trades.

115. *Royal Proclamations* (n. 104 above) 1.178: no. 1512; Ruding (n. 83 above) 1.383–84, 2.149–51.

116. Tawney (n. 108 above) 154; Ruding (n. 83 above) 2.151–52; *Journals of the House of Commons, 1547–1714* (117 vols. London 1803–63) 1.917–18.

117. *Royal Proclamations* (n. 104 above) 1.398: no. 3309; Ruding (n. 83 above) 2.3.

118. *SR* 5.451 ("An Act for the Encouragement of Trade").

119. Thomas Mun, *England's Treasure by Forraign Trade* (London 1664, rpt. Oxford 1959) chap. 4: "The Exportation of our Moneys in Trade of Merchandize is a means to encrease our Treasure." Written in the 1620s, it was published only posthumously.

By economizing on scarce, inelastic supplies of precious metals, the bill of exchange thereby directed the metals to their most profitable use, in trading with lands without banking facilities and with little demand for European merchandise. But conversely, the greater historical significance of the bill of exchange had been to conserve that generally scarce silver coinage for domestic commerce, while rapidly mobilizing capital and transferring it to whom and to where it was most needed in international trade.

Finally, if few would dispute the great importance of the bill of exchange in European economic development over the past six centuries, some may well question the significance of English economic policies and social attitudes concerning credit. Indeed, the bullionist mentality of late medieval England may appear to be nothing more than a reflection of commercial and financial backwardness.[120] But the undoubted fact that the English then were less advanced economically than the Italians or the Flemish is hardly a satisfactory explanation of their bullionist policies. English bullionism was unique only in that Parliament was so successful, usually, in forcing the crown to maintain sound money. The cost of that policy, and of the pro-gold policy, was the operation of Gresham's Law, which necessarily made the crown more zealous to conserve the nation's precious metals. If other princes were less jealous of their coinages, because they could more freely resort to debasement to reactivate their mints, almost all nevertheless imposed severe restrictions on the influx of bad coin and the efflux of bullion. Nor did public attitudes toward credit and precious metals differ substantially in other countries from English views. The one significant difference in practice is that

120. See de Roover, *Gresham* (n. 1 above) 117–19 ("The backwardness of England in trade, finance, and business organization before Elizabeth is not sufficiently emphasized"). He further portrays the English as chiefly borrowers. The evidence presented here, however, suggests that the English very frequently extended credit to the Flemish and Italians. English bullionism de Roover considers just a "phobia." See also *Lettre de change* (n. 1 above) 58–59.

public prejudice in England so often coincided with the crown's monetary management.

Late medieval England, moreover, despite its status as an "under-developed" nation, was far from being primitive or backward in the development of credit instruments. As Postan, Power, Gray, Holden, and van der Wee have conclusively demonstrated, credit was the very soul of medieval English commerce. One only has to read the published Cely papers to be convinced of that.[121] Even if Italians dominated foreign exchange banking, Englishmen in all branches of foreign and regional trade used a wide variety of credit instruments, including especially the letter obligatory and the bill of exchange. Furthermore, the latter instruments had been customarily made payable to bearer from at least the 1270s; and by the later fourteenth century, letters obligatory were freely assignable, so that merchants customarily paid debts by "setting over" their own financial claims to others.[122] As Postan comments, "a financial instrument which could pass hands so many times, and apparently without any formalities or additional documents, almost deserves the name of 'currency.' "[123] These credit instruments were not yet fully negotiable, not discountable. But in 1437 the London Mayor's

121. Postan (n. 4 above) 40–64 and "Credit" (n. 56 above) 5–27; Power, "Wool Trade in the Fifteenth Century" (n. 54 above) 54–70 and "Wool Trade in the Reign of Edward IV" (n. 56 above) 24–35; Gray (n. 56 above) 16–18; van der Wee (n. 31 above) 2.337–53; idem, "Anvers et les innovations de la technique financière aux XVIe et XVIIe siècles," *Annales: Economies, Sociétés, Civilisations* 22 (1967) 1067–89 and "Monetary, Credit, and Banking Systems, II. The World of Trade and Finance," *Cambridge Economic History of Europe* 5 (Cambridge 1977) 306–57; James Holden, *The History of Negotiable Instruments in English Law* (London 1955) 4–84; *The Cely Papers* (n. 56 above).

122. Postan (n. 4 above) 40–64; Holden (n. 121 above) 4–10, 21. The letter obligatory, like the older *instrumentum ex causa cambii,* was a two- or three-party promise to pay rather than a four-party command to pay. De Roover does "not hesitate to classify these instruments as genuine bills of exchange," *Gresham* (n. 1 above) 117. See also n. 69 above.

123. Postan (n. 4 above) 49.

Court issued a landmark decision (*Burton* v. *Davy*) that recognized the transferability of a formal bill of exchange and the bearer's legal claim to full payment, crucial steps to negotiability.[124] In Catholic countries, as noted in the introduction, the usury bans evidently prevented full negotiability with discounting until the eighteenth century. De Roover also argues that transfers by endorsement were rare on the Continent before the mid-seventeenth century. He does not, however, deny the English evidence presented by Postan and others. Indeed, he even credits the London goldsmiths of the early seventeenth century with developing true negotiability through the discounting of "inland" or domestic bills and promissory notes.[125]

Herman van der Wee, on the other hand, has found evidence that English letters obligatory were being discounted at the Antwerp fairs as early as 1536. If that was exceptional then, letters obligatory and bills of exchange, many of them issued or held by English merchants, came to be frequently discounted at the Antwerp fairs from the 1560s, with the full protection of the courts for the bearer in assigning such debts.[126] Might not the impediments of English bullionism have provided the necessary incentives to make bills and letters obligatory the much more effective payment instruments that they became by the sixteenth century? For a country that was to become the homeland of the modern Industrial Revolution, that is surely not an irrelevant question.

124. Holden (n. 121 above) 23–27.

125. See (all in n. 1 above) *Lettre de change* 83–146; "Le marché monétaire" 27–36; "New Interpretations" 190, 219–20, 230–36; *Medici* 137–40; *Gresham* 117–22; *Bruges* 350. On assignability, see also Abbott Payson Usher, *The Early History of Deposit Banking in Mediterranean Europe* (New York 1943) 94–109; van der Wee, "Monetary . . . Systems" (n. 121 above) 322–32.

126. Van der Wee (n. 31 above) 337–53; "Anvers" (n. 121 above) 1067–89; and "Monetary . . . Systems" (n. 121 above) 322–32, 347–50. See also Jacob Strieder, *Aus Antwerpener Notariatsarchiven: Quellen zur deutschen Wirtschaftsgeschichte des 16. Jahrhunderts* (Stuttgart 1930).

Appendix A.

Prohibitions against the Importation and Circulation of Counterfeit and Debased Coins and/or Foreign Coins in General

Letters and symbols (sources and notes follow this table)

C = Counterfeit coins
D = Debased and clipped coins
All = All foreign coins (see note 2)
x = Forbidden coin
n.s. = Good foreign coins not specified, since the ordinance is concerned with just counterfeit coins; see note 2 below
* = Ordinance also containing a ban on the export of precious metals

FM = Forfeiture of moneys seized
FMG = Forfeiture of money and goods
FMGL = Forfeiture of moneys, goods, and "life" (prison or execution)

Date	*Ordinance or Statute*	*Form of Coins Prohibited* C	D	All	*Penalties*	*Source*
Apr 1275	3 Ed I c. 15 Statute of Westminster	x			As for felony	*SR* 1.30
Oct 1283	Proclamation	x	x		FM	*CPR 1281–92*, 86
Sep 1284	Statutum de Moneta Magnum	x	x	x[1]	FMGL (?)	*SR* 1.219
Jan 1289	Proclamation	x	x	x	FMGL	*CCR 1288–96*, 9

(continued on following page)

Appendix A.—*continued*

Date	*Ordinance or Statute*		*Form of Coins Prohibited* C	D	All	*Penalties*	*Source*
Jun 1291	Statutum de Moneta Parvum		x	x	x	1st: FM 2nd: FMG 3rd: FMGL	*SR* 1.220
May 1299	Statutum de Falsa Moneta	*	x	x	$x^{2,3}$	FMGL	*SR* 1.131–35
Mar 1300	Proclamation	*	x	x	x^{4}	FMGL	*Foed* 1.ii.919 *CCR 1296–1302,* 385–86, 390
Aug 1310	Proclamation		x	x	x	FM	*CCR 1307–13,* 329
Jan 1317	Proclamation		x	x	n.s.	As in 1291	*CCR 1313–18,* 448 *Foed* 2.i.311
Feb 1319	Proclamation		x	x	n.s.	FM	*Foed* 2.i.386
Jan 1324	Proclamation	*	x	x	n.s.	FMGL	*Foed* 2.i.544 *CCR 1323–27,* 156
Apr 1331	Proclamation	*	x	x	n.s.	FMGL	*Foed* 2.ii.814 *CFR 1327–37,* 251–52
1335	9 Ed III stat 2, c. 2, 4, 9 (Statute of York)	*	x	x	x^{2}	FM	*SR* 1.273–74

(continued on following page)

Appendix A.—*continued*

Date	*Ordinance or Statute*		*Form of Coins Prohibited* C	D	All	*Penalties*	*Source*
Nov 1342	Proclamation	*	x	x	x[2]	FMGL	*CCR 1341–43*, 685–86
Apr 1343	17 Ed III c. 1	*	x	x	n.s.[5]	FMGL	*SR* 1.299 *Rot Parl* 2.137–38
Jul 1344	Proclamation	*	x	x	x	FMGL	*Foed* 3.i.16–17 *CCR 1343–46*, 351
Oct 1346	Proclamation	*			x	FMGL	*CCR 1346–49*, 150
Jun 1351	Proclamation	*	x	x	x	FMGL	*Foed 3.i.223*
Jan 1352	25 Ed III stat 5 c. 2		x	x	n.s.	FMGL (penalty for treason)	*SR* 1.320
Sep 1353	27 Ed III stat 2 c. 14	*	x	x	x[2, 6]	FM	*SR* 1.338 *Rot Parl* 2.249
Mar 1355	Proclamation		x	x	n.s.[7]	FM	*Foed* 3.i.297
Dec 1367	Proclamation			x	x[7]	FM	*Foed* 3.ii.838
Jun 1371	Parl. decree			x	n.s.[7]	FM	*Rot Parl* 2.308
Jun 1371	Proclamation			x	x	FM	*Foed* 3.ii.919
Feb 1389	Proclamation	*	x	x	n.s.[8]	FMGL	*CCR 1385–89*, 647
Dec 1392	Proclamation		x		n.s.[8]	FM and prison	*CCR 1392–96*, 110

(continued on following page)

Appendix A.—*continued*

Date	*Ordinance or Statute*		*Form of Coins Prohibited*			*Penalties*	*Source*
			C	D	All		
Jan 1394	17 Ric II c. 1	*	x	x	x[7]	FM	*SR* 2.87 *Rot Parl* 3.320
Jan 1401	2 Hen IV c. 6	*	x	x	x[7, 8]	FM	*SR* 2.122 *Rot Parl* 3.470
Jan 1410	11 Hen IV c. 5	*	x	x	x[7, 9]	FM	*SR* 2.163
Nov 1411	13 Hen IV c. 6		x	x	x[7, 9]	FM	*SR* 2.168
Nov 1415	3 Hen V c. 1		x	x	x[7, 9]	FM; felony	*SR* 2.191
Apr 1417	Proclamation		x	x	n.s.[8]	FM	*CCR 1413–19*, 427
Dec 1421	9 Hen V stat 2 c. 1	*	x	x	x	FM	*SR* 2.209
Aug 1423	2 Hen VI c. 9	*	x	x	n.s.[10]	FMG; felony	*SR* 2.221
Jan 1478	17 Ed IV c. 1	*	x	x	x	FM; felony	*SR* 2.452–53 *Rot Parl* 6.184
Jan 1504	19 Hen VII c. 5		x	x	n.s.[11]	FM	*SR* 2.650–51 *Rot Parl* 6.542
Sep 1560	Proclamation	*	x	x		For felony	*TSP* 1.56, no. 530
May 1627	Proclamation	*	x	x		Star Chamber	*TSP* 1.178, no. 1512

(continued on following page)

Appendix A.—*continued*

NOTES:

[1] Circulation of Scottish and Irish coins permitted.

[2] Counterfeit and debased or clipped coins to be forfeit; good foreign coins to be delivered to the Royal Exchangers and exchanged for English sterling.

[3] Limited circulation permitted for pollards and crockards; but not for wools, woolfells, leather, lead, or tin sales.

[4] Crockards and pollards demonetized and called in for recoinage from Easter 1300.

[5] If Flemish mint coins as good as sterling, they may circulate.

[6] Foreign merchants may reexport good foreign coins and are not compelled to accept sterling.

[7] Scottish coins banned in particular as fraudulent.

[8] Flemish coins banned in particular as fraudulent.

[9] Galley-halfpence banned in particular as fraudulent.

[10] French coins banned in particular as fraudulent.

[11] No one to import Irish coin above 6s. 8d. in value; but "coyne of other landys nowe curraunt in this Realme for grotes" or for 4d. and those current for 2d. are legal tender.

SOURCES:

SR = *Statutes of the Realm* (11 vols. London 1810–28)
Rot Parl = *Rotuli Parliamentorum* (6 vols. London 1767–77)
Foed = *Foedera, conventiones, litterae, et . . . acta publica, 1066–1383,* ed. Thomas Rymer et al. (Record Commission Edition, 4 vols. London 1816–69)
CCR = *Calendar of the Close Rolls*
CFR = *Calendar of the Fine Rolls*
TSP = Robert Steele, ed., *A Bibliography of Royal Proclamations of the Tudor and Stuart Sovereigns* (4 vols. London 1910)
Annals = Rogers Ruding, *The Annals of the Coinage of Great Britain and Its Dependencies* (3rd. ed. 3 vols. London 1840)

Appendix B.

Prohibitions against the Export of Precious Metals without a Royal License

Letters and symbols

SC	= English silver coins	FM	= Forfeiture of moneys seized
SB	= Silver bullion, plate, foreign silver coin	FMGL	= Forfeiture of moneys, goods, and life (prison or execution)
GC	= English gold coin (nobles)	x	= Metal whose export is banned
GB	= Gold bullion, plate, foreign gold coin	*	= Ordinance also contains a ban on the importation of foreign coins
a	= No English gold coins minted	e	= Export ban contained in an Employment Law
b	= Current English gold nobles may be exported, but no other gold coin (except d)	f	= Aliens may export half of import receipts after employing other half
c	= Current English silver coins may be exported	g	= Confirms prior statute(s)
d	= Aliens may reexport good foreign gold and silver coin		

Date	*Ordinance or Statute*		*Form of Metal Specified* SC	SB	GC	GB	*Penalties; Special Provision*	*Source*
Dec 1278	Proclamation			x	a		FM	*Foed* 1.ii.564 *CCR 1272–79*, 518
May 1299	Statutum de Falsa Moneta	*	x	x	a		FMGL	*SR* 1.131–35

(continued on following page)

Appendix B.—*continued*

Date	*Ordinance or Statute*		*Form of Metal Specified* SC	SB	GC	GB	*Penalties; Special Provision*	*Source*
Apr 1300	Proclamation	*	x	x	a		FMGL	*CCR 1296–1302*, 390
Jan 1307, Nov 1307	Proclamation		x	x	a	x	FMGL	*Foed* 1.ii.1007 *CCR 1302–07*, 522 *CCR 1307–13*, 44
Jan 1324	Proclamation	*	x	x	a		FMGL	*Foed* 2.i.544 *CCR 1323–27*, 156
Feb 1326	Proclamation		x	x	a	x	FM	*Foed.* 2.i.619
May 1331	Proclamation	*	x	x	a	x	FM	*CFR 1327–37*, 251–52
Feb 1333	Proclamation		x	x	a		FM	*CFR 1327–37*, 347
1335	9 Ed III stat 2 c. 1, 3	*	x	x	a	x	FM	*SR* 1.273
May 1338	Proclamation		x	x	a	x	FM	*CCR 1337–39*, 414
Nov 1342	Proclamation	*	x	x	a	x	FM	*CCR 1341–43*, 685–86
Apr 1343	17 Ed III c. 1	*	x	x	a		FM	*SR* 1.299 *Rot Parl* 2.137–38
Feb 1344, Jul 1344	Proclamation	*	x	x	b	x	FMGL	*CCR 1343–46*, 351 *Foed* 3.i.16–17
Jul 1345	Parl. decree		x	x	b	x	FM	*Rot Parl* 2.452 *CCR 1343–46*, 586–87

(continued on following page)

Appendix B.—*continued*

Date	*Ordinance or Statute*		*Form of Metal Specified* SC	SB	GC	GB	*Penalties; Special Provision*	*Source*
Oct 1346	Proclamation	*	x	x	b	x	FMGL	*CCR 1343–46*, 150
Jun 1351	Proclamation	*	x	x	b	x	FMGL	*Foed* 3.i.223
Sep 1353	27 Ed III stat 2, c. 14	*	x[c]	x[d]	b	x[d]	FM	*SR* 1.338 *Rot Parl* 2.249
Jan 1364	38 Ed III stat 1 c. 2		x	x	x	x	FM	*SR* 1.383 *Foed* 3.ii.728
Oct 1377	Parl. decree		x	x	x	x	FM	*Rot Parl* 3.22
Nov 1381	5 Ric II stat 1 c. 2		x	x	x	x	FMGL	*SR* 2.17–18 *Rot Parl* 3.119–20
Sep 1388	Proclamation		x	x	x	x	FM	*CCR 1385–89*, 614
Feb 1389	Proclamation	*	x	x	x	x	FMGL	*CCR 1385–89*, 647
Jun 1390	Proclamation		x	x	x	x	FM	*CCR 1389–92*, 184
Jan 1394	17 Ric II c. 1	*	x	x	x	x	FM	*SR* 2.87 *Rot Parl* 3.320
Jan 1401	2 Hen IV c. 5	*	x	x	x	x	FM[e, f]	*SR* 2.122 *Rot Parl* 3.468
Sep 1402	4 Hen IV c. 16		x	x	x	x	FM[e]	*SR* 2.142 *Rot Parl* 3.509

(continued on following page)

Appendix B.—*continued*

Date	*Ordinance or Statute*		*Form of Metal Specified* SC	SB	GC	GB	*Penalties; Special Provision*	*Source*
Jan 1404	5 Hen IV c. 9		x	x	x	x	FM[e,g]	*SR* 2.145–46 *Rot Parl* 3.543
Oct 1407	9 Hen IV c. 8		x	x	x	x	FM	*SR* 2.161 *Rot Parl* 3.621
Jan 1410	11 Hen IV c. 5	*	x	x	x	x	FM[g]	*SR* 2.163
Nov 1410	Proclamation		x	x	x	x	FM	*CCR 1409–13*, 180
Dec 1420	Parl. decree		x	x	x	x	FM[g]	*Rot Parl* 4.126–27
Dec 1421	9 Hen V stat 2 c. 1	*	x	x	x	x	FM[g]	*SR* 2.209
Oct 1423	2 Hen VI c. 6	*	x	x	x	x	FM	*SR* 2.219 *Rot Parl* 4.252
Jun 1448	Proclamation		x	x	x	x	FM	*CCR 1447–54*, 10
Feb 1449	27 Hen VI c. 3		x	x	x	x	FM[e,g]	*SR* 2.349–50 *Rot Parl* 5.155
Jan 1478	17 Ed IV c. 1	*	x	x	x	x	Pain of felony	*SR* 2.453–59 *Rot Parl* 6.184
Jan 1489	4 Hen VII c. 23		x	x	x	x	Double FM	*SR* 2.546 *Rot Parl* 6.437
Jan 1510	1 Hen VIII c. 13		x	x	x	x	Double FM[g]	*SR* 3.7

(continued on following page)

Appendix B.—*continued*

Date	*Ordinance or Statute*		*Form of Metal Specified* SC	SB	GC	GB	*Penalties; Special Provision*	*Source*
Aug 1531	3 Hen VIII c. 1		x	x	x	x	Double FM[g]	*SR* 3.23
Feb 1512	Proclamation		x	x	x	x	Double FM	*TSP* 1.14, no. 127
Mar 1553	7 Ed VI c. 6		x	x	x	x	Double FM[g]	*SR* 4.i.170
Sep 1560	Proclamation	*	x	x	x	x	Pain of felony	*TSP* 1.56, no. 530–31 *Annals* 1.334–36
Mar 1600	Proclamation		x	x	x	x	Double FM[g]	*TSP* 1.103, no. 907 *Annals* 1.353
May 1611	Proclamation		x	x	x	x	Double FM[g]	*TSP* 1.131, no. 1111
Mar 1615	Proclamation		x	x	x	x	Double FM[g]	*TSP* 1.136, no. 1157 *Annals* 1.371
Jun 1622	Proclamation		x	x	x	x	Star Chamber	*TSP* 1.157, no. 1332 *Annals* 1.377
May 1627	Proclamation	*	x	x	x	x	Star Chamber	*TSP* 1.178, no. 1512 *Annals* 1.178; 2.150
Jun 1661	Proclamation		x	x	x	x	Double FM	*TSP* 1.398, no. 3309 *Annals* 2.3
May 1663	15 Car II c. 7		x		x			*SR* 5.451, sec. 9

IV

Appendix C.

Laws or Decrees Requiring Specified Amounts of Bullion to be Delivered to the Mint for Wools or Other Goods Exported, 1340–1463

Code: n.s. = not specified; N.T. = no specified term; indefinite

Date	*Ordinance or Statute*	*Amount of Bullion to be Delivered to the Mint per Woolsack Exported*	*Duration to; or Number of Years*	*Source*
Mar 1340	14 Ed III stat 1 c. 21	Two marks (26s. 8d.) in silver plate	27 May 1341	*SR* 1.289
1340	14 Ed III stat 2 c. 4	Two marks in silver plate	n.s.	*SR* 1.291
1343	Parl. decree	Two marks in silver plate	n.s.	*Rot Parl* 2.138: no. 16
Jan 1348	Proclamation	Two marks in silver plate	n.s.	*Rot. Parl* 2.202: no. 15
Mar 1364	Proclamation	5s. (3 oz.) of fine gold	n.s.	*Foed* 3.ii.725
Apr 1379	Parl. decree	[Silver bullion worth 5% of goods exported or imported]	To the next parl.	*Rot Parl* 2.66: no. 54 *CCR 1377–81*, 193
Nov 1391	Parl. decree	One ounce of gold bullion	24 June 1392	*Rot Parl* 3.285: no. 7

(continued on following page)

Appendix C.—*continued*

Date	*Ordinance or Statute*	*Amount of Bullion to be Delivered to the Mint per Woolsack Exported*	*Duration to; or Number of Years*	*Source*
Jan 1397	Parl. decree	One ounce of gold bullion	N.T.	*Rot Parl* 3.340: no. 19 *CCR 1396–99*, 37–38
Dec 1420	8 Hen V c. 2	One ounce of gold bullion by aliens not frequenting the Calais Staple	N.T.	*SR* 2.203 *Rot Parl* 4.125: no. 15
Sep 1429	8 Hen VI c. 18	One third of the price in bullion; the rest in English coin	3 years	*SR* 2.254–55 *Rot Parl* 4.359: no. 60
Aug 1433	11 Hen VI c. 13	Reenactment of 8 Hen VI c. 18	3 years or longer	*SR* 2.287 *Rot Parl* 4.454: no. 63
Oct 1435	14 Hen VI c. 2	Reconfirmation of 11 Hen VI c. 18	N.T.	*SR* 2.289–90 *Rot Parl* 4.490: no. 19
Jan 1442	20 Hen VI c. 12	One third of the sales price in silver bullion	7 years	*SR* 2.324–25 *Rot Parl* 5.64: no. 38
Apr 1463	3 Ed IV c. 1	Half of the sales in bullion, plate, or English coin	3 years	*SR* 2.393–94 *Rot Parl* 5.503: no. 18

Appendix D.

Employment and Hosting Laws: For Imports and Bills of Exchange, 1390–1487

Code: % = Percentage of import receipts or of amount in bills of exchange to be "employed" on English goods for export

Date	*Ordinance*	%	*Special Provisions*	*Source*
Nov 1390	14 Ric II c. 1	50	For alien imports only	*SR* 2.76 *Rot Parl* 3.278
Nov 1390	14 Ric II c. 2	100	For all exchanges made abroad	*SR* 2.76 *Rot Parl* 3.278
Jan 1401	2 Hen IV c. 5	50	Aliens complying with the Employment Law may export other half in specie	*SR* 2.122 *Rot Parl* 3.468
Sep 1402	4 Hen IV c. 15	100	For all imports, by both denizens and aliens; no export of precious metals	*SR* 2.138 *Rot Parl* 3.502
Jan 1404	5 Hen IV c. 9	100	Confirmation of 4 Hen IV c. 15. Aliens to register with English "hosts"	*SR* 2.145–46 *Rot Parl* 3.543
Nov 1411	Parl. decree	100	Hosting provisions of 5 Hen IV c. 9 to be enforced	*Rot Parl* 3.661

(continued on following page)

Appendix D.—*continued*

Date	*Ordinance*	%	*Special Provisions*	*Source*
Oct 1416	Parl. decree	100	Hosting provisions of 5 Hen IV c. 9 to be enforced	*Rot Parl* 4.104
Dec 1420	Parl. decree	100	Hosting provisions of 5 Hen IV c. 9 to be enforced	*Rot Parl* 4.126
Dec 1421	9 Hen V stat 2 c. 1, 9	100	5 Hen IV c. 9 confirmed; aliens given 9 months from date of bill of exchange to "employ" funds on English goods	*SR* 2.209, 210–11
Apr 1425	Parl. decree	100	Aliens to be "hosted" within 15 days of arrival and to sell goods and employ receipts within 40 days	*Rot Parl* 4.276: no. 17
Nov 1439	18 Hen VI c. 4	100	Hosting provisions to be enforced for all aliens but the Hanse; aliens to have 8 months to sell their goods and employ their receipts. For 8 years	*SR* 2.303–05 *Rot Parl* 5.24–25: no. 38b
Jun 1448	Proclamation	100	5 Hen IV c. 9 (1404) to be enforced; aliens to provide surety	*CCR 1447–54,* 10

(continued on following page)

Appendix D.—*continued*

Date	*Ordinance*	%	*Special Provisions*	*Source*
Feb 1449	27 Hen VI c. 3	100	4 Hen IV c. 15 (1402) to be enforced; new powers for Searchers	*SR* 2.349–50 *Rot Parl* 5.155: no. 4
Jan 1465	4 Ed IV c. 6	100	Confirmation of 5 Hen IV c. 9. Aliens to employ import proceeds within 3 months, but surety provisions are relaxed	*SR* 2.413–14
Jan 1478	17 Ed IV c. 1	100	5 Hen IV c. 9 confirmed; but penalty increased to one year's imprisonment	*SR* 2.458–59 *Rot Parl* 6.186: no. 27
Jan 1484	1 Ric III c. 9	100	Aliens to sell goods and employ proceeds within 8 months, but are not to send funds abroad by bills of exchange on pain of FMG	*SR* 2.489–93 *Rot Parl* 6.263: no. 27
Nov 1485	1 Hen VII c. 10	100	Repeal of provisions of 1 Ric III c. 9 against Italian merchants	*SR* 2.507–08 *Rot Parl* 6.289–90
Nov 1487	3 Hen VII c. 9	100	Employment provisions in 17 Ed IV c. 1 confirmed and made perpetual	*SR* 2.517–18 *Rot Parl* 6.403

Appendix E.

Ordinances Banning Private Exchange or Regulating Foreign Exchange

Date	*Ordinance*	*Provisions*	*Source*
1222	Proclamation	No one to make exchange except at the Royal Exchanges of London and Canterbury	*Annals* 2.138–39
Sep 1232	Proclamation	No one to exchange new coins for old or make exchanges but at the King's Exchanger	*Foed* 1.i.207
Oct 1283	Proclamation	Ban on all letters of exchange made abroad for payment in England	*CCR 1279–88*, 244
Mar 1307	Parl. decree	Religious houses not to send money abroad to their superiors by exchange or any other such contracts	*Rot Parl* 1.217
Apr 1307	Parl. decree	Papal agents not to send money to Rome in specie or by exchange without royal licenses	*Rot Parl* 1.222
1312	Parl. decree	Manner and places of exchange (coinage) to be determined by the King-in-Parliament	*Rot Parl* 1.285: no. 30

(continued on following page)

Appendix E.—*continued*

Date	*Ordinance*	*Provisions*	*Source*
Nov 1329	Proclamation	No moneyer or changer to leave the kingdom without license	*Foed* 2.ii.774
1335	9 Ed III stat 2 c. 7	Tables of Exchange to be set up at London and Dover	*SR* 1.274
Apr 1343	17 Ed III c. 1	"None to make Exchanges with them that shall pass the Sea, of Gold, for their good sterling to the Value"	*SR* 1.299 *Rot Parl* 2.138
Jun 1351	Proclamation	"que nul eschaunge ne vente de nule manere de monoie d'or ne d'argent soit fait"	*Foed* 3.i.223–24
Jan 1352	25 Ed III stat 5 c. 12	No one to hold or to profit from Exchanges but the King's Exchanger	*SR* 1.322 *Rot Parl* 2.241: no. 38
Jun 1355	Proclamation	No one to hold private exchange on forfeiture of life & limb	*CCR 1354–60*, 222
Jul 1365	Proclamation	"Ne quis cambium de moneta . . . nisi ex causa mercaturae faciat": at the Calais Staple	*Foed* 3.ii.773

(continued on following page)

Appendix E.—*continued*

Date	*Ordinance*	*Provisions*	*Source*
Oct 1377	Parl. decree	"qe par null paiement ne par eschaunge en or, argent, plate . . . riens pluis ne soit tret" by aliens. In ban on precious metal exports	*Rot Parl* 3.22: no. 91
Jan 1380	3 Ric II c. 3	Alien ecclesiastics to be prevented from sending money, treasure, etc., abroad "par lettre d'eschange . . ."	*Rot Parl* 3.83: no. 37 *SR* 2.15
Nov 1381	5 Ric II stat 1 c. 2	No one but prelates and peers to send money or bullion abroad by "Exchanges to be made" or otherwise; latter by licenses	*SR* 2.17–18 *Rot Parl* 3.119–20: no. 107
Nov 1389	Proclamation	As in 5 Ric II stat 1 c. 2	*TSP* 1.clxx
Jan 1390	Proclamation	Richard II revokes patents that had permitted payment abroad by letters of exchange	*CCR 1389–92,* 106
Nov 1390	14 Ric II c. 2	For any sum remitted by letter of exchange the merchant must buy English goods to full value within 3 months	*SR* 2.76 *Rot Parl* 3.278: no. 7

(continued on following page)

Appendix E.—*continued*

Date	*Ordinance*	*Provisions*	*Source*
May 1391	Proclamation	"No man shall make any exchange of the King's money to foreign parts without his special license"	*CCR 1389–92,* 341
Sep 1400	Proclamation	"No one shall make any change within the realm . . . in order to receive gold or silver in foreign parts, by reason thereof, without a royal license"	*CCR 1399–1402,* 199
Sep 1402	Parl. decree	Confirmation of 14 Ric II c. 2. Merchants to provide security for "employment" of sums exchanged abroad by license	*Rot Parl* 3.510: no. 105 *CCR 1399–1402,* 596
Jun 1408	Proclamation	No one to "make any exchanges [to foreign parts] by virtue of any letters patent or writs of the king"	*CCR 1405–09,* 395
Jan 1410	11 Hen IV c. 8	14 Ric II c. 2 to be enforced. Estreats of "briefs d'Eschange" to be deposited at the Exchequer every 15 days	*SR* 2.165 *Rot Parl* 3.626: no. 27

(continued on following page)

Appendix E.—*continued*

Date	*Ordinance*	*Provisions*	*Source*
Dec 1421	9 Hen V stat 2 c. 1, 9	Confirms all prior statutes, but permits merchants 9 months to buy English goods to value of the sum exchanged abroad	*SR* 2.209, 210–11
Jan 1422	Proclamation	25 Ed III stat 5 c. 12 (1352) to be enforced	*CCR 1419–22,* 221
Sep 1429	8 Hen VI c. 18	No sales credit to be allowed in Staple wool sales	*SR* 2.255–56 *Rot Parl* 5.359
Sep 1429	8 Hen VI c. 24	No sales credit to be allowed for any goods to aliens	*SR* 2.257 *Rot Parl* 5.360–61: no. 66
Jan 1431	9 Hen VI c. 2	8 Hen VI c. 24 amended to allow credit for "six months to six months" in the cloth trade; but credit ban confirmed for all other commodities	*SR* 2.263–64 *Rot Parl* 4.377: no. 31
Feb 1473	Parl. decree	Use of bills of exchange at the Calais Staple explicitly permitted for 16 years	*Rot Parl* 6.60: no. 59

(continued on following page)

Appendix E.—*continued*

Date	*Ordinance*	*Provisions*	*Source*
Jan 1484	1 Ric III c. 9	Italians to "employ" all import proceeds on English goods and forbidden "to make [any suche Moneye] over the See by Exchaunge" on pain of FMG	*SR* 2.489–93 *Rot Parl* 6.263: no. 27
Nov 1485	1 Hen VII c. 10	Repeal of 1 Ric III c. 9: of provisions against bills and Italian merchants	*SR* 2.507–08 *Rot Parl* 6.289–90
Nov 1487	Parl. decree	Permission to use bills of exchange at Calais Staple extended for 16 years from April 1488	*Rot Parl* 6.395–97: no. 14
Nov 1487	3 Hen VII c. 6	Prohibition of "drye exchaunge" and "newe chevessaunce"	*SR* 2.514 *Rot Parl* 6.403: no. 29
Nov 1487	3 Hen VII c. 7	Prohibition of "exchaunge and rechaunge without the Kynges lycence." Confirmation of 25 Ed III stat 5 c. 12 and 5 Ric II stat 1 c. 2	*SR* 2.515 *Rot Parl* 6.403: no. 28
Jan 1489	4 Hen VII c. 23	No one to "pay or deliver wittingly by way of eschaunge or otherwise" any precious metals to aliens	*SR* 2.546 *Rot Parl* 6.437: no. 52

(continued on following page)

Appendix E.—*continued*

Date	*Ordinance*	*Provisions*	*Source*
1503	Parl. decree	Permission to use bills of exchange at Calais Staple extended for 16 years from April 1504	*Rot Parl* 6.525: no. 3
Jul 1531 (Sep 1530?)	Proclamation	No one to make exchanges contrary to 5 Ric II stat 1 c. 2 on pain of FMGL	*TSP* 1.14, no. 127 *Annals* 1.307, 2.147 *EHP* 2.631–32, no. 155
Jul 1538	Proclamation	Right of merchants "to make their exchaunge and rechaunges" restored to 1 Nov 1538	*TSP* 1.19, no. 172 *EHP* 2.634, no. 157
Aug 1538	Proclamation	Decree "freely licencinge Exchaunges and Rechaunges by Marchaunts" indefinitely	*TSP* 1.19, no. 173
1546	Proclamation	3 Hen VII c. 7 and 25 Ed III stat 5 c. 12 to be enforced	*Annals* 2.148
Jun 1551	Proclamation	3 Hen VII c. 7 to be strictly enforced; "eschaunge and reeschaunge" prohibited	*TSP* 1.42, no. 398
Jan 1552	5–6 Ed VI c. 19	25 Ed III stat 5 c. 12 to be enforced, with 1 year's imprisonment for violations	*SR* 3.154

(continued on following page)

Appendix E.—*continued*

Date	*Ordinance*	*Provisions*	*Source*
Mar 1552	Proclamation	Proclamation of 10 June 1552 prohibiting bills of exchange is annulled	*Discourse*, p. 146
1558	Proclamation	Prohibition of carrying money abroad by way of exchange	*Annals* 2.148
Sep 1576	Proclamation	Existing statutes and laws "upon bargains of exchange" to be enforced. Bills of exchange not valid unless endorsed by a deputy-Exchanger. Exchangers not to endorse bills in which money is "deliuered vnder the iust values of their standerd"	*TSP* 1.76, nos. 706–07 *Annals* 2.148 *TED* 2.167–69: no. iii.15
Mar 1601	Proclamation	5–6 Ed VI c. 19, 5 Ric II stat 1 c. 2 and 25 Ed III stat 5 c. 12 to be strictly enforced	*TSP* 1.103, no. 907 *Annals* 1.353
Feb 1619	Proclamation	Official coinage rates to be respected; gold and silver not to be exchanged for profit	*TSP* 1.147, no. 1240

(continued on following page)

Appendix E.—*continued*

Date	*Ordinance*	*Provisions*	*Source*
May 1627	Proclamation	Royal Exchanger to have sole control over exchanges from 29 Sep 1627. Goldsmiths condemned for culling & exporting coins	*TSP* 1.178, no. 1512 *Annals* 1.383–84
Jun 1661	Proclamation	5 Ed VI c. 19, 5 Ric II stat 1 c. 2 and 25 Ed III stat 5 c. 12 to be enforced	*TSP* 1.398, no. 3309 *Annals* 2.3
May 1663	15 Car II c. 7	Free export of foreign coins and of bullion to be lawful from 1 Aug 1663	*SR* 5.451, sec. 9

SOURCES:

EHP = Georg Schanz, *Englische Handelspolitik gegen Ende des Mittelalters* (2 vols. Leipzig 1881)
TED = *Tudor Economic Documents*, ed. Richard H. Tawney and Eileen E. Power (3 vols. London and New York 1924)
Discourse = Thomas Wilson, *Discourse upon Usury* [1572], ed. Richard H. Tawney (New York 1925)

ABBREVIATIONS

AJ	*Archaeological Journal*
ANSMN	*American Numismatic Society Museum Notes*
BCH	*Bulletin de correspondance hellénique*
BMC	*British Museum Catalogue* (with suffix)
BMQ	*British Museum Quarterly*
BNJ	*British Numismatic Journal*
BSA	*Annual of the British School at Athens*
BSFN	*Bulletin de la société française de numismatique*
CR	*Classical Review*
DOC	*Dumbarton Oaks Catalogue*
FMRD	*Die Fundmünzen der römischen Zeit in Deutschland*
HN	*Historia Numorum*
IG	*Inscriptiones Graecae*
IGCH	*Inventory of Greek Coin Hoards*
JASB	*Journal of the Asiatic Society of Bengal*
JHS	*Journal of Hellenic Studies*
JNG	*Jahrbüch für Numismatik und Geldgeschichte*
JNSI	*Journal of the Numismatic Society of India*
JRS	*Journal of Roman Studies*
NC	*Numismatic Chronicle*
NCirc	*Numismatic Circular*
NNÅ	*Nordisk Numismatisk Årsskrift*
NNM	*Numismatic Notes and Monographs*
RBN	*Revue belge de numismatique*
RIC	Mattingly, Sydenham, and others, *Roman Imperial Coinage*
RN	*Revue numismatique*
SCBI	*Sylloge of Coins of the British Isles*
SCMB	*Seaby's Coin and Medal Bulletin*
SNG	*Sylloge Nummorum Graecorum*
Traité	E. Babelon, *Traité des monnaies grecques et romaines*
VCH	*Victoria County History*
WN	*Wiadomości Numizmatyczne*
ZfN	*Zeitschrift für Numismatik*

V

Mint Policies, Ratios, and Outputs in the Low Countries and England, 1335–1420: Some Reflections on New Data

1

In his recent magisterial study of the medieval English wool trade, Mr Terence Lloyd has attacked my views on Anglo-Flemish mint competition from 1388 to 1402, an episode that I had described in a much broader study as 'the war of the gold nobles'.[1] In brief, I had contended that the Flemish mints were aggressively luring both metals: gold (from 1388), by counterfeiting the much-prized English noble; and silver (from 1390), by offering a higher price or 'bimetallic ratio' than were the English mints. The English crown responded to at least the gold threat by banning Flemish nobles and by forcing Flemish wool buyers to pay partly in gold bullion at the Calais Staple. Mr Lloyd rejected my *supposed* conclusion that England subsequently lost 'the war of the nobles', in terms of coinage output. To begin with, he notes that even my own statistics fail to demonstrate any major defeat for England: a total fourteen-year production of 22,348 gold *marcs* by the Flemish mints *v.* 21,098 gold *marcs* by London's Tower Mint. But England then had another mint in production; and Mr Lloyd's discovery of the Calais mint accounts for this very period, accounts that I (and everybody else) had missed, enabled him to present a far graver challenge to my views. Thus 'when the Calais figures are added to those of London total English production of gold considerably exceeded that of Burgundy. The surviving Calais accounts record the coinage of £107,288 in gold [or] 10,221 *marcs de Troyes*, while accounts are missing for two important years [1388–9], when production may easily have reached £50,000 [in gold, or] 4,763 *marcs de Troyes*.' England therefore won the 'war of the gold nobles . . .'.[2]

Certainly I must heartily congratulate Mr Lloyd for having discovered these

[1] T. H. Lloyd, *The English Wool Trade in the Middle Ages* (Cambridge, 1977), pp. 246–7. For my views, see J. H. Munro, *Wool, Cloth, and Gold: The Struggle for Bullion in Anglo-Burgundian Trade, 1340–1478* (Brussels and Toronto, 1973), pp. 43–63.

[2] Lloyd, *Wool Trade* (n. 1), p. 246. The conclusion of his sentence is: 'but only at the cost of losing the "battle" for silver'. See my comments below, p. 74.

hitherto unknown Calais mint accounts. Having myself found the Calais mint seignorage records from July 1422 to March 1436 in the very same source (in 1966), the Calais Treasurer's reports in the Enrolled Foreign Accounts, L.T.R. Exchequer Series E. 364, I obviously should have searched through these earlier accounts as well. Regrettably I had maintained the erroneous view that the Calais mint had been dormant for the entire thirty-eight years between its well-known closure in January 1384 and its later re-establishment by parliament in 1422.[3] Mr Lloyd's new evidence on Calais mint production during the entire 'war of the nobles' unquestionably provides important new perspectives on that Anglo-Flemish conflict.

Nevertheless I cannot accept Mr Lloyd's own conclusions about this monetary conflict. In the first place, his statistical comparison is a biased one that exaggerates the English leadership in gold coinage output: by setting over sixteen years of Calais output (17 January 1387 to 30 March 1403) against less than fourteen years of Flemish output (1 October 1388 to 16 June 1402). In the second place, almost a third of Calais' sixteen-year output is contained in the first mint account—£32,537 (= 2,169.1 Tower lb. = 3,101 *marcs*)—which commences over twenty months *before* the war began in October 1388, when the Flemish mint struck the first counterfeit gold nobles. In the third place, I must reject Mr Lloyd's supposition that this first account is followed by a gap of almost two years, from 28 February 1388 to 17 January 1390, during which time Calais could well have struck an additional '£50,000', in his view. Having now checked these Calais mint accounts myself, I find no such gap. My reading of that initial account in E. 364/25 m. 5 is that the notation of 28 February 1388 refers only to a change of comptrollers, and that this same account then continues 'ab eodem xxviii die ffebruari anno xi [1388] usque xvii diem januari anno xiii [1390] per visium et testimonium Roberti Selby, contrarotulator regis, *ibidem scilicet de tribus annis integris*'. Hence that princely sum of £32,537 was coined instead over the full three-year period 17 January 1387–17 January 1390. It is, of course, quite impossible to state how much of this amount was struck before or after the outbreak of the 'war of the nobles' in October 1388—though the next account, also for three full years (to 17 January 1393), indicates a far smaller volume of output: £6,618 sterling. All the remaining Calais mint accounts proceed quite intact, without a single break, until the final one of 30 March 1403–30 March 1404.

[3] By 9 Hen. V stat. 1 c. 6, in *Statutes of the Realm*, vol. 2, p. 206. The Calais mint accounts from 20 Feb. 1363 to 7 Jan. 1384 were published by C. G. Crump and C. Johnson, 'Tables of bullion coined under Edward I, II, and III', *NC*[4] 13 (1913), 235, 243–5; but no accounts were given in the sequel, G. C. Brookes and E. Stokes, 'Tables of bullion coined from 1377 to 1550', *NC*[5] 9 (1929), 27–69. My series for 1422–36 were published in my *Wool, Cloth, and Gold* (1973), pp. 187–97. See also P. Spufford and P. Woodhead, 'Calais and its mint', in *Coinage in the Low Countries (880–1500)*, ed. N. J. Mayhew (*BAR* International Ser. 54, Oxford, 1979), pp. 171–202.

This final account, it must be noted, extends Mr Lloyd's series of Calais mint statistics by precisely one more year—and the total gold output by a mere £301. 8*s.* 7*d.* sterling = 20.1 Tower lb. = 28.7 *marcs*. No wonder the Calais mint closed that year! Mr Lloyd himself had found no references to coinage in this 1403–4 account, which appeared to be incomplete. In fact this account, on m. 2 of E. 364/39, is interrupted and followed on m. 3 by other quite unrelated 'foreign accounts'; but then on m. 4 the Calais account is resumed, with an entry recording 70*s.* 4*d.* in Calais mint seignorage in the closing section. The next Calais Treasurer's account, of 30 March 1404–9 May 1405, explicitly states 'nulla moneta'; the next, of 9 May 1405–5 March 1406, records the sale of the mint pix (for 5*s.*); and the following accounts up to the re-establishment of the Calais mint in July 1422 either state explicitly 'quod nulla moneta fabricata fuit', or make no mention of coinage at all.[4]

2

This final correction of Mr Lloyd's statistics, while important in establishing the true record of Calais' mint output, does not of course detract from his central argument: that the English mints surpassed the Flemish in gold output during this era. And while the other corrections do seriously undermine his contentions about the *extent* of the English gold supremacy, one cannot dispute the fact of that supremacy. But I had never contended the converse, of a Flemish superiority in gold output. Indeed I had never even aggregated and compared the two countries' mint outputs from 1388 to 1402, because too many other factors affected actual levels of output: military expenditures abroad; ransom and booty; changes in export receipts; international credit arrangements; effects of taxation and domestic dishoardings; and mint-competition with other, third, countries. Furthermore, I had contended that Duke Philip of Burgundy was successful in attracting gold only from 1393, when he perfected his counterfeiting policy, until January 1397, when Richard II retaliated by imposing his *Ordenance de la Bullion* on the wool trade, with some considerable success for English minting, to 1399. Nevertheless, I did state that Richard II—not England—subsequently lost this phase of the 'war of the nobles' on the specific grounds that Burgundian counter-measures finally forced the English to abandon the *Ordenance de la Bullion* after 1399. But I had also concluded that Richard's successor Henry IV (1399–1413) had much greater success in foiling the Flemish counterfeiting, above all by issuing a much lighter noble, in 1412. Almost incredibly that constituted the first English debasement since 1351; and I commented that 'by clinging so

[4] Public Record Office, LTR Exchequer, E 364/39 m. 2, 4 (1403–4); 43 m. 8 (1404–5); 46 m. 4 (1405–6); 46 m. 4 (5.iii.1406–7.vii.1407); 46 m. 3 (7.vii.1407–28.xii.1409); 50 m. 3 (28.xii.1409–29.iii.1412); 55 m. 1 (6.viii.1413–6.viii.1417); 56 m. 3 (4.ii.1421–9.vi.1421). Accounts are missing for 29.iii.1412–6.viii.1413 and 6.viii.1417–4.ii.1421. See Lloyd, *Wool Trade* (n. 1), pp. 241, 245.

obstinately to "sound money", the English had taken a long time—some 23 years—*to defeat the Flemish*'.[5] Whether or not the English victory over Flemish counterfeiting had really taken so long will be reconsidered, in the light of new evidence, near the end of this article.

3

My principal objection, however, to Lloyd's attack (and to those who have repeated his arguments) is that insufficient attention was paid to my discussion of that other metal, silver.[6] Thus, if we accept Mr Lloyd's terms and compare the two countries' aggregate mint outputs for the entire period of the conflict from Mich. 1388 to Mich. 1402, as set out in Table 4, we find that: (*a*) the Flemish coined 82.7 per cent as much pure gold as the English, *but* (*b*) that the English coined only 4.4 per cent as much pure silver as did the Flemish. The gold figures depend on apportioning (estimating by monthly averages) the Calais output for Mich. 1388–9; but the silver figures for both countries during this period are complete and exact.[7] To be fair to Lloyd, he has indeed admitted that the Flemish had a superiority in silver minting by a ratio of 22.6 : 1. But for reasons that elude me, he has regarded the competition for silver merely as a 'battle'; that for gold, on the other hand, was the true 'war', won by the English. Furthermore, he has charged elsewhere that my silver statistics 'exaggerate the advantage enjoyed by Burgundy' because the latter's 'frequent manipulation of the currency' meant that the same silver was being reminted several times in Flanders, while England's stable coinage meant that for her any 'mint output was a genuine addition to the money supply'.[8] Apart from the fact this argument ignores international bullion and credit flows, it is unfair on the face of it: for the Flemish in this era altered the coinage with a major debasement only once, in October 1388, and thereafter only with a *renforcement* in January 1390 and then in January 1391 with a quite insignificant reduction of 0.87 per cent in the silver coinage weight

[5] Munro, *Wool, Cloth, and Gold*, pp. 43, 61. But see below p. 92 and n. 59.

[6] See M. Prestwich's review of Lloyd's *Wool Trade* in the *English Historical Review*, 93 (1978), 388–90; and Spufford, 'Calais' (n. 3 above), 176.

[7] See above, p. 72 for the discussion of the Calais account of 17 Jan. 1387 to 17 Jan. 1390. All mint outputs have been given for Michaelmas years ending 29 September. For this Calais account, 23.5 per cent of the coinage was assigned to the period 17 Jan.–Mich. 1387 (8.45 months); 33.3 per cent to Mich. 1387–Mich. 1388 (12 months); 33.3 per cent to Mich. 1388–Mich. 1389 (12 months); and 9.9 per cent to Mich. 1389–17 Jan. 1390 (3.55 months). This method of apportionment was used for all English and Flemish-Brabantine mint accounts not coinciding with, or falling within, Michaelmas years. Since the Flemish accounts began on 1 Oct. 1388 and terminate on 16 June 1402, and since no accounts are missing, the totals given in Table 4 for Flemish output Mich. 1388–Mich. 1402 are complete and exact. But the year-by-year figures given for both Flemish and English mint outputs from 1380 to 1419 in Tables 1–3 have been estimated by this method of apportionment, necessarily.

[8] Lloyd, *Wool Trade* (n. 1), p. 246 and T. H. Lloyd, 'Overseas trade and the English money supply in the fourteenth century', in *Edwardian Monetary Affairs (1279–1344)*, ed. N. J. Mayhew (*BAR* 36, Oxford, 1977), p. 119.

(0.037 g!), a change fully annulled in June 1393 (see Table 8). Thereafter the fully restored, strong coinage remained quite unchanged until the *renforcement* of August 1409 (—or, if one prefers, to the closure of the Flemish mints in June 1402). It must be stressed that normally a mint will produce much larger outputs with a debasement than with a *renforcement* and strong money.

But let us obviate Mr Lloyd's objection entirely by comparing the Flemish and English silver outputs only for those years 1393 to 1402, when both countries' mint indentures were unchanged and operative. The statistical comparison for this latter period turns out to be even less favourable for Lloyd's case. The Flemish mints in fact outproduced the English in silver by an even greater ratio of 35.9 : 1—i.e. 42,970.4 kg *v.* 1,198.3 kg of pure silver.

While it may seem preferable to have a supremacy in gold coinage, as the more 'valuable' metal, the only rational method of comparing the two countries' aggregate gold and silver outputs is to assign them their corresponding money-of-account values. In this case, to facilitate the international comparisons, I have used as the common denominator for both countries the English pound sterling values for gold and silver, on the grounds that these values were stable, quite unchanged from 1351 to 1411. By these calculations, set out in Table 4, the Flemish mints win the contest decisively: the sterling value of the total Flemish gold and silver coinage outputs combined, from 1388 to 1402, was 54.4 per cent greater than that of the English mint outputs. If one also compares the coinage output values from 1393 to 1402, the period of perfect mint stability, or the mean output values for the quinquenniums 1390–4 and 1395–9, as given in Tables 3 and 5, the results remain the same: the Flemish mints win by a decisively large margin.

4

The central point, which my critics seem to have missed, is that the Flemish (or Duke Philip of Burgundy) deliberately *chose to attract silver over gold* by switching from a pro-gold to a pro-silver bimetallic ratio in 1389–90. Normally the opportunity cost of altering the mint ratio to favour one metal is to lose the other. The striking novelty of the Flemish policy was to reduce this opportunity cost, to stem the expected outflow of gold to mints favouring that metal—the English in particular—by counterfeiting English gold nobles. Thus some merchants would still bring gold to Flemish mints for the expected gain in acquiring more nobles for their bullion. But only those who could successfully pass the counterfeit nobles abroad (and accept the risks of confiscation) would derive enough gain to offset the unfavourable mint ratio and exchange rate. Undoubtedly the Flemish monetary officials neither expected nor desired to have even half their coinage output in gold, after changing the mint ratio in 1390. Hence, perhaps the most surprising feature of the comparisons portrayed in Table 4 is that the Flemish succeeded in coining as much gold as they did in this period. Why one metal should be preferred at times to the other, and specifically why the Flemish converted to a pro-silver policy in the late fourteenth century will be reconsidered at the end of this article, after examining new evidence on bimetallism, mint ratios, and mint outputs in the Low Countries, France, and England.

Since medieval bimetallism is not the easiest theory to elucidate, and since my earlier model in *Wool, Cloth, and Gold* (1973) lacked some refinements, I should bear some blame for my critics' confusion on the silver issue.[9] Furthermore, the theory that mint-ratio alterations can influence international monetary flows—a variant of Gresham's Law—has often been expressed in oversimplified, unhistorical terms that have deservedly received much attack.[10] My own particular, further refined model that seeks to meet these legitimate objections is given in Appendix A.

In view of the considerable scepticism about the validity of the bimetallic theory, it requires not only more refined models but a great deal more empirical evidence to sustain it. Elsewhere I have attempted to demonstrate with Chi-Square tests and elaborate graphs that major alterations of mint ratios in the fifteenth century dramatically affected the relative flows of gold and silver to the Burgundian and English mints, each receiving the much greater share of its 'favoured' metal over long periods.[11] Now, thanks to the prodigious labours and analyses of Professor Wim Blockmans and his late father Frans Blockmans on Flemish mint outputs and coinage rates from 1332 to 1384, to the researches of Dr Pierre Cockshaw, and to some ancillary detective work of my own, especially on the Brabant mints (1375–1420), I am now able to make similar analyses of mint outputs and mint ratios for the fourteenth century as well (but omitting the more elaborate statistical tests).[12]

5

These mint statistics, presented in the accompanying ten tables, provide a much better perspective on fourteenth-century monetary history in general and on the Anglo-Flemish monetary conflict of 1388–1402 in particular. First, Table 8 supports the contention of Professor Andrew Watson and others that the gold : silver ratios in north-west Europe, having been extraordinarily high (pro-gold) in the earlier fourteenth century, were dropping

[9] *Wool, Cloth, and Gold*, pp. 29–32.

[10] See in particular H. A. Miskimin, *Money, Prices, and Foreign Exchange in Fourteenth Century France* (New Haven, 1963), chapter 8 and *passim*. For the application of the mint-ratio theory on a broad scale, see A. M. Watson, 'Back to gold—and silver', *Econ. Hist. Rev.*[2] 20 (1967), 1–34; and for a criticism of his thesis, see E. Ashtor, 'Recent researches on Levantine trade', *Journal of European Economic History*, 2 (1973), 193.

[11] Munro, *Wool, Cloth, and Gold*, pp. 29–32, 70–92, 157–75; J. H. Munro, 'Monetary contraction and industrial change in the late-medieval Low Countries, 1335–1500', *Coinage in the Low Countries (880–1500)*, ed. N. J. Mayhew (*BAR* International Ser. 54, Oxford, 1979), pp. 95–110, 147–8.

[12] See the sources for Tables 1–10 below.

sharply in the 1330s;[13] and that this fall in the relative price of gold may have facilitated Flanders' and England's belated adoption of gold coinages, in June 1335 and January 1344, respectively. Even though both countries' gold : silver ratios continued to fall gently until the early 1350s, both evidently continued to favour gold over silver. So did France—usually; but France's monetary instability, periodically utter chaos, during the earlier phase of the Hundred Years War, with eighty alterations of the silver coinage and thirty-four (known) changes of the gold, from January 1337 to December 1360, makes comparisons difficult and certainly most tedious to make.[14] As Table 9 shows, when France did re-establish a sound coinage in April 1365, one that endured for twenty years, her gold : silver ratio (10.22 : 1) was very close to the Flemish. The differences between the French and Flemish ratios of the *traites* (coined value of a *marc* of metal) were usually too small to make any significant impact on their relative mintings of gold and silver. The Flemish and French ratios were, however, almost always lower than the English, except very briefly in 1361–3, when the Flemish ratio rose to 11.38 (*v*. England's 11.16). Thereafter the Flemish ratio declined, dropping surprisingly sharply in favour of silver in 1369–70; but, after a three-year hiatus in the mint accounts, it rose again in the mid 1370s and early 1380s, ranging from 10.12 to 10.67—lower than, but not out of line with, the English ratio.

The significance of (*a*) the relatively high ratios in favour of gold that both the English and Flemish (usually) maintained, and of (*b*) the usually higher English bimetallic ratio, can be seen in Tables 5, 6, and 7, the latter two especially. The over-all predominance of gold is most striking, fully supporting Professor Watson's views on fourteenth-century European coinages.[15] From the very beginning of gold minting in England, this metal accounted for over half of the total value of coinage struck. Once the 1351 silver debasement had run its course, once the bimetallic ratios had been stabilized—the ratio of *traites* in 1351 (11.16), the mint's gold bullion ratio in 1361 (10.97)—that gold predominance became overwhelming. Usually over 90 per cent of the total coinage (by value) was in gold—as high as 98.6 per cent in the later 1360s. During this era the smallest share of total English coinage that gold commanded was a still impressive 84–5 per cent in 1375–84, when the Flemish bimetallic ratio had again risen sharply in favour of gold, to 10.67 (Tables 9 and 6). In England, from the mid 1380s to the next mint-ratio alterations of

[13] Watson, 'Back to gold' (n. 10), 21–31. See also M. Prestwich, 'Early fourteenth-century exchange rates', *Econ. Hist. Rev.*[2] 32 (1979), 470–82; F. C. Lane, 'The Venetian galleys to Alexandria, 1344', *Wirtschaftskräfte und Wirtschaftswege: Festschrift für Hermann Kellenbenz*, vol. 1, *Mittelmeer und Kontinent*, ed. J. Schneider (Bamberg, 1978), pp. 431–6.

[14] Taken from E. Fournial, *Histoire monétaire de l'occident médiéval* (Paris, 1970), pp. 98–119. See also the sources for the Tables, below.

[15] Watson, 'Back to gold' (n. 10), 11–34. See also W. A. Shaw, *The History of the Currency, 1252–1894* (London, 1896), pp. 44–58, for similar observations.

November 1411, gold fully reasserted its overwhelming dominance, averaging 96–8 per cent of the total English coinage. That the proportion of total coinage in gold form then fell to 'just' 92 per cent during the final quinquennium of our series, 1415–19, can perhaps be attributed to the debasement and mint-ratio alterations of 1411–12, which slightly reduced the ratio of *traites*, from 11.16 to 10.33, and the mint's gold bullion ratio, from 10.97 to 10.15 (Tables 8 and 10). In view of these mint alterations, it may seem surprising that silver did not account for more of the English coinage in the years 1412–19; but in fact other countries by that time had also altered their mint ratios in favour of that metal, and more strongly than England.[16]

Similarly in Flanders, for much of the fourteenth century, the leadership of gold in her mint outputs is also very striking. Except for the period 1338–49, mostly years of revolution and civil war when the Flemish coined virtually no gold, that metal consistently accounted for at least 60 per cent of the total value of coinage struck, until the 1390s. Indeed from the mid 1350s to the late 1380s, as Table 5 shows, the average *volume* of pure gold struck in Flanders exceeded the English mean in all quinquenniums except (possibly) 1370–4. But we must keep in mind that the English coinage remained quite unchanged during this entire period, while Flanders' gold coinage was altered no fewer than twenty-four times, for an over-all debasement of 59 per cent. Thus much of these large Flemish gold mint outputs, to the 1380s, undoubtedly represented a 'recycling' of her own domestic coinages. Furthermore, gold clearly accounted for a far less impressive proportion of the total value of Flemish coinages than of the English. Only in the years 1355–9, 1360–4, and 1375–9, when the Flemish bimetallic ratio rose to approach the English ratio (and briefly exceed it in 1361–3, as noted), did the proportion of total Flemish minting in gold reach and exceed the 80 per cent mark. Just as in England, therefore, the performance of gold in Flemish minting closely corresponds to the mint-ratio alterations.

6

But perhaps the most striking feature of Tables 5, 6, 8, 9, and 10 is the abrupt changes in Flemish mint prices and ratios during the 1380s: revolutionary changes indeed that provide a new perspective on the Anglo-Flemish monetary conflict of 1388–1402. First, from July to September 1384, shortly after succeeding Louis de Mäle as count of Flanders, Duke Philip the Bold of Burgundy instituted the very first *renforcement* or strengthening of the silver coinage (by 21.1 per cent) recorded in Flemish history—certainly the first since March 1331 (Table 8). It was, one might say, a very bold move; and precisely why he did so remains one of the several monetary paradoxes of his twenty-year reign. Secondly, he also strengthened the gold coinage, but by an

[16] See below, pp. 93–4.

even greater amount (29.8 per cent), so that he consequently altered the mint ratio in favour of silver: from 10.60 to 9.89. Such a fall in the ratio below 10 : 1 to favour silver so strongly had occurred in Flanders only twice before, as very brief anomalies in 1351 and 1369 (Table 8). Thirdly, and at the same

FIG. 1. Flemish and Brabantine 'monnaies de convention' of 1384: roosebekers (named from the chapelet of roses which forms part of the type).

time, Duke Philip concluded a monetary convention with his aunt and neighbour, Duchess Joanna of Brabant, to strike a common, unified coinage for five years at Mechelen for Flanders and Leuven for Brabant (see Fig. 1).[17] This treaty of 16 July 1384 was evidently modelled on two prior conventions for Flemish-Brabantine monetary unity, of 1299–1300 and 1339.[18] By

[17] Archives Générales du Royaume de Belgique—Algemeen Rijksarchief [AGR], Chambre de Comptes [CC], carton 65: *bis* 1; *Les Ordonnances de Philippe le Hardi, de Marguerite de Mäle, et Jean sans Peur, 1381–1419:* I: *Les ordonnances du 16 octobre 1381 au 31 décembre 1393*, ed. J. Bartier and A. Van Nieuwenhuysen (Brussels, 1965), pp. 50–3. Minting did not commence at Mechelen until 9 Sept. 1384. (AGR, Comptes en Rouleau [CR] no. 2143a.) By the new Flemish coinage, £1 groot represented: (*a*) 281.47 g pure silver = 21.04 per cent more than the 232.53 g in the 1383 £ groot; (*b*) 28.476 g pure gold = 29.77 per cent more than the 21.944 g in the 1383 £ groot. For Flemish-Brabantine monetary relations, 1384–90, see H. Laurent, *La loi de Gresham au moyen âge: essai sur la circulation monétaire entre la Flandre et le Brabant à la fin du XIVe siècle* (Brussels, 1933); A. de Witte, *Histoire monétaire des comtes de Louvain, ducs de Brabant, et marquis de saint-empire romain* (3 vols., Antwerp, 1894), vol. 1, pp. 164–79; H. Van Werveke, 'De Vlaamse munthervorming van 1389–90', *Nederlandsche historiebladen*, 1 (1938), 336–47, reprinted in his *Miscellanea Mediaevalia* (Ghent, 1968), pp. 268–80; and especially P. Cockshaw, 'A propos de la circulation monétaire entre la Flandre et le Brabant de 1384 à 1390', *Contributions à l'histoire économique et sociale*, 6 (1970–1), 107–41.

[18] *Inventaire analytique et chronologique des chartes et documents appartenant aux archives de la ville d'Ypres*, ed. I. L. A. Diegerick (5 vols., Bruges, 1853–60), vol. 2, p. 109, no. 504 (Dec. 1339); *Recherches sur les monnaies des comtes de Flandre*, ed. V. Gaillard, vol. 1 (Ghent, 1852), pp. 23–6, no. 13 (Oct. 1299), pp. 27–8, no. 14 (Apr. 1300); de Witte, *Histoire monétaire* (n. 17), vol. 1, pp. 90–2, 112, 131–2.

adopting the new 1384 Flemish coinage, Duchess Joanna also instituted a *renforcement*, though a more modest one for Brabant: making silver 17.3 per cent stronger and gold 17.6 per cent stronger than her previous coinages, struck from 1382 (Table 9). But as these figures indicate, the consequent change in Brabant's mint ratio was virtually imperceptible: from 9.90 to 9.89.[19] As Table 9 also indicates, Brabant's mint-ratio policy from at least 1375 had differed markedly from those of England, France, and Flanders in favouring silver so strongly, with ratios varying from a low of 8.74 to the more recent high of 9.90. Possibly, therefore, Philip's shift to a pro-silver policy, adopting almost precisely the same mint ratio already in force in Brabant, was the price he paid for securing Joanna's agreement to strike a common 'strong' coinage (and thus not to resume her silver debasements).[20]

But the 1384 monetary convention, with its radical changes, was not destined to last much longer than its two predecessors. In March 1385 the French crown (Charles VI) debased both the gold and silver coinages for the first time in twenty years: by 5.18 and 4.00 per cent respectively, thus raising the bimetallic ratio slightly more in favour of gold, from 10.22 to 10.35 (Table 9). At least two historians have cited these French mint alterations as a *casus belli* to excuse Duke Philip's total abandonment of his coinage agreement with Brabant—and thus also of his strong-money policy.[21] For in the next two years, Duke Philip debased his Flemish coinage three times; in April 1386, October 1386, and April 1387. But surely the very minor French changes, so minor after twenty years of stability, can hardly justify Duke Philip's over-all debasement of gold by 29.5 per cent and of silver by 27.6 per cent, which thus altered the mint ratio back in favour of gold, from 9.89 to 10.14 (Table 8). The subsequent French debasement of gold—silver remained untouched—by an exceptionally modest 2.17 per cent in February

[19] Minting at Leuven did not commence until 3 Sept. 1384 (AGR, CR no. 2589). By the new Brabantine coinage, £1 *groot* Brabant represented: (*a*) 93.822 g pure silver = 17.33 per cent more than the 79.962 g in the 1382 £ *groot*; (*b*) 9.492 g pure gold = 17.56 per cent more than the 8.073 g in the 1382 £ *groot*. By this convention Joanna also revalued the money-of-account and tied it to the Flemish pound *groot* so that 1 new Flemish *groot* (1.173 g pure silver) = 3 Brabant *groots* (3 × 0.391 g) = 12*s*. 'payment'. On this see especially H. Van der Wee, *Growth of the Antwerp Market and the European Economy, Fourteenth to Sixteenth Centuries* (3 vols., The Hague, 1963), vol. 1, pp. 123–7.

[20] Duke Wenceslas and Joanna had debased the silver coinage in April 1380 (4.12 per cent), in April 1381 (0.51 per cent), and January 1382 (0.28 per cent), AGR, CR no. 2591 (Leuven mint accounts 1375–83); Van der Wee, *Antwerp Market* (n. 19), 1, p. 125. During that time the Flemish coinage had been debased only once, in September 1383, but by 4.17 per cent (Table 8). See also C. Piot, 'Ancienne administration monétaire de la Belgique' and his 'Discussions entre le duc de Wenceslas et les états de Brabant au sujet de ses monnaies', both in *RBN* 1 (1842–5), 56–8, no. 10; 173–200; de Witte, *Histoire monétaire* (n. 17), vol. 1, pp. 145–50, 165–6; Laurent, *Loi de Gresham* (n. 17), pp. 111–16, 131–40, nos. 1, 2, and 6.

[21] H. Enno van Gelder, 'Aantekeningen bij de Vlaamse muntslag, 1384–1434', *RBN*, 107 (1961), 138–41; Cockshaw, 'Circulation monétaire' (n. 17), 108. I also cannot agree that the English were partly to blame; for their coinage had remained perfectly stable.

1388 was, therefore, undoubtedly a purely defensive reaction to the Flemish alterations.

Nor can one blame the commendably patient Duchess Joanna, who held her peace until months after Philip's third debasement, until September 1387, when she finally followed suit. Her new gold and silver coinages in fact contained precisely the same amount of precious metals as Philip's current Flemish coins; and with the same relative values, the Brabant mint ratio was also identical at 10.14 (Table 9).[22] Nevertheless, Duke Philip was enraged by Joanna's new coinages, demanding that she withdraw them. Joanna meekly protested that her new coins were perfectly honest, loyal imitations of the Flemish, struck in full legal accordance with the terms of the 1384 convention. But, requiring Philip's assistance in the Guelders war, she capitulated to his terms, signing a new convention on 5 January 1388. Valid until 25 July 1389, it required her to close down her Leuven mint, to cease minting anywhere, and to have all bullion sent from Brabant to the Flemish mint (Ghent), in return for half of the Flemish mint profits. That month the Leuven mint did indeed close down, under Flemish supervision.[23] Several historians have contended that Joanna was still minting, or had resumed minting, in early 1389; but the balance of evidence convinces me that the Brabant mints remained closed for almost five years (to mid 1392).[24] In any

[22] Text in Piot, 'Administration' (n. 20), 59–61, no. 12; and de Witte, *Histoire monétaire* (n. 17), vol. 1, pp. 167–8. The text given in Laurent, *Loi de Gresham* (n. 17), p. 156, no. 15 is badly garbled; it has been corrected by Cockshaw, 'Circulation monétaire' (n. 17), 119. Note that Cockshaw has also made some very important corrections of, and additions to, the previously published monetary ordinances of April and October 1386 and April 1387, correcting errors of Laurent, Deschamps de Pas [in his *Histoire monétaire des comtes de la maison de Bourgogne* (Paris, 1863)], Van Werveke, and Bartier–Van Nieuwenhuysen. Hence the difference between my statistics and those of Van Werveke (n. 17), 270–4. Joanna's new gold angels were identical to the Flemish: 47¾ struck to a *marc* of 23½ carats (= 5.019 g fine gold). The silver double *groots* were slightly lighter than the Flemish (*taille* of 60 to the *marc v.* 59½ to the *marc*, for the Flemish); but they also had a slightly better fineness (5 den. 5 gr. *argent-le-roy v.* 5 den. 4 gr. in the Flemish), so that the silver contents of both were identical at 1.697 g.

[23] Text of Joanna's letter to Duke Philip (undated) published in Piot, 'Notice sur les monnaies de Jeanne, duchesse de Brabant (1383–1406)', *RBN* 2 (1846), 133–6, no. 2; with analysis on pp. 120–2. The text of the convention of 5 Jan. 1388 was discovered and published by Cockshaw, 'Circulation monétaire' (n. 17), 136–8, annexe III, with analysis on pp. 117–20 and n. 68. See also de Witte, *Histoire monétaire* (n. 17), vol. 1, pp. 167–8; Laurent, *Loi de Gresham* (n. 17), pp. 54–6, 59; pp. 154–6, nos. 13–14; p. 158, no. 16: 4 (with closure of the Leuven mint); C. Cumont, 'Mélanges numismatiques: Règne de Jeanne de Brabant veuve (1383–1406)', *TMP* 10 (1902), 197–9.

[24] In referring to Joanna's supposed 1389 coinage, Piot, de Witte, Cumont, and Laurent all assumed that Joanna's undated letter (n. 23) defending her current coinages and herself against Duke Philip's charges of counterfeiting was written just before the convention signed on 12 June 1389 (n. 25), because they were ignorant of the earlier convention signed on 5 Jan. 1388 (n. 23). Surprisingly Cockshaw, even though he discovered the text of the January 1388 convention, repeated these assertions of Piot, de Witte, Cumont, and Laurent. But Joanna's letter refers to 'les angeles, qu'on forge en la monnoie de monseigneur de Bourgogne à Gand': i.e. the angels issued by Duke Philip from April 1387 and by Joanna

event, on 12 June 1389, shortly before the convention was to expire, Joanna renewed it for another five years on virtually identical terms, making Flemish coinage Brabant's legal currency.[25]

Does Duke Philip therefore stand convicted of monetary aggression in the years 1385–8? Perhaps not. Perhaps he deserves at least a Scottish verdict of 'not proven'. Possibly, as Enno Van Gelder and others suggest, his debasements were indeed defensive measures to protect Flanders against marauding mints in Holland or elsewhere in the eastern Low Countries.[26] Furthermore, his debasements may have been necessary to reactivate the Flemish mints after the dismal failure of his 1384 *renforcement*. In general, *renforcements* and 'strong money' policies, which necessarily mean a deflationary contraction of the money supply, producing at least the illusion of falling incomes, are highly unpopular and thus difficult to implement.[27] This was no exception: from 9 September 1384 to 4 December 1385 his Mechelen mint coined only 232.5 kg of the new gold and 2,155.0 kg of silver, singularly unimpressive amounts, compared to his predecessor Louis de Mäle's mint outputs (1346–84), as shown in Tables 1–3 and 5–6. Then from 4 December to 2 May 1386 the Flemish mint was completely shut down.[28] Excessively high mintage fees may also have contributed to the failure of this 1384 *renforcement*. For, as Table 10 shows, Philip's two debasements of 1386 were accompanied by very sharp reductions in those fees; and though they were increased with the April 1387 debasement, they still remained well below the 1384 fees. How

from September 1387. But the Ghent mint accounts for the period 1 Oct. 1388 to 18 Nov. 1389 show that only gold nobles were struck (even though the 1 Oct. 1388 ordinance had prescribed gold angels as well). AGR, CR no. 824. Consequently I believe that Joanna's letter was written just prior to the 5 Jan. 1388 convention and that her mints remained inactive in 1389.

[25] Full text in Bartier–Van Nieuwenhuysen, *Ordonnances* (n. 17) vol. 1, pp. 327–9, nos. 217–18. See also de Witte, *Histoire monétaire* (n. 17), vol. 1, pp. 167–9; Piot, 'Notice' (n. 23), pp. 136–7, no. 3 and pp. 120–2; pp. 133–6, no. 2; Laurent, *Loi de Gresham* (n. 17), pp. 59–61; Cockshaw, 'Circulation monétaire' (n. 17), 124–6; Cumont, 'Mélanges numismatiques' (n. 23), 197–9. The 1388 convention had not specified that Flemish coins be legal tender.

[26] See n. 21 above and Enno Van Gelder, *De Nederlandse munten* (Utrecht, 1968), pp. 35–6, 41. In particular he blames Albert of Bavaria (*ruwaard* of Holland), the bishop of Utrecht, the count of Loon, the lords of Batenburg and Bergh (in Guelders), Rummen and Reckheim and of Hoorne-Gronsveld (in Limburg), and of Schoonvorst (the Rhineland) for their debasements.

[27] See my *Wool, Cloth, and Gold*, pp. 25–34; and my 'Monetary Contraction' (n. 11), pp. 95–110; and Van der Wee, *Antwerp Market* (n. 19), vol. 1, pp. 123–7 (for the failure of the 1384 renforcement).

[28] AGR, CR no. 2142b, published in part in Laurent, *Loi de Gresham* (n. 17), pp. 147–9, no. 9. See also Cockshaw, 'Circulation monétaire' (n. 17), 112; and Pierre Cockshaw, 'Le fonctionnement des ateliers monétaires sous Philippe le Hardi', *CENB* 7 (1970), 24–36. 24–36. See also expressions of Philip's concern about the lack of bullion for his mints in ordinances banning all foreign coins, on 25 Sept. 1386 (Laurent, *Loi de Gresham* (n. 17), pp. 150–2, no. 11; also pp. 50–1); and in ordering the reminting of all former Flemish coins of Louis de Mäle, on 27 Apr. 1387. Bartier–Van Nieuwenhuysen, *Ordonnances* (n. 17), vol. 1, pp. 231–2, no. 147.

successful these three debasements were we cannot say, since we have no Flemish mint accounts from 2 May 1386 to 1 October 1388.

7

On that latter date, Duke Philip undertook the last major debasement of his reign, and perhaps his most significant. In debasing gold by 10.4 per cent and silver by 9.0 per cent, he certainly did not make his most drastic alterations; but since he sharply increased his mintage fees, as Table 10 shows, his debasement hardly seems to be defensive. Indeed by this debasement Philip commenced his infamous counterfeiting of the English noble. This venture was obviously inspired by the very recent restoration of the English wool staple from Middelburg in Zeeland to Calais, now free from French attacks.[29] Some reports indicate that the Staple had reimposed payment regulations first enacted by Edward III in 1363–4, requiring that only good English coin be used in making wool purchases, and that all foreign coin be reminted at Calais.[30] These regulations had been designed to prevent the importation of fraudulent and debased foreign coins, chiefly Flemish.[31] Perhaps now in 1387 the English were similarly concerned by the current Flemish and Brabantine debasements. In any event, thanks to Mr Lloyd, we now know that the Calais mint, closed in January 1384 with the move to Middelburg, had been reopened on 17 January 1387, even before the formal

[29] See Lloyd, *Wool Trade* (n. 1), pp. 229–33, arguing that French intervention in the Flemish civil war during 1382, with French forces led by Philip, made the Calais Staple trade untenable by cutting off Flemish access.

[30] Merchants later contended (in the 1390s) that 'lesditz suppliantz ne resceivent au dit lieu de Caleys pur leurs Merchandises illoeques venduz autre Monoie de vostre coigne'. *Rotuli Parliamentorum* (6 vols., London, 1767–77), vol. 3, p. 369, no. 80. For Edward III's payment regulations see *Foedera, conventiones, litterae et acta publica, 1066–1383*, ed. Thomas Rymer *et al.* (Record Commission edn. 4 vols., London, 1816–69), vol. 3/2, 699 (10 May 1363), 724 (22 Feb. 1364), 725 (1 Mar. 1364), 773 (26 July 1363).

[31] Merchants had been complaining that 'les monoies que feurent receux pur leines estoient si febles que les dites leines et merchandises ne poent estre venduz au pris convenables', with losses up to a third (*Foedera* (n. 30), vol. 3/2, p. 725, Mar. 1364). The fact that Count Louis de Mäle had debased his gold coinage eight times between 1356 and 1363, by a total of 23.7 per cent, as Tables 5 and 8 show, seems to justify the English complaints. The new payment regulations of 1363–4, however, evidently impeded many merchants' commerce by tying up their working capital at the Calais mint. Consequently they sought to evade these regulations by resorting more and more to credit transactions, 'par voi d'apprest sanz rien paiere d'or ou d'argent'. To thwart this move and to defend the new Calais mint, Edward III in March 1364 issued a decree requiring that 5*s.* weight or 3 oz. Tower fine gold be brought to the Calais mint for each woolsack sold. Whether or not this onerous regulation was enforced for long is uncertain; but certainly Calais coined much gold in the next decade, an average of 864.02 kg a year during 1365–74, 62.3 per cent of the total English gold output. In my view, this Calais ordinance, rather than the earlier bullion laws of 1340, 1343, and 1348, is the true, direct ancestor of the 1397 *Ordenance de la Bullion*. See Munro, *Wool, Cloth, and Gold*, pp. 34–41; J. H. Munro, 'Bullionism and the bill of exchange in England, 1272–1663: a study in monetary management and popular prejudice', in *The Dawn of Modern Banking*, ed. F. Chiappelli (New Haven, 1979), pp. 192–6. I can find no discussion of this important ordinance in Lloyd, *Wool Trade* (n. 1).

edict restoring the Staple to Calais.[32] The very large initial gold output, already noted, does suggest that the Staplers were indeed requiring foreign coin to be reminted and were exacting payment in English gold nobles. Thus, from the Flemish point of view, if payment had to be made in nobles alone, and if nobles were scarce, why not substitute a Flemish brand of gold nobles?

FIG. 2. Flemish gold noble of Duke Philip the Bold, 1388–1402.

Duke Philip had stated, in March 1388, that it was 'son intencion de eulz faire un denier d'or semblable au noble d'Angleterre de tel pois et aloy et aussi bon *ou milleur* que les dis nobles sont'.[33] That was, or turned out to be, patent nonsense. The English noble, 45 to the Tower pound (349.9144 g) of 23 carats $3\frac{1}{2}$ grains, was designed to contain 7.7354 g pure gold; the Flemish noble (Fig. 2), $31\frac{2}{3}$ to the *marc de Troyes* (244.7529 g) of $23\frac{3}{4}$ carats, was designed therefore to have only 7.6485 g pure gold, or 98.88 per cent of the English noble's gold content.[34] In Brabant, the authorities certainly recognized this difference: for a subsequent coinage ordinance assigned an exchange rate of 9*s.* 7*d. groot* (Brabant) to the English noble but only 9*s.* 4*d. groot* to the Flemish (in fact undervaluing the latter by $1\frac{1}{2}$*d.*).[35] Since the fineness and

[32] Lloyd, *Wool Trade* (n. 1), pp. 229–33, 241–5. PRO, E 364/22 m. 8 ('quod nulla moneta ibidem fuit fabricata': 7 Jan. 1384–17 Jan. 1387); E 364/25 m. 5. See note 3.

[33] Archives départmentales du Nord (Lille), Sér. B. 632/14. 534, now published in Cockshaw, 'Circulation monétaire' (n. 17), 138–41, annexe 4. For the petition of the Ghent échevins to strike the new nobles, see Louis Deschamps de Pas, *Histoire monétaire des comtes de Flandre de la maison de Bourgogne* (Paris, 1863), p. cxi, no. 7.

[34] For the English mint indenture, unchanged from 2 Dec. 1361 to November 1411, see *Calendar of Close Rolls, 1360–64*, pp. 293–5 and *CCR 1399–1402*, pp. 579–80; for the Flemish mint indenture see Bartier–Van Nieuwenhuysen, *Ordonnances* (n. 17), vol. 1, pp. 292–4, no. 193; and AGR CR no. 824 (Ghent mint account).

[35] When Joanna renewed the 1388 monetary convention on 15 June 1389, she was forced to give the English and Flemish nobles identical exchange rates. Piot, 'Notice' (n. 23), 136–7, no. 3; Bartier–Van Nieuwenhuysen, *Ordonnances* (n. 17) vol. 1, p. 329, no. 218. But when freed from that convention, and striking her own coinages, she stipulated on 15 July 1393 these new and different exchange rates. Text in Laurent, *Loi de Gresham* (n. 17), pp. 186–90, no. 33. Subsequently, on 10 Aug. 1405, Duke Anthony published at Antwerp a coinage ordinance assigning rates of 6*s.* 6*d.* (78*d.*) to the Flemish noble and 6*s.* 8*d.* (80*d.*) to the English. Charles Piot, 'Documents sur quelques monnaies frappées par Antoine, duc de Brabant', *RBN* 1 (1842–5), 251–6, no. 1. Risks of confiscation in England, of course, lowered the Flemish noble's market value. Crown and parliament several times ordered the confiscation and reminting of Flemish nobles. See *CCR 1385–89*,

weight of the Flemish noble remained unchanged, and were once more prescribed in the coinage ordinance of 30 April 1407, that difference in gold content was hardly accidental.[36] Furthermore, if Philip's motives had been purely altruistic, to give his wool-buying subjects a 'cheaper' noble, his evident lust for profit certainly hindered that objective. For he initially exacted a seignorage of 1⅔ nobles (= 5.26 per cent) and a brassage of ½ noble per *marc* of 23¾ carats, totalling a high 6.84 per cent of the *traite*; the English total mintage fees, on the other hand, were only 1.67 per cent of the *traite* (Table 10). That meant that merchants received only 29½ fraudulent nobles per *marc* of 23¾ carats, while from the Calais or Tower mints they could have obtained 30.789 good nobles per *marc* of this fineness (= 30.951 nobles per *marc* English fineness = 44.25 nobles per Tower lb.). Duke Philip's very large gold coinages of 1388–90, as shown in Tables 1 and 3, are therefore very surprising, especially in exceeding the combined Calais and Tower mint outputs. Evidently they must reflect a considerable reminting of former Flemish gold coins; but even so, merchants would not have had them reminted unless that proved to be profitable. Perhaps one can attribute Philip's success to his having altered the bimetallic ratio even more strongly in favour of gold: from 10.14 to 10.41. Nevertheless, as Table 10 shows, his mintage fees on both metals were so high from October 1388 to January 1390 that the mint bullion ratios for both metals fell. *Both* were inferior to the English bullion ratios, a singularly unusual situation.

By that latter date of January 1390, Duke Philip had effected his most significant monetary revolution, which by its very nature threatened to extinguish his gold minting: a brutal *renforcement* of both coinages, gold by 41.7 per cent and silver by 31.8 per cent. Along with mintage fees changes, that also produced a radical alteration of the three ratios in favour of silver: the ratio of *traites* from 10.41 to 9.68, the mint's gold bullion ratio from 10.04 to 9.38, and the silver bullion ratio from 11.76 to 10.82. Why Duke Philip had again decided to effect a *renforcement* and mint-ratio alterations to favour silver so strongly is not clear, especially in light of the 1384–5 fiasco. Furthermore, these *renforcements*, first decreed on 20 December 1389 (effected by 31

p. 647 (2 Feb. 1389); *CCR 1392–96*, p. 110 (2 Dec. 1392); *Rot. Parl.*, vol. 3, p. 320, no. 38 (Jan. 1394), and n. 59, for 1401. For proof that the Flemish noble appeared to be almost identical to the English, see photographs in J. D. A. Thompson, 'Continental imitations of the rose noble', *BNJ* 25 (1949), pl. A: 1, p. 184; and C. Oman, *The Coinage of England* (Oxford, 1931), pl. 19, 1 and 4. In England, a Commons petitioner subsequently maintained (1401) that out of every 15 nobles in circulation 3 or 4 were Flemish, and that they were 'pire et pluis feble qu le Noble Engleys par iid.'. *Rot. Parl.*, vol. 3, p. 470, no. 61. But Peter Spufford has correctly noted that the difference in intrinsic value was really only 1*d.*, in 'Continental coins in late medieval England', *BNJ* 32 (1963), 130. See also Woodhead, 'Calais' (n. 3), p. 192.

[36] AGR, Chambre de Comptes [CC], carton 65: *bis* 1. See also P. Cockshaw, 'Les premières monnaies de Jean sans Peur: l'émission de 1407', *CENB* 8 (1971), 41–52. See n. 61.

January 1390), were far more severe and unpopular than the former. As Van Werveke and others have shown, the sharp fall in money values provoked serious unrest, almost a rebellion.[37] Possibly, as Tables 8 and 9 suggest, Philip's move had been inspired or provoked by the slightly earlier alteration of the French bimetallic ratio from 10.58 to 9.80 in September 1389. That was certainly the first such pro-silver shift in ratios by the French since the 1350s. But since the French alteration was part of a silver debasement, of 7.4 per cent, which evidently produced very substantial silver outputs in 1390–1 (Tables 2 and 9), Duke Philip's move seems all the more courageous.

What is so remarkable about Philip's 1389–90 mint alterations is that both the *renforcement* and shift to silver succeeded for so long, when the few previous attempts had failed so badly. Apart from a very minor, temporary debasement of silver by 0.87 per cent in 1391, fully annulled in 1393, Flanders retained a very strong, stable silver coinage until December 1416. Indeed Philip's son and successor Duke John the Fearless, had strengthened the silver coinage even more in August 1409, by 16.33 per cent. The pro-silver mint-ratio policy was retained even longer, until June 1425: a total of thirty-five years.[38]

Since, as previously stressed, the built-in cost of a pro-silver policy is the loss of gold, actual or potential, what steps did Duke Philip take, when his gold output began to fall? As Table 1 shows, it did fall sharply from 1390 to 1393. Since the two mint-bullion ratios arc not mirror images of each other, as Table 10 shows, one remedy was to adjust these two ratios. Very grudgingly, slowly, and by miserly steps, Duke Philip reduced his gold mintage fees: in February, July, and November 1389, and finally, effectively in June 1393, to $\frac{2}{3}$ noble (= 4*s*.), thus allowing a mint price of 31 nobles per *marc*. He had in fact permitted such a gold price earlier, in November 1392, but almost immediately rescinded this order, demanding proof first from his officials that 'les gens du roy d'Angleterre de ses monnoies à Calais donnent xxxi nobles d'Angleterre pour marc d'or ainsi qu'il nous a esté affermé'.[39] The mint accounts show that he actually reduced the mint price from 30$\frac{2}{3}$ nobles to

[37] See H. Van Werveke, 'De economische en sociale gevolgen van de muntpolitiek der graven van Vlaanderen (1337–1433)', *Annales de la Société d'Emulation de Bruges*, 74 (1931), reprinted in his *Miscellanea Mediaevalia* (Ghent, 1968), pp. 246–54; and his 'Vlaamse munthervorming' (n. 17) 126–30; Raymond De Roover, *Money, Banking, and Credit in Mediaeval Bruges* (Cambridge, Mass., 1948), pp. 227–9; De Roover, *The Bruges Money Market Around 1400* (Brussels, 1968), pp. 39–40; Munro, 'Monetary Contraction' (n. 11), p. 112, 132. See also Bartier–Van Nieuwenhuysen, *Ordonnances* (n. 17), vol. 1, pp. 345–8, no. 231; pp. 358–61, no. 239; pp. 399–400, no. 262.

[38] See Munro, *Wool, Cloth, and Gold*, pp. 70–84 (esp. graph 3, p. 71), 198–211 (tables C–J). See also Munro, 'Monetary Contraction' (n. 11), pp. 101, 142–8.

[39] Bartier–Van Nieuwenhuysen, *Ordonnances* (n. 17), vol. 1, pp. 536–7, no. 333. For other instructions to mint officials, from 10 Jan. 1389 to 20 Jan. 1393, see ibid., vol. 1, pp. 309–12, 335–6, 403–4, 535–41, nos. 203–5, 223, 266, 332–5; ADN (Lille), carton 623–4; AGR, CC, carton 65: *bis* 1; Deschamps de Pas, *Histoire monétaire* (n. 33), pp. v, x–xii, nos. 18, 40, 44, 45; Laurent, *Loi de Gresham* (n. 17), pp. 160–3, nos. 19–20.

30½ nobles per *marc* after 19 November 1392; and, though Philip promised to raise the price to 31 nobles in January 1393, the mint adopted this price only after 27 June 1393.[40] At that last price, merchants could indeed gain from minting their gold into fraudulent nobles: about 0.211 noble (Flemish) per *marc* of 23¾ carats = 1*s.* 3*d.* *groot* Flemish = 1*s.* 5*d.* sterling—about three times the daily wage of a master mason. The Flemish mint's gold bullion ratio, while still distinctly inferior to England's 10.97, was at least increased from the 9.38 set in January 1390 to 9.48 in June 1393. Table 1 does show that Flemish gold coinage did increase very substantially, more than doubling from 1392 to 1394, though declining to about two-thirds the peak level in 1395–6.

In England, as would be expected, the mints, having that superior gold ratio, continued to produce more gold coinage than the Flemish after the 1390 changes—but only until 1395. As Table 1 shows, the combined London and Calais gold output declined very sharply from its peak in 1393 to well less than half by 1396, when total English gold output was inferior to the Flemish. Then, in January 1397, Richard II's parliament imposed the notorious *Ordenance de la Bullion*, requiring merchants to supply the Tower Mint with one ounce of foreign gold per woolsack sold.[41] Perhaps parliament's correct move should have been to order a debasement of 2–5 per cent that would eliminate the Flemish noble's advantage; but parliament, ever since enacting the Statute of Purveyors in January 1352, in reaction to Edward III's debasements, had obdurately refused to countenance any such coinage alterations.[42] In the light of the Flemish and French monetary experiences, there is much to be said for that stand. In any event, the *Ordenance de la Bullion* may have succeeded, initially; for the Tower's gold coinage output more than doubled from 1396 to 1398. But total English gold output increased by far less (29.4 per cent), because a major effect of the *Ordenance* was to transfer much minting from Calais to London. Indeed Calais minted hardly any gold in

[40] For the mint accounts, see AGR, CR nos. 824–6 (Ghent: 1 Oct. 1388–22 Oct. 1390); CC nos. 48, 976–7 (Mechelen: 3 Nov. 1390–29 Oct. 1392); CR nos. 776–8 (Bruges: 1 June 1392–20 June 1393–7 Mar. 1394); and Laurent, *Loi de Gresham* (n. 17), pp. 164–86, nos. 21–2, 25, 28, 32.

[41] *Rot. Parl.* vol. 3, p. 340, no. 19. Earlier, in November 1391, parliamen thad enacted a similar bullionist ordinance; but it was to endure only to 24 June 1392, during which time the Staple was temporarily fixed in English home ports (*Rot. Parl.*, vol. 3, p. 285, no. 7) This ordinance seems to be related more to the recent Employment Laws to curb bullion exports (14 Ric. II c. 1–2 of Nov. 1390) than to Flemish counterfeiting of English nobles. See also Eileen Power, 'The wool trade in the fifteenth century', in *Studies in English Trade in the Fifteenth Century*, ed. E. Power and M. Postan (London, 1933), p. 80; Munro, *Wool, Cloth, and Gold*, pp. 44–7, 53–7; Munro, 'Bullionism' (n. 11), pp. 192–205; Lloyd, *Wool Trade* (n. 1), pp. 244–7. I fully agree with Lloyd's argument that the 1397 *Ordenance* was also partly designed to curb the increasing resort to credit at the Staple; but see my comments in n. 31.

[42] 25 Ed. III stat. 5 c. 13 in *Stat. Realm*, vol. 1, p. 322; *Rot. Parl.*, vol. 2, p. 240, no. 32. See Munro, 'Bullionism' (n. 11), pp. 190–2, 202–5.

1398 and 1399: under 10 kg and 20 kg respectively. Why the *Ordenance* required the gold to be brought to the Tower's mint instead of to the Calais mint is far from clear, unless the crown no longer trusted Calais to keep out the Flemish nobles. The requirement to transport gold to London at such cost and inconvenience, for provincial merchants especially, as well as the difficulty of extracting gold bullion from reluctant wool-buyers, certainly made the *Ordenance* most unpopular with the Staplers, and helps to explain its later abandonment.[43]

8

What remains to be added to the history of Anglo-Flemish monetary relations in this era is the significance of mint competition from third parties, principally Brabant and France. Or more precisely: the Flemish perception of that competition. In Brabant, Duchess Joanna, an unwilling signatory to the 1388 and 1389 conventions, subsequently demanded the right to resume minting, in particular to combat an influx of foreign debased coins. Philip reluctantly agreed to her demands in a revised convention dated 28 April 1392, stipulating that any coins struck in Brabant be entirely different from the Flemish, and that the combined profits of all their mints be equally shared.[44] To Philip's great consternation, however, Joanna's new Vilvoorde mint began striking double *groots*, from 25 June 1392, whose size and stamp closely resembled those of his own Flemish double *groots* (Fig. 3), but which contained only 81.8 per cent as much silver. Angry Flemish protests resulted only in a further Brabantine debasement of 3.2 per cent in July 1393, at the very time that Duke Philip had restored his temporarily reduced silver coinage to its full 1390 strength.[45] Table 2 shows that Joanna's debasements

[43] See the petition in the parliament of January 1398 demanding the revocation of the *Ordenance de la Bullion*: *inter alia*, it stated that Burgundian officials 'ne voillent suffrer nully porter Bullion hors ne parmy la dite pais de Flandres vers vostre dite Ville de Caleys . . . si qe les ditz suppliantz ne purront nullement acquere Bullion pur perfourner vostre dit Ordenance'. *Rot. Parl.*, vol. 3, pp. 369–70, no. 80. See Munro, *Wool, Cloth, and Gold*, p. 56; Lloyd, *Wool Trade* (n. 1), p. 245.

[44] See Bartier–Van Nieuwenhuysen, *Ordonnances* (n. 17), vol. 1, pp. 467–8, no. 306 (May 1392); Deschamps de Pas, *Histoire monétaire* (n. 33), p. viii, nos. 30–1 (Apr.–May 1392); Laurent, *Loi de Gresham* (n. 17), p. 173, no. 26 (Apr. 1392), pp. 178–83, nos. 29–30 (Aug.–Sept. 1392), 186–90, no. 33, and discussion, pp. 69–81; Piot, 'Notice' (n. 23), 122–5, 137–9, no. 4; Cumont, 'Mélanges' (n. 23), 203–10; de Witte, *Histoire monétaire* (n. 17), vol. 1, pp. 169–70; Cockshaw, 'Circulation monétaire' (n. 17), 130–1; R. Chalon, 'Nouvelle classification des monnaies de Jeanne, duchesse de Brabant', *RBN* 14 (1858), 356–7.

[45] Laurent, *Loi de Gresham* (n. 17) pp. 69–71, and 178–83, nos. 29–30 (letters of Flemish officials, 30 Aug. and 9 Sept. 1392), 186–7, no. 33 (15 July 1393 ordinance). Duke Philip closed his Mechelen mint in October 1392, perhaps because of the Brabantine mint competition. AGR, CC no. 48,977. Philip's Flemish double *groots* had a *taille* of 57 (as restored June 1393) to a *marc* of 6 deniers *argent-le-roy* = 2.057 g pure silver. Joanna's double *groots* had a *taille* of 60 to a *marc* of 5 den. 4 gr. = 1.683 g pure silver; the fineness was reduced to 5 den. in July 1393, so that the silver content became 1.629 g. AGR, CR nos. 2590,

produced respectably large silver outputs in 1393–4. Possibly these were achieved at the expense of the Flemish silver output, which did decline from 1392 to 1394; but the Flemish silver output nevertheless still exceeded Brabant's by 30 per cent in 1393–4. In her gold coinage, Duchess Joanna was

FIG. 3. Flemish and Brabantine double *groots* of the 1390s.

considerably less successful. Although gold *pieters* had been prescribed in the June 1392 ordinance, no gold at all was struck until August 1393 (as gold *towers*).[46] From then until January 1395 only 255.7 kg was minted, just 19.0 per cent as much as the Flemish output and 12.8 per cent as much as the English (Table 1). Tables 8 and 9 suggest the reason why: the Brabant mint ratios, as in the past, were even more strongly pro-silver and unfavourable to gold than the Flemish ratio. Even Joanna's success in silver minting proved transitory. Her mints closed on 25 January 1395, purportedly for lack of bullion.[47] The Brabant *recettes générales* suggest that mints were later open at Leuven, from 25 December 1395 to 20 January 1396, and then at Maastricht, to perhaps late June 1396: but if so, neither the accounts nor any coins from them have survived.[48] Duchess Joanna, failing thereafter to reactivate her

2592, and 2588 (Vilvoorde and Leuven mint accounts, 25 June 1392–28 Jan. 1395). Ordinance of 25 June 1392 and accounts to 19 Apr. 1394 published in Piot, 'Notice' (n. 23), 137–46, nos. 4–5. See also de Witte, *Histoire monetaire* (n. 17), vol. 1, pp. 170–1; Cumont, 'Melanges' (n. 23), 207–14.

[46] See sources cited in nn. 44–5.

[47] AGR, CR no. 2588 (Leuven mint account 15.v.1394–28.i.1395: 'ende niet meer ghemunten en const mids dat tgelt soe op liep'.); Cumont, 'Mélanges' (n. 23), 217–20; de Witte, *Histoire monétaire* (n. 17), vol. 1, p. 172; Laurent, *Loi de Gresham* (n. 17), pp. 81–2.

[48] See Laurent, *Loi de Gresham* (n. 17), pp. 81–2; Cumont, 'Mélanges' (n. 23), 214–15, 224–30; Piot, 'Notice' (n. 23), 126–7; de Witte, *Histoire monétaire* (n. 17) vol. 1, p. 172.

mints, leased them to the Brabantine towns for ten years from 1 October 1396, for 2,000 *towers* a year. Again there are no records nor distinguishable coins to indicate whether the towns in fact ever did operate these mints.[49] Then in 1399 Joanna terminated this lease and once more adopted the current Flemish coinage as the official Brabantine currency (until April 1409).[50] In any event, from January 1395 Brabant evidently ceased to be any threat to even the Flemish silver coinage, which strongly recovered and remained large in output until 1399 (Table 2).

For Philip's gold coinage, the major threat was seen to come from France—and England. In July 1394, the French government again reduced the weight of the *couronne*, by 1.1 per cent (from 61⅓ to 62 per *marc* fine), thus adjusting the mint ratio slightly in favour of gold (Table 9). Of particular concern to the Flemish was the mint of Tournai, a small French enclave within Flanders itself. Philip quickly voiced fears that, at the present rate of 37*d. groot* for the couronne, merchants would be 'grandement decuz' and that 'les ouvrages de noz monnoies de beaucop amenri, pour ce que les diz nobles seroient portez au feu' at the Tournai and other French mints.[51] My own calculations, however, indicate that the Tournai gold mint price was still slightly less than the Flemish (£9.284 *groot* per *marc* of 24 carats *v* £9.398 *groot* at Ghent);[52] and Table 1 does not indicate particularly substantial gold coinages in France in 1394–5 (when the Miskimin mint statistics unfortunately terminate). But it is the perceived threat that is important: important enough for Duke Philip's officials and the Four Members of Flanders to hold at least a dozen meetings in 1396 concerning the 'overvalued French *couronnes*' from Tournai.[53]

We should therefore also view Philip's reactions to the *Ordenance de la*

[49] Text in Laurent, *Loi de Gresham* (n. 17), pp. 197–208, no. 38. De Witte, while doubting that the towns did exercise their new minting rights, does cite a billon coin of doubtful provenance that may have been struck in Brussels *c.*1396–9. *Histoire monétaire* (n. 17), vol. 1, pp. 172–4, pl. xxi, no. 428. See also Piot, 'Notice' (n. 23), 126–7; Cumont, 'Mélanges' (n. 23), 227–38, noting payments of *Torrenghelde* only from 1400 to 1406. But Van der Wee cites exchange rates indicating a decline in the value of Brabantine silver coinage from 1395 to 1399. *Antwerp Market* (n. 19), vol. 1, pp. 123–4.

[50] Van der Wee, *Antwerp Market* (n. 19), vol. 1, pp. 123–4. In July–August 1405, however, Duke Anthony, Joanna's heir-presumptive, struck slightly debased coins for circulation in Antwerp and his Limburg lands, within the duchy of Brabant. Joanna died 1 Dec. 1406. See Piot, 'Antoine' (n. 35) 247–60; Cumont, 'Mélanges' (n. 23), 238–46; de Witte, *Histoire monétaire* (n. 17), vol. 1, p. 180; Table 9 below.

[51] Laurent, *Loi de Gresham* (n. 17), pp. 193–5, no. 36 (18 Feb. 1395). His edition erroneously gives a *taille* of 72 per *marc*; Deschamps de Pas, *Histoire monétaire* (n. 33), p. xiv, no. 61.

[52] According to a report of monetary officials dated 3 Feb. 1395 (in Laurent, *Loi de Gresham* (n. 17), p. 191, no. 35), the Tournai mint, striking 62 *couronnes* to a *marc* of pure gold, purchased bullion at 60 *couronnes* and 5*s.* tournois = 97.13 per cent of the *traite* of £67.750 tournois = 60.222 *couronnes*, which, at the current rate of 37*d. groot* Flemish = £9.284 *groot* per pure *marc* gold. The Bruges mint price for gold at 23¾ carats was then £9.300 *groot* (or 31 nobles at 6*s.*) = £9.398 per *marc* of fine gold.

[53] *Handelingen van de leden en van de staten van Vlaanderen, 1384–1405*, ed. Walter Prevenier (Brussels, 1959), pp. 118–24, nos. 330–45 (7 Feb. 1396–12 May 1396).

Bullion of 1397 in the light of these threats from various foreign mints. Imposing the strictest controls to prevent the transport of bullion to Calais was, to be sure, perfectly correct and rational; and ultimately successful. But Philip's other response, in banning all English nobles, declaring them to be bullion (*billon*), was less sagacious.[54] Certainly that ban placed his subjects in a most difficult position; for they could not buy English wools without some English nobles. Indeed they complained that because of Philip's ban they were forced to buy English nobles from money-changers at Calais at rates 4*d.* and 5*d. groot* above that of the Flemish noble.[55] In response to numerous demands from the Four Members, from October 1397 to March 1400, that the English noble be restored to legal tender at 6*s. groot*, Philip replied that only when the English removed their ban on his nobles would he reconsider his own ban.[56] But Philip's ban never succeeded in achieving this objective; nor does Table 1 suggest that it succeeded in refueling his rapidly declining mints with gold bullion. In seeking revocation or modification of the *Ordenance de la Bullion*, however, Duke Philip and the Staplers seem to have had greater success—once Richard II had been overthrown in 1399. That October, during the first parliament of Henry IV, the new king accepted the Staplers' petition that they be released from the stipulated bullion obligations to the Tower Mint, that all securities exacted to ensure compliance be returned, and that 'la dite Bullion serra à Caleys' until the next parliament.[57] While no decree exists that specifically annulled the *Ordenance de la Bullion*, the latter was never enrolled in the Statutes; nor is there any evidence to show that it was enforced after 1399. Perhaps, therefore, Henry IV's concessions explain why Duke Philip did restore the English noble to legal tender at

[54] Descamps de Pas, *Histoire monétaire* (n. 33), p. xvi, no. 78 (6 Oct. 1397), xvii, no. 80 (Nov. 1397); *Précis analytique des archives de la Flandre-Occidentale: comptes du Franc*, ed. F. Priem, vol. 2/1 (1844) 12. For confiscations of English nobles as bullion (*billon*) see AGR, CR nos. 785–6 (Bruges mint account, Aug. 1397–June 1400); CC no. 13,925, fols. 4–5 (Bailiff of Sluis account, Jan.–Sept. 1400). Duke Philip had in fact banned the English gold noble, and other foreign gold coins, as *billon* once before, in January 1390. Bartier–Van Nieuwenhuysen, *Ordonnances* (n. 17), vol. 1, pp. 358–61, no. 239. That ban, requiring such coins to be sold to the mint (the English noble at 69⅝*d. groot*), was evidently designed to protect his gold coinage at the very time that he was implementing his *renforcement* and shift to silver. But obviously the English noble was shortly thereafter restored to circulation, at 6*s. groot*.

[55] ADN (Lille), Sér. B. 630/14.238 (26 Dec. 1399).

[56] Ibid. See also Prevenier, *Handelingen* (n. 53), pp. 142–52, nos. 389–409; 179–86, nos. 463–76; 194, nos. 495–7; 222, no. 542; Munro, *Wool, Cloth, and Gold*, pp. 55–7; P. Cockshaw, 'La politique monétaire en Flandre des ducs de Bourgogne de la maison de Valois, 1384–1430', in *Coinage in the Low Countries* (n. 3), pp. 163–8, attributing the ban on English nobles to 'pride and wounded vanity'. In my view, these emotional factors may have influenced but did not determine Philip's actions.

[57] *Rot. Parl.*, vol. 3, p. 429, no. 86; PRO, Treaty Rolls, C. 76/84 m. 16 (16 Nov. 1399). See Munro, *Wool, Cloth, and Gold*, pp. 56–7; Lloyd, *Wool Trade* (n. 1), p. 245. The 1397 *Ordenance* was not, as I had stated earlier, among those acts of 21 Ric. II repealed by Henry IV's first parliament; for the *Ordenance* was in fact enacted during 20 Ric. II.

6*s*. *groot*, on or after 31 July 1400, though undoubtedly pressure from the Four Members had forced him to do so, as well.[58]

Certainly the English did not respond in similar fashion. Indeed in January 1401 parliament again ordered that all Flemish nobles and other foreign coin be 'voided from the realm' or reminted at Calais.[59] Very possibly, therefore, the large Calais gold output of 295.8 kg from 25 August 1399 to Mich. 1401 reflects in part this forced recoinage (as well as the resumption of Calais minting in general). If so, then this recoinage may well deserve more credit in thwarting the Flemish counterfeits than Henry IV's subsequent debasement of the English noble. In any event, neither party continued to find much profit in minting. The Bruges mint closed on 16 June 1402, despite repeated demands from the Flemish towns to keep it open; and the Calais mint, as noted earlier, closed some time between April 1403 and March 1404.[60] A few years later, in April 1407, a Flemish coinage ordinance prescribed the reissue of Philip's gold noble; but this ordinance evidently never took effect.[61] An attempt to restore Flemish minting that October proved abortive—only a few coins were struck; and minting did not successfully resume until January 1410, following upon a new ordinance of August 1409. At that time, London's Tower Mint output had fallen to a mere trickle.[62]

Who, therefore, 'won' the Anglo-Flemish monetary war? Despite my

[58] Deschamps de Pas, *Histoire monétaire* (n. 33), p. xx, nos. 100, 112.

[59] 2 Hen. IV c. 6 in *Stat. Realm*, vol. 2, p. 122; *Rot. Parl.*, vol. 3, p. 470, no. 61; see also n. 35 on the earlier bans. While Lloyd's new Calais evidence now makes it possible to argue that the 1401 recoinage effectively stemmed the influx of Flemish nobles, P. Spufford in 'Calais', *Coinage in the Low Countries* (1979), p. 175, still argues, as I had, that only the 1412 debasement and recoinage fully resolved this problem. (See n. 3.) This argument was also advanced by C. Oman, *Coinage* (n. 35), pp. 199–202 and J. D. A. Thompson, *Inventory of British Coin Hoards, A.D. 500–1500* (Oxford, 1956), p. xlv.

[60] See Prevenier, *Handelingen* (n. 53), pp. 212–24, nos. 524, 527, 534–6, 539, 544 (25 Jan. 1402: 'van der munte, die men meende te slutene'); 545–6 (30 Jan. 1402: a delegation to beg the duke 'dat hi zine munte opene wilde doen houden'); AGR, CR no. 787 (Bruges mint account). It is possible that Duke Philip's Fauquemont mint in southern Limburg, established in November 1396, was still open at this time; for a letter of his officials dated 20 July 1402 discusses a 'commission au sujet de la fabrication de deniers d'or et d'argent' at that mint. *Inventaire sommaire des archives départementales antérieures à 1790: Nord, Série B*, ed. l'abbé Dehaisnes and Jules Finot (Lille, 1906), vol. 1/2, p. 532. See also Van Gelder, 'Aantekeningen' (n. 21), 143. But our last extant mint account for Fauquemont, of 1 Dec. 1398 to 1 Nov. 1399, shows that only 6 *marcs* of fine gold and 1150.5 *marcs argent-le-roy* (= 269.86 kg pure silver) were then struck. AGR, CR no. 2587. See also C. Piot, 'Monnaies battues à Fauquemont par Philippe le Hardi, comte de Flandre', *RBN* 1 (1842–5), 122–32. For the closure of the Calais mint in 1403–4, see above, p. 73 and n. 4.

[61] Cockshaw, 'Les premières monnaies de Jean sans Peur' (n. 36), 41–52; H. Van der Wee, 'L'échec de la réforme monétaire de 1407 en Flandre vu par les marchands italiens de Bruges', in *Studi in onore di Amintore Fanfani* (Milan, 1962), vol. 3, pp. 579–89. Another proposal to reissue these Philip nobles in August 1409 was also abortive. AGR, CC, carton 65: *bis* 1; and subsequently, from December 1416, a new issue of Flemish nobles, struck as counterfeits of Henry IV's 1412 nobles, proved a failure, because it was much too inferior to pass effectively. See Munro, *Wool, Cloth, and Gold*, p. 61 n. 63; and Tables 1 and 10 below.

[62] See Tables 1 and 2, and sources; Munro, *Wool, Cloth, and Gold*, pp. 60–2.

statistics in Table 4 demonstrating that decisive Flemish supremacy in the value of total gold and silver outputs, I still see no reason to alter my earlier view: nobody won. Both sides had proved to be, as I had remarked, 'Bourbons': learning nothing and forgetting nothing, the English and Burgundians continued their monetary conflicts into the fifteenth century, to the mutual harm of their interdependent wool and cloth trades.[63] At the same time, I also fully concur with Dr Peter Spufford's recently expressed view that 'the English and Burgundians alike were the common victims of a general bullion famine' in the later fourteenth and early fifteenth centuries.[64] I myself had earlier argued that 'a severe scarcity of specie' seems to have been chiefly responsible for the rapid decline in both countries' minting from the late 1390s, but had regarded this scarcity as essentially a regional and transitory problem.[65] My own subsequent researches and those of several other scholars (Miskimin, Patterson, Day, Mayhew, and Spufford) have now persuaded me that late-medieval Europe experienced a much more significant monetary contraction over a much wider area for a far longer period, from about the 1370s to the 1470s.[66] Having already discussed this issue at considerable length elsewhere, I need only refer to these publications; and also to the accompanying Tables 5, 6, and 7, covering the period 1335–1419.[67] The decline, the almost parallel decline in English and Flemish minting from the end of the 1360s, is so readily apparent, so stark, that only one further comment seems necessary. If one should object that periodic debasements followed by varying periods of stable coinage distort our perception of monetary trends, then the outputs following the two major English debasements and recoinages, those of 1351 and 1411, should be compared in terms of *constant* pounds sterling, as in Tables 5 and 7. Clearly the outputs following the latter (1411–19) were no more than 60 per cent of the former (1351–9).

Finally, and perhaps more definitively, these new monetary statistics offer further proof that mint-ratio alterations could have a profound long-term impact upon international gold and silver bullion flows. Note in particular from Table 6 the striking change in the relative amounts of gold and silver

[63] Munro, *Wool, Cloth, and Gold*, pp. 63 and et seq.

[64] Spufford, 'Calais' (n. 3), pp. 176–7.

[65] Munro, *Wool, Cloth, and Gold*, pp. 58–63; but see also pp. 155–7.

[66] H. A. Miskimin, 'Monetary movements and market structures: forces for contraction in fourteenth and fifteenth century England', *Journal of Economic History*, 24 (1964), 470–90; Miskimin, *Economy of Early Renaissance Europe, 1300–1460* (Cambridge, 1975), pp. 25–72, 132–57; C. C. Patterson, 'Silver stocks and losses in ancient and medieval times', *Econ. Hist. Rev.*[2], 25 (1972), 205–35; N. J. Mayhew, 'Numismatic evidence and falling prices in the fourteenth century', ibid. 27 (1974), 1–15; Mayhew, 'Monetary background to the Yorkist recoinage of 1464–71', *BNJ* 44 (1974), 62–73; J. Day, 'The great bullion famine of the fifteenth century', *Past and Present*, 79 (1978), 3–54; Spufford, 'Calais' (n. 3), pp. 171–83.

[67] Munro, 'Monetary Contraction' (n. 11), pp. 95–161; Munro, 'Bullionism' (n. 31), pp. 169–239.

minted in Flanders following the mint-ratio changes of 1390–3. After almost forty years of dominance by gold, silver's share of total mint outputs in pounds *groot* more than doubled in the early 1390s, from 20.6 to 45.9 per cent. Once the mint adjustments had been completed and the countervailing force of gold counterfeiting had waned, silver's share jumped to over 60 per cent, then 70 per cent, reaching a maximum of 93.7 per cent in 1410–14, almost diametrically the opposite of England's minting pattern. Almost—for, as noted earlier, even England, the most strongly pro-gold country in western Europe, had also adjusted its mint ratio slightly more towards silver in the 1412 debasement, though far less so than her neighbours had done.

Why, therefore, did these countries, Flanders and Brabant especially, make such a shift towards silver in the late fourteenth century? Clearly it was a deliberate shift, not just a more rapid fall in the mint ratio, which had begun in the 1330s or earlier. Did this mint-ratio alteration reflect a relatively more severe scarcity of silver in the later fourteenth century? Did mints just follow the market? Possibly, But regression analyses of fifteenth-century Burgundian mint statistics suggest, on the contrary, that the volume of gold minting declined more so than did the silver.[68] Did this shift then reflect a deliberate preference by governments for silver over gold? Gold, on the one hand, was usually considered to be the more useful metal for international trade, banking, finance, diplomacy, and certainly warfare; it was also the much more commanding symbol of regal power. Silver, on the other hand, while far from absent in international trade, was generally considered the more useful metal for domestic commerce: above all for retail trades and the payment of wages, since in England especially the value of the smallest gold coin, the rarely struck ferlin at 20*d.* (quarter-noble), was more than three times a mason's daily wage.[69] It has been argued, however, that one of the beneficial consequences for the domestic economy of adopting a gold coinage was to liberate a significant amount of silver that had previously been reserved for international uses.[70] That argument may be theoretically sound, at least for a

[68] Munro, 'Monetary Contraction' graphs I–III (pp. 106–8); tables 3–5 (pp. 140–2). Note that in the early fifteenth century Near Eastern lands were favouring gold at their mints; and Watson has noted a flow of Italian gold coins to the Levant, in 'Black to Gold' (n. 10), 18. See also E. Ashtor, *Les Métaux précieux et la balance des payements du Proche-Orient à la basse époque* (Paris, 1971), pp. 31–6, 51, 65–96; Miskimin, *Economy*, pp. 151–8. The fact that prices of gold coins were rising, in Flanders especially, from the late 1390s reflects the serious undervaluation of gold in Flanders, and higher gold values elsewhere. For rising gold values, see Cockshaw, 'Circulation monétaire' (n. 17), 126 n. 95; Van der Wee, *Antwerp Market* (n. 19), vol. 1, pp. 129–31 (table xvi).

[69] See M. Bloch, 'Le problème de l'or au moyen âge', *Annales d'histoire économique et sociale*, 5 (1933), 1–34, reprinted as 'The Problem of Gold in the Middle Ages', in *Land and Work in Mediaeval Europe: Selected Papers of Marc Bloch*, trans. J. E. Anderson (London, 1967), pp. 186-229; Watson, 'Back to Gold' (n. 10), pp. 1–34; Munro, 'Bullionism' (n. 31), pp. 183–7; and *Wool, Cloth, and Gold*, pp. 31–3.

[70] Lloyd, 'Overseas Trade' (n. 8), p. 113; M. Mate, 'The role of gold in the English economy, 1338–1400', *NC*7 18 (1978), 126–41.

generation following the adoption of a gold coinage. But gold, after initial dishoardings, can be acquired only at the expense of silver: either purchased by silver or received in lieu of silver. (Neither England nor the Low Countries had any significant active gold mines in this area.) How much silver, whose short life-spans have now been demonstrated by Mayhew, Patterson, and Archibald, could be so 'liberated' for the domestic economy when, as in England's case, over 95 per cent of the coinage was being struck in gold?[71] Did countries such as Flanders make these mint-ratio alterations because their governments, after having long glorified gold, finally recognized their economies' need for a constantly replenished supply of silver, especially with the sharp decline in European silver mining during the fourteenth century?[72] If so, the Brabantine government may have perceived this need for silver at least a decade before the Flemish. Obviously this subject of medieval precious-metal preferences and mint-ratio alterations demands further investigation—possibly also in the realms of social and cultural history.

APPENDICES

A. The Theory of Medieval Mint Ratios Under Bimetallism

1. *Arbitrage trade in precious metals*

The theory of bimetallic ratios most commonly presented is defective in utilizing only one ratio and in describing an arbitrage trade in precious metals that makes unrealistic assumptions. Thus it is supposed that if, say, England's mint ratio were 11 : 1 and Flanders' only 10 : 1, a merchant could take 1 pound of gold to the English mint, exchange it for 11 pounds of silver, which he would then take to the Flemish mint, exchanging the silver for 1.1 pound of gold (i.e. $\frac{1}{10}$th of 11 lb.). But in fact the two metals could not be so easily exchanged internationally; and the costs of undertaking this arbitrage trade in metals, assumed to be minimal, could in fact easily eliminate the gains suggested here.

First, bullion in one metal could not be exchanged for bullion in the other at the mint or money-changer, but would be sold for current coin. Second, in buying bullion, the mint or exchange official would deduct the minting costs of *brassage* (for the mintmaster) and the prince's *seignorage* tax from the official coined value of the metal concerned, a value called the *traite*. That residual is thus the mint price for bullion. For this arbitrage theory, the operative mint ratio is neither the ratio of the *traites*, the coined value of gold and silver, nor the ratio of the mint prices for gold and silver bullion. Instead there is a separate ratio for each metal: (*a*) the gold bullion mint ratio, as the ratio of the mint price for gold bullion to the *traite* of

[71] Mayhew, 'Numismatic evidence' (n. 66), pp. 1–13; Patterson, 'Silver stocks' (n. 66), pp. 205–35; M. Archibald, 'Wastage from currency: Long-Cross and the recoinage of 1279', in *Edwardian Monetary Affairs, 1279–1344*, ed. N. J. Mayhew (*BAR* 36, Oxford, 1977), pp. 167–86.

[72] See sources cited in n. 66 and J. U. Nef, 'Mining and metallurgy in medieval civilisation', *Cambridge Economic History*, vol. 2 (Camb. 1952), pp. 456–73; Nef, 'Silver production in central Europe, 1450–1618', *Journal of Political Economy*, 49 (1941), 575–91.

silver, per pound or *marc* of fine metal; and similarly (*b*) the silver bullion mint ratio, as the ratio of the mint price for silver bullion to the *traite* value of gold. As Table 10 clearly demonstrates, because the minting fees were not necessarily proportional on both metals, the one mint ratio was not the inverse or reciprocal of the other.

As De Roover has noted, high minting charges could protect a prince's mint by discouraging the export of his coins to foreign mints, since those exporting coin would lose the equivalent value of the *brassage* and seignorage on the coins;[1] but those minting charges similarly discouraged the influx of metals into the prince's mints. Note from Table 10 that *ceteris paribus*, the higher the total minting fees, the less 'favourable' will be the mint ratio for that metal. Thus the gold ratio, as $x/1$, will fall with an increase in minting fees. The silver ratio appears to rise with an increase in the minting fees; but actually it also falls, as $1/x$. (Thus, 1/11 is smaller than 1/10.) At the same time, a *wider* gap between these two mint bullion ratios, reflecting the high minting fees, will normally narrow the gap between that country's mint ratios and the corresponding ratios in foreign mints.

There are also many problems concerning the coins received in exchange for the bullion. Thus a merchant supplying a mint with silver bullion will normally receive not gold but silver coin in return; and to obtain gold coins, he would have to deal with a money-changer, who would exact more exchange fees, and might well give him worn and clipped coins in return. If the merchant took these coins as bullion to a foreign mint, he would have to pay another set of mintage and exchange fees, and transport costs. And if he tried to export bullion (demonetized or decried coins or plate) to foreign mints, he ran the risk of having such bullion confiscated by frontier officials. Most countries banned bullion exports, requiring that such precious metals be sold directly to the domestic mint.

The differences between two countries' mint ratios, therefore, had to be very large indeed before merchants could hope to profit from such an international arbitrage in precious metals alone. For these reasons, a pure arbitrage trade in metals, as just described, was rarely a significant force in late-medieval monetary and bullion flows.

2. *Arbitrage in goods and metals*

Nevertheless, although small differences in mint ratios could not in themselves instigate international bullion movements divorced from trade, even small differences did have a powerful influence in determining which of the two metals would predominate in a country's foreign-trade receipts (and expenditures) and thus in its mint outputs. For merchants buying goods in several countries would seek to have their gold and silver bullion coined in those mints offering the higher purchasing power for each metal. Their arbitrage profits would be realized not directly through a straight exchange of metals, but indirectly through international trade: exchanging metal for goods and goods for metal. The following example for 1396, using the mint prices, ratios, and exchange rates for that year, will clearly demonstrate why a merchant would maximize his profits by having his gold bullion minted in England and his silver bullion minted in Flanders when trading in and between these

[1] R. De Roover, *Gresham on Foreign Exchange* (Cambridge, Mass., 1948), p. 82.

two countries. The prices are based on 1 kg of pure gold and pure silver and are given in pounds sterling English and pounds *groot* Flemish, respectively:

	Values of the traite		*Mint prices for bullion*	
Country	*Gold*	*Silver*	*Gold*	*Silver*
England	£43.092	£3.862	£42.374	£3.733
Flanders	£39.223	£4.050	£38.397	£3.730

	Monetary and mint ratios			
	Ratio of traites	*Gold bullion to silver* traite	*Silver bullion to gold* traite	*Gold bullion to silver bullion price*
England	11.16	10.97	11.54	11.35
Flanders	9.68	9.48	10.51	10.29

The current exchange rate, based on the relative values of the florin and ducat in the two currencies, was £1 sterling (20*s.*) = 19*s.* groot = £0.950.[2] Let us suppose that a merchant intended to buy £100 sterling worth of goods in England and goods of equivalent value in Flanders, £95 groot—goods commonly featured in this era's international trade. The merchant making these purchases would require the following amounts of pure metals, taking into account the minting fees to be deducted from the bullion supplied in each country:

Country where goods purchased	*Value in £*	*Value in nobles*	*Gold in kg (mint price)*	*Silver in kg (mint price)*
England	£100 st.	300	2.360	26.788
Flanders	£95 gr.	316⅔	2.474	25.469

If the merchant exported the English goods to Flanders he would logically demand not silver but gold coins (nobles) in payment; and conversely when importing the Flemish goods for sale in England he should demand not gold but silver coins in payment. The following examples make the assumptions that: (*a*) the goods were sold in the country at cost price, permitting a profit only from the indirect exchange of metals; and then that (*b*) the goods were sold for 20 per cent more than their purchase price.

Country where goods sold	*Value in £*	*Value in nobles*	*Gold in kg* (traite)	*Silver in kg* (traite)
England	£100 st.	300	2.321	25.893
Flanders	£95 gr.	316⅔	2.422	23.457
England	£120 st.	360	2.785	31.072
Flanders	£114 gr.	380	2.906	28.148

Thus, in the most profitable case, a merchant would buy £100 sterling worth of goods in England for 300 nobles+5 nobles in minting fees = 305 nobles = 2.360 kg pure gold (= 305×7.736 g or £100/42.374). Selling them in Flanders for £114 groot, at a 20 per cent markup, he would receive 380 nobles = 2.906 kg pure gold

[2] The florin and ducat were then worth about 35–36*d.* sterling in England and 33½*d.*–34½*d. groot* in Flanders. P. Spufford and W. Wilkinson, *Interim Listing of the Exchange Rates of Medieval Europe* (Keele, 1977), pp. 250, 264, 266.

(= £114/39.223). Conversely he would buy £95 *groot* worth of Flemish goods with 25.469 kg of pure silver (= £95/3.730) and sell them in England for £120 sterling, at a 20 per cent markup, receiving the coined equivalent of 31.072 kg pure silver (= £120/3.862).[3]

One might object, however, that the market's pricing system for precious metals and other commodities would quickly restore an equilibrium to eliminate these disparities and thus the arbitrage profits. Indeed, one can argue that the frequent and evidently fruitless edicts of late-medieval European princes forbidding merchants to accept gold coins (rarely silver) above official rates must indicate that the 'mint ratios' were quite irrelevant, that market values and market equilibriums always prevailed. That contention is, in my view, quite oversimplified. The rising values of gold coins condemned in such edicts in fact often reflected an increased demand for such gold coins on the parts of money-changers, bankers, and international merchants *precisely* because better mint ratios, higher values or purchasing power for gold coins could be obtained abroad. Indeed, in this respect, the just-discussed arbitrage trade and the market were in the process of making the expected equilibrium adjustments, continuing to raise gold prices until the international differences disappeared. But medieval market economies, especially because of their primitive transport and communication facilities, were far from perfect. They did not make equilibrium adjustments with any great rapidity, so that ample time usually remained to effect such arbitrage trades in goods.

Nevertheless, of the two sets of transactions examined in this goods-and-metals model, the *purchase* transactions would continue in this fashion much longer and have the more powerful impact on mint outputs. For the operation of the mint ratio, as examined in this model, would finally make gold so scarce in Flanders that merchants selling goods there would encounter difficulty in demanding gold coins in payment. Conversely, they would have the same difficulty in securing silver coins for the goods they sold in England. But if these merchants merely intended to reinvest their sales receipts in that country's own goods, it would not matter whether the £114 *groot* Flemish or £120 sterling was received and then re-spent in gold or silver. But obviously, if in Flanders, for example, the merchant selling his goods there wanted money to buy English wool at the Calais Staple, he would gain by receiving gold nobles in payment, since gold commanded a much higher purchasing power than silver at the Staple. That is, with £114 gr. in nobles (380 = 2.906 kg gold) our merchant could buy at Calais $15\frac{5}{6}$ sacks of wool, priced at £8 sterling, or 24 nobles per sack. But if he received his £114 *groot* in silver coin (= 28.148 kg of pure silver), and then exchanged that silver for gold coin at Calais he would receive, after deductions, just 315.23 nobles (28.148 × £3.733 × 3, at 3 nobles to the £ sterling), enabling him to buy only 13.135 woolsacks.

Finally, the various methods of mint ratio alterations were themselves significant in international bullion flows. Most commonly such alterations occurred indirectly when the prince or government decided to debase one metal more severely than the other. Consequently one would expect the mint to receive a much larger influx of the metal so 'favoured' by the debasement, in so far as it succeeded in augmenting

[3] The arbitrage profit from the difference between the bimetallic ratios that is included in this 20 per cent markup is: (*a*) 2.906–2.422 = 0.484 kg pure gold; and (*b*) 31.072–25.893 = 5.179 kg pure silver.

the premium on that coinage over bullion. Thus the mint, by so raising the *traite* of the debased coinage, was able to offer merchants more coins, a greater money-of-account value, for their bullion than before, or than other mints. So long as merchants could spend these coins quickly before any inflation ensued, they stood to gain. So did the prince, who frequently increased his seignorage exactions with each debasement, except those that were purely defensive. Frequently, as Table 10 indicates, these exactions were much too steep, impeding the influx of metal and so forcing the prince to 'fine-tune' his mint ratios by reducing minting fees. The prince could, of course, also alter his mint ratios to 'favour' one or the other metal by a *renforcement* that strengthened the 'favoured' coinage *less* than the other, in precious-metal contents. Historically such *renforcements* by not offering the quick gains of debasement to merchants and princes occurred far less frequently: usually only after a series of drastic debasements had seriously undermined confidence in the coinage, with a destructive inflation. As Table 8 shows, Flanders experienced *renforcements* only twice in the fourteenth century (and only three times in the fifteenth century).[4]

B. Problems with the Flemish Mint Statistics, 1334–1384

The bulk of the Flemish mint accounts of Counts Louis de Nevers and of Louis de Mäle, from 16 September 1334 to 29 February 1384, were first published in 1856 by Victor Gaillard, from documents in Belgium's Algemeen Rijksarchief—Archives Générales du Royaume (Comptes en Rouleau).[5] Almost a century later, in 1949, Professor Hans Van Werveke published another dozen accounts in résumé from documents in the Lille archives (Archives départementales du Nord, France), which Gaillard had missed. These cover the period September 1353 to June 1365. Even despite these additions, Van Werveke reported that 'more than one fifth of the original records are still lacking'.[6] Professor Wim Blockmans, as well as correcting a number of errors in the accounts presented by Gaillard and Van Werveke, has now published (1979) an estimate of gold output from 28 June 1335 to 16 June 1336 and two previously missing mint accounts from Mechelen, from 7 August 1380 to 3 May 1382.[7] The unfilled gaps now remaining in the Flemish mint accounts, up to the beginning of the Burgundian era in 1384, are the following:

1. 7 Nov. 1338–16 Apr. 1343	53.3 months
2. 17 Oct. 1343–20 Jan. 1346	27.1 months
3. 11 Aug. 1347–24 Dec. 1347	4.4 months
4. 21 Feb. 1349–6 May 1349	2.2 months
5. 24 Nov. 1355–20 Feb. 1356	2.7 months
6. 11 May 1364–10 Feb. 1365	8.4 months
7. 18 June 1368–21 Apr. 1369	10.1 months

[4] In August 1409, October 1433, and December 1489.

[5] *Recherches sur les monnaies des comtes de Flandre*, vol. 2, *Sous les règnes de Louis de Crécy et de Louis de Mäle*, ed. V. Gaillard (Ghent, 1856).

[6] H. Van Werveke, *De muntslag in Vlaanderen onder Lodewijk van Mäle*, Brussels, 1949; H. Van Werveke, 'Currency manipulation in the middle ages: the case of Louis de Male, Count of Flanders', *Transactions of the Royal Historical Society*[4], 31 (1949), reprinted in his *Miscellanea Mediaevalia* (Ghent, 1968), pp. 255–6.

[7] F. and W. P. Blockmans, 'Devaluation, coinage, and seignorage under Louis de Nevers and Louis de Male, Counts of Flanders', in *Coinage in the Low Countries (880–1500)*, ed. N. J. Mayhew (*BAR* International Ser. 54, Oxford, 1979), pp. 69–94.

*8. 5 Aug. 1370–18 June 1373 — 34.4 months
9. 26 June 1376–6 Nov. 1376 — 4.3 months
*10. 27 June 1377–30 Jan. 1380 — 31.1 months

I fully accept Professor Blockmans's cogent argument that gaps nos. 1 and 2, for 1338–46, do not reflect any missing mint accounts, but actual closures of the mints during the troubled Artevelde years. Gap nos. 3 to 7 and no. 9 are all for less than a year each. The Flemish mints may have been closed for these short periods as well; no great statistical damage will be created by assigning nil production to these very short periods. Thus the only significant gaps to remain are nos. 8 and 10: for 1370–3 and 1377–80, totalling 65.1 months—far less serious lacunae than Van Werveke had suggested. Since we also have no extant coinage ordinances for these two periods, a closure of the Flemish mints during both is thus a very distinct possibility. Consequently I have computed the mean outputs by: (1) first assigning a nil value to these gaps, and dividing the total output by five to obtain the quinquennial mean; and (2) by also dividing the total mint outputs recorded in each quinquennium by the number of years of the extant mint accounts only. These latter means, given in square brackets in the tables, are necessarily larger than the former, being divided by a number less than 5.

My own presentation of the Flemish mint statistics differs from Professor Blockmans's in one major and several minor respects. The major difference is that I have included all of the Mechelen mint accounts, while he omitted those from 8 August 1357 to 4 March 1364 (fifteen accounts for gold and seven for silver), perhaps because the Mechelen seigneurie was an enclave in neighbouring Brabant. But from 1357 it did strike purely Flemish coinage for the profit of the Count of Flanders.

Specifically my figures differ from Professor Blockmans's as noted in the following (including the addition of Mechelen outputs):

A. *Accounts of gold outputs*: (*a*) 28.vi.1338–16.x.1338: I have added 393.194 *marcs*; (*b*) 8.viii.1357–17.vi.1358: from the Mechelen mint I have added 3,442.308 *marcs*; (*c*) 22.x.1359–1.ii.1360: I calculate 2,989.286 *marcs* (the mint-master gives 2,900 m. 2 oz.); (*d*) 22.x.1359–24.vi.1360: from the Mechelen mint I have added 2,527.529 *marcs*; (*e*) 24.vi.1360–28.xii.1360: from the Mechelen mint I have added 2,029.088 *marcs*; (*f*) 14.iii.1360–25.vi.1360: I calculate 3,524.67 *marcs* (the mint-master gives 3,670 m. 6 oz. 15 est.); (*g*) 25.vi.1360–19.ix.1360: I calculate 1,215.70 *marcs* (the mint-master gives 1,256 m. 4 oz. 9 est.); (*h*) 17.iii.1361–16.vi.1361: I calculate 1.320.66 *marcs* (the mint-master gives 1,365 m. 1 oz.); (*i*) 28.xii.1360–26.vi.1361: from the Mechelen mint I have added 2,982.41 *marcs* (by my calculations; the mint-master gives 2,988 m.); (*j*) 12.ix.1363–23.x.1363: I read 1,564.25 *marcs* (the 1,925.23 *marcs* given are *marcs d'oeuvre*); (*k*) 29.i.1364–4.iii.1364: I read 820.09 *marcs* (the 1,009.38 *marcs* given are *marcs d'oeuvre*).

B. *Accounts of silver outputs*: (*a*) 24.xi.1346–27.v.1351: I calculate 122,232.06 *marcs* (the mint-master gives 121,030 m. 2 oz); (*b*) 20.ii.1356–3.xii.1356: I read 31,656.58 *marcs* rather than 31,857.31 *marcs*; (*c*) 4.xi.1357–18.x.1359: I read 54,934.71 *marcs* rather than 54,834.06 *marcs*; (*d*) for 8.x.1357–17.vi.1358, I have added from the Mechelen mint account 10,444.79 *marcs*; (*e*) 22.x.1359–26.vi.1361: from the Mechelen mint account I have added 10,525.00 *marcs*; (*f*) 1.xii.1363–2.iii.1364: from the Mechelen mint account I have added 2,925.00 *marcs*; (*g*) 18.vi.1373–27.vi.1377: I have added another 408.35 *marcs* from striking 6,533.50 *marcs d'oeuvre* in double *mites*.

Since these mint accounts provide (*a*) the number of coins 'in the box' for assay, representing the total number of coins of alloyed *marcs* struck, (*b*) the total number of alloyed *marcs d'oeuvre*, (*c*) the number of fine *marcs* in each metal, (*d*) the fineness and *taille* per *marc* of the coin (usually), (*e*) the *seignorage* rate per pure *marc* struck, and (*f*) the *seignorage* revenue, one can quite easily determine the accuracy of the accounts and make any necessary corrections. The number of differences or actual errors involved here is really remarkably small, in relation to the total number of accounts from 1334 to 1384: 103 for gold and 98 for silver. And of course it is always easier to detect slips when going over someone else's work. At the same time, I must acknowledge my great indebtedness to Blockmans's study in allowing me to detect errors made by Gaillard, Van Werveke, and indeed myself in handling these same accounts.

I was also able to find or to estimate the gold and silver values for all those mint accounts in Blockmans's publication that did not list them (twenty-five accounts); and I have thus also computed the values of the Flemish mint outputs from 1334 to 1419 in current pounds *groot*, coin by coin, as well as in constant pounds sterling (of 1351–1411 values). The mint outputs and coinage values for Flanders from 1384 to 1419 and for Brabant from 1375 to 1420 are derived from my own researches in Belgium's Algemeen Rijksarchief, supplemented by the invaluable researches of Dr Pierre Cockshaw. All of these accounts were carefully rechecked during a visit to Brussels in October 1979. Finally, I wish to express my gratitude to Dr Peter Spufford for his most valuable advice and assistance to me when I was revising this article for publication.

Table 1

Output of Gold Coinage, in Kilograms of Pure Metal, from the Mints of England, Flanders, and Brabant, 1380–1419, and of France, 1380–95

Mich. year (29 Sept.)	London	Calais	Total England	Flanders	Brabant	France
1380	108.84	124.94	233.78	283.13	284.29	275.59
1381	108.84	78.38	187.22	477.38	96.28	851.01
1382	108.84	0.79	109.62	440.10	7.27	598.42
1383	108.84	0.79	109.62	439.82	-nil-	337.02
1384	136.68	0.21	136.90	1,093.28	8.03	467.48
1385	265.82	-nil-[a]	265.82	198.47	160.62	1,399.74
1386	265.82	-nil-[a]	265.82	[21.98][b]	100.66	704.40
1387	265.82	177.23	443.04	missing[b]	-?-	41.12
1388	261.49	251.69	513.18	missing[b]	missing[c]	-nil-
1389	373.56	251.69	625.25	1,130.57	-nil-[c]	253.32
1390	566.26	110.51	676.77	962.96	-nil-	351.22
1391	534.44	51.19	585.64	276.33	-nil-	254.30
1392	495.02	51.19	546.22	223.19	-nil-	173.78
1393	397.41	377.65	775.06	386.91	42.57	200.45
1394	314.53	336.06	650.59	572.16	176.03	142.69
1395	314.53	260.97	575.50	384.48	[37.07][d]	123.36[e]
1396	186.83	128.92	315.75	379.49	missing[f]	
1397	398.58	122.58	521.16	517.81		
1398	398.58	9.95	408.53	353.31		
1399	370.61	18.06	388.67	209.12		
1400	180.72	140.90	321.61	163.21		
1401	172.46	140.90	313.36	92.16		
1402	172.46	40.19	212.65	65.51[g]		
1403	103.96	23.59	127.55	-nil-[g]		
1404	109.25	3.50[h]	112.74			
1405	77.06	-nil-[h]	77.06		1.01[i]	
1406	125.49		125.49			
1407	69.18		69.18	missing ?[j]		
1408	50.35		50.35			
1409	[50][k]		[50][k]		51.50	
1410	[50][k]		[50][k]	95.13	110.41	
1411	[50][k]		[50][k]	22.45	[67.97][l]	
1412	2,608.42		2,608.42	-nil-	missing[l]	
1413	3,421.06		3,421.06	1.30		
1414	1,636.93		1,636.93	3.86		
1415	1,636.93		1,636.93	1.81		
1416	1,636.93		1,636.93			
1417	1,636.93		1,636.93		11.36	
1418	664.84		664.84	11.39	2.62	
1419	633.12		633.12		53.00	

Notes

a. No minting at Calais from 7 Jan. 1384 to 17 Jan. 1387 (Calais Treasurer's account in PRO, E 364/22 m. 8).
b. The Mechelen mint was closed from 4 Dec. 1385 to 2 May 1386 (mint-master's account in AGR, CR no. 2143b). The mint accounts from 2 May 1386 to 30 Sept. 1388 are missing.
c. There are no mint accounts extant for the new Brabantine coinage proclaimed on 9 Sept. 1387. On or before 5 Jan. 1388 Duchess Joanna agreed to close her Brabantine mints and have all bullion sent to Flemish mints. See nn. 23–4 in the text.
d. The Leuven mint was closed on 28 Jan. 1395 'for lack of bullion', and this mint may have remained closed until 25 Dec. 1395. The subsequent mint accounts for 25 Dec. 1395 to 20 Jan. 1396 (Leuven) and from 20 Jan. 1396 to 22 May or to 1 Oct. 1396 (Maastricht) are missing; but there is no convincing evidence—and no coins at all—to indicate any substantial volume of minting in this period. See AGR, CR no. 2588; Alphonse de Witte, *Histoire monétaire des comtes de Louvain, ducs de Brabant*, 3 vols. (Antwerp, 1894), vol. 1, pp. 172–4; G. Cumont, 'Mélanges numismatiques: règne de Jeanne de Brabant veuve (1383–1406)', *Tijdschrift van het koninklijk Nederlandsch genootschap voor munt- en penningkunde*, vol. 10 (1902), pp. 224–38.
e. Professor H. A. Miskimin's series of French mint statistics terminates with those of 1395. (See Sources.)
f. On 1 Oct. 1396 Duchess Joanna leased her mints to the Brabantine towns for ten years; but in 1399 she terminated that lease, once more adopting the Flemish coinage. Again there is no numismatic or literary evidence indicating any Brabantine minting between 1396 and 1399. See de Witte, vol. 1, pp. 172–4, 178–9; Cumont, pp. 230–8; and note 36 in the text.
g. The Bruges mint closed on 16 June 1402. AGR, CR no. 787.
h. The Calais mint closed some time between 30 Mar. 1403 and 30 Mar. 1404, having coined only £301. 8*s*. 7*d*. sterling (in gold) during that period. (Calais Treasurer's account, PRO, E 364/39 m. 4).
i. Coinage by Anthony, son of Duke Philip of Burgundy, Joanna's designated heir, and *ruwaard* of Brabant, for circulation only in his own territories of Antwerp and Limburg within Brabant. The Antwerp mint struck coinage only from 5 Sept. to 10 Sept. 1405, but did not formally close until 29 Aug. 1406. See de Witte, vol. 1, p. 180; Cumont, pp. 238–46.
j. No mint accounts are extant for the new Flemish coinage proclaimed in July 1407; evidently that coinage was abortive.
k. Output estimated from the previous Tower Mint accounts and from the parliamentary complaints about the current scarcity of coinage.
l. The Leuven mint accounts are missing for the period 21 Mar. 1411 to 25 June 1412, during which time a total *seignorage* of £354 *groot* on gold and silver coinage was recorded. The Brabantine mints were closed from 25 June 1412 to 28 June 1417. See AGR, Ch. de C. no. 18,064; and de Witte, vol. 1, p. 186.

TABLE 2

Output of Silver Coinage, in Kilograms of Pure Metal, from the Mints of England, Flanders, and Brabant, 1380–1419, and of France, 1380–95

Mich. year	England[a]	Flanders	Brabant	France
1380	326.15	2,808.38	234.56	160.67
1381	326.15	3,072.39	276.25	129.24
1382	326.15	3,559.52	1,984.51	437.91
1383	326.15	3,881.20	970.03	59.34
1384	326.15	1,824.03	76.07	128.07
1385	282.45	1,747.28	1,022.88	143.08
1386	282.45	[310.14][b]	644.49	83.50
1387	282.45	missing[b]	—	4.46
1388	37.79	missing[b]	missing[c]	18.06
1389	53.98	2,064.71	-nil-[c]	590.37
1390	580.91	6,563.72	-nil-[c]	6,416.48
1391	708.35	3,319.57	-nil-[c]	2,788.15
1392	89.13	4,495.20	329.08	434.40
1393	74.65	2,371.60	1,764.21	2,133.28
1394	47.65	3,610.70	2,821.70	635.41
1395	47.65	4,583.25	[855.54][d]	563.17[e]
1396	54.83	5,150.84	missing[f]	
1397	190.15	7,324.48		
1398	190.15	7,426.13		
1399	355.95	5,202.12		
1400	86.89	3,852.96		
1401	75.20	2,021.42		
1402	75.20	1,436.89[g]		
1403	41.80			
1404	117.00[h]			
1405	22.52		136.58[i]	
1406	26.26			
1407	20.63	missing ?[j]		
1408	2.08			
1409	[2][k]		1,424.84	
1410	[2][k]	5,568.50[m]	3,249.66	
1411	[2][k]	3,371.52[m]	[2,048.99][l]	
1412	523.44	6,957.88[m]	missing[l]	
1413	1,283.58	769.60[m]		
1414	1,514.20	875.80		
1415	1,514.20	446.54		
1416	1,514.20			
1417	1,514.20		755.75	
1418	454.22	464.96	174.40	
1419	371.95		1,246.84	

Notes

a. Coinage from the Tower Mint of London only. Calais evidently struck only gold in this period.

b to l. See the corresponding notes for Table 1.

m. There are two separate sets of Ghent mint accounts for the two periods 17 Jan. 1410–17. Feb. 1411 and 2 July 1412–3 July 1413 (in fact with no more coinage given after 28 Feb. 1413): one giving aggregate outputs for each period to compute the *seignorage*, and the other giving periodic production and delivery figures. I have chosen to utilize the latter, which exceeds the former by only 0.33 per cent (i.e. 47,350.881 *v.* 47,193.75 *marcs argent-le-roy*). AGR, CR nos. 827–8 and AGR, Acquits de Lille no. 936: 1–3.

TABLE 3

Values of the Combined Gold and Silver Coinage Outputs of Flanders, Brabant, and England, 1380–1419: in Current Domestic Pounds and in English Pounds Sterling

Mich. year (29 Sept.)	Flanders £ *groot* Flemish	Brabant £ payment 000s	England £ sterl.	Flanders £ sterl.	Brabant £ sterl.
1380	23,541.4	1,648.98	11,333.5	23,046.3	13,156.3
1381	32,997.9	703.07	9,327.2	32,436.8	5,315.6
1382	33,417.2	1,232.64	5,983.5	32,711.4	7,977.2
1383	34,986.5	582.30	5,983.5	33,941.9	3,746.2
1384	57,466.2	79.54	7,158.7	54,155.9	639.9
1385	13,177.9	1,335.18	12,545.3[a]	15,300.2	10,871.8
1386	[1,874.4][b]	838.32	12,545.3[a]	[2,145.6][b]	6,826.5
1387	missing[b]	—	20,182.6[a]	missing[b]	—
1388	missing[b]	missing[c]	22,259.8	missing[b]	missing[b]
1389	73,869.1	missing[c]	27,151.6	56,692.4	-nil-[c]
1390	67,547.5	—	31,406.9	66,844.8	—
1391	24,341.8	—	27,971.9	24,727.5	—
1392	27,108.7	312.83	23,881.8	26,978.1	1,270.9
1393	24,818.6	2,093.69	33,687.1	25,831.7	8,647.9
1394	37,107.6	4,396.06	28,219.4	38,600.0	18,482.5
1395	33,706.5	[1,182.46][d]	24,983.5	34,268.3	[4,901.3][d]
1396	35,795.1	missing[f]	13,817.9	36,245.3	missing[f]
1397	50,014.0		23,192.1	50,600.4	
1398	43,970.5		18,338.7	43,904.0	
1399	29,338.2	£ *groot*	18,123.3	29,101.9	
1400	22,076.9	(from 1399)	14,194.5	21,913.1	
1401	11,875.6		13,793.5	11,778.1	
1402	8,441.6[g]		9,453.9	8,372.2[g]	
1403			5,657.7		
1404			5,310.2[h]		
1405		695.9[i]	3,407.7		570.9[i]
1406			5,508.9		
1407	missing?[j]		3,061.0	missing?[j]	
1408			2,177.8		
1409		9,134.8	[2,162.3][k]		7,721.9
1410	22,621.2[m]	20,710.4	[2,162.3][k]	25,604.4[m]	17,307.7
1411	12,502.7[m]	[13,027.2][l]	[2,162.3][k]	13,988.1[m]	[10,842.2][l]
1412	24,258.5[m]	missing[l]	127,317.4	32,245.2[m]	missing[l]
1413	2,736.6		169,749.3	3,628.7	
1414	3,194.6		85,393.6	4,243.4	
1415	1,620.5		85,393.6	2,156.2	
1416			85,393.6		
1417		5,520.7	85,393.6		4,406.3
1418	2,410.1	1,274.0	33,937.4	2,700.2	933.7
1419		13,411.4	32,037.6		8,315.8

Notes

See the corresponding notes in Tables 1 and 2. For the nature of the Brabantine monetary system, see note a of Table 9.

1 kilogram pure gold = £43.092065 English sterling up to 1411.
= £47.880072 English sterling after 1411.
1 kilogram pure silver = £3.861948 English sterling up to 1411.
= £4.634338 English sterling after 1411.

TABLE 4

Total and Mean Outputs of the Flemish and English Mints from Michaelmas 1388 to Michaelmas 1402: in Kilograms of Pure Metal Struck and in Current Pounds Sterling

	Flanders			England		
	Kilograms of pure metal	Pounds sterling value	Percentage of total	Kilograms of pure metal	Pounds sterling value	Percentage of total
Metals						
Gold	5,717.222	246,366.90	51.77	6,916.736	298,056.44	96.70
Silver	59,423.574	229,490.75	48.23	2,630.705	10,159.65	3.30
Combined value		475,857.65	100.00		308,216.09	100.00
14-year means						
Gold	408.373	17,597.64	51.77	494.053	21,289.75	96.70
Silver	4,244.541	16,392.20	48.23	187.908	725.69	3.30
Combined value		33,989.84	100.00		22,015.44	100.00

1 kilogram of pure gold = £43.092065 sterling.
1 kilogram of pure silver = £3.861948 sterling.

TABLE 5

The Mint Outputs of Flanders and England, 1335–1419: Quinquennial Means of Kilograms of Pure Gold and Silver Struck and of Total Coinage Values in Constant Pounds Sterling of 1351–1411 Values[a]

Mich. years (29 Sept.)	Gold in kilograms		Silver in kilograms		Total value of coinage in constant pounds sterling[a]	
	Flanders	England	Flanders	England	Flanders	England
1335–9	295.06		5,244.71	483.08	32,969.68	1,865.64
1340–4[b]	[1.32]	187.30	[176.76]	3,629.67	739.61	22,088.53
1345–9[b]	94.73	602.84	3,787.61	3,111.00	18,709.44	37,992.01
1350–4	914.93	1,734.56	5,761.30	15,583.84	61,676.03	134,929.78
1355–9	2,898.65	1,765.65	7,839.63	6,401.07	155,184.97	100,806.23
1360–4	2,575.95	2,403.54	4,107.57	1,858.76	126,866.38	110,752.05
1365–9	2,084.87	1,818.20	9,232.03	283.28	125,495.06	79,444.17
1370–4[c]	815.35	953.77	4,213.83	198.82	51,408.61	41,867.94
[d]	[1,913.96]		[9,891.61]		[120,677.47]	
1375–9[e]	466.15	251.91	1,203.27	510.55	24,734.45	12,826.91
[f]	[850.13]		[2,194.41]		[45,108.41]	
1380–4[g]	546.74	155.43	3,029.10	326.15	35,258.47	7,957.28
[h]	[585.48]		[3,243.73]		[37,756.71]	
1385–9[i]	[521.97]	422.62	[1,592.58]	187.82	[28,643.20]	18,936.90
1390–4	484.31	646.86	4,072.16	300.14	36,596.40	29,033.43
1395–9	368.84	441.92	5,937.36	167.75	38,823.98	19,691.10
1400–4[j]	64.18	217.58	1,462.25	79.22	8,412.68	9,681.97
1405–9		74.42		14.70		3,263.54
1410–14	24.55	1,553.28	3,508.66	665.04	14,608.00	69,502.54
1415–19	2.64	1,241.75	182.30	1,073.75	817.79	57,656.31

Notes

a. 1 kilogram pure gold = £43.092065; 1 kilogram pure silver = £3.861948.

b. For Flanders, these are the gold and silver coinages for the period 16 Apr. to 17 Oct. 1343 only. No Flemish coinage is recorded from 16 Oct. 1338 to 16 Apr. 1343 and from 17 Oct. 1343 to 20 Jan. 1346 (and no further gold until 6 May 1349). These lacunae correspond with the Artevelde Revolt and the revolutionary urban regime in Flanders. In England, gold coinage commenced only on 20 Jan. 1344. From then until Mich. 1344, the Tower minted 936.474 kg pure gold; and the mean computed here is that amount divided by 5 to produce a quinquennial mean for 1340–4.

c. There are no records of Flemish minting from 5 Aug. 1370 to 18 June 1373 (34.44 months); but the means computed here are based on 60 months, for the full quinquennium.

d. The Flemish means for 1370–4 are computed on the basis of the 25.56 months of recorded mint activity, as explained in note e.

e. There are no records of Flemish minting from 27 June 1377 to 30 Jan. 1380 (27.10 months for this quinquennium; 3.97 for the next); but the means computed here are based on 60 months for the full quinquennium 1375–9.

f. The Flemish means are computed on the basis of 32.9 months of recorded mint activity from Mich. 1374 to 27 June 1377 (though no minting is recorded from 26 June to 6 Nov. 1376).

g. See note e. Mean based on the full 60 months of the quinquennium, for Flanders.

h. The Flemish means are computed on the basis of the 56.03 months of recorded mint activity, from 30 Jan. 1380 to Mich. 1384. See note e.

i. The Flemish mint accounts are missing from 2 May 1386 to 30 Sept. 1388, a period of 28.94 months. The Flemish means are therefore computed on the basis of the remaining 31.06 months, including 4.93 months when the Flemish mints were definitely closed, from 4 Dec. 1385 to 2 May 1386.

j. The Bruges mint closed on 16 June 1402; and there are no further Flemish mint accounts extant until 17 Jan. 1410. The Calais mint closed some time between 30 Mar. 1403 and 30 Mar. 1404, and did not reopen until 20 July 1422.

The mints whose outputs are included in these tables are:

Flanders

(*a*) Ghent: Sept. 1334–June 1338; Apr. 1343–Feb. 1349; Dec. 1354–May 1370; June 1373–June 1377; Oct. 1388–July 1390; Jan. 1410–Apr. 1415; Oct. 1417–Mar. 1418.
(*b*) Bruges: Sept. 1349–Oct. 1354; June 1393–June 1402.
(*c*) Mechelen (Malines): Aug. 1357–June 1358; Oct. 1359–June 1361; Dec. 1363–Mar. 1364; Jan. 1380–Dec. 1385; Nov. 1390–Oct. 1392.
(*d*) Fauquemont: Nov. 1396–Nov. 1399.

England

(*a*) London Tower Mint: Mich. 1334–Mich. 1419.
(*b*) Canterbury: Mich. 1344–Dec. 1346.
(*c*) York: July 1353–May 1355.
(*d*) Calais: Feb. 1363–Jan. 1384; Jan. 1387–Mar. 1404.

TABLE 6

Values of the Flemish Mint Outputs: Quinquennial Means of Coinage Outputs in Current Pounds Groot *and Constant Pounds Sterling of 1351–1411 Values,*[a] *1335–1419 (Michaelmas Years)*

Years (29 Sept.)	Gold		Silver		Total coinage outputs	
	£ *groot* Flemish	Per-centage	£ *groot* Flemish	Per-centage	£ *groot* Flemish	£ sterling English[a]
1335–9	4,389.93	39.2	6,814.58	60.8	11,204.51	32,969.68
1340–4[b]	[26.60]	7.9	[310.86]	92.1	[337.46]	[739.61]
1345–9[b]	1,977.56	20.7	7,576.29	79.3	9,553.85	18,709.44
1350–4	19,781.09	62.0	12,137.37	38.0	31,918.46	61,676.03
1355–9	71,800.16	79.3	18,698.30	20.7	90.498.46	155,184.97
1360–4	72,956.89	87.6	10,292.48	12.4	83,249.37	126,866.38
1365–9	65,037.95	69.6	28,378.34	30.4	93,416.29	125,495.06
1370–4[c]	30,760.72	66.9	15,224.95	33.1	45,985.67	51,408.61
,, [d]	[72,208.27]		[35,739.31]		[107,947.58]	[120,677.47]
1375–9[e]	18,597.49	80.4	4,540.43	19.6	23,137.93	24,734.45
,, [f]	[33,916.40]		[8,280.43]		[42,196.83]	[45,108.41]
1380–4[g]	23,941.05	65.6	12,540.77	34.4	36,481.82	35,258.47
,, [h]	[25,637.39]		[13,429.34]		[39,066.73]	[37,756.71]
1385–9[i]	[27,262.38]	79.4	[7,092.29]	20.6	[34,354.67]	[28,643.20]
1390–4	19,589.24	54.1	16,595.61	45.9	36,184.84	36,596.40
1395–9	14,467.19	37.5	24,097.69	62.5	38,564.87	38,823.98
1400–4[j]	2,517.25	29.7	5,961.57	70.3	8,478.82	8,412.68
1405–9[j]	—		—		—	—
1410–14	820.89	6.3	12,241.85	93.7	13,062.75	14,608.00
1415–19	97.67	12.1	708.44	87.9	806.11	817.79

See the corresponding notes for Table 5.

TABLE 7

Values of the English Mint Outputs: Quinquennial Means of Coinage Outputs in Current Pounds Sterling and Constant Pounds Sterling of 1351–1411 Values, 1335–1419 (Michaelmas Years)

Years (29 Sept.)	Gold		Silver		Total coinage outputs	
	£ sterling current	Percentage	£ sterling current	Percentage	£ sterling current	£ sterling constant
1335–9	—	0.0	1,737.43	100.0	1,737.43	1,865.64
1340–4	7,865.45	38.1	12,762.99	61.9	20,628.44	22,088.53
1345–9	24,061.09	68.9	10,855.94	31.1	34,917.03	37,992.01
1350–4	74,363.36	55.4	59,947.26	44.6	134,310.63	134,929.78
1355–9	76,085.64	75.5	24,720.61	24.5	100,806.25	100,806.23
1360–4	103,573.62	93.5	7,178.43	6.5	110,752.05	110,752.05
1365–9	78,350.15	98.6	1,094.02	1.4	79,444.17	79,444.17
1370–4	41,100.09	98.2	767.85	1.8	41,867.94	41,867.94
1375–9	10,855.17	84.6	1,971.73	15.4	12,826.90	12,836.91
1380–4	6,697.70	84.2	1,259.58	15.8	7,957.28	7,957.28
1385–9	18,211.54	96.2	725.36	3.8	18,936.90	18,936.90
1390–4	27,874.31	96.0	1,159.13	4.0	29,033.44	29,033.44
1395–9	19,043.26	96.7	647.84	3.3	19,691.10	19,691.10
1400–4	9,376.03	96.8	305.94	3.2	9,681.97	9,681.97
1405–9	3,206.79	98.3	56.76	1.7	3,263.54	3,263.54
1410–14	74,275.57	96.0	3,081.42	4.0	77,356.99	69,502.54
1415–19	59,455.03	92.3	4,976.14	7.7	64,431.17	57,656.31

See the notes accompanying Tables 1–3 and 5.

TABLE 8

Official Values of Gold and Silver in Flanders and England, 1279–1418: in Pounds Groot *Flemish and Pounds Sterling English, Respectively, per Kilogram of Pure Metal, with the Gold: Silver Ratios*

Date	Flanders			England		
	Gold £ *groot*	Silver £ *groot*	Ratio of values	Gold £ sterling	Silver £ sterling	Ratio of values
Dec. 1279					3.128	
Apr. 1300		1.098				
Mar. 1331	16.786	1.157	14.51			
Mar. 1332	14.811	1.196	12.38			
May 1335			12.38		3.601	
June 1335	14.641	1.196	12.24			
June 1337	16.394	1.433	11.44			
Apr. 1343		1.759	—			
Jan. 1344				43.092	3.476	12.40
Aug. 1344				37.825	3.424	11.05
June 1345				37.825	3.450	10.96
Jan. 1346		1.835	—			10.96
Aug. 1346				40.219	3.476	11.57
Nov. 1346		2.016				11.57
May 1349	20.877	2.016	10.36			11.57
May 1351	20.877	2.164	9.65			11.57
July 1351			9.65	43.092	3.862	11.16
Jan. 1352	22.300	2.164	10.30			11.16
Sept. 1352	22.775	2.164	10.52			11.16
Sept. 1353	22.775	2.221*	10.25			11.16
Dec. 1354	23.945	2.385	10.04			11.16
July 1356	24.787	2.385	10.39			11.16
Sept. 1357	25.682	2.385	10.77			11.16
Oct. 1357	24.787	2.385	10.39			11.16
July 1358	25.558	2.385	10.72			11.16
Oct. 1359	25.833	2.487	10.39			11.16
Nov. 1359	26.966	2.487	10.84			11.16
Feb. 1360	27.251	2.487	10.96			11.16
Sept. 1361 }	28.201	2.558	11.02			11.16
Dec. 1361 }	29.111	,,	11.38			11.16
Dec. 1363	31.387	2.771	11.33			11.16
Mar. 1364	29.111	2.771	10.51			11.16
Apr. 1365	30.813	3.038	10.14			11.16
Jan. 1368	32.405	3.240	10.00			11.16
Apr. 1369	32.405	3.391	9.56			11.16
Sept. 1369	32.865	3.553*	9.25*			11.16
Apr. 1370	33.124	3.553*	9.32*			11.16
June 1373	39.530	3.739	10.57			11.16
	39.896	,,	10.67			
Jan. 1380	41.692	4.121	10.12			11.16
	42.598	,,	10.34			

Date	Flanders			England		
	Gold £ *groot*	Silver £ *groot*	Ratio of values	Gold £ sterling	Silver £ sterling	Ratio of values
Sept. 1383	45.570	4.300	10.60			11.16
Sept. 1384	35.120	3.553	9.89			11.16
Apr. 1386	41.727	4.050	10.30			11.16
Oct. 1386	41.727	4.050	10.30			11.16
	,,	4.107	10.16			
Apr. 1387	49.811	4.910	10.14			11.16
Oct. 1388	55.566	5.337	10.41			11.16
Jan. 1390	39.223	4.050	9.68			11.16
Jan. 1391	39.223	4.086	9.60			11.16
June 1393	39.223	4.050	9.68			11.16
July 1407	39.636	4.050	9.79			11.16
Aug. 1409	33.443	3.482	9.60			11.16
Nov. 1411			9.60	47.880	4.634	10.33
Dec. 1416	37.554	4.263	8.81			10.33
June 1418	47.290	4.832	9.79			10.33

* Estimated.

TABLE 9

Official Values of Gold and Silver in France and Brabant, 1365–1420: in Livres Tournois and Pounds Groot *Brabant, with their Gold: Silver Ratios and the Flemish Gold: Silver Ratios*

Date	France			Brabant[a]			Flanders
	Gold £ tourn.	Silver £ tourn.	Ratio of values	Gold £ payment	Silver £ payment	Ratio values	Ratio of values
Apr. 1365	261.488	25.580	10.22				10.14
Jan. 1368			10.22				10.00
Apr. 1369			10.22				9.56
Sept. 1369			10.22				9.25[b]
Apr. 1370			10.22				9.32[b]
June 1373			10.22				10.57
July 1375			10.22	3,468.1	380.6	9.11	10.57
				5,202.2[c]	571.0[c]	9.11	
Jan. 1380			10.22			9.11	10.12
Apr. 1380			10.22	5,202.2	595.5	8.74	10.12
Nov. 1380			10.22	5,573.8	598.6	9.31	10.12
May 1381			10.22	5,697.7	598.6	9.52	10.12
Jan. 1382			10.22	5,945.4	600.3	9.90	10.12
Sept. 1383			10.22			9.90	10.60
Sept. 1384			10.22	5,057.3	511.6	9.89	9.89
Mar. 1385	275.788	26.646	10.35			9.89	9.89
Apr. 1386			10.35			9.89	10.30
Oct. 1386			10.35			9.89	10.30
							10.16
Apr. 1387			10.35				10.14
Sept. 1387			10.35	7,172.8	707.2	10.14	10.14
Feb. 1388	281.917	26.646	10.58			10.14	10.14
Oct. 1388			10.58			10.14	10.41
Sept. 1389	281.917	28.778	9.80			10.14	10.41
Jan. 1390			9.80				9.68
Jan. 1391			9.80				9.60
June 1392			9.80		950.6		9.60
June 1393			9.80	9,206.4	982.3	9.37	9.68
July 1394	284.981	28.778	9.90			9.37	9.68
1399			9.90	11,296.3	1,166.4	9.68	9.68
				=39.223[d]	=4.050[d]		
Apr. 1405	284.981	31.062	9.17				9.68
Sept. 1405			9.17	45.550	4.759	9.57	9.68
July 1407			9.17			9.57	9.79
Apr. 1409			9.17	44.856	4.789	9.37	
Aug. 1409			9.17			9.37	9.60
Jan. 1410			9.17	44.856	4.867	9.22	9.60
Oct. 1411	294.174	34.107	8.63			9.22	9.60
June 1413	294.174	30.879	9.53			9.22	9.60
Nov. 1413	294.174	30.791	9.55			9.22	9.60
June 1414	294.174	34.107	8.63			9.22	9.60
Dec. 1416			8.63			9.22	8.81
May 1417	409.286	42.634	9.60				8.81
June 1417			9.60	63.842	6.340	10.07	8.81

Date	France			Brabant[a]			Flanders
	Gold £ tourn.	Silver £ tourn.	Ratio of values	Gold £ *groot*	Silver £ *groot*	Ratio values	Ratio of values
Oct. 1417	427.890	63.951	6.69			10.07	8.81
June 1418			6.69			10.07	9.79
Dec. 1418			6.69	72.967[e]	7.181	10.16	9.79
				78.446	8.100	9.68	
Mar. 1419	409.286	102.321	4.00			10.16	9.79
Apr. 1419				76.139[f]	7.319	10.40	9.79
				76.139	8.202	9.28	
June 1419	409.286	85.268	4.80			10.40	9.79
July 1419	409.286	102.321	4.00			10.40	9.79
Mar. 1420			4.00	57.270[g]	5.898	9.71	9.79
				59.675	6.075	9.82	
May 1420	409.286	170.536	2.40			9.71	9.79
Dec. 1420	303.367	31.883	9.52			9.71	9.79

Notes

a. The chief money-of-account in fourteenth-century Brabant was the 'pound payment', based on the current silver coinage: £1 = 20*s.* = 240*d.* About 1360, this pound was tied to a new silver coin, the *groot* or large penny, copied from the Flemish, as follows: 1 *groot* = 4*s.* 0*d.* payment. Subsequently, in July 1384 (effective September), Flanders and Brabant agreed to establish a common coinage; and by the convention: 1 new *groot* of Flanders and Brabant = 3 old Brabant *groots* = 12*s.* 0*d.* payment.

b. Estimated. See Table 8 for the Flemish coinage values and ratios.

c. In 1374–5 the duke of Brabant attempted to impose a new, much heavier, stronger silver *groot*, called the *schuerman* or *scuerken*, as the 'link money' of 4*s.* payment. But the Brabantine towns refused to accept this *renforcement* and raised the value of the *schuerman* 50 per cent to 6*s.* payment. The gold Peter (*pieter*), valued at 70 *schuermans*, rose proportionally from £14 to £21 payment.

d. In 1399 Duchess Joanna once more agreed to adopt the current Flemish coinage, so that the heavy Flemish *groot* of 1389/90 became the common link money: 1 strong Flemish *groot* = 1 new Brabant *groot* = 2 'weak' Flemish *groots* (in fact Brabant *groots* based on the 1384 convention) = 6 old Brabant *groots* = 24*s.* payment; and thus £1 *groot* = £288 payment.

e. Gold values based on the Brabant *écu* and *mouton*; silver values, on the double *groot* and the *thunen.*

f. Gold value based on the *écu*; silver values, on the double *groot* and *thunen.*

g. Gold values based on the angel and florin; silver values, on the double *groot* ('drielander') and the single *groot.*

TABLE 10

Minting Charges and Mint Bullion-price Ratios in England, 1351–1411, and Flanders, 1384–1418

Date	Minting charges on gold: % of *traite*	Minting charges on silver: % of *traite*	GOLD Ratio. Gold bullion price ÷ silver *traite* $(x/1)$[a]	SILVER Ratio. Silver bullion price ÷ gold *traite* $(1/x)$[b]	GOLD Ratio of Flemish to English gold mint ratios[c]	SILVER Ratio of Flemish to English silver mint ratios[c]
ENGLAND						
June 1351	3.08	5.83	10.81	11.85	n.a.	n.a.
May 1355	2.22	3.85	10.91	11.61	n.a.	n.a.
Mar. 1361	1.67	3.33	10.97	11.54	n.a.	n.a.
Nov. 1411[d]	1.75	3.33	10.15	10.69	0.92	1.03[e]
FLANDERS						
July 1384	3.76	14.00	9.51	11.50	0.87	1.00
Apr. 1386	2.50	8.77	10.04	11.29	0.92	1.02
Oct. 1386	2.50	7.02	10.04	11.08	0.92	1.04
	2.00	7.44	9.96	10.98	0.91	1.05
Apr. 1387	3.25	9.92	9.81	11.26	0.90	1.03
Oct. 1388	6.84	12.46	9.66	11.85	0.88	0.97
Feb. 1389	6.05	11.80	9.77	11.76	0.89	0.98
July 1389	3.68	11.80	9.99	11.76	0.91	0.98
Nov. 1389	3.16	11.80	10.04	11.76	0.92	0.98
Jan. 1390	3.16	10.53	9.38	10.82	0.85	1.07
Jan. 1391	3.16	10.43	9.30	10.72	0.85	1.08
Nov. 1392	3.68	11.30	9.25	10.82	0.84	1.07
		13.91	9.25	11.15	0.84	1.04
June 1393	2.11	7.89	9.48	10.51	0.86	1.10
July 1407	2.78	7.89	9.51	10.63	0.87	1.09
Aug. 1409	3.09	7.14	9.31	10.34	0.85	1.12
Nov. 1411	3.09	7.14	9.31	10.34	0.92	1.03
Jan. 1414	1.95	7.14	9.42	10.34	0.93	1.03
Dec. 1416	5.56	13.75	8.32	10.21	0.82	1.05
June 1418[f]	2.21	6.62	9.57	10.48	0.94	1.02

Notes

a. In the gold ratio, the ratio between the mint price for gold bullion and the coined value (*traite*) of the same weight of silver, the value x serves as the numerator: i.e. the gold bullion price at the mint is 10.15 times the value of the same weight of pure silver in coined form.

b. In the silver ratio, the ratio between the mint price for silver bullion and the coined value of the same weight of gold (*traite*), the value x serves as the demoninator: i.e. the silver bullion price at the mint is 1/10.69 the value of the same weight of pure gold in coin.

c. In these relative ratios, the Flemish ratio serves as the numerator and the English ratio as the denominator. Because of the way that the silver ratio is computed (in note b), the English and Flemish ratios seem to be reversed in the relative silver ratio; but in fact the English ratio remains the denominator, as this example shows:

$$\text{Jan. 1390} \quad \frac{\text{Flemish ratio}}{\text{English ratio}} \quad \frac{1/10.82}{1/11.54} = 1.06654 = 1.07$$

d. English ratios valid until July 1421.

e. See below, the Flemish ratios for November 1411.

f. Flemish ratios valid until November 1422.

SOURCES FOR THE TABLES

A. ENGLAND: LONDON, CANTERBURY, YORK, AND CALAIS

C. G. Crump and C. Johnson, 'Tables of bullion coined under Edward I, II, and III', *NC*[4] 13 (1913), 200–45.

G. C. Brooke and E. Stokes, 'Tables of bullion coined from 1377 to 1550', *NC*[5] 9 (1929), 27–69.

Public Record Office, Lord Treasurer's Remembrancer Exchequer, E 364/22, 25, 28, 30, 34, 36, 37; King's Remembrancer Exchequer, E 101/184/10.

J. Craig, *The Mint: A History of the London Mint from A.D. 287 to 1948* (Cambridge, 1953), pp. 408, 412.

T. H. Lloyd, *The English Wool Trade in the Middle Ages* (Cambridge, 1977), p. 241, table 15.

B. FLANDERS

1. 1334 to 1384: GHENT, BRUGES, AND MECHELEN

V. Gaillard, ed. *Recherches sur les monnaies des comtes de Flandre*, II: *Sous les règnes de Louis de Crécy et de Louis de Mäle* (Ghent, 1856).

H. Van Werveke, *De muntslag in Vlaanderen onder Lodewjik Van Mäle* (Mededelingen van de koninklijke Vlaamse Academie voor Wetenschappen, Letteren, en Schone Kunsten van België, Klasse der Letteren, no. 11/5, Brussels, 1949).

C. Piot, 'Quatre comptes de monnaies frappées par Louis de Crécy, comte de Flandre', *RBN* 8 (1852), 45–76.

—— 'Notice sur six comptes de monnaies frappées à Bruges par Louis de Male, comte de Flandre', ibid. 190–9.

—— review of Frederic Verachter, *Documents pour servir à l'histoire monétaire des Pays-Bas* (1841), in *RBN* 1 (1842–5), 83–92, 133–46 [Mechelen mint accounts].

J. Ghyssens, 'Le monnayage d'argent en Flandre, Hainaut, et Brabant au début de la guerre de Cent Ans', *RBN* 120 (1974), 109–91.

F. and W. P. Blockmans, 'Devaluation, coinage, and seignorage under Louis de Nevers and Louis de Mäle, Counts of Flanders, 1330–84', in N. Mayhew, ed., *Coinage in the Low Countries (880–1500): The Third Oxford Symposium on Coinage and Monetary History* (BAR International Series 54, Oxford, 1979), pp. 69–94.

2. 1384 to 1419: BRUGES, GHENT, MECHELEN, AND FAUQUEMONT

Algemeen Rijksarchief—Archives Générales du Royaume de Belgique, Rolrekeningen—Comptes en rouleau, nos. 776–87 (Bruges), 824–31 (Ghent), 2142–3 (Mechelen), 2586–7 (Fauquemont); Rekenkamer—Chambre des Comptes, nos. 48,976–7 (Mechelen); Acquits de Lille: liasses des monnaies, nos. 931 (various), 936 (Ghent); Cartons nos. 65, 65: *bis* 1, 65: *bis* 2.

C. Piot, 'Monnaies battues à Fauquemont par Philippe-le-Hardi, comte de Flandre', *RBN* 1 (1842–5), 122–32.

H. Laurent, *La loi de Gresham au moyen âge: essai sur la circulation monétaire entre la Flandre et le Brabant à la fin du XIV*[e] *siècle* (Brussels, 1933), appendices and documents.

P. Cockshaw, 'A propos de la circulation monétaire entre la Flandre et le Brabant de 1384 à 1390', *Contribution à l'histoire économique et sociale*, 6 (1970–1), 107–41.

—— 'Les premières monnaies de Jean sans Peur: l'émission de 1407', *CENB* 8 (1971), 41–52.

J. Bartier and A. Van Nieuwenhuysen, eds. *Les Ordonnances de Philippe le Hardi, de Marguerite de Mäle, et de Jean Sans Peur, 1381–1419*, vol. 1: *du 16 octobre 1381 au 31 décembre 1393* (*Recueil des ordonnances des Pays-Bas*, 1re série, Brussels, 1965).

L. Deschamps de Pas, *Essai sur l'histoire monétaire des comtes de Flandre de la maison de Bourgogne* (Paris, 1863).

J. H. Munro, *Wool, Cloth, and Gold: The Struggle for Bullion in Anglo-Burgundian Trade, ca. 1340–1478* (Brussels and Toronto, 1973), appendices I and II, pp. 188–214.

C. BRABANT: LEUVEN, VILVOORDE, MAASTRICHT, AND BRUSSELS

ARA-AGR de Belgique, Rolrekeningen nos. 2588–9 (Leuven), 2590 (Vilvoorde), 2591 (Leuven), 2592 (Vilvoorde); Rekenkamer nos. 17,985 (Brussels); 18,064 (Leuven); 18,071 and 18,073 (Maastricht); 18,094 (Vilvoorde).

F. Verachter, ed. *Documents pour servir à l'histoire monétaire des Pays-Bas* (Antwerp, 1841), pp. 107–8, 110–14, 119–20, 125, 140–3.

A. de Witte, *Histoire monétaire des comtes de Louvain, ducs de Brabant, et marquis du Saint-Empire romain*, 2 vols. (Antwerp, 1894–6), 1.

H. Laurent, *La loi de Gresham au moyen âge* (Brussels, 1933).

C. Piot, 'Discussions entre le duc de Wenceslas et les états de Brabant au sujet de ses monnaies', *RBN* 1 (1842–5), 173–200.

—— 'Notice sur les monnaies de Jeanne, duchesse de Brabant (1383–1406), *RBN* 2 (1846), 116–46, 285–9.

—— 'Documents sur quelques monnaies frappées par Antoine, duc de Brabant', *RBN* 1 (1842–5), 247–60.

R. Chalon, 'Nouvelle classification des monnaies de Jeanne, duchesse de Brabant', *RBN* 14 (1858), 353–61.

G. Cumont, 'Mélanges numismatiques: règne de Jeanne de Brabant, veuve, 1383–1406', *TMP* 10 (1902), 197–246.

—— 'Un officier monétaire au XIVe siècle: Nicolas Chavre (mort en 1397), maître de la monnaie de Louvain', *Gazette numismatique française*, 1 (1897), 187–232.

D. FRANCE

H. A. Miskimin, *Money, Prices, and Foreign Exchange in Fourteenth Century France* (New Haven, 1963), appendix D, pp. 158–60.

J. Lafaurie, *Les Monnaies des rois de France*, vol. 1: *Hughes Capet à Louis XII* (Paris, 1951).

A. Dieudonné, 'La monnaie royale depuis la réforme de Charles V jusqu'à la restauration monétaire par Charles VII', *Bibliotheque de l'école des chartes*, 72 (1911), 473–99; 73 (1912), 263–82.

A. Blanchet and A. Dieudonné, *Manuel de numismatique française*, vol. 2 (Paris, 1916).

E. Fournial, *Histoire monétaire de l'occident médiéval* (Paris, 1970), pp. 100–2, 118–19.

Note that these French sources do not always agree: Dieudonné is sometimes inexact on coinage weights by omitting fractions in the *taille* per *marc*; Lafaurie and Fournial do not list the restoration of the October 1411 silver coinage in June 1414; and Fournial estimates silver contents of coins on the basis of the *pied*, not always an exact method.

VI

Bullion flows and monetary contraction in late-medieval England and the Low Countries

Bullion flows and monetary contraction

For almost a century now, many economic historians have contended that Europe's aggregate stock of precious metals was declining in the late Middle Ages.[1] But even amongst those who support this proposition in general, there is still no agreement on four vital questions: (1) What were the principal causes of this reduction in Europe's precious metal stocks—in particular of

1. The major studies in chronological order are: W. A. Shaw, *The History of Currency, 1252-1894* (London, 1896), pp. 1-60; Sir Albert Feavearyear, *The Pound Sterling: A History of English Money* (Oxford, 1931); 2nd rev. edn. by E. Victor Morgan (Oxford, 1963), pp. 10-15; Marc Bloch, "Le problème de l'or au moyen âge," *Annales d'histoire économique et sociale,* V (1933), 1-34 [reprinted as "The Problem of Gold in the Middle Ages," in *Land and Work in Medieval Europe: Selected Papers by Marc Bloch,* ed. J. E. Anderson (London, 1967), pp. 186-229]; Marc Bloch, *Esquisse d'une histoire monétaire de l'Europe* (Paris, 1954), pp. 35-77 [but written before 1940]; Henri Laurent, "Crise monétaire et difficultés économiques en Flandre aux XIVe et XVe siècles," *Annales d'histoire économique et sociale,* V (1933), 156-61; Henri Laurent, *La loi de Gresham au moyen âge* (Brussels, 1933), pp. 3-36; A. Girard, "Un phénomène économique: la guerre monétaire, XIVe-XVe siècles," *Annales: E. S. C.*, II (1940); F. Graus, "La crise monétaire du XIVe siècle," *Revue belge de philologie et d'histoire,* XXIX (1951), 445-54; Johan Schreiner, "Wages and Prices in the Later Middle Ages," *Scandinavian Economic History Review,* II (1954), 61-73; W. C. Robinson, "Money, Population, and Economic Change in Late-Medieval Europe," *Economic History Review,* 2nd ser. XII (1959), 63-76; Harry A. Miskimin, "Monetary Movements and Market Structure: Forces for Contraction in Fourteenth and Fifteenth Century England," *Journal of Economic History,* XXIV (1964), 470-90; R. Cazelles, "Quelques reflexions à propos des mutations de la monnaie royale française (1295-1360)," *Le moyen âge,* LXXII (1966), 83-105, 251-78; Harry A. Miskimin, *The Economy of Early Renaissance Europe, 1300-1460* (Englewood Cliffs, N.J., 1969; reissued Cambridge, 1975), especially pp. 25-72, 132-57; E. Fournial, *Histoire monétaire de l'occident médiéval* (Paris, 1970); R. S. Lopez, H. A. Miskimin, and A. L. Udovitch, "England to Egypt, 1350-1500: Long-Term Trends and Long-Distance Trade," *Studies in the Economic History of the Middle East,* ed. M. A. Cook (London, 1970), pp. 93-128; C. C. Patterson, "Silver Stocks and Losses in Ancient and Medieval Times," *Economic History Review,* 2nd ser. XXV (1972), 205-35; Nicholas Mayhew, "Numismatic Evidence and Falling Prices in the Fourteenth Century," *Ibid.*, 2nd ser. XXVII (1974), 1-15; Nicholas Mayhew, "The Monetary Background to the Yorkist Recoinage of 1464-1471," *British Numismatic Journal,* XLIV (1974), 62-73; John Day, "The Decline of a Money Economy: Sardinia in the Late Middle Ages," in *Studi in memoria di Federigo Melis,* 3

monetized metals? (2) When did this monetary contraction commence: in the late-thirteenth, early-, mid-, or late fourteenth century? And when did it terminate? (3) Was this contraction ever serious enough to constitute a "bullion famine:" i.e., was there a serious scarcity of coined money in relation to the transactions demand for money? Did the frequent coinage debasements and the spread of credit instruments counteract any deflationary effects of reductions in bullion supplies? (4) What was the relationship between monetary factors and general economic movements—*conjoncture*—in late-medieval Europe? In particular, were monetary factors a primary or even a secondary cause of the so-called "Great Depression" of late medieval Europe? Or was a contraction in monetary flows merely a passive response to, an adaptation to, general demographic and economic contraction? Did monetary factors behave, as Marc Bloch suggested, like a "seismograph that not only registers earth tremors but sometimes brings them about"?[2]

This last question, the most complex of all, is quite beyond the scope of this modest study, and indeed transcends the theme of this volume on international monetary flows. But one can hardly pose the first three questions without being aware of the fourth; and any subsequent answers to the fourth question will ultimately depend on answers given to the first three. Answers to these questions in turn will depend upon how we interpret the admittedly meagre quantitative data at our disposal, chiefly mint statistics. In doing so, it is imperative to distinguish clearly between those forces that instigated bullion flows and those that resulted in monetary contraction; between transient and purely regional monetary scarcities produced by trade and bullion flows and a long-term, secular decline in Europe's total specie stocks.

The causes of monetary contraction and specie outflows

For many historians, the earliest and principal cause of a general European monetary contraction per se was a severe slump in European silver mining,

---

vols. (Florence, 1978), III, 155-76; John Day, "The Great Bullion Famine of the Fifteenth Century," *Past and Present*, no. 79 (1978), 3-54. The most impressively documented study so far on this issue, Day's article appeared the year following the presentation of my paper to the 1977 Wisconsin Conference, and after I had prepared a paper on "Monetary Contraction and Industrial Change in the Late-Medieval Low Countries" for the Third Oxford Symposium on Coinage and Monetary History, held in September 1978. My arguments, essentially unchanged from those two conferences of 1977-78, are similar to Day's on monetary contraction itself, though we differ on minor points.

2. Bloch, "Problem of Gold," p. 186. See also Carlo Cipolla, "Currency Depreciation in Medieval Europe," *Economic History Review*, 2nd ser. XV (1963), 413-22 [reprinted in *Change in Medieval Society: Europe North of the Alps, 1050-1500*, ed. Sylvia Thrupp (New York, 1964), pp. 227-36]; R. S. Lopez and H. A. Miskimin, "The Economic Depression of the Renaissance," *Economic History Review*, 2nd ser. XIV (1962), 408-26; Carlo Cipolla, R. S. Lopez, and H. A. Miskimin, "Economic Depression of the Renaissance? Rejoinder and Reply," *Ibid.*, XVI (1964), 519-29; and the writings of Miskimin in n. 1 above.

from the late thirteenth or early fourteenth centuries, variously in Saxony, Bohemia, the Tyrol, Alsace, England, and Sweden. Prof. John Nef has argued that because there had been no real progress in mining technology since Classical times, indeed because medieval mining and drainage technology were generally inferior to that of the Romans, diminishing returns would soon afflict any mining ventures.[3] Whether or not mines became physically depleted, rising marginal costs—or quite simply, rising waters and flooding—were bound to force many mines to halt production in this era. To be sure, as some other historians have countered, new mines, especially gold mines, were opened in Hungary, Bosnia, Serbia, Bohemia (Kutna Hora for silver), and Sardinia.[4] But Nef does not agree that their combined outputs offset the sharp decline in production from older centres in Saxony, Bohemia, and elsewhere in Europe. More recently Prof. John Day has contended that production from new mines compensated for the decline of the old, if at all, only until the 1360s, when some of the new mines, especially at Kutna Hora and in Sardinia, also began to decline.[5] Europe did not in fact enjoy a genuine silver mining boom, comparable to that of the twelfth and thirteenth centuries, again until the 1460s, when South German mining engineers achieved two crucial technological breakthroughs: mechanical drainage pumps to eliminate flooding, and a lead-chemical process to separate the metals in those argentiferous-cupric ores that were so very plentiful in Central Europe.[6] Naturally one is tempted to believe that a "bullion famine" and high metal prices provided the necessary economic incentives to produce these innovations.

In the post-war years, however, this "mining slump" theory did not fare so well (until recently) in the literature on late-medieval economic changes, thanks in particular to the persuasive writings of Prof. Michael Postan.[7]

3. John U. Nef, "Mining and Metallurgy in Medieval Civilisation," *Cambridge Economic History of Europe*, II (ed. M. M. Postan, Cambridge, 1952), 456-69; and his "Silver Production in Central Europe, 1450-1618," *Journal of Political Economy*, XLIX (1941), 575-91. See also Schreiner, "Wages" (n. 1 above), pp. 67-71.

4. D. Kovačević, "Les mines d'or et d'argent en Serbie et en Bosnie médiévales," *Annales: E. S. C.*, XV (1960), 248-58; Graus, "Crise monétaire," pp. 450-2; Day, "Bullion Famine," pp. 35-7; Day, "Sardinia," pp. 156-65; Andrew Watson, "Back to Gold—and Silver," *Economic History Review*, 2nd ser. XX (1967), 30-2; Marian Malowist, "Problems of the Growth of the National Economy of Central-Eastern Europe in the Late Middle Ages," *Journal of European Economic History*, III (1974), 331-57.

5. Day, "Bullion Famine," p. 35.

6. Nef, "Mining," pp. 458-73 and "Silver Production," pp. 575-91.

7. In particular, Michael Postan, "Rapport," *IXe congrès international des sciences historiques* (2 vols. Paris, 1950), I, 225-41 [revised and republished as "The Economic Foundations of Medieval Society," in his *Essays on Medieval Agriculture and General Problems of the Medieval Economy* (Cambridge, 1973), pp. 3-27, especially 7-13]; "The Trade of Medieval Europe: The North," *Cambridge Economic History*, II (1952), 191-222, especially 211-16; and his "Note" to W. C. Robinson's "Money, Population, and Economic Change in Late-Medieval Europe," *Economic History Review*, 2nd ser. XII (1959), 77-82. Another of his arguments, a contentious one too complex to discuss here, is that only demographic and not monetary factors would explain divergent trends in grain prices and industrial prices and wages. See also n. 22 below.

While in no way denying that medieval silver mining did suffer a slump, he firmly rejected the contention that any decline in mined output could in itself have produced a bullion famine. In the first place, he argued, no mining slump could have seriously diminished the European money supply when Europe's total stock of precious metals, amassed over two or three centuries of economic expansion, was "two hundred to five hundred times its annual accretions." In the second place, most countries did not possess gold or silver mines and were consequently dependent upon foreign trade and their international balance of payments for their monetary stocks. Indeed for much of the medieval and early-modern era Europe generally received much more gold from its African trade than from its own mines. In any event, Postan observed that in late-medieval Europe "changes in trade balances did not synchronize with the ups and downs of silver mining" and that England in particular continued to enjoy a large influx of precious metals long after the mining slump had commenced.

Then came his final point, constituting the most devastating refutation of the "mining slump" thesis: the very severe declines in European population, of 30 to 40 percent during the fourteenth and fifteenth centuries, which must have increased the per capita supplies of precious metals. Or in the *aggregate* terms of the Fisher Identity, M.V. = P.T: the fall in the volume of transactions (T) resulting from depopulation and various economic dislocations of the era would have been much greater than any decline in money stocks (M) attributable to the mining slump. Consequently, unless coinage velocity of circulation (V) also declined sharply, the general price level (P) should have risen. In fact, during the quarter-century following the Black Death, much of Europe did experience very considerable inflations. As David Herlihy has so aptly observed, "men were dying, but coins were not."[8]

But Postan's fundamental contention that late-medieval Europe possessed vast accumulated stocks of immortal moneys, more than adequate for a contracted, depopulated economy, has recently been undermined by several studies contending that medieval coins were indeed highly perishable. The principal authors, C. C. Patterson, Marion Archibald, and Nicholas Mayhew, thus suggest a second reason for a late-medieval monetary contraction, a more powerful one when combined with the mining-slump thesis: precious metal losses from normal wear and tear in coinage circulation, from ship-

8. David Herlihy, *Medieval and Renaissance Pistoia: The Social History of an Italian Town, 1200-1430* (New Haven-London, 1967), pp. 125, 122-47; Karl Helleiner, "Population Movement and Agrarian Depression in the Later Middle Ages," *Canadian Journal of Economics and Political Science*, XV (1949); E. J. Hamilton, *Money, Prices, and Wages in Valencia, Aragon, and Navarre, 1351-1500* (Cambridge, Mass. 1936), appendices; Léopold Genicot, "Crisis: From Middle Ages to Modern Times," *Cambridge Economic History of Europe*, I (rev. edn. 1966), 677-94 (tables 5-17); Harry Miskimin, *Money, Prices, and Foreign Exchange in Fourteenth Century France* (New Haven, 1963), pp. 53-71; Schreiner, "Wages," pp. 69-73; E. H. Phelps Brown and Sheila Hopkins, "Seven Centuries of the Prices of Consumables, Compared with Builders' Wage-Rates," *Economica*, new ser. XXIII (1956) [reprinted in *Essays in Economic History*, ed. E. M. Carus-Wilson, II (London, 1962), 193-6.]

wrecks, from unretrieved hoards, indeed from "losses in the fire" during recoinages.[9] Patterson believes that the average annual rate of precious metal loss from such causes was as much as 1.0 percent per annum. Subsequently Mayhew, citing earlier analyses of Sir John Craig, adopted a much more conservative estimate of 0.2 percent weight loss per annum; nevertheless he calculates that in early fourteenth century England such a loss rate would have meant that "seven tons of silver vanished into thin air through wear alone every decade."[10] Consequently these authors contend that unless a country's money supply was frequently and abundantly replenished with fresh mintings it would inevitably, and over a century drastically, diminish.

With insufficient mining production, was late-medieval Europe collectively able to fuel its mints and fully replenish its coinage supplies from its balance of payments with the rest of the world? The simple answer, according to many historians, is no. Indeed in the most recent analysis of this issue, John Day contends that the principal if not sole cause of the late-medieval "Great Bullion Famine" was a severe balance of payments deficit with the Islamic Near East.[11] I believe Day's thesis—in fact a quite traditional thesis—to be a thoroughly sound one, particularly because it can be buttressed by some additional statistical evidence from the meticulously researched publications of the eminent Orientalist Prof. Eliyahu Ashtor.[12] By his calculations for the later fifteenth century, Western Europe's annual deficit amounted to about 400,000 gold ducats: the difference between total oriental imports from Syria and Egypt valued at 660,000 ducats per annum on the average (= 2,345 kg. pure gold) and total European exports to the Islamic East valued at an annual average of 260,000 ducats (=925 kg. gold). For the second half of the fifteenth century, that average annual specie drain to the East, the equivalent of 1,420 kg. pure gold or about 16,500 kg. pure silver, exceeded by some 30 percent the *combined* annual average mint outputs of both England and the Burgundian Low Countries: the equivalent of 1,093 kg. gold or 12,703 kg. silver (Tables 7, 9).

9. Patterson, "Silver Stocks," pp. 205-34; Mayhew, "Numismatic Evidence," pp. 1-15; Marion Archibald, "Wastage from Currency: Long-Cross and the Recoinage of 1279," in *Edwardian Monetary Affairs (1279-1344)*, ed. Nicholas Mayhew (*British Archeological Reports* 36, Oxford, 1977), pp. 167-86; Sir John Craig, *The Mint: A History of the London Mint from A. D. 278 to 1948* (Cambridge, 1953), pp. xvi, 60.

10. Mayhew, "Numismatic Evidence," p. 3. It should be noted, however, that an annual average weight loss of 0.2 percent would mean a loss of 1.83 percent in the first decade—not 2.0 percent; and in the second decade, a loss of 3.32 percent, not 4.0 percent.

11. Day, "Bullion Famine," pp. 5-12, 35-40.

12. For the following see Eliyahu Ashtor, *Les métaux précieux et la balance des payements du Proche-Orient à la basse époque* (Paris, 1971), pp. 65-96; Ashtor, "The Venetian Supremacy in Levantine Trade: Monopoly or Pre-Colonialism?," *Journal of European Economic History*, III (1974), 5-53; Ashtor, "The Volume of Levantine Trade in the Later Middle Ages (1370-1498)," *Ibid.*, IV (1975), 573-612; Ashtor, "Observations on Venetian Trade in the Levant in the XIVth Century," *Ibid.*, V (1976), 533-86; Ashtor, *A Social and Economic History of the Near East in the Middle Ages* (London, 1976), pp. 319-31. See also Day, "Bullion Famine," pp. 7, 10-11. The Venetian ducat = 3.56 g. pure gold.

Nevertheless, before agreeing that such a specie outflow produced or contributed to a bullion famine in late-medieval Europe, we must answer a number of rather crucial questions. First, since Day himself dates the onset of this "bullion famine" only from the 1390s—much later than does any other monetarist historian in this debate—must we assume therefore that trade deficits with the Near East became a serious problem only from that era? That question, with its overtones of negative doubt, naturally arises from a long tradition of historical scholarship maintaining that Europe in almost every era from the ancient Classical period to modern times has suffered a chronic payments deficit with "The East"—with the possible exception of the mid-thirteenth century.[13] Ashtor, however, does cautiously suggest that the European deficits resulted in serious specie drainages only from the late fourteenth or early fifteenth centuries. His investigations indicate that Venetian imports from Syria and Egypt grew by at least a third during the fifteenth century.[14] Even though some of that expansion was at the expense of other ports in the Levantine trade, principally Genoa, Marseilles, and Barcelona, western specie exports may well have expanded considerably, to reach those very high levels in the late fifteenth century. Secondly, if western imports of oriental goods evidently increased during the fifteenth century, did European exports to the Near East also decline? Both Ashtor and Prof. Abraham Udovitch have concluded that the Levantine market in this era seriously diminished as the result of depopulations, deflation, and depression that afflicted Mamluk Egypt in particular. Ashtor notes that Italian exports to the Near East changed in their composition from higher priced goods to become "mainly olive oil, cheap and dried fruits, copper (for small coins), and cheap cloth." Udovitch believes that the Levant itself also suffered an overall balance of payments deficit with a growing outflow of specie to India and other Asian states, principally in payment for oriental luxury goods and spices—as much for domestic consumption as for re-export.[15] Prof. Jere Bacharach (in this volume) would also agree that Mamluk Egypt suffered from economic depressions and crises, a growing deficit in its balance of payments, severe monetary difficulties, a "silver famine" in particular, from ca. 1400. Bacharach also ascribes part of Mamluk Egypt's

13. See Robert Lopez, "Back to Gold, 1252," *Economic History Review*, 2nd ser. IX (1956), 219-41; and also in this volume Thomas Walker, "The Italian Gold Revolution of 1252: Shifting Currents in the Pan-Mediterranean Flow of Gold" and Louise Robbert, "Monetary Flows: Venice, 1150 to 1400 A.D."

14. See n. 12 above, especially Ashtor's "Volume of Levantine Trade," pp. 605-12; "Venetian Supremacy," pp. 5-17, 23-40, 46-53.

15. A. L. Udovitch, "England to Egypt, 1350-1500," *Studies in the Economic History of the Middle East*, ed. M. A. Cook (London, 1970), pp. 115-28: Ashtor, "Venetian Supremacy," and his *Economic History*, pp. 280-331. In his *Métaux précieux* (1971), pp. 13, 41-53, 97-110, Ashtor had however attributed the increasingly severe monetary scarcity of fifteenth-century Egypt to Mamluk military expenditures abroad and especially to hoarding, not to the balance of trade, which he believed remained favourable overall for the Levant. But subsequent views expressed in "Volume of Levantine Trade" (1975) are more in accordance with Udovitch's (see p. 612).

balance of payments deficit to imports of European manufactured goods, in apparent contradiction of Ashtor's observations.[16] But the Levant was much more than just Egypt; and if fifteenth-century Egypt was as economically depressed and crisis-ridden as all these authorites state, its market could hardly have consumed enough European goods to offset Europe's evident deficits.

Next, one must inquire whether Western Europe had earlier been able to finance its (previously smaller) trade deficits with the Levant from trade surpluses with other parts of the world; and then found itself unable to earn such surpluses, from the later fourteenth century. In particular did Italian revenues from their trade with Tunisia, the Maghreb, and Morocco—once Europe's chief source of gold—diminish in the later Middle Ages?[17] Did other indigenous African factors sharply diminish the flow of 'Sudanese' gold from the Niger basin: in particular, as Day contends, the disintegration of the Mali Empire and nomadic disruptions of Saharan trade routes, from the later fourteenth century?[18] Furthermore, did Western Europe also develop a trade deficit with the eastern Baltic and Russia, especially during the fifteenth century, in purchasing grain, lumber, naval stores, and luxury furs, while failing to expand its textile exports?[19] Day himself believes that, although Europe's growing balance of payments deficit with the Near East remained the principal cause of the late-medieval monetary contraction, that scarcity became an acute "bullion famine" only from the 1390s when the combination of a severe diminution in Sudanese gold supplies and the worsening European mining slump further reduced precious metal stocks.

Another vigorous proponent of the thesis of a late-medieval bullion famine who assigns an even greater responsibility to Europe's balance of payments deficit with the East, indeed the rest of the world, is Prof. Harry Miskimin, also a contributor to this volume.[20] Of all the participants in the current debate he is the most original. For he offers a tightly organized economic model that explains *why* that balance of payments deficit became so

16. Jere Bacharach, "Circassion Monetary History: Silver," *Numismatic Chronicle*, 7th ser. XI (1972), 267-81; Bacharach, "The Dinar versus the Ducat," *International Journal of Middle East Studies*, IV (1973), 77-96; Bacharach, "Monetary Movements in Egypt, 1171-1517" in this volume; Boaz Shoshan, "Exchange-Rate Policies in Fifteenth-Century Egypt," forthcoming (draft version kindly communicated to me, 1981).

17. See Lopez, "Back to Gold," pp. 232-40; Bloch, "Problem of Gold," pp. 212-18; Ashtor, *Métaux précieux* (n. 12), pp. 65-96; Marian Malowist, "Quelques observations sur le commerce de l'or dans le Soudan occidentale au moyen âge," *Annales: E. S. C.*, XXV (1970), 1630-6; E. W. Bovill, *The Golden Trade of the Moors*, 2nd ed. (London, 1968), pp. 13-44, 79-131.

18. Day, "Bullion Famine," pp. 36-40.

19. As suggested by Miskimin in "England to Egypt," pp. 102-04 and in his *Economy* (n. 1), pp. 138-42. See also Artur Attman, *The Russian and Polish Markets in International Trade, 1500-1650* (Goteborg, 1973), pp. 103-93 (especially 103-18 on influxes of specie into Russia from the 11th century).

20. See the works of Miskimin cited in n. 1 above; and also in this volume, his "Money and Money Movements in France and England at the End of the Middle Ages."

severe, from perhaps the mid-fourteenth century, in the context of a thesis that also seeks to explain the nature of the late-medieval "Great Depression." He has adroitly avoided the pitfalls of other, earlier monetarists such as W. C. Robinson, who rashly argued (1959) that an earlier monetary contraction, ca. 1290-ca. 1330, was directly responsible for that Depression.[21] His arguments were devastatingly demolished by Postan, who has long maintained, just as strongly, that demographic decline, various fourteenth-century dislocations and other "real" factors were instead the chief culprits—and that the Depression commenced well before the Black Death of 1348.[22] In almost full accordance with Postan's thesis, Miskimin also assigns prime responsibility to demographic decline, though much more to the Black Death, demonstrating with economic models how falling population first produced a European-wide agrarian depression, whose chief economic consequence was to alter the barter terms of trade sharply in favour of the urban industrial sector, thus "making it a magnet for the nation's bullion." Without contradicting the logic of the Postan thesis, he further argued that another, more immediate consequence of the mid-century depopulations was to increase per capita wealth, in particular permitting some survivors to become very prosperous from inherited cash balances. Miskimin contends that the general reaction of such survivors to the various plagues and other catastrophes of this era was to spend those cash balances rapidly in a spirit of unbridled hedonism. The previously discussed inflations following the Black Death are certainly evidence supporting his thesis. Miskimin's model in particular seeks to demonstrate that such a hedonistic consumption pattern, as it became firmly implanted in late-medieval European society, led to an increased importation of costly luxury goods: from Italy into northern Europe, and from the Near East into Europe as a whole, chiefly by Italian trade. The result was "a growing outflow of bullion that in turn generated the monetary shortage so much commented upon after the Black Death." Miskimin's ultimate conclusion is that a protracted, worsening monetary scarcity exacerbated and prolonged the medieval "Great Depression" into the late fifteenth century.[23] This second part of his thesis has not, of course, won favour with the "real school" followers of Postan, who firmly deny that any monetary factors contributed

21. Robinson, "Money, Population, and Economic Change," pp. 63-76, followed by Postan's devastating "Note," pp. 77-82.

22. See above n. 7, and also M. M. Postan, "Some Economic Evidence of Declining Population in the Later Middle Ages," *Economic History Review,* 2nd ser. II (1950), 221-46 [reprinted in his *Essays* (n. 7), pp. 186-213]; Postan, "Medieval Agrarian Society in Its Prime: England," *Cambridge Economic History,* I (2nd edn. 1966), 560-70; Postan, *The Medieval Economy and Society: An Economic History of Britain, 1100-1500* (London, 1972), pp. 27-40, 224-46. See also n. 24 below.

23. Quotations from Miskimin, "Monetary Movements," p. 490. Some additional support for Miskimin's theses of the "inheritance effect" and "hedonistic consumption pattern," along with a more highly skewed income distribution after the depopulations, can be found in Herlihy, *Pistoia* (n. 8), pp. 86-105, 134-44; and in R. S. Lopez, "Hard Times and Investment in Culture," *The Renaissance: A Symposium* (New York, 1953), pp. 19-32.

to that Depression.[24] But such a debate, beyond the scope of this study, cannot be resolved here—or indeed elsewhere, I suspect.

Miskimin's thesis, so directly based upon English evidence, in particular contradicts Postan's assertion that late-medieval England consistently enjoyed favourable trade balances, so that there was "every reason why silver should have continued to be imported."[25] More recently Terence Lloyd has supported Postan's contentions, at least for most of the fourteenth century. I have found Lloyd's analysis of the English customs accounts to be both brilliant and provocative; but having myself worked with the enrolled customs accounts in the London Public Record Office from the 1270s to the 1520s I cannot accept his conclusions for reasons that I have elaborated elsewhere.[26] In any event, Lloyd himself admits that England's "favourable" trade balances were probably diminishing from the 1360s; and he thus implicitly also admits the possibility that England did suffer trade deficits in the fifteenth century. For in that century England's chief exports, raw wool and woollen cloths, indisputably suffered a severe decline, despite temporary upsurges in the 1420s and early 1440s. Such exports reached their dismal nadir in the 1460s, with an aggregate volume that was only 47 percent of the exports achieved in that Indian Summer boom of the early 1390s—and just 38 percent of the late 1350s' export volume.[27]

While it remains impossible to make definitive statistical assertions about English balance of payments in the late Middle Ages, Miskimin did support his contentions with impressive and voluminous citations of sumptuary, anti-luxury, anti-Italian, and bullionist legislation. Indeed from both official ordinances and popular writings one can amplify his list quite considerably. In my view, the period of most intense bullionist legislation was from the 1360s, when Parliament first banned the export of both precious metals without royal licences, to about the 1490s.[28] As early as 1381, a parliamentary commission concluded that a combination of foreign coinage debasements

24. See in particular John Hatcher, *Plague, Population, and the English Economy, 1348-1530* (London, 1977), pp. 47-54; and M. M. Postan and John Hatcher, "Population and Class Relations in Feudal Society," *Past and Present,* No. 78 (1978), 24-37.

25. Postan, "Trade of Medieval Europe," pp. 212-13.

26. T. H. Lloyd, "Overseas Trade and the English Money Supply in the Fourteenth Century," *Edwardian Monetary Affairs (1279-1344),* ed. Nicholas Mayhew (Oxford, 1977), pp. 96-124; John H. Munro, "Monetary Contraction and Industrial Change in the Late-Medieval Low Countries, 1335-1500," in *Coinage in the Low Countries (880-1500): Third Oxford Symposium on Coinage and Monetary History,* ed. Nicholas Mayhew (*BAR* International 54, Oxford, 1979), pp. 97-8, 126 nn. 13-14.

27. Calculated from E. M. Carus-Wilson and Olive Coleman, eds. *England's Export Trade, 1275-1547* (Oxford, 1963). Such a decline could not have been offset by higher values for wool and cloth, nor by wool export duties, which were already at virtually their highest levels by the late 1330s, and which were in fact reduced in the 1420s. See n. 60.

28. John Munro, "Bullionism and the Bill of Exchange in England, 1272-1663: A Study in Monetary Management and Popular Prejudice," in *The Dawn of Modern Banking* (Center for Medieval and Renaissance Studies, University of California; New Haven-London, 1978), pp. 169-243.

(see below) and a deficit in the balance of payments—excessive imports, excessive papal taxes, and other specie transfers by Italian merchants—were primarily responsible for the current and truly serious dearth of coinage (Tables 1-3).[29] Parliament subsequently responded by enacting two sets of remedies to stem this (supposed) external haemorrhaging of specie. The most sophisticated and impressive were a series of Employment Acts (1390-1487) that required all aliens to export as much in value in English goods as they imported or remitted abroad by bills of exchange. More deleterious and counter-productive were several bullionist impositions on the wool export trade, which variously forced English merchants (Staplers) to exact full payment in ready English money and bullion to be coined at the king's mints.[30] There is no evidence that such measures were at all successful in protecting and augmenting England's money supplies; and by often hindering trade seriously they may actually have curbed English bullion inflows. But such legislation remains very significant in demonstrating late-medieval England's very genuine concerns about the money supply—and in blaming Italian importers for that dearth.

Further evidence that both England and the cross-Channel Low Countries experienced chronic balance of payments deficits with Italy in the later fourteenth and fifteenth centuries can be found in the late Raymond De Roover's analyses of Italian commercial and bills of exchange transactions. But he also discovered that Flanders often enjoyed a payments surplus in its Spanish trade, thus permitting some merchants to settle Italian debts by tri-lateral bills that drew on accumulated credits in Spain.[31] Yet it hardly seems likely that Spanish trade could compare in value with the Italian trade of this era, to permit north-western Europe as a whole to balance its deficits with the rest of the Mediterranean—above all, the Near East![32]

As sympathetic as I am, however, to the Miskimin thesis on specie outflows, I would not ignore the importance, albeit much lesser importance, of other factors in explaining a late-medieval monetary contraction. Apart from the two previously discussed, the European mining slump and the constant "leakage" from physical losses of metal, there are two more factors

29. *Rotuli Parliamentorum*, III, 126-27: nos. 1-2. See Munro, "Bullionism," pp. 169-90 for its long-term significance.

30. Munro, "Bullionism," pp. 169-243; J. H. Munro, *Wool, Cloth, and Gold: The Struggle for Bullion in Anglo-Burgundian Trade, 1340-1478* (Brussels-Toronto, 1973), chapters 1, 2, 4; Eileen Power, "The Wool Trade in the Fifteenth Century," in *Studies in English Trade in the Fifteenth Century*, ed. E. Power and M. Postan (London, 1933), 79-90.

31. Raymond De Roover, "La balance commerciale entre les Pays Bas et l'Italie au XVe siècle," *Revue belge de philologie et d'histoire*, XXXVII (1959), 374-86; De Roover, *L'evolution de la lettre de change, XIVe-XVIIIe siècles* (Paris, 1953), pp. 64-5; De Roover, *The Bruges Money Market Around 1400* (Brussels, 1968).

32. See also Wendy Childs, *Anglo-Castilian Trade in the Later Middle Ages* (Manchester, 1978), chapters 3-4; G. A. Holmes, "Florentine Merchants in England, 1346-1436," *Economic History Review*, 2nd ser. XIII (1960), 193-208; E. B. Fryde, "Anglo-Italian Commerce in the Fifteenth Century," *Revue belge de philologie et d'histoire*, L (1972), 345-55.

to consider, both variations on one theme: hoarding and other circumstances that reduced coinage velocity; and an increased industrial use of precious metals. According to J. D. A. Thompson and others, proportionately more European coin hoards can be attributed to the late Middle Ages, the later fourteenth century in particular, than to the adjacent eras.[33] Yet for the specific shorter period of 1440-1465, which Day and others (myself included) believe to be the most severe phase of the bullion famine, very few coin hoards have been documented.[34] Certainly in the later fourteenth and early fifteenth centuries hoarding can be regarded as perfectly natural reactions to the various plagues and epidemics, famines, wars, peasant jacqueries and urban rebellions, economic dislocations and general insecurity that afflicted so much of Europe. Indeed one would expect to find a significant decline in coinage velocity in general in late-medieval Europe with such depopulations, such a large drop in the number of spenders, with market contractions and periodically severe depressions. Hence the previous question in revised form: did coinage velocity fall just passively in response to this economic contraction, in direct proportion to the decline in the volume of transactions (T); or did a fall in V exacerbate that economic contraction? Thus increased hoarding may have been again a rational response to the deflations (however caused) that beset many parts of Europe from the 1370s and 1380s. But extensive hoarding would then have accelerated that deflation, which in turn would have squeezed profit margins, bred a pessimistic business psychology, and curtailed investments and production. In particular, monetary scarcity and deflation would have constricted investment by increasing the real burden of debt, both the cost of previously borrowed capital in the repayments and of future borrowing in possibly higher interest rates.

Furthermore, various government reactions to depressed trade, monetary scarcity, and fiscal stringency in protectionist and bullionist legislation, especially the almost universally imposed bans on precious metal exports, undoubtedly interfered with the international flow of specie and depressed coinage velocities in the late Middle Ages. On the other hand such bullionist restrictions undoubtedly also encouraged a greater use of bills of exchange, letters

33. J. D. A. Thompson, *Inventory of British Coin Hoards, 600-1500 A.D.* (Oxford, 1956), p. xxvi and passim. See also Jean Lafaurie, *Les monnaies des rois de France: Hughes Capet à Louis XII* (Paris, 1951); Peter Spufford, *Monetary Problems and Policies in the Burgundian Netherlands, 1433-1496* (Leiden, 1970), pp. 55-73 (but see also Appendix D: Coin Hoards, 1425-40, pp. 203-13); Day, "Bullion Famine," pp. 44-5. See also Erik Aerts and Herman Van der Wee, *The Leuven Coin Find of 1851 and the Currency of the Burgundian Netherlands in the Middle of the Fifteenth Century: A Case Study* (Katholieke Universiteit te Leuven, Centrum voor Economische Studiën, 1980, in mimeo), pp. 1-37.

34. For late medieval price trends and variations, see the sources cited in n. 8 above; and also, for the Low Countries, Herman Van der Wee, *The Growth of the Antwerp Market and the European Economy, Fourteenth to Sixteenth Centuries,* 3 vols. (The Hague, 1963), I (Tables, from the 1360s) and III (Graphs); and his "Prices and Wages as Development Variables: A Comparison between England and the Southern Netherlands, 1400-1700," *Acta Historiae Neerlandicae,* X (1978), 58-78.

obligatory, and other credit instruments to obviate the physical transport of specie; and such credit instruments would admittedly have increased coinage velocity by economizing on the use of specie within countries. But surely the use of such international credit instruments in the fourteenth and fifteenth centuries was largely restricted to a very few international centres dominated by Italian commerce. It has yet to be proven that the use of credit instruments, most of them still tied to specie payments, expanded sufficiently and universally to counteract fully the various forces of monetary contraction.[35]

Such arguments concerning hoarding and coinage velocity are not, however, necessarily a contradiction of the Miskimin thesis, provided that one specifies differences between periods and social classes. Thus the widespread, hedonistic spending sprees in the inflationary post-Black Death era of ca. 1350-1375 may have been followed by a dolorous parsimony and hoarding amongst some of the population in that subsequent, deflationary era from the late 1370s. Some segments of society—nobles, upper echelons of the Church, gentry, wealthy bourgeoisie, even "kulak" peasants may have continued to engage in conspicuous consumption of imported luxuries throughout both eras. Poorer peasants and artisans, on the other hand, likely responded to crises and chronically bleak times by increased hoarding: the more so that plagues, epidemics, and wars became more fixed in the rhythm of later medieval life.

Furthermore, the increased industrial consumption of gold and silver in church and other building construction and in resplendent luxury display, including brocaded textiles, which so many art historians of late-medieval Europe have described, is fully in accord with the Miskimin thesis.[36] Such display still constitutes hoarding of metals, albeit in a more aesthetic and useful form. Of course hoarding, even in this respect, differs sharply from all other forms of metal losses discussed earlier in that hoarded metals can easily be restored to monetary circulation as minted coins (with some obvious exceptions). As the mint accounts discussed below will demonstrate, and as Postan rightly reminds us, there were occasional, perhaps frequent circumstances at times, in some regions, that stimulated or forced dishoarding:

35. Even for the 16th-17th centuries, Frank Spooner contends that "the arrival and distribution of bullion . . . was enough to set in motion a series of credit transactions under the virtual monopoly of the great fairs and commercial centers. And yet the opposite conditions could also occur: an unexpected delay in the arrivals of bullion could precipitate a sudden spate of bankruptcies." *The International Economy and Monetary Movements in France, 1493-1725* (Cambridge, Mass. 1972), p. 3. See the writings of De Roover in n. 31 above; Munro, "Bullionism," pp. 169-243; Paul Einzig, *History of Foreign Exchange*, 2nd edn. (London, 1970), pp. 76-112; Michael Postan, "Credit in Medieval Trade' and 'Private Financial Instruments in Medieval England," both reprinted in his *Medieval Trade and Finance* (Cambridge, 1973), pp. 1-27, 28-64.

36. See Miskimin, *Economy*, pp. 92-104, 134-44; the works of Lopez and Herlihy in n. 23 above; Johan Huizinga, *The Waning of the Middle Ages* (London, 1926), pp. 140-52; Philip Ziegler, *The Black Death* (London, 1969), pp. 240-88; Françoise Piponnier, *Costume et vie sociale: la cour d'Anjou, XIVe-XVe siècle* (Paris, 1970), chapters 7-10; Agnes Geijer, *A History of Textile Art* (London, 1979), pp. 141-55.

government taxes and forced loans, purveyances, etc. in time of war, ransoms, booty and plunder, and even those late-medieval cyclical movements that temporarily restored some prosperity, as in the 1420s.

Short-term and long-term forces in international bullion flows

Insofar as we all must rely heavily on mint and coinage statistics for evidence of late-medieval Europe's monetary contraction and bullion flows, we must distinguish carefully between those forces that merely circulated metals amongst regional mints, or caused only temporary regional coinage scarcities, and those that produced a permanent outflow of bullion from Europe. And insofar as we assert that a drainage of specie to the East was the major if not the sole cause of that contraction, we must understand how the mechanics of minting influenced the form or nature of those specie outflows.

First we return to the issue of "leakage," of physical deterioration of coins through wear and tear, and especially also from the nefarious but common practice of clipping and "sweating" coins to extract bullion. Such metallic losses could further contract the domestic money supply by curtailing, even halting, domestic mint production and by instigating bullion outflows. Thus since silver coins in particular normally circulated by "tale," at decreed face values, and not by weight, merchants would collectively respond to a significant presence of underweight or fraudulent coins in circulation by discounting the entire coinage, bad and good alike: that is, by bidding up all prices. Once the market price for bullion had risen above the mint price, the premium that coins normally commanded over bullion, by virtue of their portability and convenience, would disappear. Without the premium, necessary to cover at least the minting costs (brassage and seignorage), merchants would instead export their bullion to foreign mints offering better prices, and would cull out good, full weight coins for foreign trade.[37] The coinage standard and the money supply would thus continue to diminish until the prince either: (1) imposed a total recoinage on his subjects at their expense, as a *renforcement* (strengthening) that would also further contract the money supply—with better but necessarily fewer coins; or more likely, (2) he debased the coinage in weight, perhaps also in fineness, to match the inferior standard of the current circulating coinage. Such a debasement, in striking more but inferior coins from the same amount of metal, necessarily raised the mint's money-of-account price for bullion (and the value of metal in the coin) above the market price, thereby restoring the coinage premium. If the new mint price was

37. See Feavearyear, *Pound Sterling* (n. 1), pp. 10-15; John Munro, "An Aspect of Medieval Public Finance: The Profits of Counterfeiting in the Fifteenth-Century Low Countries," *Revue belge de numismatique,* CXVIII (1972), 127-48; N.J. Mayhew and D. R. Walker, "Crockards and Pollards: Imitation and the Problem of Fineness in a Silver Coinage," *Edwardian Monetary Affairs,* ed. N.J. Mayhew (Oxford, 1977), pp. 125-46; and Mavis Mate, 'Monetary Problems in England, 1272-1307', *British Numismatic Journal,* XLI (1972), 37-45 (with analyses of such discounting and consequent price increases).

raised high enough, it would succeed in attracting foreign bullion and specie as well. Foreign princes, faced with a consequent outflow of bullion and a closure of their own mints, could normally respond by similar debasements. But debasements were frequently undertaken also for aggressive as well as for these defensive reasons: to produce seignorage revenues, as the prince's own tax on coinage.[38] Unfortunately, debasements, whether defensive or aggressive in origin, provoked retaliatory *guerres monétaires*. Indeed Western Europe, after having enjoyed a century of monetary stability until Philip the Fair's aggressive debasements of 1295-1305, was thereupon plagued by two centuries of such monetary wars and mint manipulations.[39]

One aspect of medieval mint manipulation that is crucially important for understanding the nature of international bullion flows was the deliberate alteration of the so-called mint-ratio in order to attract either gold or silver by "favouring" the one metal over the other. The mint could do so either by physically debasing the one coinage *more* than the other, in weight and/or fineness, by physically strengthening that coinage in question *less* than the other (in a *renforcement*), or simply by raising its money-of-account and exchange value. But any influx of the one metal so "favoured" would normally be mirrored, though not necessarily in proportion, by an efflux of the other metal in effecting international payments. For that other metal would now be relatively "favoured" by those foreign mints (and money-changers) that had maintained the former mint-ratio, or had raised it in favour of that other metal. Such flows would seem to be a reflection of Gresham's Law in which the cheap, i.e., debased and "favoured," metal drives out the dear metal.

Thus in that seminal article of 1967 discussed in the editor's introduction, "Back to Gold—and Silver," Andrew Watson contended that late-medieval Europe, by adopting strongly pro-gold mint ratios, minted large quantities of this metal, while suffering large outflows of silver to the Islamic Near East, whose mints generally "favoured" that metal just as strongly. Watson also

38. See A. Blanchet and A. Dieudonné, *Manuel de numismatique française*, II (Paris, 1916), chapters 3-7; A. Grunzweig, "Les incidences internationales des mutations monétaires de Philippe le Bel," *Le moyen âge*, LIX (1953), 117-72; Cazelles, "Mutations," pp. 83-105; Girard, "Guerre monétaire;" Hans Van Werveke, "Currency Manipulation in the Middle Ages: The Case of Louis de Male, Count of Flanders," *Transactions of the Royal Historical Society*, 4th ser. XXXI (1949), 115-27 [reprinted in his *Miscellanea Mediaevalia* (Ghent, 1968), pp. 255-67]; Munro, *Wool, Cloth, and Gold* (n. 30), chapter 1. In that work, on pp. 14-23, I had argued against the theses of Carlo Cipolla (n. 3) and Henri Laurent (n. 1) that later medieval coinage debasements were undertaken chiefly to remedy scarcities of specie. Citing Postan et al to deny that later-medieval Europe ever experienced any such scarcity, I instead contended that the princes' principal motivation for aggressive, autonomous debasement was to acquire seignorage profits. Obviously my subsequent researches, providing me with a greater spatial and temporal perspective, have forced me to alter my views on late-medieval money supplies, by 180 degrees; nevertheless, I still maintain my former views on the principal causes of aggressive and defensive debasements.

39. Watson, "Back to Gold," pp. 1-34 (esp. 31-4).

contended that, while late-medieval Europe might have experienced a "silver famine" of its own making, there was no general monetary scarcity, as silver outflows were generally marched by gold inflows. On both issues, Watson's views have been attacked by several historians—not surprisingly by Miskimin in particular.[40] I myself have argued that any medieval international arbitrage trade in precious metals had to surmount a number of quite formidable barriers.[41] In the first place, no mint would act as a market to exchange metals freely in either bullion or coined form. The operative mint ratio was not that generally given in the literature—the ratio of official coined values (the *traite* ratio)—nor of the two mint prices for bullion: instead it was the ratio of the mint's price for bullion in the one metal to the coined or *traite* value of the other metal, to take account of the mintage fees. Furthermore any merchant seeking to trade in metals would have had to pay money changers' fees and transport costs; and he would have had to face the prospect of receiving worn or clipped coins in return; or of having his bullion and coin seized by customs inspectors and frontier guards, or by pirates and brigands— would have had to pay insurance costs, in effect. Consequently the difference between two countries' effective mint ratios had to be very large indeed before merchants could have hoped to cover all these costs and to profit from a purely arbitrage trade in precious metals. Therefore I believe that very, very rarely indeed were such mint-ratio alterations and arbitrage trades in themselves able to instigate international bullion flows in the late-medieval world.[42]

Nevertheless it would be equally wrong, in my view, to dismiss the significance of mint-ratios in medieval bullion flows. For even small differences in such ratios, or even *traite* ratios, indisputably had a powerful influence in determining which of the two metals would predominate in a country's foreign trade receipts and expenditures, and thus in its annual mint outputs. For merchants buying goods in several countries would seek to have

40. Miskimin, *Money*, pp. 117-19 (on this aspect of Gresham's Law) and "Money and Money Movements" in this volume; Ashtor, *Métaux précieux* (n. 12), pp. 31-6 (though a qualified agreement with Watson on p. 51); Ashtor, "Recent Research on Levantine Trade," *Journal of European Economic History*, II (1973), 193; see also Day, "Bullion Famine," pp. 5-6. But a position similar to Watson's, though for a more limited time and area, can be found in R. H. Bautier, "L'or et l'argent en Occident de la fin du XIIIe siècle au début du XIVe siècle," *Académie des inscriptions et belles lettres: comptes rendus* (1951), 169-74.

41. See John Munro, "Mint Policies, Ratios, and Outputs in the Low Countries and England, 1335-1420: Some Reflections on New Data," *Numismatic Chronicle*, 8th ser. I (1981), 71-116 (especially Appendix A, 95-9); *Wool, Cloth, and Gold* (n. 30), pp. 29-32, and "Bullionism," pp. 185-7, in which I am much less resolute in denying that mint-ratio alterations could instigate bullion flows.

42. Watson (nn. 4, 39 above) does cite evidence, particularly from Jacques Coeur's trial of 1453 (pp. 20-2), to demonstrate that silver was being shipped to the Levant precisely to profit from such an arbitrage trade in metals; but the evidence does not prove that such bullion shipments were divorced from concurrent trading ventures in goods. See n. 41 above.

their gold and silver bullion coined in those mints offering the higher purchasing power for each metal. Thus their arbitrage profits would be realized not directly through an exchange of metals but indirectly through normal channels of international trade: exchanging metal for goods and ultimately goods for metal. In a recent article, I have sought to demonstrate this indirect arbitrage in an economic model employing actual trade, price, and coinage statistics for England and Flanders in 1396.[43] Eventually, one would suppose, the market would adjust the prices of both the metals and the goods, would impose equilibrium prices, to eliminate such disparities and thus the arbitrage profits. But with the primitive transport and communication facilities of the late Middle Ages, with so many impediments to free trade, these very imperfect markets made equilibrium adjustments very, very slowly indeed.

Finally, to complete this theoretical section, we must realize that the effect of any given debasement (or *renforcement*) upon mint outputs, the country's "net" money supply, and international bullion flows are all quite unpredictable. The consequences of a debasement could depend upon a complex combination of the following factors: (1) how much of the current coinage was actually surrendered and reminted into the more plentiful but inferior new coinage; (2) how much domestic bullion from dishoarding, and how much foreign bullion and specie would be attracted by higher mint prices (as in the previous analysis); (3) how much of a balance of trade surplus might then be earned, if any, from any increase in exports and any reduction in imports resulting from an accompanying fall in the exchange rate; (4) how much inflation then ensued from the debasement and increase in the money supply to curb exports and encourage imports; (5) how much of the newly debased coinage might be more profitably spent abroad, in places as yet unaware of the debasement, especially if such debased coins were counterfeits of much more respectable earlier coins or of good, popular foreign coins:[44] (6) how much of the other, now "disfavoured" metal was sent abroad; (7) how much inflation and monetary instability from excessive debasements encouraged hoarding or a flight of capital. All of these caveats must be kept clearly in mind in considering the following, final section.

Monetary contraction and bullion outflows: Trends in the mint outputs of late-medieval England and the Low Countries

Faute de mieux, we are all necessarily dependent upon mint production statistics for quantitative evidence of late-medieval monetary contractions and bullion flows. In the Appendix, I discuss a number of technical problems in utilizing these mint data; and explain why I believe that my mint statistics

43. Munro, "Mint Policies," pp. 95-9.

44. On this point see Munro, *Wool, Cloth, and Gold* (n. 30), chapter 2; and Munro, "Profits of Counterfeiting."

for England (1235-1500) and the Low Countries (1335-1500) are more complete and accurate than those that were employed in the articles of Harry Miskimin (1964) and John Day (1978). My English mint statistics, furthermore, cover a far longer time-span than did Miskimin's (1273-1470) and Day's (1340-1500).

A comparison of the mint outputs for these two regions in the late Middle Ages is particularly illuminating because of the similarities and differences in their economic and monetary experiences. On the one hand, their economies were closely intertwined, more so than with any of their other neighbours.[45] The Low Countries were by far the most important market for English wools, and by the mid-fifteenth century also became the most important market for English woolens as well (except in Flanders, where they had long been banned). Through the fairs of Flanders and Brabant, Bruges and Antwerp, the Low Countries were also one of England's chief sources of imported manufactured goods. On the other hand, their "states" of economic development were certainly different. The Low Countries were the most highly industrialized, commercialized, and urbanized region in northern Europe; England, despite its important cloth industry and trade, was still essentially agrarian. Furthermore, the monetary experiences of the two regions were also radically different. England's was indeed unique. No other late-medieval European country (of importance) maintained stable coinages for such long periods—fifty to sixty years at a time, so rarely engaged in mint-manipulation, and so consistently favoured a gold coinage, from its adoption in the 1340s. The Low Countries had a much more typically medieval European monetary history, with cycles of often frenetic debasements, sometimes terminating in brutal *renforcements*, and with periodic alterations of the mint-ratio to favour one or the other metal. Consequently, we wish to determine if these economically related regions demonstrated similar long term trends in their mint outputs, despite different stages of economic development and despite their radical monetary differences.

In testing a hypothesis of monetary contraction and bullion outflows, we must use the mint statistics as only very general indicators of trends, since they can hardly serve as year-to-year statistical proxies of the money supply, for the reasons already explained. Above all, we must clearly distinguish between those mint outputs that resulted from balance of payments surpluses and from increased levels of economic activity on the one hand, and those, on the other hand, from mint-manipulations in debasements, *renforcements* and mint-ratio alterations. Sometimes the differences are obvious; sometimes the distinctions cannot be clearly made.

For England, with its remarkable monetary stability, the relatively few mint alterations are simply summarized: (1) recoinages to eliminate underweight and fraudulent coins in 1247-49, 1279-82, 1300-02, and 1421-22

45. See J. H. Munro, "The Costs of Anglo-Burgundian Interdependence," *Revue belge de philologie et d'historie*, XLI (1968), 1228-38; *Wool, Cloth, and Gold* (n. 30), pp. 1-10, 181-7.

(partially); and (2) coinage debasements in 1335, 1345-46, 1351, 1411, and 1464-65; only those of 1335 and 1411 were purely defensive. For Flanders and then the Burgundian Low Countries, as Table 10 summarizes, the forty-year period 1349-1389 was punctuated by 22 debasements of the gold coinage and 18 debasements of the silver, most of them aggressive, with one abortive *renforcement* in 1384. A highly successful if brutal *renforcement* was imposed in 1389-90 (gold by 41.7 percent and silver by 31.8 percent). Thereafter, Flanders maintained a perfectly stable, strong money policy (indeed with another small *renforcement* in 1409) until 1416.[46] From then until 1433, the Burgundian Low Countries suffered from another round of often drastic debasements (12 for gold, 7 for silver), especially in the years 1426-33. Then a *renforcement* and general unification of the Burgundian coinage in 1433-34 was followed by 33 years of strong, stable money, interrupted only in 1454 by a minor debasement of gold. During the last third of the century, from 1466 to 1497, the Low Countries were again plagued by aggressive debasements, 22 of them, especially during the misrule of Archduke Maximilian and the civil war years of ca. 1483-92. Two *renforcements* intervened, in 1484 and 1489; a final modest debasement of 1496 (adjusted 1497-1500) successfully ushered in a quarter-century of monetary stability (until February 1521).[47]

As a cursory examination of the tables and graphs reveals, all of these mint alterations were associated with some increases in coinage outputs, some great and some small. Indeed the truly massive English silver outputs following the recoinages of 1247-49, 1279-82, and 1300-02 are, so to speak, especially striking.[48] Certainly they produced far and away the largest silver outputs recorded in our entire series. But in this period England had no gold to compete with silver; and since English sterlings then served as an international medium of exchange in northern Europe, these large outputs may reflect for this reason an international demand for English silver coinage.[49] Nevertheless the generally high levels of coinage output, in terms of both kilograms of metal and sterling values, in the thirteenth century may be taken as evidence of that era's plentiful money supply.

46. Munro, "Mint Policies," pp. 78-95.

47. Spufford, *Monetary Problems,* pp. 141-6; Munro, *Wool, Cloth, and Gold,* pp. 65-180; Van der Wee, *Antwerp Market,* I, 127-8.

48. The thirteenth-century silver coinages and especially the outputs resulting from the recoinages of 1247-49 and 1279-82 are even greater than those indicated in Table 1, because we lack the accounts for a number of provincial mints. Marion Archibald has estimated that such missing provincial mints accounted for perhaps 50 percent of total English coinage in 1247-50; for about 5 percent, from 1250-1278; and for 20-25 percent from 1278 to 1290: "Wastage from Currency," pp. 167-86.

49. Jules Chautard, *Imitations des monnaies au type esterlin frappées en Europe pendant le XIIIe et XIVe siècle* (Nancy, 1871); S. E. Rigold, "The Trail of the Easterlings," *British Numismatic Journal,* XXVI (1949-51), 31-55; Mayhew and Walker, "Crockards and Pollards," pp. 125-46; N.J. Mayhew, "The Circulation and Imitation of Sterlings in the Low Countries," *Coinage in the Low Countries (880-1500),* ed. N. J. Mayhew (Oxford, 1979), pp. 54-68.

As the graph shows, there are three other major, if less impressive, coinage upsurges common to both England and the Low Countries; and these upsurges are only partly explained by mint policies: those of ca. 1350-70, ca. 1415-35, and ca. 1465-80. In each of them, coinage alterations initially played a significant role. For Flanders in particular, during the first of these upsurges, the mints' debasements were very drastic: gold by 36.5 percent and silver by 43.3 percent, from 1350 to 1369.[50] But the same cannot be said for England, which terminated its brief experimentation with aggressive debasement at the very outset of this period, in July 1351: thereafter England maintained a perfectly stable coinage for 60 years exactly, until 1411.[51] Nor can the Flemish debasements in themselves be called upon to explain the equally impressive English mint outputs, since all foreign coins imported into England had to be reminted anyway, whether they were good or bad.[52] Thus since the mint outputs for both countries in this period ca. 1350-70 are so very large and so remarkably similar, we must look for additional explanations. These should include the following: (1) the Miskimin thesis concerning the "inheritance effect" of the Black Death and subsequent depopulations: the aforementioned hedonistic spending sprees of inherited cash balances, associated with Death, Disaster, and Display; (2) a remarkably strong boom in both English wool and cloth exports and also in Flemish cloth production for most of this period: in part stimulated by devaluations, by English royal finances, especially royal intervention in the wool export trade to generate large revenues, and also by a general boom in the European economy;[53] (3) bullion flows from royal taxation and military expenditures in this very active phase of the Hundred Years War; (4) the profits of war and associated piracy, in ransom and plunder; (5) dishoardings periodically encouraged by these factors. Finally, since England had only just recently adopted a gold coinage (1344), fully establishing it in 1351, the veritable explosion in English gold

50. See Munro, "Mint Policies," pp. 76-8, 110-11 (Table 8); Van Werveke, "Currency Manipulation," pp. 255-67; and Tables 4-6, 10, below.

51. In January 1352, Parliament responded to Edward III's recent debasements (1344-51) by forbidding the crown to impair the coinage in any way (25 Ed. III stat. 5 c. 13, in *Statutes of the Realm,* I, 322; *Rot. Parl.* II, 240: n. 32). Subsequently, after a long and severe deterioration of the coinage, an influx of foreign counterfeits (Galley Halfpence), and "la graunde Escarcité de Money" finally forced the crown to adopt a defensive debasement, Henry IV first had to obtain Parliament's assent, in November 1411. (*Rot. Parl.* III, 658-9: no. 28; *S. R.* II, 163, 168). See Feavearyear, *Pound Sterling* (n. 1), pp. 15-39; Munro, "Bullionism," pp. 186-91.

52. See Munro, "Bullionism," pp. 187-96. One of the purposes of establishing the Calais mint in 1363 was to facilitate such recoinages of specie from Anglo-Flemish trade.

53. See Munro, "Low Countries," pp. 110-12, 138 (Table 1); Hans Van Werveke, "De economische en sociale gevolgen van de munt politiek der graven van Vlaanderen (1337-1433)" and his "Currency Manipulation" both in *Miscellanea Mediaevalia* (n. 38), pp. 243-54, 264-6; E. M. Carus-Wilson, "Trends in the Export of English Woollens in the Fourteenth Century," *Economic History Review,* 2nd ser. III (1950) [reprinted in her *Medieval Merchant Venturers* (London, 1954), pp. 247-52 (though I do not agree with all her references to Flanders).] Miskimin, furthermore, has shown that for France the years 1355-75 were also ones of very large coinage outputs: *Money,* pp. 87-8, 90-4, 100-15.

mint outputs might be regarded as that generational "one shot" coinage of England's long accumulated stocks of gold plate, jewelry, bullion, and foreign coins, some of which had already served a monetary function in the economy. But such a hypothesis could hardly apply to Flanders, where a gold coinage had been implanted much longer, since 1335.

For the second of these major coinage upsurges, somewhat similar explanations can be offered as for the first, except the "inheritance effect" thesis. For England, the initial major factor was undoubtedly the debasement (gold by 10 percent, silver by 16.7 percent) and general recoinage from 1411-12 which possibly took several years to complete. That was followed in 1421-22 by an official (though unverified) recoinage of all underweight or fraudulent specie.[54] For the Burgundian Low Countries, certainly the debasements of 1426-33 and the *renforcement* recoinages of 1433-34 again played a very major role in their large coinage outputs. But again, with such a similarity in the upsurges, we must look to additional factors, for both countries:[55] (1) a significant expansion in Anglo-Burgundian trade in general, following upon the English conquest of Normandy (1415-17), Burgundian seizure of Paris (1417), and their Treaty of Troyes alliance, in 1420; (2) a boom in the English cloth trade, while both the English wool trade and the Low Countries' textile industries temporarily halted a steep decline that had begun in the 1370s; (3) taxation and military expenditures in this very active phase of the Hundred Years' War; (4) coinage of booty and ransoms from both English and Burgundian campaigns in northern France; (5) for England, the re-opening of the Calais mint from July 1422 (closed since 1404). One of its chief tasks, following upon the partial recoinage of that year, was to prevent the importation of fraudulent coin by requiring that all foreign specie received from wool sales at the Calais Staple be reminted there into good English coin.[56] In 1430 the English crown, responding to Burgundian debasements and counterfeiting of English gold nobles, imposed its most onerous bullionist laws yet on the Calais Staple: forbidding the use of credit, requiring payment in good English coin for two thirds of the wool price, and in bullion for the remainder.[57] As Table 1 indicates, the Calais mint had been spectacularly successful from the very beginning, vastly exceeding the London Tower Mint in coinage outputs in the 1420s and early 1430s. But the 1430 bullion laws had only a very limited, short term success in maintaining coinage outputs. Insofar as they severely damaged the English wool trade, which plunged by over 50 percent, provoked a Burgundian ban on English cloth,

54. 9 Hen. V stat. 1 c. 11 in *S.R.* II, 208. The recoinage, principally of underweight gold nobles, was mintage-free.

55. See Munro, *Wool, Cloth, and Gold,* chapter 3; Munro, "Low Countries," pp. 112-14 and 151 (Table 15).

56. *Calendar of Patent Rolls, 1422-29,* p. 337; Munro, *Wool, Cloth, and Gold,* pp. 75-92.

57. 8 Hen. VI c. 18 in *S.R.* II, 254-5; *Rot. Parl.* IV, 359: no. 60. See Power, "Wool Trade," pp. 82-3; Munro, *Wool, Cloth, and Gold,* pp. 74-126; T. H. Lloyd, *The English Wool Trade in the Middle Ages* (Cambridge, 1977), pp. 257-72.

and then became an issue in the Anglo-Burgundian war of 1436-40, they were clearly self-defeating. Calais mint outputs dropped dramatically from 1433, ceasing entirely by 1440.[58] Other reasons for that latter decline will be considered subsequently.

For the third and final upsurge in mint outputs under consideration, ca. 1465-1480, coinage debasements and monetary ordinances possibly played a relatively greater role, particularly because warfare was so much less a factor than in the two previous periods—apart from the duke of Burgundy's ultimately fatal campaigns against Louis XI of France and the Swiss. For England certainly the single most important cause of its coinage upsurge in the 1460s was Edward IV's debasements of 1464-65: silver by 20 percent and gold by 26 percent (in total). His reimposition of the Calais bullion laws, in modified form, in 1463 may have contributed to those high mint outputs.[59] According to many historians, these debasements were also important in stimulating, through foreign exchange devaluation, a revival and then strong boom in English cloth exports, which continued almost unabated into the sixteenth century.[60] That cloth export boom may have contributed to, but did not long sustain any high level of English mint outputs after the 1470s.

For the Low Countries, obviously one must cite the impact of the previously mentioned, very drastic coinage debasements and *renforcements* from 1466 to 1497. But in Prof. Herman Van der Wee's view, the initial silver debasements of the 1460s and 1470s were especially important for another reason: in offering such a high price and exchange-ratio for silver, they were very instrumental in attracting South German merchants with large quantities of silver from their recently developed Central European mines to the Brabant Fairs.[61] According to Prof. Nef, South German mining technology and enterprise succeeded in increasing that silver production five-fold from the 1460s and the 1530s.[62] Table 4 indicates a dramatic upsurge in Brabantine silver coinage outputs (at Antwerp) from the 1470s, surpassing the Flemish coinage outputs for the last two decades of the fifteenth century. These events

58. Munro, *Wool, Cloth, and Gold*, pp. 93-126; Lloyd, *Wool Trade*, pp. 261-70. See also Table 1 below.

59. *C. P. R. 1461-67*, pp. 370-1; Craig, *The Mint*, pp. 72-5; Munro, *Wool, Cloth, and Gold*, pp. 155-79; Lloyd, *Wool Trade*, pp. 278-81.

60. Van der Wee, *Antwerp Market*, II, 82-3. The English cloth trade to the Low Countries, however, was interrupted by a Burgundian ban from 1464 to 1467. By this era, lost markets or lost access routes to other European regions had forced the English to concentrate more and more of their cloth exports on the Antwerp market. See Munro, "Industrial Protectionism in Medieval Flanders: Urban or National?" in *The Medieval City*, ed. H. A. Miskimin, et al (New Haven-London, 1977), pp. 246-53 and Tables 4-5; Munro, "Low Countries," pp. 116-22; Munro, *Wool, Cloth, and Gold*, pp. 155-86; M. M. Postan, "Economic and Political Relations of England and the Hanse, 1400-1475," in *Studies in English Trade*, pp. 151-3.

61. Van der Wee, *Antwerp Market*, II, 80-3, 104-05.

62. See n. 3 above.

also benefited the English insofar as their cloth trade boom was directly dependent upon expansion of the Brabant Fairs and South German trade. Undoubtedly the Low Countries' mint outputs could have been even higher had it not been for the very destructive effects of the revolt against Maximilian (1483-1492). Indeed Maximilian's debasements and *renforcements* were both so drastic that they may well have encouraged a flight of bullion and capital.[63] At the same time, in view of the previous discussion of contemporary Mediterranean economic and monetary history, and of the Miskimin and Day theses, one wonders whether the influx of this new South German silver into the Low Countries was still not exceeded by an outflow of bullion through trade to Italy and the Islamic East.

What conclusions may be drawn about these three coinage upsurges? The strong emphasis given to the role of coinage debasements may well lead one to believe that they so distorted late-medieval mint statistics that no trends can be safely gleaned from them.[64] As the tables and graphs suggest, so great were the fluctuations evidently engendered by debasements, even when combined with other factors, that the standard deviations of mint outputs for various periods were generally greater than their corresponding means, especially (and surprisingly) in the English mint data. Nevertheless the most striking feature of the three upsurges as viewed together in the graphs is the very dramatic diminution in the intensity of those upsurges. Indeed, if one believes that debasements hopelessly bias the mint data, it is most instructive to compare the relative power of such debasements to draw metals into the English and Flemish mints at various periods. To make such a comparison comprehensible, with two metals and fluctuations in their money-of-account values—with the problem of combining monetary "apples and oranges"—I have converted all the mint output data into a "constant" pound sterling, using the official English gold and silver values from 1351 to 1411.[65] I have chosen this period because it neatly bisects the whole period under discussion (from 1235) and because it represents the longest period of stability (sixty years) in medieval English monetary history. The consequent gold to silver ratio of 11.16:1 is certainly not unrealistic for late-medieval Europe. All of the means are comparable: decennial outputs of aggregate gold and silver coinages; and the decades chosen are those of the most intensive monetary changes in debasements or recoinages. The decade 1420-9 has been included for England because of all the special monetary circumstances discussed above:

63. Spufford, *Monetary Problems*, pp. 141-6; Van der Wee, *Antwerp Market*, I, 127-8; and II, 105-11.

64. Such is the criticism that R. D. Ware made of Miskimin's "Monetary Movements," in the appended "Discussion," *Journal of Economic History*, XXIV (1964), 491-5.

65. From 24 June 1351 to 29 November 1411, 1 Tower Pound (= 349.9144 g.) of gold at 23 7/8 carats (99.479166% pure) was worth £15.Os.Od. ster., so that 1 kilogram of pure gold = 1000 × £15.00/349.9144 × 0.99479166 = £43.092065. Similarly, 1 Tower Pound of silver at 11 oz. 2 dwt = 92.50% pure was worth 25s. (£1.25), so that 1 kilogram of pure silver = £3.861948. See n. 51 above and Table 10 below.

A comparison of mint outputs during monetary changes

ENGLAND		
Decade	Mean Annual Value of Total Mint Outputs in Constant £ Sterling	Percentage of 1350-9 Mean
1300–09	113,054	95.9
1350–59	117,867	100.0
1410–19	63,579	53.9
1420–29	85,004	72.1
1465–74	65,392	55.5

LOW COUNTRIES		
Decade	Mean Annual Value of Total Mint Outputs in Constant £ Sterling	Percentage of 1355-64 Mean
1355–64	141,026	100.0
1390–99	41,040	29.1
1425–35	83,035	58.9
1470–79	45,112	32.0
1480–89	33,141	23.5

Those who would deny that there was any monetary contraction in the late Middle Ages, and also that there was any relation between mint outputs and money supplies, would have to explain why so much less metal passed through the mints of both countries during recoinages or debasements in the fifteenth than in the fourteenth century—and in the case of the Low Countries so much less than through the *Flemish* mints alone in the mid-fourteenth century. Surely Archduke Maximilian and Edward IV were as avaricious as were Count Louis de Mäle of Flanders and Edward III of England a century earlier?

If we are to contend that there was such a late-medieval monetary contraction (a contention I myself had once opposed),[66] when did it commence? By the late thirteenth century, as Robinson suggested? Or by the early fourteenth century, well prior to the Black Death, as Nicholas Mayhew contends?[67] Tables 1, 2, 3, and 9 do offer some support for those contentions:

66. See Munro, *Wool, Cloth, and Gold*, pp. 14-23; and n. 38 above.
67. Robinson, "Money," pp. 63-76; Mayhew, "Numismatic Evidence," pp. 1-15.

that the mean English coinage output (constant pounds sterling) in the half century 1250-99 was 39.2 percent higher than the corresponding mean in 1300-49; that English mint outputs were very low indeed in the 1290s and especially in the 1320s and 1330s. When measured in terms of the above-defined constant pound sterling, the mean English mint ouput in the 1330s was lower than in any decade of the fifteenth century. But the first of these disastrous minting slumps, in the 1290s, a very brief one, can be attributed to: (1) an influx of counterfeit sterlings from the Low Countries, the famous Pollards and Crockards; and (2) Edward I's diplomatic and military expenditures abroad, estimated by Prestwich at £350,000 in 1294-98.[68] The subsequent general recoinage from 1300, to eliminate those counterfeit sterlings, produced the largest silver and the second largest aggregate mint output in English medieval history. The severe minting slump in the second period, the 1320s and 1330s, may also be explained in part by another influx of counterfeit sterlings and other debased coins from the continent.[69] A more complete explanation would include Edward III's very lavish expenditures abroad, first on diplomacy and then on warfare, at the outset of the Hundred Years' War. One historian has estimated that the bullion outflow in the later 1330s from such financing was about one million pounds; another termed this outflow a veritable "sterling crisis."[70] But there is no hard evidence that such a dearth of coinage was at all general in Europe. Flemish silver coinage outputs in 1335-39 (the earliest accounts available) averaged 91 percent of those in 1350-54; incomplete French mint accounts do show a very large silver coinage at the end of the 1330s.[71] The fact remains in any event that

68. Michael Prestwich, "Edward I's Monetary Policies and Their Consequences," *Economic History Review*, 2nd ser. XXI (1969), 409-12; Mavis Mate, "Monetary Problems," pp. 57-8, 63-6. On counterfeit sterlings, see n. 49 above. For the subsequent, massive coinage outputs, from 1300, see also Mavis Mate, "High Prices in Early Fourteenth-Century England: Causes and Consequences," *Economic History Review*, 2nd ser. XXVIII (1975), 1-16.

69. Mate, "High Prices," pp. 12-15; Cazelles, "Mutations," pp. 88-94, 256-62 (French debasements of 1323-9, 1337-43); Miskimin, *Money* (n. 8), pp. 143-44 (Appendix C); Joseph Ghyssens, "Le monnayage d'argent en Flandre, Hainaut, et Brabant au début de la guerre de Cent Ans," *Revue belge de numismatique*, CXX (1974), 109-91; Hans Van Werveke, "Currency Manipulation," pp. 255-67. For English complaints about foreign counterfeit coins, see *Foedera, conventiones, litterae et acta publica, 1066-1383*, ed. Thomas Rymer et al (4 vols. Record Commission, London, 1816-69), II.i, 544 (1324), II.ii, 814 (1331); *S.R.* I, 273-4 (1335: 9 Ed. III stat. 2, "Statute of York"); *Calendar of Close Rolls 1341-43*, pp. 685-6 (1342); *S.R.* I, 299 (1343: 17 Ed. III c. 1); *Foedera* III.i, 16-17 (1344); *Rot. Parl.* II, 160: nos. 15-16 (1346).

70. See Michael Prestwich, "Currency and the Economy of Early Fourteenth Century England," in *Edwardian Monetary Affairs (1279-1344)*, ed. N. J. Mayhew (*BAR* 36, Oxford, 1977), pp. 45-58 (who also attributes the silver coinage slump to silver exports in exchange for gold, not yet legally monetized); Mate, "High Prices," pp. 12-15; Mayhew, "Numismatic Evidence," pp. 11-15; E. B. Fryde, "Financial Resources of Edward III in the Netherlands, 1337-40," *Revue belge de philologie et d'histoire*, XL (1962), 1168-87; XLIV (1967), 1142-1216; E. B. Fryde, 'Loans to the English Crown, 1328-1331', *English Historical Review*, LXX (1955); Feavearyear, *Pound Sterling*, pp. 15-20; and especially Edward Ames, "The Sterling Crisis of 1337-39," *Journal of Economic History*, XXV (1965), 496-522.

71. Miskimin, *Money*, pp. 90 (fig. 13), 93 (fig. 14), 158 (App. D); Cazelles, "Mutations," pp. 83-105. See Tables 4-6 below.

this deep trough in English minting was followed by a sharp upswing in the later 1340s and then by truly enormous outputs of coinage in the period 1350-69, as demonstrated earlier, with the largest gold and one of the largest silver outputs recorded in medieval England. Certainly the available supply of precious metals had remained most abundant.

Consequently, I would date the onset of a late-medieval monetary contraction, in terms of a definite secular trend, from the late 1360s or early 1370s, certainly for both England and the Low Countries. Although Day would prefer to commence a definite bullion famine from the 1390s, my dating of the onset of general contraction seems to be quite consistent with his published graphs; only the Florentine downswing on his graph commences later, from the 1390s.[72] Similarly, despite Miskimin's strong emphasis on the role of the Black Death, and a suggested commencement of contraction in the 1350s, my dating does not conflict with the logic of his thesis. I certainly agree that a general demographic and economic contraction, a secular depression, may well have had its true beginnings long before this monetary contraction. Nevertheless, my other research in late-medieval economic history also indicates to me that whatever the true origins of such a "depression," the most severe and prolonged phase of economic contraction also commenced about the 1370s and lasted to perhaps the late 1460s in northern Europe, though in some regions certainly (e.g., Flanders) until the early sixteenth century.[73]

All of my statistical investigations suggest that in such secular terms the century 1370-1470 also marked the most severe monetary contraction for both England and the Low Countries, when their aggregate gold and silver coinages are evaluated in "constant" pounds sterling (1351-1411 values) and in current moneys-of-account. The graphs and Tables 1-6 lend strong support to the views of Day and Peter Spufford that the most acute bullion famine, the true nadir of this monetary contraction was in the 1440s and 1450s (ignoring the Burgundian gold debasement of 1454).[74] From the late 1440s to the mid 1460s also appears to be the period of the most severe, acute depression in northern Europe during the fifteenth century.[75] But monetary contraction itself continued to ca. 1500.

72. Day, "Bullion Famine," Graph II, pp. 50-1.

73. See Munro, "Low Countries," pp. 95-161; Munro, "Industrial Protectionism," pp. 247-53; Carus-Wilson, "Trends," pp. 252-61; Van der Wee, *Antwerp Market,* II, 7-18, 28-30, 289-95, 309-14; and G. A. Holmes, *The Estates of the Higher Nobility in Fourteenth-Century England* (Cambridge, 1957), pp. 115-20; and especially for the 1370s as the watershed, A. R. Bridbury, "The Black Death," *Economic History Review,* 2nd ser. XXVI (1973), 577-92 (esp. 584-5, 592).

74. Day, "Bullion Famine," pp. 40-6; Spufford, *Monetary Problems,* pp. 115-21. See also n. 83 below.

75. Munro, "Low Countries," pp. 109-10, 115-18, 151-2 (Tables 12-3); Munro, *Wool, Cloth, and Gold,* pp. 131-54, 181-6; Van der Wee, *Antwerp Market,* II, 61-73; H. L. Gray, "English Foreign Trade from 1446 to 1482," in *Studies in English Trade,* pp. 1-38; Postan, "Economic and Political Relations of the Hanse," *Ibid.*, pp. 149-53; E. M. Carus-Wilson, "The Iceland Trade" and "The Overseas Trade of Bristol," *Ibid.*, pp. 155-246; Postan, "Trade," pp. 246-56.

My statistical comparisons of mint outputs in England and the Low Countries are summarized in Table 9, which presents their long-term trends in terms of both fifty- and hundred-year means. Note that for England, even in terms of debasement-inflated current pounds sterling, the annual mean for 1370-1469 of the total value of coinages struck is only 71.0 percent of the corresponding mean for the preceding century 1270-1369; in terms of the constant pound sterling, to eliminate the effects of debasement, the English mean of total coinage struck in 1370-1469 is only 55.8 percent of 1270-1369 mean. If one were to agree that the *greater* part of the demographic decline had already occurred by the 1370s, from the major plagues, then it becomes very difficult to defend the notion that per capita money supplies were maintained during the later fourteenth and fifteenth centuries. But admittedly there are eminent historians who do contend that English population continued to plunge drastically, not just to decline slowly, until the later fifteenth century.[76]

If we now turn, however, to more useful fifty-year means for both England and the Low Countries, the pattern of decline for both from the mid- to later-fourteenth century through both halves of the fifteenth century is much clearer, much starker. (Since Flemish mint statistics begin only in 1335, we obviously cannot make the same century-long comparisons as for England). Indeed when we combine gold and silver coinages together in constant pounds sterling values (1351-1411), we find that the extent of decline is on the same drastic order of magnitude for both countries. Thus in these terms the mean annual such value of total English coinage output for 1450-99 is only 39.5 percent of the comparable mean for 1350-99, while in the Low Countries the same mean for 1450-99 is just 37.0 percent of the corresponding 1350-99 mean. When we remember that in fact we are comparing combined outputs for all the Burgundian mints in the fifteenth century with chiefly Flemish mint outputs alone in the fourteenth century, the extent of that decline appears to be all the greater. Would anyone contend that the population of the two countries declined in the same proportion as evidently did the aggregate coinage outputs—by some 60-65 percent from 1350-99 to 1450-99? In terms of current moneys-of-account values, of course, the minting slump appears to be less severe. In England, the mean value of total coinage struck in these terms for 1450-99 is a perhaps more respectable 57.4

76. Hatcher, *Plague,* pp. 55-73. Even so, his graph on p. 71 does indicate that by his estimates by far the greatest depopulation had occurred by the late 1370s. For the Low Countries, see especially W. P. Blockmans, "The Social and Economic Effects of the Plague in the Low Countries, 1349-1500," *Revue belge de philologie et d'histoire,* LVIII (1980), 833-63, in particular rejecting the widely-cited contention that the Black Death spared much of this region, as expounded in Hans Van Werveke, *De Zwarte Dood in de zuidelijke Nederlanden, 1349-1351* (Brussels, 1950). In the fifteenth-century Low Countries, the rate of decline in their mint outputs exceeds the most severe estimates of population decline there. See also Joseph Cuvelier, *Les dénombrements de foyers en Brabant, XIVe-XVe siècles* (Brussels, 1912); Maurice Arnould, *Les dénombrements de foyers dans le comté de Hainaut, XIVe-XVIe siècles* (Brussels, 1956); Van der Wee, *Antwerp Market* (n. 34), I, 545-48 (Appendix 49), II, 7-9, 31-7, 61-7.

percent (!) of the corresponding 1350-99 mean. In the Low Countries, thanks to the severe debasements of Charles the Rash and Maximilian, the mean values of total coinage outputs in current pounds *groot* Flemish are about the same for these two periods. The significant decline in current money-of-account values of total coinage struck is instead in the first half of the fifteenth century. Thus, as suggested, the fifteenth-century remains overall a century of significant monetary contraction. It is a moot point whether the decline was more severe in the hundred years 1370-1469 or 1400-1499, in terms of the weight of both metals struck, and their values in constant pounds sterling or current moneys-of-account. But clearly the influx of Central European silver into north-western Europe in the second half of the fifteenth century did little to offset the overall trend of monetary contraction—and presumably of the bullion outflows.

If we now consider the two precious metals separately, and look at the first, far-left column of Table 9, we might think that the most drastic monetary contraction of all, over the 250-year period 1250-1499, is that of English silver: for the mean output in 1450-99 is just a miserable 14.2 percent of the mean silver output in 1250-99. But some considerable proportion of that silver decline is illusory and is accounted for by England's adoption of a gold coinage in January 1344-July 1351. Once the existing stocks of gold bullion, plate, and foreign coin had been minted, further gold coinages necessarily had to be struck at the direct expense of silver. Gold was either purchased directly with silver, or more commonly, gold was received instead of silver in foreign trade transactions.

That question necessarily returns us to the vexing problem of bimetallic ratios. When most countries in north-west Europe adopted gold coinages in the fourteenth century, they did so with a vengeance: Flanders in 1335, England in 1344, the Rhine Electors in 1356 (France had already done so in 1266).[77] For England and the Low Countries in particular the impact of imposing a strongly pro-gold mint ratio upon the relative mintings of the two precious metals can be readily discerned in Tables 3 (England) and 6 (Low Countries). Thus in England, in the first full decade of gold coinage, the 1360s, gold accounted for almost two-thirds (64 percent) of the total value of coinage struck. In the next decade, gold's share of total coinage values leaped fantastically to 95.7 percent (mean value), reaching a peak of 97.2 percent of total coinage values in the decade 1400-09. No wonder historians have commented on a "silver famine" in the later fourteenth century! England consistently maintained this pro-gold mint policy for the rest of the fifteenth century, though not always at the same drastic expense of the silver coinage.

At first glance, from Table 6, a similar if less drastic pattern emerges in Flanders' and Brabants' fourteenth-century mint outputs. Count Louis de Mäle also imposed a pro-gold mint policy on Flanders, so that gold coinages

77. See Watson, "Back to Gold," pp. 9-21; Shaw, *History of Currency*, pp. 1-60; Lopez, "Back to Gold," pp. 219-40.

accounted for an average of almost 75 percent of total mint output values in the 1350s, 78 percent in the 1360s, and 71 percent in the 1370s. But almost immediately after Count Louis' death in 1384, his successor Duke Philip the Bold of Burgundy made an abrupt volte-face in this policy by adopting a much more pro-silver mint-ratio. He did so as part of a sweeping monetary reform: a *renforcement* and the striking of new common coinages for both Flanders and Brabant, in fact adopting Brabant's current mint-ratio. Although that reform failed, and was temporarily followed by more pro-gold debasements, the pro-silver *renforcement* of 1389-90 fully succeeded, at the very time that France also shifted to a more pro-silver mint ratio.[78] That pro-silver mint policy was rigidly maintained in the Low Countries for the next 35 years; and the results show clearly in Table 5. Thus silver's share of total mint output values in the Low Countries rose from 32 percent in the 1380s to 56 percent in the 1390s, when the policy had been fully implemented, to a peak of 87 percent of total coinage values in the decade 1410-19.

Then in 1425-26, Duke Philip the Good of Burgundy (1419-67) made another monetary volte-face, abruptly switching back to a strongly pro-gold mint ratio, for reasons discussed elsewhere, chiefly military.[79] Despite his withdrawal from the French war and his *renforcement*-monetary reform in the 1430s, Duke Philip maintained that pro-gold mint policy until the very eve of his death, to 1466. Again the table demonstrates that between 1425 and 1465 the pattern of Burgundian minting dramatically altered in accordance with this change in ratios: so that gold's share of total mint output values rose from a mean of 37 percent in the 1420s to just over 98 percent in the 1450s. The Burgundian mint ratio in this forty-year period was in fact even more strongly pro-gold than England's, so that the English mints, against their will, were consequently favouring silver. Thus in the 1430s and again in the 1450s, silver accounted for an average of 71-72 percent of total English mint output values. Indeed England's mint at Calais, almost entirely at the mercy of Burgundian commerce, coined little gold after 1425, none from 1431, but vast quantities of silver, until the outbreak of the Anglo-Burgundian war in 1436.[80]

Then, in May 1466, the Burgundian mints effected the third, and for our period final, change in the bimetallic ratio, again to favour silver.[81] As suggested earlier, that mint-ratio alteration, with such a high price for silver, was a significant factor in luring South German silver and commerce to Antwerp. Similarly Tables 3 and 6 demonstrate once more that after this mint-ratio alteration the Low Countries were coining predominantly silver,

78. See Munro, "Mint Policies," pp. 65-88.

79. Munro, *Wool, Cloth, and Gold*, chapters 3-4, especially Graph III, on p. 71 (See p. 51 n. 28 for an explanation of the ratio lines.)

80. *Ibid.*, pp. 188 (Table A: gold), 191 (Table B: silver); and in the text, pp. 81-126.

81. *Ibid.*, pp. 155-73, especially Graph VI on p. 156. See also the Chi-Square Contingency tables, to demonstrate the importance of mint-ratios (1425-99) in Munro, "Low Countries," pp. 147-8, Table 9 (with commentary on pp. 101-02).

accounting for an average of 77 percent of total mint output values in 1470-99; and England was coining predominantly gold, though by no means in the overwhelming proportions of the previous century.

Several important conclusions can be drawn from these analyses and from another consideration of Table 9 on long-term means of the mint productions. First, even though mint-ratio alterations in themselves rarely if ever instigated international bullion flows, clearly they played a decisive role through international payments in determining which metal would predominate in a country's bullion flows and mint outputs. Secondly, the much discussed "silver famine" of late medieval Europe was as much a product of these strongly pro-gold mint ratios as it was a feature of that era's general monetary contraction. In England indeed that "silver famine" preceded the general monetary contraction by almost a generation.

Insofar as late-medieval countries did favour gold so strongly, they undoubtedly did their domestic economies a disservice. While gold, by its high and generally stable values, was the preferred metal for international trade and finance, for diplomacy and warfare, such high values severely limited its usefulness in domestic transactions. Consider that in England the smallest gold coin, the rarely struck ferlin (quarter-noble), at 20d was worth three times the daily wage of a master mason.[82] Since most countries' money-of-account pricing systems were based directly on the silver penny, not on gold, the effect of such mint policies in driving away silver was clearly deflationary. Witness again the general deflation in England during the later fourteenth and fifteenth centuries—and also in the Burgundian Low Countries during much of the pro-gold period, ca. 1435-1465.[83]

But thirdly, the so-called "silver famine" was much more a transitory and then a regional problem than is generally stated. As stressed earlier, England was the only major northern European country to pursue so consistently for so long a pro-gold policy. As we have seen, Flanders, Brabant, and France all switched to a more pro-silver mint ratio in the late 1380s. Thereafter, the Low Countries maintained that ratio for 70 of the next 110 years (i.e., except 1425-1465). Insofar as they successfully attracted silver, that policy may have contributed to supposed "silver famines" elsewhere—perhaps in the Near East (early fifteenth century), as well as in England?[84]

Fourthly and finally, as Table 9 demonstrates, while the mint outputs of both metals declined sharply in both England and the Low Countries from the later fourteenth century, in both the decline was by the greater in gold outputs! Thus in the Low Countries, the mean silver output for 1450-99 is

82. E. H. Phelps Brown and Sheila Hopkins, "Seven Centuries of Building Wages," *Economica*, new ser. XXII (1955) [reprinted in *Essays in Economic History*, ed. Carus-Wilson (London, 1962), 177-8: ca. 1360-1412, at 5d. per day; 1412-1532, at 6d. per day (plus food and drink on occasion). See also Bloch, "Problem of Gold," pp. 186-229.

83. Van der Wee, "Prices and Wages," pp. 58-78; Munro, "Low Countries," pp. 109-10 and Table 18 (p. 157: regressions of prices on coinage outputs). See also n. 34 above.

84. See above pp. 14-15 and n. 16.

virtually identical (99.1 percent) to that for the first half of the century, and 85.7 percent of the silver mean for 1350-99. The Low Countries' mean gold output for the period 1450-99, on the other hand, is just 62.4 percent of the mean output for 1400-49—and just a miserable 19.3 percent of the mean for 1350-99. Even in pro-gold England, the mean gold coinage output for 1450-99 was just half that for 1400-49, 49.2 percent, and only 31.8 percent of the mean gold output in 1350-99. (The English mean silver output for 1450-99 was, however, a much higher 75.0 percent of the 1350-99 mean silver output). Such a situation should have been deduced from the fact that, despite frequently cited complaints about silver scarcities in the fifteenth century, the most consistent monetary concern of that era in both countries was rising gold prices.[85]

Where was all the northern gold going? Into hoards, jewelry, plate church ornamentation? Into thin air, from wear? To Italy? To the East? Was indeed Asia's appetite for European gold just as voracious as for its silver? Presumably if Europe had a chronic deficit in its balance of payments with Asia, both metals would flow there, and not just silver. But not all questions can be fully answered by the papers published in this volume.

85. See Spufford, *Monetary Problems*, pp. 115-21; Munro, *Wool, Cloth, and Gold*, pp. 134-6; and Munro, "Low Countries," pp. 144-5, Table 7: values of fine gold on the Antwerp Market and official gold values, 1420-99. See also the perspicacious comments of John Day concerning the rising bimetallic ratios as indicators of increasing scarcity of gold relative to the silver supplies, in "Bullion Famine," pp. 40-3. I do not believe, however, that this situation can be fully explained by the opening of new European silver mines; for the decline in gold minting comes much too early and is much too drastic. More rapid declines in European gold mining and in imports of African gold are reasonable conjectures, but only conjectures.

Appendix: The mint production statistics for England, 1235-1500 and the Low Countries, 1335-1500

Miskimin's seminal article of 1964 on late-medieval monetary contraction was based fundamentally on English mint statistics for 1273-1470, specifically:[1] (a) Sir John Craig's occasionally careless rendition of the London Tower Mint accounts (in *A History of the London Mint*, 1953) published by C. G. Crump and C. Johnson (1272-1377) and then by G. C. Brooke and E. Stokes (1377-1550) in the 1913 and 1929 volumes respectively of the *Numismatic Chronicle*; (b) Crump and Johnson's publication of the Calais mint accounts from 1363 to 1384 in the same journal. Since then a number of important additional mint accounts have appeared. First and foremost, in the *British Numismatic Journal* of 1980, C. E. Blunt and J. D. Brand published the London and Canterbury mint accounts of Henry III (from the Pipe Rolls), 1220 to 1272; they are virtually complete for both mints from 1234. (The complete Canterbury mint accounts from 1272 to the mint's final closure in December 1346 were also published by Crump and Johnson). Then in my 1973 monograph *Wool, Cloth, and Gold*, I published the complete set of Calais mint production figures from July 1422 to September 1440, extracted from the K.R. and L.T.R. Exchequer accounts in the London Public Record Office. From the same sources, T. H. Lloyd supplied the hitherto unknown Calais mint accounts from January 1387 to March 1403, in his 1977 monograph *The English Wool Trade in the Middle Ages*. Subsequently, in the *Numismatic Chronicle* for 1981, I amended some of his Calais mint figures, filled a non-existent gap in the accounts from February 1388 to January 1390, and extended the Calais mint figures to March 1404. Finally, in his 1978 monograph *The Tudor Coinage*, C. E. Challis has presented a new set of London Tower Mint accounts from November 1485 to July 1603, correcting and expanding on those accounts previously published by Brooke and Stokes in 1929.

Therefore, on the basis of these newer studies, I decided that Miskimin's hypotheses should be retested with a new, more complete, and much longer run of English mint statistics, from 1235 to 1500 (265 years). The tables presented here provide production statistics for London's Tower Mint for this entire period and from all the extant provincial mint accounts as follows: Canterbury, 1235-1346; Exeter, Newcastle, Bristol, Chester, and York, 1300-02; York, again from 1353 to 1355, 1423-24, and 1470-75; Bristol again, from 1470-72; and Calais, from 1363-1384, 1387-1404, and 1422-1440. The only important provincial mint accounts that appear to be missing are from lesser mints partaking in the recoinages of 1274-49 and 1280-82. The London mint accounts themselves are remarkably complete from 1235, with lacunae for only 15 years from then to 1500: for 1310-11, 1322, 1409-11, 1461-62, 1467-68 and 1490-94. I have deduced that only a trickle of coinage, if any, flowed from the Mint in 1409-11 and 1461-62, in each case just prior to a major debasement.

For the 1977 Wisconsin conference I also presented a set of mint statistics for the

1. For complete citations of all the following publications, see the sources for the ten monetary tables.

Low Countries from 1335 to 1500. As it happened, the very next year an apparently similar set of mint statistics for the Low Countries, though in graphic form, was published in John Day's article, "The Great Bullion Famine of the Fifteenth Century." A singularly brilliant tour de force, in my opinion, Day's article documented the most convincing case yet for a late-medieval monetary contraction, with coinage production statistics for France (or various regions), Navarre, Barcelona, Valencia, Sardinia, Florence, Genoa, and Lübeck, as well as for England and the Low Countries—representing a very broad geographic sweep. But I am compelled to note that his mint production figures for both England and the Low Countries are incomplete. His English statistics, which commence only in 1340, a full century after mine, are based on Sir John Craig's London figures; they differ from those of Miskimin only in that Day has used my Calais mint figures for 1422-1440. No other provincial English mint accounts seem to have been used.

Secondly, while those for the Burgundian Low Countries seem to be quite complete, based on my published figures (to 1480) and those of Peter Spufford (to 1499), they are regrettably defective in many places for the preceding century.[2] For the Flemish outputs from 1334 to 1384, Day utilized the forty-seven mint accounts of Counts Louis de Crécy and Louis de Mäle, preserved in the Algemeen Rijksarchief at Brussels, and published in 1856 by Victor Gaillard in his *Recherches sur les monnaies des comtes de Flandre*. But Gaillard was unaware that another nine mint accounts for Louis de Mäle (for various years, 1353-1365) were to be found in France's Archives départementales du Nord at Lille; and Day furthermore was evidently also unaware that Prof. Hans Van Werveke had published synopses of these nine accounts in his *De muntslag in Vlaanderen onder Lodewijk Van Male,* in 1949. Much more recently, in 1979, Wim Blockmans has published synopses of three more important Flemish mint accounts, found much earlier by his late father Frans: for Ghent, from 28 June 1335 to 16 June 1336 (?); and for Mechelen, from 7 August 1380-28 April 1381, and from then to 3 May 1382, in his essay "Devaluation, Coinage, and Seignorage Under Louis de Nevers and Louis de Male, Counts of Flanders, 1330-84," in Nicholas Mayhew, ed. *Coinage in the Low Countries, 880-1500*. This essay also corrects a number of errors by Gaillard and Van Werveke, and provides much additional information on Flemish coinage in this era.

Elsewhere, in the 1949 *Transactions of the Royal Historical Society,* Hans Van Werveke rather gloomily reported that "more than one fifth of the original [Flemish mint] records are still lacking."[3] Perhaps that comment had inspired Day to extrapolate Flemish mint data for all those years not covered by the Gaillard collection. Apart from the fact that we can now utilize another 12 accounts without such extrapolation, I do not believe that the remaining lacunae up to 1384 are that serious:

(1) 7 November 1338-16 April 1343: 4.44 years
(2) 17 October 1343-20 January 1346: 2.26 years
(3) 11 August 1347-24 December 1347: 0.37 year
(4) 21 February 1349-6 May 1349: 0.18 year
(5) 24 November-20 February 1356: 0.23 year

2. John Day, "The Great Bullion Famine of the Fifteenth Century," *Past and Present,* no. 79 (1978), 52.

3. Hans Van Werveke, "Currency Manipulation in the Middle Ages: The Case of Louis de Male, Count of Flanders," *Transactions of the Royal Historical Society,* 4th ser. XXXI (1949), 116.

(6) 11 May 1364-10 February 1365: 0.70 year
(7) 18 June 1368-21 April 1369: 0.84 year
*(8) 5 August 1370-18 June 1373: 2.87 years
(9) 26 June 1376-6 November 1376: 0.36 year
*(10) 27 June 1377-30 January 1380: 2.59 years

I fully accept Blockman's contention that gaps nos. 1-2 almost certainly reflect actual mint closures during the Artevelde revolt and Count Louis' exile.[4] Since the next five gaps (nos. 3-7) and no. 9 are all so short, for less than a year, one may also reasonably conclude that the Flemish mints were closed in those periods as well. For all these periods I have assigned a nil value in computing quinquennial or decennial means of mint outputs. The only significant gaps remaining are nos. 8 and 10, marked by an asterisk, totalling just 5.46 years. From a comparison of Flemish and Brabantine monetary history in this period, which reveals no references at all to Flemish coinages during these gaps, I strongly suspect that they also reflect mint closures.[5] In the tables on Flemish mint production, nos. 4-7, I have computed two sets of means, quinquennial and decennial, for the period of these gaps: (a) by again assigning a value of zero to these periods, dividing total output by 5 and 10 respectively, and (b) by computing a mean based only upon the actual number of recorded years of mint activity: i.e. dividing total output in 1370-74 by 2.13 and in 1375-79 by 2.74 years. These means, necessarily larger than the former, are given in square brackets. For the long-term means in Table 9, I have assigned zero values to all the gaps. In many places, therefore, my Flemish mint statistics will differ considerably from Day's. (He also used semi-log or ratio-scale graphs, which are good for demonstrating comparative rates of change, relative change; but not so good for showing absolute changes—the actual extent of decline, my primary concern here).

For fourteenth-century Brabant, the 1380s and 1390s, Day unfortunately had to rely on texts and précis in Henri Laurent's often inaccurate *La loi de Gresham au moyen âge* (1933), which provided figures only for September 1384-May 1386 and May 1394-January 1395.[6] Laurent was surprisingly unaware of some other Brabant mint accounts, and neglected to supply data from some already published accounts. I currently have in press synopses of all the available Brabantine mint accounts, from the earliest extant archival records up to the Burgundian coinage unification of 1433-35, as follows: July 1375-March 1383 (Leuven), September 1384-May 1386 (Leuven), June 1392-January 1395 (Vilvoorde and Leuven), September-October 1405 (Antwerp), April 1409-June 1412 (Vilvoorde and Leuven), June 1417-December 1417 (Vilvoorde), December 1418-October 1421 (Maastricht and Brussels), September 1429-March 1432 (Leuven). Figures for 1420-21 and 1429-32 have been given in Day's graphs.[7]

4. Willem Blockmans, "Devaluation, Coinage, and Seignorage Under Louis de Nevers and Louis de Male, Counts of Flanders, 1330-84," *Coinage in the Low Countries (880-1500)*, ed. N. J. Mayhew (*BAR* International 54, Oxford, 1979), pp. 72-4.

5. See John H. Munro, "Le monnayage, monnaies de comptes, et mutations monétaires au Brabant à la fin du moyen âge," in *Etudes d'histoire monétaire médiévale*, ed. John Day (Cahiers Jussieu, Université Paris 7, Presses Universitaires de Lille, forthcoming, 1982).

6. Henri Laurent, *La loi de Gresham au moyen âge: essai sur la circulation monétaire entre la Flandre et le Brabant à la fin du XIVe siècle* (Brussels, 1933), pp. 80-1 (précis only), 149-50, doc. no. 10; Day, p. 52.

7. See n. 5 above.

In my tables, all data on mint production in the Low Countries, except for Flanders 1334-1384 (as above), are based upon my own research in the Belgian and Dutch archives. All data have been computed to run for Michaelmas years ending 29 September, in accordance with the English mint accounts, using monthly averages where necessary to apportion the mint data into Michaelmas years.

The mint statistics for the Low Countries, commencing in 1334-34 with the earliest Flemish account, are necessarily restricted to Flanders until 1375, when the first surviving Brabantine account becomes available. From the 1380s, we may legitimately combine the Flemish and Brabantine mint outputs in our tables. For in 1384, with accession of the ducal house of Burgundy in Flanders (Philip the Bold), the two principalities agreed to strike a common, unified coinage; and in 1388, to have the Flemish mints strike all the coinage for both, sharing mint profits equally.[8] Even when the duchess of Brabant temporarily broke that agreement in the early 1390s (restoring it in 1399), the Brabantine coinages remained within the dominant Flemish monetary orbit, as did subsequent Brabantine coinages, after the duchy passed into Burgundian hands in 1406.[9] From 1421 to 1430, we must also add the neighbouring mints in Namur, Hainaut, and Holland-Zealand, as the third duke of Burgundy (Philip the Good) personally acquired these provinces (and also Brabant in his own name). Indeed having promised the Flemish Estates in 1418 not to alter the coinage again for fifteen years, Philip proceeded to utilize these new mints in order to strike debased imitations of Flemish coins.[10] Finally, from October 1433, Duke Philip unified the coinages of all the Burgundian Low Countries on the basis of the newly reformed Flemish coinage. Thereafter, as Tables 4 and 5 demonstrate, minting leadership in the Low Countries alternated between Flanders and Brabant.

Although I have published elsewhere parts of these statistical series on mint ouputs in England and the Low Countries, this is the first time that they are presented completely, correctly, and in their entirety for the Late Middle Ages: in kilograms of *pure* metal, in current moneys-of-account values (pounds sterling and pounds groot Flemish), and in constant pounds sterling of 1351-1411 values.[11]

8. John Munro, "Mint Policies, Ratios, and Outputs in the Low Countries and England, 1335-1420: Some Reflections on New Data," *Numismatic Chronicle,* 8th ser. I (1981), 78-90.

9. See n. 5 above, and n. 10 below.

10. John Munro, *Wool, Cloth, and Gold: The Struggle for Bullion in Anglo-Burgundian Trade, 1340-1478* (Brussels-Toronto, 1973), pp. 65-103.

11. See nn. 5, 8, 10, and also "Monetary Contraction and Industrial Change in the Late-Medieval Low Countries, 1335-1500," in *Coinage in the Low Countries*, pp. 139-44. The mint statistics published in this volume differ in some places from those previously published because of: (a) discovery of new mint accounts, especially for Calais, Mechelen, and the 14th-century Brabantine towns; (b) different methods of handling lacunae in mint-data; except for London in 1409-11 and 1461-62 (when output was evidently almost nil), I have not this time extrapolated for missing years; instead I have taken averages of extant data only, as explained above; (c) different methods of apportioning uneven accounts into consistent Michaelmas years (ending on 29 September).

Table 1. Silver coinage outputs of the English mints: decennial means in kilograms of pure metal, current and constant pounds sterling, 1240–9 to 1495–99

Decade	London kg. of silver	Provincial kg. of silver	Total kg. of silver	Value in current £ sterling	Value in constant £ sterling*
1240–9	10,906.25	8,366.89	19,273.14	60,041.73	74,431.90
1250–9	10,655.67	10,500.85	21,156.52	65,908.98	81,705.36
1260–9	6,923.69	5,192.88	12,116.57	37,746.79	46,793.55
1270–9	6,219.53	312.98	6,532.51	20,379.62	25,228.20
1280–9	19,223.84	6,958.80	26,182.64	81,889.30	101,116.01
1290–9	1,925.87	162.24	2,088.11	6,531.98	8,064.18
1300–9	18,425.41	10,848.36	29,273.77	91,573.58	113,053.79
1310–9[a]	3,858.70	5,050.61	8,909.31	27,869.91	34,407.30
1320–9[b]	798.81	813.87	1,612.68	5,044.73	6,228.06
1330–9	320.72	20.39	341.11	1,180.17	1,317.34
1340–9	3,304.83	65.51	3,370.34	11,809.47	13,016.05
1350–9	10,323.96	668.50	10,992.46	42,333.94	42,452.29
1360–9	971.73	99.29	1,071.02	4,136.23	4,136.23
1370–9	354.69	–	354.69	1,369.79	1,369.79
1380–9	256.99	–	256.99	992.47	992.47
1390–9	233.94	–	233.94	903.48	903.48
1400–9[c]	46.96	–	46.96	181.35	181.35
1410–9[c]	869.40	–	869.40	4,028.78	3,357.57
1420–9	588.49	3,547.53	4,136.02	19,167.69	15,973.08
1430–9	424.62	4,936.23	5,360.85	24,843.99	20,703.32
1440–9	250.64	–	250.64	1,161.53	967.94
1450–9	1,360.46	–	1,360.46	6,304.81	5,254.01
1460–9[d]	3,834.76	–	3,834.76	20,747.32	14,809.65

Table 1. *(continued)*

Decade	London kg. of silver	Pronvincial kg. of silver	Total kg. of silver	Value in current £ sterling	Value in constant £ sterling*
1470–9	1,792.17	113.27	1,905.44	11,038.11	7,358.74
1480–9	926.38	–	926.38	5,366.46	3,577.64
1495–9[e]	2,123.97	–	2,123.97	12,303.99	8,202.66

*Values of constant pound sterling (1351–1411 values)
1 kg. of silver = £3.861948
[a]Mean of 8 years: 1312–19 (1310–11 missing)
[b]Mean of 9 years: 1320–21, 1323–29 (1322 missing)
[c]Accounts for 1409–11 missing: amounts have been extrapolated
[d]Mean of 8 years: 1460–66 and 1469 (1467–68 missing); 1461–2 extrapolated
[e]Mean of 5 years: accounts missing for 1490–94

Table 2. Gold coinage outputs of the English mints: decennial means in kilograms of pure metal and in current and constant pounds sterling, 1340–9 to 1495–9

Decade	London mint kg. gold	Provincial mints kg. gold	Total mints kg. gold	Value in current £ sterling	Value in constant £ sterling*
1340–9	395.07	–	395.07	15,963.27	17,024.20
[a]	[658.44]	–	[658.44]	[26,605.44]	[28,373.67]
1350–9	1,750.11	–	1,750.11	75,224.50	75,415.57
1360–9	1,395.53	715.34	2,110.87	90,961.88	90,961.88
1370–9	263.14	339.70	602.84	25,977.63	25,977.63
1380–9	200.45	88.57	289.02	12,454.62	12,454.62
1390–9	397.68	146.71	544.39	23,458.78	23,458.78
1400–9[b]	111.09	34.91	146.00	6,291.41	6,291.41
1410–9[b]	1,397.52	–	1,397.52	66,865.30	60,221.85
1420–9	1,302.11	299.83	1,601.94	76,701.38	69,031.25
1430–9	191.40	8.22	199.62	9,557.86	8,602.08
1440–9	78.72	–	78.72	3,768.99	3,392.08
1450–9	53.77	–	53.77	2,574.57	2,317.10
1460–9[c]	657.73	–	657.73	41,294.58	28,342.97
1470–9	499.03	14.00	513.03	33,160.84	22,107.24
1480–9	206.77	–	206.77	13,365.40	8,910.28
1495–9[d]	296.41	–	296.41	19,159.40	12,772.92

*Values of constant pound sterling (1351–1411 values)
1 kg. of gold = £43.092065
[a]Gold first struck in January 1344: mean of 1344–49
[b]Accounts missing for 1409–11: amounts extrapolated
[c]8-year mean for 1460–66 and 1469 (1467–68 missing); amounts extrapolated for 1461–62 (also missing)
[d]5-year: mean only: accounts missing for 1490–94

Table 3. Silver and gold coinage outputs of the English mints: decennial means in current and constant pounds sterling, 1240–49 to 1490–99

Decade	Silver current £ sterling	% of total	Gold current £ sterling	% of total	Total coinage current £ sterling	Outputs in: constant £ sterling*
1240–9	60,041.73	100.0	–	–	60,041.73	74,431.90
1250–9	65,908.98	100.0	–	–	65,908.98	81,705.36
1260–9	37,746.79	100.0	–	–	37,746.79	46,793.55
1270–9	20,379.62	100.0	–	–	20,379.62	25,228.20
1280–9	81,889.30	100.0	–	–	81,889.30	101,116.01
1290–9	6,531.98	100.0	–	–	6,531.98	8,064.18
1300–9	91,573.58	100.0	–	–	91,573.58	113,053.79
1310–9[a]	27,869.91	100.0	–	–	27,869.91	34,407.30
1320–9[b]	5,044.73	100.0	–	–	5,044.73	6,228.06
1330–9	1,180.17	100.0	–	–	1,180.17	1,317.34
1340–9	11,809.47	42.5	15,963.27	57.5	27,772.74	30,040.25
1350–9	42,333.94	36.0	75,224.50	64.0	117,558.44	117,867.86
1360–9	4,136.23	4.3	90,961.88	95.7	95,098.11	95,098.11
1370–9	1,369.79	5.0	25,977.63	95.0	27,347.42	27,347.42
1380–9	992.47	7.4	12,454.62	92.6	13,447.09	13,447.09
1390–9	903.48	3.7	23,458.78	96.3	24,362.26	24,362.26
1400–9[c]	181.35	2.8	6,291.41	97.2	6,472.76	6,472.76
1410–9[c]	4,028.78	5.7	66,865.30	94.3	70,894.08	63,579.42
1420–9	19,167.69	20.0	76,701.38	80.0	95,869.07	85,004.33
1430–9	24,843.99	72.2	9,557.86	27.8	34,401.85	29,305.40
1440–9	1,161.53	23.6	3,768.99	76.4	4,930.52	4,360.02
1450–9	6,304.81	71.0	2,574.57	29.0	8,879.38	7,571.11
1460–9[d]	20,747.32	33.4	41,294.58	66.6	62,041.90	43,152.62

Table 3. (*continued*)

Decade	London mint kg. gold	Provincial mints kg. gold		Total mints kg. gold	Value in current £ sterling	Value in constant £ sterling*
1470–9	11,038.11	25.0	33,160.84	75.0	44,198.95	29,465.98
1480–9	5,366.46	28.6	13,365.40	71.4	18,731.86	12,487.92
1495–9[e]	12,303.99	39.1	19,159.40	60.9	31,463.39	20,975.58

*Constant pounds sterling values, of 1351–1441:
1 kg. of gold = £43.092065 1 kg. of silver = £3.861948

[a]Mean of 8 years: accounts missing for 1310–11

[b]Mean of 9 years: accounts missing for 1322

[c]Accounts missing for 1409–11; but outputs have been extrapolated

[d]Mean of 8 years: accounts missing for 1467–68; accounts also missing for 1461–62, but outputs have been extrapolated.

[e]Mean of 5 years: accounts missing for 1490–94.

Table 4. Silver coinage outputs of the Low Countries' mints: decennial means in kilograms of pure metal and in current pounds groot Flemish, 1335–9 to 1490–9

	Kilograms					
Decade	Flanders	Brabant	Holland	Namur & Hainaut	Total silver	Values in pounds groot
1335–9[a]	5,244.71					6,814.58
1340–9[b]	1,982.18					3,943.57
1350–9	6,800.46					15,417.83
1360–9	6,669.80					19,335.41
1370–9[c]	2,708.55					9,882.69
	[5,559.80][d]	[558.45][g]				
1380–9	2,539.11[e]	580.44[h]			3,119.55	13,121.03
	[2,654.86][f]					
1390–9	5,004.76	577.05			5,581.81	22,696.94
1400–9	731.13	156.14			887.27	3,617.37
1410–9	1,845.48	926.64			2,772.12	9,794.69
		[855.63][i]				
1420–9	9,000.26	438.16		449.70	9,888.12	49,086.20
1430–9	4,792.21	1,088.91	844.50	554.99	7,280.61	38,167.37
1440–9	119.78	–	42.67	–	162.46	849.34
1450–9	52.23	29.93	4.67	27.51	114.34	644.31
1460–9	1,036.73	501.11	36.83	51.83	1,626.50	9,767.56
1470–9	4,284.99	3,637.40	–	–	7,922.39	52,339.77
1480–9	1,962.03	4,032.04	1,540.26	–	7,534.34	73,534.33
1490–9	1,292.68	1,959.39	191.05	168.15	3,611.27	28,616.41

[a]5-year mean only; Flemish accounts Sept. 1334 to Sept. 1339.
[b]10-year mean; but no record of minting in 1340–42; 1344–45.

Table 4. *(continued)*

[c]No record of Flemish minting from 5 Aug. 1370 to 18 June 1373 (34.44 months) and from 27 June 1377 to 30 Jan. 1380 (31.07 months). Zero values have been assigned to these gaps, and the mean is based upon the full ten years.
[d]Mean is calculated on the basis of the 4.872 years of recorded mint activity.
[e]For Mich. 1379 to 30 Jan. 1380, see note c above. There are no mint accounts available for the period 2 May 1386 to 30 Sept. 1388 (28.94 months), when the mints were evidently still active. The mean is therefore calculated on the basis of the remaining 91.06 months in the decade = 7.58833 years.
[f]Mean is calculated on the basis of 7.26 years of recorded mint activity, as explained in note c and e above: i.e. from 30 Jan. 1380 to 2 May 1386, and from 1 Oct. 1388 to 30 Sept. 1389.
[g]Leuven mint account commences only on 1 July 1375; the mean is therefore calculated on the remaining 4.25 years to 30 Sept. 1379. The value of this output is not included in the totals in the two final columns.
[h]Mean computed on the same basis as the one for Flanders, as in e above. Approximately the same number of months are also missing for the Leuven mint accounts.
[i]To be consistent with the Flemish mean, Brabant mean computed on basis of full ten years, even though accounts are missing from 21 March 1411 to 25 June 1412. On basis of 3.737 years of recorded output, mean would be 855.63 kg.

Table 5. Gold coinage outputs of the Low Countries' mints: decennial means in kilograms of pure metal and in current pounds groot Flemish, 1335–9 to 1490–9

	Kilograms					
Decade	Flanders	Brabant	Holland	Namur & Hainaut	Total gold	Values in pounds groot
1335–9[a]	295.06					4,389.93
1340–9[b]	48.02					1,002.08
1350–9	1,906.79					45,790.63
1360–9	2,330.41					68,997.42
1370–9[c]	640.75					24,679.11
	[1,315.26][d]	[734.23][g]				
1380–9[e]	538.29	69.99[h]			608.28	28,289.20
[f]	[562.83]					
1390–9	426.58	25.57			452.15	18,057.78
1400–9	32.09	5.25			37.34	1,464.57
1410–9	13.59	30.56[i]			44.15[i]	1,505.25
		[28.08]				
1420–9	201.19	2.77	121.69	135.77	461.43	28,586.05
1430–9	275.55	389.57	154.88	427.06	1,247.06	78,742.35
1440–9	62.88	–	3.35	–	66.24	3,808.70
1450–9	239.34	160.65	29.34	107.31	536.64	32,888.71
1460–9	82.18	24.32	1.71	3.50	111.71	7,194.08
1470–9	177.48	159.39	–	–	336.87	25,017.80
1480–9	16.37	59.01	18.46	–	93.84	12,930.40
1490–9	39.06	39.90	0.76	–	79.71	8,127.79

[a] 5-year mean only; Flemish accounts Sept. 1334 to Sept. 1339.
[b] 10-year mean; but no record of minting in 1340–42; 1344–45.

Table 5. *(continued)*

[c]No record of Flemish minting from 5 Aug. 1370 to 18 June 1373 (34.44 months) and from 27 June 1377 to 30 Jan. 1380 (31.07 months). Zero values have been assigned to these gaps, and the mean is based upon the full ten years.

[d]Mean is calculated on the basis of the 4.872 years of recorded mint activity.

[e]For Mich. 1379 to 30 Jan. 1380, see note *c* above. There are no mint accounts available for the period 2 May 1386 to 30 Sept. 1388 (28.94 months), when the mints were evidently still active. The mean is therefore calculated on the basis of the remaining 91.06 months in the decade = 7.58833 years.

[f]Mean is calculated on the basis of 7.26 years of recorded mint activity, as explained in note c and e above: i.e. from 30 Jan. 1380 to 2 May 1386, and from 1 Oct. 1388 to 30 Sept. 1389.

[g]Leuven mint account commences only on 1 July 1375; the mean is therefore calculated on the remaining 4.25 years to 30 Sept. 1379. The value of this output is not included in the totals in the two final columns.

[h]Mean computed on the same basis as the one for Flanders, as in e above. Approximately the same number of months are also missing for the Leuven mint accounts.

[i]To be consistent with the Flemish mean, Brabant mean computed on basis of full ten years, even though accounts are missing from 21 March 1411 to 25 June 1412.

Table 6. Silver and gold coinage outputs of the Low Countries' mints: decennial means in current pounds groot Flemish and in constant pounds sterling,* 1335–9 to 1490–9

Decade	Silver current £ groot	% of total	Gold current £ groot	% of total	Total coinage current £ groot	Outputs in: constant £ sterling*
A. *Flanders, 1335 to 1399*						
1335–9[a]	6,814.58	60.8	4,389.93	39.2	11,204.51	32,969.68
1340–9	3,943.57	79.7	1,002.08	20.3	4,945.65	9,724.53
1350–9	15,417.83	25.2	45,790.63	74.8	61,208.46	108,430.50
1360–9	19,335.41	21.9	68,997.42	78.1	88,332.83	126,180.72
1370–9[b]	9,882.69	28.6	24,679.11	71.4	34,561.80	38,071.54
[c]	[20,286.06]		[50,658.45]		[70,944.51]	[78,148.86]
1380–9[d]	10,682.33	29.9	25,073.94	70.1	35,756.27	33,002.05
[e]	[11,169.28]		26,216.93		[37,386.21]	[34,506.44]
1390–9	20,346.65	54.4	17,028.22	45.6	37,374.87	37,710.21
B. *Low Countries, 1380–1499*						
1380–9[d]	13,121.03	31.7	28,289.20	68.3	41,410.23	38,259.73
1390–9	22,696.94	55.7	18,057.78	44.3	40,754.72	41,040.47
1400–9	3,617.37	71.2	1,464.57	28.8	5,081.94	5,035.60
1410–9	9,794.69	86.7	1,505.25	13.3	11,299.93	12,608.63
1420–9	49,086.20	63.2	28,586.05	36.8	77,672.25	58,071.36
1430–9	38,167.37	32.6	78,742.35	67.4	116,909.72	81,855.47
1440–9	849.34	18.2	3,808.70	81.8	4,658.04	3,481.76
1450–9	644.31	1.9	32,888.71	98.1	33,533.02	23,566.54
1460–9	9,767.56	57.6	7,194.08	42.4	16,961.64	11,095.60
1470–9	52,339.77	67.7	25,017.80	32.3	77,357.57	45,112.03
1480–9	73,534.33	85.0	12,930.40	15.0	86,464.73	33,141.03
1490–9	28,616.41	77.9	8,127.79	22.1	36,744.20	17,381.41

Table 6. *(continued)*

*Values in constant pounds sterling (1351–1441 Values):
1 kg. of gold = £43.092065 1 kg. of silver = £3.861948

[a]5-year mean only, for 1335–9 (first account commences in Sept. 1334).

[b]There are no records of Flemish minting from 5 Aug. 1370 to 18 June 1373 (34.44 months) and from 27 June 1377 to 30 Jan. 1380 (31.07 months). Zero values have been assigned to these gaps, and the mean is based upon the full ten years.

[c]Mean calculated on the basis of 4.872 years of recorded mint activity.

[d]For Mich. 1379 to 30 Jan. 1380, see note b above. There are no mint accounts available for the period 2 May 1386 to 30 Sept. 1388 (28.94 months), when the mints were evidently active. The mean is therefore calculated on the basis of the remaining 91.06 months in the decade = 7.58833 years.

[e]Mean calculated on the basis of 7.26 years of recorded activity, as explained in notes b and d above: i.e. from 30 Jan. 1380 to 2 May 1386, and from 1 Oct. 1388 to 30 Sept. 1389.

Table 7. Output of silver and gold coinages in England and the Low Countries: quinquennial means in kilograms of pure metal, 1335–9 to 1495–9

	Silver kilograms			Gold kilograms		
Years	England	Flanders	Low Countries	England	Flanders	Low Countries
1335–9	483.08	5,244.71		–	295.06	
1340–4	3,629.67	[176.76][b]		187.30	[1.32][b]	
1345–9	3,111.00	3,787.61		602.84	94.73	
1350–4	15,583.84	5,761.30		1,734.56	914.93	
1355–9	6,401.07	7,839.63		1,765.65	2,898.65	
1360–4	1,858.76	4,107.57		2,403.54	2,575.95	
1365–9	283.28	9,232.03		1,818.20	2,084.87	
1370–4	198.82	4,213.83[c]		953.77	815.35[c]	
		[9,891.61][d]			[1,913.96][d]	
1375–9	510.55	1,203.27[e]	1,761.72	251.91	466.15[e]	1,200.38[j]
		[2,194.41][f]	[2,752.86]		[850.13][f]	[1,584.36]
1380–4	326.15	3,029.10[g]	3,737.39	155.43	546.74[g]	625.91
		[3,243.73][h]	[3,952.02]		[585.48][h]	[664.65]
1385–9	187.82	1,592.58[i]	1,926.05	422.62	521.97[i]	574.23
1390–4	300.14	4,072.16	5,055.16	646.86	484.31	528.03
1395–9	167.75	5,937.36	6,108.47	441.92	368.84	376.25
1400–4	79.22	1,462.25	1,462.25	217.58	64.18	64.18
1405–9	14.70	–	312.28	74.42	–	10.50
1410–4	665.04	3,508.66	4,926.55[k]	1,553.28	24.55	72.28[k]
1415–9	1,073.75	182.30	517.70	1,241.75	2.64	16.04
1420–4	1,953.69	12,910.53	13,382.67	2,375.36	11.27	14.39
1425–9	6,318.34	5,089.98	5,393.58	828.54	319.11	908.46
1430–4	9,006.56	4,812.88	7,554.38	266.30	189.52	1,731.18
1435–9	1,715.14	4,771.55	6,906.84	132.94	361.58	762.93

Table 7. *(continued)*

Years	Silver kilograms			Gold kilograms		
	England	Flanders	Low Countries	England	Flanders	Low Countries
1440–4	271.56	226.65	311.99	107.00	102.73	109.44
1445–9	229.71	12.92	12.92	50.43	23.04	23.04
1450–4	1,578.57	15.06	42.45	83.32	161.99	346.22
1455–9	1,142.35	89.41	186.22	24.22	316.69	727.06
1460–4	2,169.42	–	–	81.97	11.12	13.75
1465–9	6,610.33[a]	2,073.46	3,253.00	1,617.34[a]	153.24	209.69
1470–4	2,567.15	5,117.94	7,407.07	595.17	74.31	96.04
1475–9	1,243.75	3,452.06	8,437.72	430.88	280.64	577.69
1480–4	955.91	2,853.73	6,793.23	284.92	30.68	65.32
1485–9	896.86	1,070.34	8,275.45	128.62	2.07	122.37
1490–4	n.a.	950.51	2,894.03	n.a.	8.90	46.45
1495–9	2,123.97	1,634.85	4,328.51	296.41	69.21	112.97

[a]3-year mean: 1465–66, 1469.
[b]Flanders: gold and silver coinages for 16 Apr. to 17 Oct. 1343 only.
[c]There are no records of Flemish minting from 5 Aug. 1370 to 18 June 1373 (34.44 months); but the means computed here are based on 60 months (5 years).
[d]The Flemish means for 1370–4 are computed on the basis of the 25.56 months of recorded mint activity, as explained in note c.
[e]There are no records of Flemish minting from 27 June 1377 to 30 Jan. 1380 (27.10 months for this quinquennium; 3.97 for the next); but the means computed here are based on 60 months for the full quinquennium 1375–9.
[f]The Flemish means are computed on the basis of 32.9 months of recorded mint activity from Mich. 1374 to 27 June 1377.
[g]See note e. Mean based on the full 60 months of the quinquennium.
[h]Flemish means are computed on the basis of the 56.03 months of recorded mint activity, from 30 Jan. 1380 to Mich. 1384. See note e.
[i]The Flemish mint accounts are missing from 2 May 1386 to 30 Sept. 1388, 28.94 months. The Flemish means are therefore computed on the basis of the remaining 31.06 months, including 4.93 months when the mints were definitely closed, from 4 Dec. 1385 to 2 May 1386.
[j]Mean of 4.25 years. Account available only from 1 July 1375 (9 months missing).
[k]For Brabant (Leuven), mean based on 3.737 years of recorded mint activity: accounts missing from 21 Mar. 1411 to 25 June 1412.

Table 8. Values of the coinage outputs of England and the Low Countries: quinquennial means in current moneys-of-account and in constant pounds sterling (1351–1411 values)

	Total coinage values in current £			Total coinage values in constant £		
Years	England £ sterl.	Flanders £ groot	Low Countries £ groot	England £ sterl.*	Flanders £ sterl.*	Low Countries £ sterl.*
1335–9	1,737.43	11,204.51		1,865.64	32,969.68	
1340–4	20,628.44	[337.46][b]		22,088.53	[739.61][b]	
1345–9	34,917.03	9,553.85		37,992.00	18,709.44	
1350–4	134,310.62	31,918.46		134,929.78	61,676.03	
1355–9	100,806.24	90,498.46		100,806.23	155,184.97	
1360–4	110,752.03	83,249.37		110,752.05	126,866.38	
1365–9	79,444.17	93,416.29		79,444.17	125,495.06	
1370–4	41,867.94	45,985.67[c]		41,867.94	51,408.61[c]	
		[107,947.58][d]			[120,677.47][d]	
1375–9	12,826.91	23,137.93[e]	54,537.83[j]	12,826.91	24,734.45	58,530.68[j]
		[42,196.83][f]			[45,108.42][f]	
1380–4	7,957.28	36,481.82[g]	42,881.01	7,957.28	35,258.48[g]	41,405.53
		[39,066.73][h]			[37,756.71][h]	
1385–9	18,936.90	34,354.67[i]	38,569.06	18,936.90	28,643.20[i]	32,182.88
1390–4	29,033.43	36,184.84	41,959.32	29,033.43	36,596.42	42,276.69
1395–9	19,691.10	38,564.87	39,550.11	19,691.10	38,824.00	39,804.25
1400–4	9,681.97	8,478.82	8,478.82	9,681.97	8,412.66	8,412.66
1405–9	3,263.54	–	1,685.06	3,263.54	–	1,658.53
1410–4	77,356.99	13,062.75	19,606.13[k]	69,502.54	14,608.00	22,140.72[k]
1415–9	64,431.16	806.11	2,993.73	57,656.31	817.79	3,076.54
1420–4	122,786.43	63,093.00	67,946.44	109,904.20	50,345.45	54,234.51
1425–9	68,951.70	50,153.92	87,398.05	60,104.45	36,510.98	61,908.22
1430–4	54,489.94	35,938.47	155,836.00	46,258.34	26,753.90	104,160.96
1435–9	14,313.75	44,611.30	77,983.43	12,352.47	34,008.71	59,549.98

Table 8. *(continued)*

Years	Total coinage values in current £			Total coinage values in constant £		
	England £ sterl.	Flanders £ groot	Low Countries £ groot	England £ sterl.*	Flanders £ sterl.*	Low Countries £ sterl.*
1440–4	6,381.66	7,077.30	7,901.58	5,659.60	5,302.16	5,920.67
1445–9	3,479.38	1,414.50	1,414.50	3,060.44	1,042.84	1,042.84
1450–4	11,305.14	10,009.21	21,442.17	9,686.90	7,038.64	15,083.42
1455–9	6,453.63	19,947.79	45,623.89	5,455.33	13,992.12	32,049.65
1460–4	14,557.49	681.41	842.41	11,910.37	479.18	592.30
1465–9	141,182.56[a]	22,403.18	33,080.89	95,223.05[a]	14,611.03	21,598.91
1470–4	53,341.60	35,818.13	51,002.14	35,561.09	22,967.39	32,744.41
1475–9	35,056.29	45,299.40	[101,867.52] 103,712.98[l]	23,370.88	25,425.04	57,479.64
1480–4	23,954.35	25,535.80	[57,264.52] 59,458.24[l]	15,969.58	12,343.02	29,049.63
1485–9	13,509.38	10,205.67	113,471.24	9,006.26	4,222.80	37,232.43
1490–4	n.a.	7,507.11	26,466.58	n.a.	4,054.34	13,178.36
1495–9	31,463.39	20,241.50	47,021.80	20,975.58	9,296.11	21,584.46

*Values of constant pound sterling (1351–1411 values)
1 kg. of gold = £43.092065 1 kg. of silver = £3.861948
[a]3-year mean: 1465–66, 1469.
[b]Flanders: gold and silver coinages for 16 Apr. to 17 Oct. 1343 only.
[c]There are no records of Flemish minting from 5 Aug. 1370 to 18 June 1373 (34.44 months); but the means computed here are based on 60 months (5 years).
[d]The Flemish means for 1370–4 are computed on the basis of the 25.56 months of recorded mint activity, as explained in note c.
[e]There are no records of Flemish minting from 27 June 1377 to 30 Jan. 1380 (27.10 months for this quinquennium; 3.97 for the next); but the means computed here are based on 60 months for the full quinquennium 1375–9.
[f]The Flemish means are computed on the basis of 32.9 months of recorded mint activity from Mich. 1374 to 27 June 1377.
[g]See note e. Mean based on the full 60 months of the quinquennium.

Table 8. *(continued)*

[h]Flemish means are computed on the basis of the 56.03 months of recorded mint activity, from 30 Jan. 1380 to Mich. 1384. See note e.

[i]The Flemish mint accounts are missing from 2 May 1386 to 30 Sept. 1388, 28.94 months. The Flemish means are therefore computed on the basis of the remaining 31.06 months, including 4.93 months when the mints were definitely closed, from 4 Dec. 1385 to 2 May 1386.

[j]Mean of 4.25 years. Account available only from 1 July 1375 (9 months missing).

[k]For Brabant (Leuven), mean based on 3.737 years of recorded mint activity: accounts missing from 21 Mar. 1411 to 25 June 1412.

[l]Coinage of Brabant as 'weak coinage' (by 12.5%).

Table 9. A comparison of long-term averages of mint outputs in England and the Low Countries: in kilograms of pure metal, constant pounds sterling (1351–1411 values), and current moneys, 1250–1499

	England (1250–1499)				Low Countries (1350–1499)			
			Total coinage values				Total coinage values	
Period of the mean	Silver kg.	Gold kg.	Constant £ sterl.	Current £ sterl.	Silver kg.	Gold kg.	Constant £ sterl.	Current £ groot Flemish
1250–99	13,615.3	–	52,581.5	42,491.3				
1300–49	8,843.4[a]	84.1[a]	37,775.0[a]	31,353.8[a]				
1350–99	2,581.8	1,059.5	55,624.6	55,562.6	4,856.3[e]	1,200.5[e]	70,487.0[e]	52,242.0[e]
1400–99	2,132.8	684.8	37,744.4	42,513.7	4,198.1	371.2	32,210.6	43,124.4
1450–99	1,935.4[b]	336.7[b]	21,984.9[b]	31,901.3[b]	4,161.8	231.8	26,059.3	50,212.2
1300–99	5,615.8[a]	586.8[a]	46,975.8[a]	43,832.6				
1400–99	2,041.5[b]	523.9[b]	30,457.7[b]	37,606.9[b]	4,179.9	301.5	29,134.9	46,668.3
1270–1369	9,116.6[c]	438.8[c]	54,115.1[c]	48,332.0[c]				
1370–1469	1,626.3[d]	555.1[d]	30,201.2[d]	34,310.0[d]	3,450.0[f]	453.6[f]	32,868.5[f]	39,815.9[f]

*Gold values (1351–1411): 1 kg. = £43.092065; Silver values (1351–1411): 1 kg. = £3.861948.
[a]Mean of 47 (97) years: data missing for 1310–11 and 1322.
[b]Mean of 43 (53) years: data missing for 1467–68 and 1490–94.
[c]Mean of 97 years (see a).
[d]Mean of 98 years (see b).
[e]Mean of 47.5883 years: data missing for 1386–88, when mints were active.
[f]Mean of 97.5883 years: data missing, see e.

Table 10. Official values of gold and silver in the Low Countries and England, 1335–1504: in pounds groot Flemish and pounds sterling English, respectively, per kilogram of pure metal, with the official gold to silver ratios (ratios of traites)

	Low Countries (Flanders)*			England		
Date	Gold £ groot	Silver £ groot	Ratio	Gold £ ster.	Silver £ ster.	Ratio
May 1335					3.601	
Jun 1335	14.641	1.196	12.24			
Jun 1337	16.394	1.433	11.44			
Apr 1343		1.759				
Jan 1344				43.092	3.476	12.40
Aug 1344				37.825	3.424	11.05
Jun 1345				37.825	3.450	10.96
Jan 1346		1.835				10.96
Aug 1346				40.219	3.476	11.57
Nov 1346		2.016				11.57
May 1349	20.877	2.016	10.36			11.57
May 1351	20.877	2.164	9.65			11.57
Jul 1351			9.65	43.092	3.862	11.16
Jan 1352	22.300	2.164	10.30			11.16
Sep 1352	22.775	2.164	10.52			11.16
Sep 1353	22.775	2.221	10.25			11.16
Dec 1354	23.945	2.385	10.04			11.16
Jul 1356	24.787	2.385	10.39			11.16
Sep 1357	25.682	2.385	10.77			11.16
Oct 1357	24.787	2.385	10.39			11.16
Jul 1358	25.558	2.385	10.72			11.16
Oct 1359	25.833	2.487	10.39			11.16
Nov 1359	26.966	2.487	10.84			11.16
Feb 1360	27.251	2.487	10.96			11.16
Sep 1361	28.201	2.558	11.02			11.16

Table 10. *(continued)*

Date	Low Countries (Flanders)*			England		
	Gold £ groot	Silver £ groot	Ratio	Gold £ ster.	Silver £ ster.	Ratio
Dec 1361	29.111	2.558	11.38			11.16
Dec 1363	31.387	2.771	11.33			11.16
Mar 1364	29.111	2.771	10.51			11.16
Apr 1365	30.813	3.038	10.14			11.16
Jan 1368	32.405	3.240	10.00			11.16
Apr 1369	32.405	3.391	9.56			11.16
Sep 1369	32.865	3.553**	9.25**			11.16
Apr 1370	33.124	3.553**	9.32**			11.16
Jun 1373	39.530	3.739	10.57			11.16
	39.896	3.739	10.67			
Jan 1380	41.692	4.121	10.12			11.16
	42.598	4.121	10.34			
Sep 1383	45.570	4.300	10.60			11.16
Sep 1384	35.120	3.553	9.89			11.16
Apr 1386	41.727	4.050	10.30			11.16
Oct 1386	41.727	4.050	10.30			11.16
	41.727	4.107	10.16			
Apr 1387	49.811	4.910	10.14			11.16
Oct 1388	55.566	5.337	10.41			11.16
Jan 1390	39.223	4.050	9.68			11.16
Jan 1391	39.223	4.086	9.60			11.16
Jun 1393	39.223	4.050	9.68			11.16
Jul 1407	39.636	4.050	9.79			11.16
Aug 1409	33.443	3.482	9.60			11.16
Nov 1411			9.60	47.880	4.634	10.33
Dec 1416	37.554	4.263	8.81			10.33

Table 10. *(continued)*

Date	Low Countries (Flanders)*			England		
	Gold £ groot	Silver £ groot	Ratio	Gold £ ster.	Silver £ ster.	Ratio
Jun 1418	47.290[a]	4.832[a]	9.79			10.33
Oct 1421		4.832[c]				10.33
Aug 1423		4.263[c]				10.33
Jun 1425	56.784[a]	4.832[a]	11.75			10.33
Jul 1425	56.784[c]	4.519[c]	12.57			10.33
Jul 1426	64.412[c]	4.558[c]	14.13			10.33
Nov 1426	64.412[a]	4.832[a]	13.33			10.33
Sep 1427	50.672[a]	4.832[a]	10.49			10.33
Jun 1428	62.054[c]	5.116[c]	12.13			10.33
Nov 1428	58.835[a]	5.474[a]	10.75			10.33
Feb 1429	64.052[c]	5.525[c]	11.59			10.33
Jun 1429	65.834[c]	5.756[c]	11.44			10.33
Sep 1429	64.248[b]	5.453[b]	11.78			10.33
Jan 1430	65.834[c]	5.756[c]	11.44			10.33
May 1430	64.248[b]	5.453[b]	11.78			10.33
Dec 1430	65.985[c]	5.756[c]	11.46			10.33
Mar 1431	64.722[b]	5.453[b]	11.87			10.33
Mar 1431	65.985[c]	5.756[c]	11.46			10.33
Apr 1431	66.504[c]	5.815[c]	11.44			10.33
Sep 1431	67.031[c]					10.33
Dec 1431	70.381[c]	6.139[c]	11.46			10.33
Oct 1432	73.110[c]	6.139[c]	11.91			10.33
May 1433	77.176[c]	6.634[c]	11.63			10.33
Aug 1433	57.883[c]	4.975[c]	11.63			10.33
Oct 1433	55.591[a,b]	5.116[a,b]	10.87			10.33
Mar 1443	57.907	5.116	11.32			10.33

Table 10. *(continued)*

	Low Countries (Flanders)*			England		
Date	Gold £ groot	Silver £ groot	Ratio	Gold £ ster.	Silver £ ster.	Ratio
Jan 1454	61.286	5.116	11.98			10.33
Aug 1464			11.98	59.850	5.793	10.33
Mar 1465			11.98	64.638	5.793	11.16
Jun 1466	63.480	5.862	10.83			11.16
Oct 1467	65.029	6.004	10.83			11.16
Dec 1474	74.316	6.821	10.90			11.16
Sep 1477	83.607[a]	6.821[a]	12.26			11.16
Sep 1477	83.607[b]	7.674[b]	10.89			11.16
Jul 1482	92.898[a]	8.527[a]	10.89			11.16
Mar 1484	74.316	6.821	10.90			11.16
Apr 1485	92.898[a]	10.232[a]	9.08			11.16
	102.189[a]	10.232[a]	9.99			
Dec 1485	92.898[b]	8.527[b]	10.89			11.16
Mar 1486	92.898[a]	8.527[a]	10.89			11.16
Aug 1486	102.189[b]	9.379[b]	10.89			11.16
Jul 1487	121.347[b]	10.386[b]	11.68			11.16
	121.347[b]	11.750[b]	10.33			
Jun 1488		14.244[d]				11.16
Nov 1488	168.832[d]	17.480[d]	9.66			11.16
	204.643[d]	17.480[d]	11.71			
Jun 1489		13.643[a]				11.16
		15.000[a]				
Jul 1489		15.348				11.16
		15.804				
Jan 1490	61.932	5.683	10.90			11.16
Mar 1492	74.316	7.248	10.25			11.16

Table 10. *(continued)*

Date	Low Countries (Flanders)*			England		
	Gold £ groot	Silver £ groot	Ratio	Gold £ ster.	Silver £ ster.	Ratio
Dec 1492	76.196[v]	7.248[v]	10.51			11.16
Sep 1493	74.316[a]	7.248[a]	10.25			11.16
Sep 1493	74.316[b]	8.156[b]	9.11			11.16
Aug 1494	[74.316]	7.248	10.25			11.16
Jan 1495	74.316	7.248	10.25			11.16
	86.704	8.156	10.63			
May 1496	90.704[a]	8.420[a]	10.77			11.16
May 1496	90.704[b]	8.527[b]	10.64			11.16
	98.262[b]	9.593[b]	10.24			
Sep 1497	90.704[b]	8.420[b]	10.77			11.16
May 1499	94.483	8.527	11.08			11.16
Feb 1500	94.977	8.527	11.14			11.16
May 1503	94.977	8.527	11.14			11.16
	94.977	8.898	10.67			
Jan 1504	94.977	8.527	11.14			11.16

*The monetary values for the Low Countries for the period 1335 tɔ 1418 are for Flanders only; thereafter, the principality concerned is indicated as follows:

[a]Flanders.

[b]Brabant.

[c]Namur.

[d]Mechelen (seigneurie of).

Where there is no such indication, the data refer to all of the Burgundian Low Countries, whose coinages were unified after 1433; but as indicated, regional mints occasionally differed from the 1470s, particularly during the era of revolt against Maximilian.

**silver values estimated (interpolated) for 1369 and 1370.

Table 10. *(continued)*

Note: all of these monetary data have been taken directly from the mint accounts or mint indentures, not from official proclamations (except for the Low Countries in March 1443, when the value of the gold *rijder* or *philippus* was raised from 48d. to 50d. groot Flemish). When one or the other metal was not struck, no value was given for that metal.

All of these values are in terms of 100% pure metal, not in terms of official standards of fineness. In England sterling silver was 92.5% pure; in the Low Countries silver *argent-le-roy* was 23/24th or 95.833% pure. The English gold noble at 23 7/8 carats was thus 99.479166% pure gold. In both England and the Low Countries this was often taken as the standard for 'fine' gold.

When two sets of values are given for one date, that means that an alteration in the coinage(s) took place some time after the mint account commenced.

Sources for the Monetary Tables

A. *ENGLAND*

1. *London and Canterbury: 1235-1272*
   C. E. Blunt and J. D. Brand, "Mint Output of Henry III," *British Numismatic Journal,* XXXIX (1970), 61-6.
2. *London, Canterbury, and Other Provincial Mints: 1272-1377*
   C. G. Crump and C. Johnson, "Tables of Bullion Coined Under Edward I, II, and III," *The Numismatic Chronicle,* 4th ser. XIII (1913), 200-45.
3. *London, 1377-1485 (and Bristol, 1470-72; York, 1470-75)*
   G. C. Brooke and E. Stokes, "Tables of Bullion Coined from 1377 to 1550," *The Numismatic Chronicle,* 5th ser. IX (1929), 27-69.
   The London statistics for 1432 and 1433 have been corrected by information in:
   Sir John Craig, *The Mint: A History of the London Mint from A. D. 287 to 1948* (Cambridge, 1953), pp. 408, 412.
4. *London, 1485-1499*
   C. E. Challis, *The Tudor Coinage* (Manchester, 1978), pp. 305, 307.
5. *Calais*
   a) 1363-1384: Crump and Johnson, "Tables of Bullion Coined," *N.C.*, XIII (1913), 235, 243-45.
   b) 1387-1404: T. H. Lloyd, *The English Wool Trade in the Middle Ages* (Cambridge, 1977), p. 241: Table 15, as verified, corrected, and extended, from: Public Record Office, Lord Treasurer's Remembrancer Exchequer, E. 364/22, 25, 28, 30, 34, 36, 37; King's Remembrancer Exchequer, E. 101/184/10
   c) 1422-1440: Public Record Office, L. T. R. Exchequer, E. 364/59, 61-3, 65-6, 69, 72; K. R. Exchequer, E. 101/192-3; and *Calendars of Patent Rolls, 1422-29,* pp. 337-8, 502; *Calendar of Patent Rolls, 1429-1436,* pp. 256-7, and 259.
   F. A. Walters, "Supplementary Notes on the Coinage of Henry VI," *Numismatic Chronicle,* 4th ser. XI (1911), 171-2 (for Calais in 1436 and 1439-40; for York in 1423-24).

B. *THE LOW COUNTRIES*

1. *Flanders, 1334 to 1384:* Ghent, Bruges, and Mechelen
   Victor Gaillard, ed. *Recherches sur les monnaies des comtes de Flandre, II: Sous les règnes de Louis de Crécy et de Louis de Mäle* (1856); Hans Van Werveke, *De muntslag in Vlaanderen onder Lodewijk van Male* (Mededeligen van de koninklijke Vlaamse Academie voor Wetenschappen, Letteren, en Schone Kunsten van België, Klasse der Letteren, no. XI: 5, Brussels, 1949).
   Frans and Willem P. Blockmans, "Devaluation, Coinage, and Seignorage Under Louis de Nevers and Louis de Male, Counts of Flanders, 1330-84," in *Coinage in the Low Countries (880-1500),* ed. Nicholas Mayhew (*BAR* International series 54, Oxford, 1979), pp. 69-94 (mint accounts of Ghent, 1335-6, and Mechelen, 1380-82).
2. *Flanders, 1384-1499*
   a) *Ghent:*
   Archives générales du royaume (Belgique), Comptes en rouleau nos. 824-26 (1388-90), nos. 827-31 (1410-19); Acquits de Lille, nos. 936: 1-8 (1410-22) and nos. 937: 1-26 (1422-47); Chambre de Comptes, reg. no. 580 (1419-29) and reg. nos. 18,195-200 (1459-89); Archives départmentales du Nord (Lille), Chambre de Comptes, Série B, no. 1606 (1441-42)
   b) *Bruges:*
   A. G. R., Comptes en rouleau nos. 776-87 (1392-1402); Acquits de Lille, no. 1512: 1-4 (1454-56, 1466-67); Chambre de Comptes, reg. nos. 18,103-124 (1455-1499); A. D. N.

(Lille), Chambre de Comptes, Série B., no. 644/15,939 (1454-55); no. 19,960/19,312 (1454-55)

c) *Mechelen*
A. G. R., Comptes en rouleau nos. 2142-43 (1384-85); Chambre de Comptes, reg. nos. 48,976-77 (1390-92); Comptes en rouleau nos. 2145-46 (copies of 1390-92); Acquits de Lille nos 1512: 2-3 (1454-56) and 1512: 5 (1459-60); Chambre de Comptes, reg. no. 18,242: 1-3 (1485, 1488-89)

d) *Fauquemont*
A. G. R., Comptes en rouleau nos. 2586-87 (1396-98)

3. *Brabant, 1375-1499*

a) *Leuven (Louvain)*
A. G. R., Comptes en rouleau no. 2591 (1375-1383); nos. 2144 and 2589 (1384-86); no. 2590 (1393-94), no. 2588 (1394-95); Chambre de Comptes, no. 18,064 (1410-11), nos. 18,065-68 (1429-32); nos. 18,069-72 (1466-74);
Frederic Verachter, ed. *Documents pour servir à l'histoire monétaire des Pays Bas* (Antwerp, 1841), pp. 108-10; and Alphonse de Witte, *Histoire monétaire des comtes de Louvain, ducs de Brabant,* 2 vols. (Antwerp, 1894-96), I, 185-86:Jan.-July 1410 (both from private MSS).

b) *Vilvoorde*
A. G. R., Comptes en rouleau nos. 2590, 2592 (1392-93); Chambre de Comptes, no. 18,094 (1417); Verachter, *Documents monétaires,* pp. 107-8 (1409: from A. G. R., Chambre de Comptes no. 48,967, missing since June 1940)

c) *Maastricht*
A. G. R., Chambre de Comptes, nos. 18,071 and 18,073 (1419)

d) *Brussels*
A. G. R., Chambre de Comptes no. 17,985 (1420-21); nos. 17,986-89 (1434-37)

e) *Antwerp*
Alphonse de Witte, *Histoire monétaire,* I, 181 (1405)
A. G. R., Chambre de Comptes, reg. nos. 17,880-82 (1474-99)

4. *Holland, 1425-1493:* Dordrecht, Zevenbergen, The Hague
Algemeen Rijksarchief der Nederlanden, Rekeningen van de grafelijkheids-rekenkamer, nos. 4937: I-XVIII (1425-27, 1434-40, 1454-55, 1466-67, 1481-88, 1489-93);
Accounts in précis in P.O. Van der Chijs, *De munten der voormalige graafschappen Holland en Zeeland* (Haarlem, 1858), corrected by Peter Spufford, *Monetary Problems and Policies in the Burgundian Netherlands, 1433-1496* (Leiden, 1970), appendices (which I used for the Dordrecht account for 1489-93, unavailable to me).

5. *Namur, 1421-1499*
A. G. R., Chambre de Comptes reg. nos. 18,203: 1-21 (1421-33); reg. nos. 18,204 (1497-1500)

6. *Valenciennes (Hainaut)*
A. D. N. (Lille), Chambre de Comptes, Série B., no. 17,651 (1434); no. 31 and 19,975/19,402 (1454-55); A. G. R., Acquits de Lille, no. 1512: 4 (1466-67); Spufford, *Monetary Problems.* p. 184 (for 1455-56: from Acquits de Lille, no. 937bis, now missing from the A. G. R.) The Valenciennes mint accounts for Feb. 1437-Mar. 1439 and July 1441-Oct. 1444 are missing (Spufford, p. 177)

Graph I: England's Coinage Outputs

Silver and gold coinage outputs of the English mints, 1300-1499: Decennial means in kilograms of pure metal

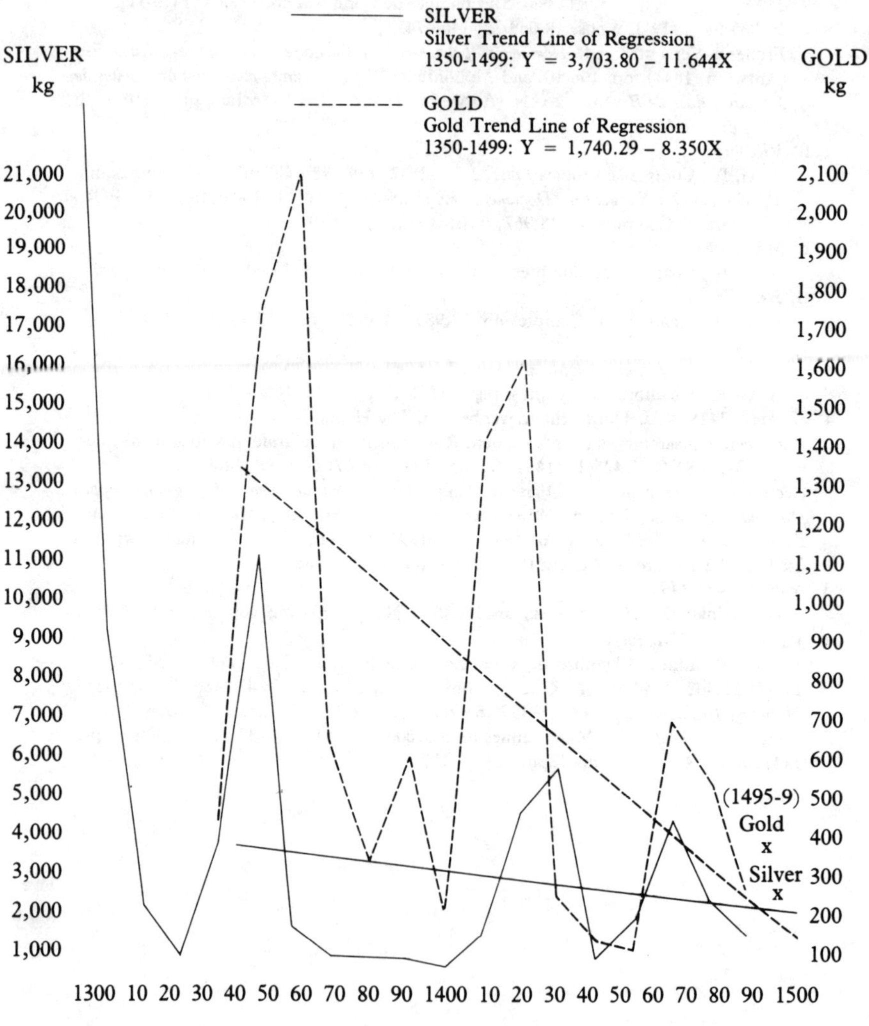

Graph II: The Low Countries' Coinage Outputs

Silver and gold coinage outputs of the Low Countries' mints, 1350-1499: Decennial means in kilograms of pure metal

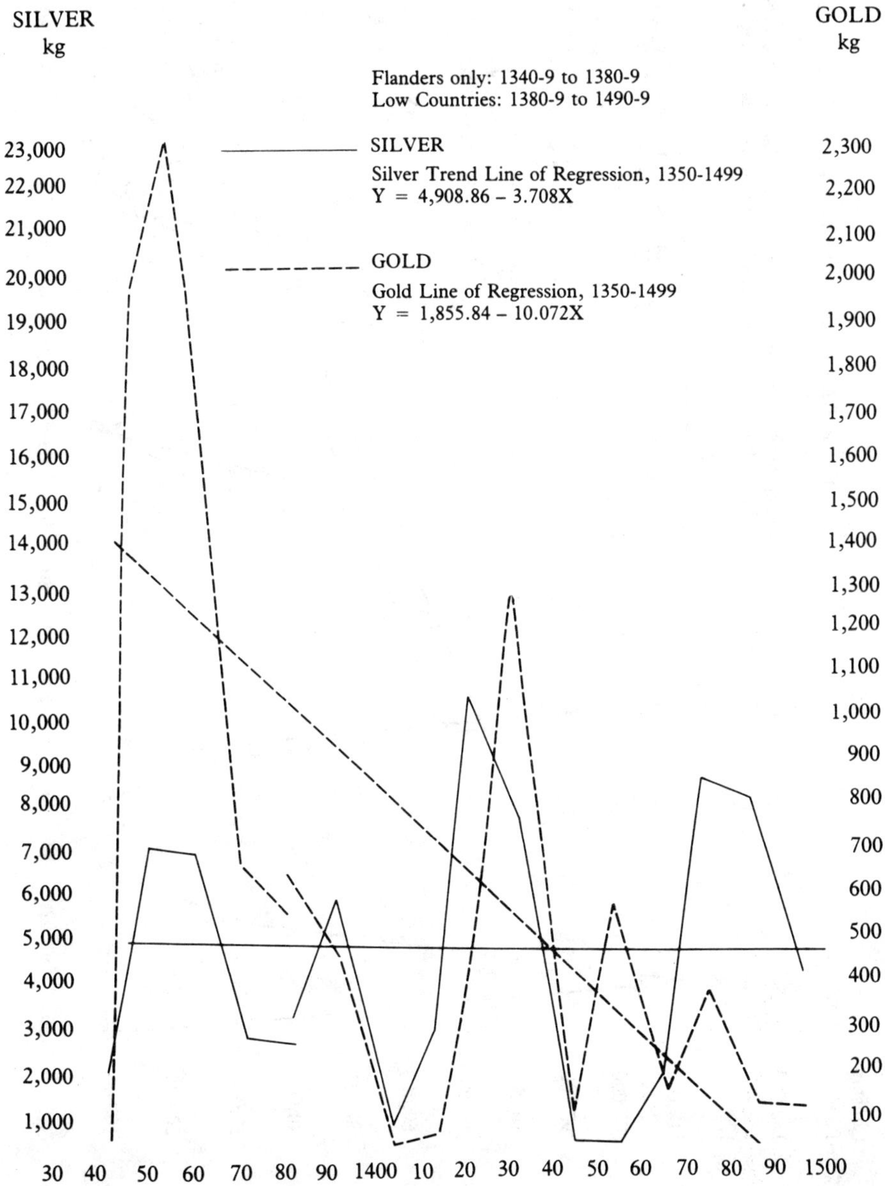

Graph III: Coinage Outputs of England and the Low Countries

The aggregate silver and gold coinage outputs of England (1290-1499) and the Low Countries (1340-1499): Decennial means in constant pounds sterling of 1351-1411 values

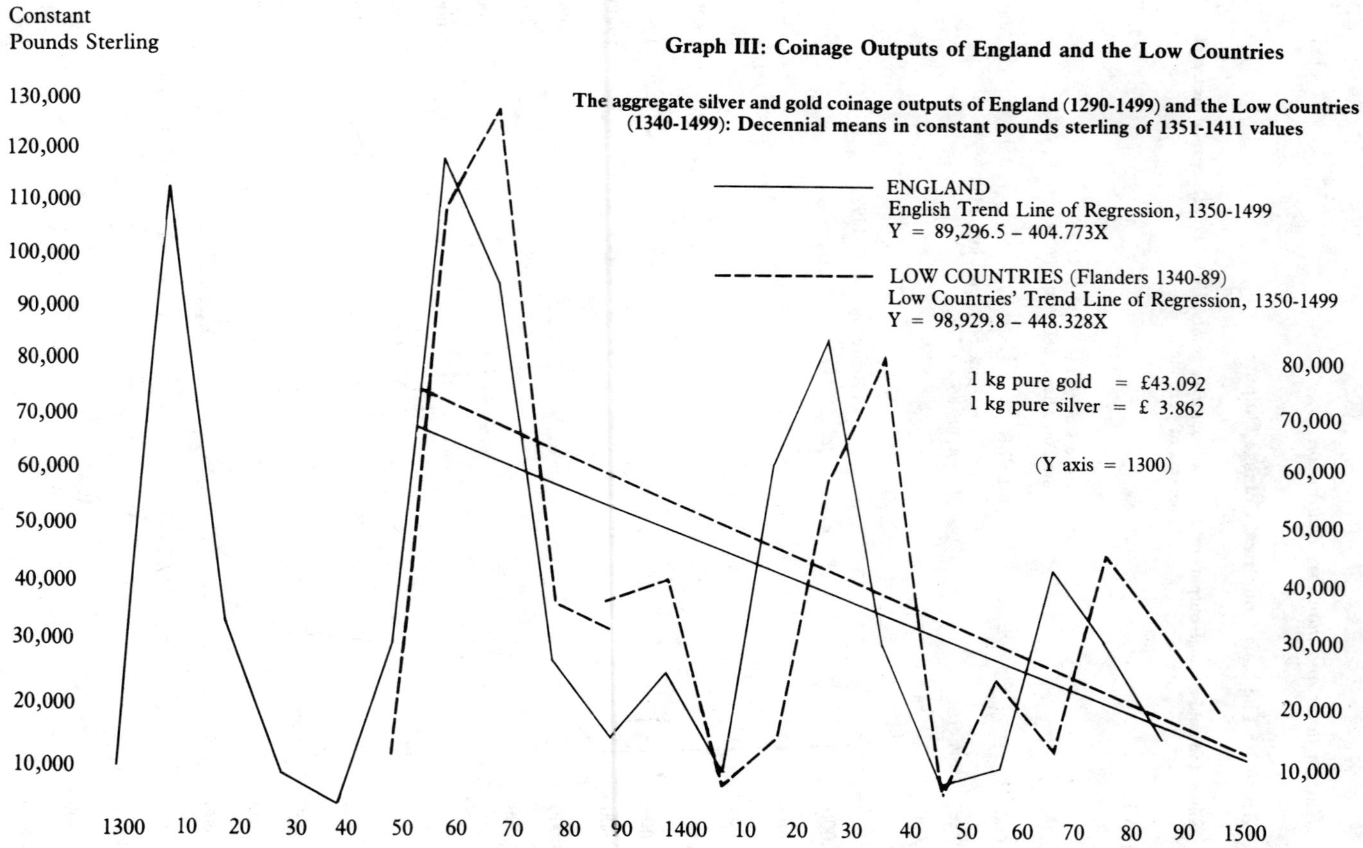

VII

Monnayage, monnaies de compte et mutations monétaires au Brabant à la fin du Moyen Age

En dépit des nombreuses publications au cours de ces 140 dernières années concernant la frappe des monnaies au Brabant, l'histoire monétaire de ce grand duché impérial, au XIVe et au début du XVe siècle, reste bien plus mal connue que celle de son voisin occidental, le comté de Flandre [1]. Peut-être sera-t-il impossible de faire toute la lumière sur ce sujet, car nous ne pourrons probablement jamais posséder pour le Brabant des comptes de la Monnaie comparables à ceux de Flandres qui remontent pratiquement sans interruption jusqu'à 1334. Néanmoins, je pense qu'il est maintenant possible de dresser un tableau relativement complet et précis des productions des Hôtels de la Monnaie du Brabant, ainsi que des mutations monétaires et des taux de change, entre 1375 et la réunification monétaire des Pays-Bas bourguignons de 1433-34. Pour beaucoup d'historiens de la monnaie — et surtout pour les économistes — l'intérêt principal de ces comptes réside dans le fait qu'ils permettent d'établir les volumes et les valeurs de la production monétaire brabançonne. Donc, avec l'aide de ces statistiques et aussi de celles déjà publiées pour les ateliers anglais, français et flamands, on peut mieux suivre les mouvements internationaux de métaux précieux à la fin du Moyen Age [2].

Cependant, il est tout aussi important — et ceci constitue le but essentiel de cette étude — de tirer parti de tous les chiffres sur le monnayage trouvés aussi bien dans les comptes des Hôtels brabançons que dans ceux de Flandre, de façon à dresser un tableau plus précis des changements monétaires survenus au Brabant, et en particulier des relations qui existaient entre les monnaies métalliques et les monnaies de compte. Pour des raisons d'ordre pratique, je n'aurai pas la possibilité d'effectuer cette analyse jusqu'à l'époque de la réunification. Nous devrons nous arrêter à la génération précédente avec les monnayages intervenus sous le duc Antoine en

1409-12 qui établirent l'avant-dernière forme des monnaies de compte brabançonnes, à savoir le *pond groot* ou la livre de gros, tout à fait indépendante de celle de Flandre.

Afin de pouvoir comprendre ces comptes de la Monnaie, ainsi que tous les problèmes monétaires soulevés dans le présent article, nous devons d'abord expliquer les mécanismes de la frappe et ses rapports avec les monnaies de compte au XIVe siècle en Flandre et au Brabant. Dans ces deux principautés, le titre standard utilisé pour la frappe de l'or, correspondant à un or parfaitement pur, était, là comme ailleurs, de 24 carats. Pour l'argent, le standard ne correspondait qu'à une pureté de 23/24e (95,833 %) exprimé en termes de 12 deniers *argent-le-roy*, avec 24 grains par denier. Aussi bien pour les monnaies d'or que pour celles d'argent, le standard de poids utilisé par les Hôtels de la Monnaie aux Pays-Bas était le marc de Troyes français, correspondant à un poids théorique de 244,7529 grammes. Il contenait 8 *onces* avec 20 *esterlins* (*ingelschen*) par once et 32 *azen* par esterlin, soit 5120 *azen* par marc (aux Pays-Bas) [3]. Cependant, les poids des pièces n'étaient pas exprimés en fonction de ces petites subdivisions dans les ordonnances monétaires médiévales, parce que les techniques de frappe étaient trop imprécises pour assurer des pièces uniformes. Au contraire, les ordonnances spécifiaient simplement que telle quantité de pièces d'un type donné devait être frappée ou découpée à partir d'un marc de métal de titre fixé : c'était la taille au marc. Aussi bien pour le titre que pour la taille, on acceptait en général une certaine tolérance raisonnable ou *remède* [4].

Ainsi, par exemple, le gros flamand d'argent (*groot*), ou denier, frappé de décembre 1361 à septembre 1362 à raison de 6 deniers *argent-le-roy* et à la taille de 72 pour un marc, avait un poids théorique de 3,399 gr et contenait 1,629 gr d'argent pur (théoriquement 244,7529/72 × 6/12 × 23/24) [5]. Ce gros d'argent s'était vu assigner une valeur ou un taux de change de ld. dans le système de monnaie de compte flamand connu sous le nom de livre de gros (*pond groot*). C'était une variante d'un système très répandu en Europe où 1 livre valait 20 sous ou 240 deniers. A son tour, ce denier gros avait été subdivisé en 3 esterlins (ou *ingelschen*), parce que, à l'origine (de 1300 à 1340), le gros flamand valait 3d. sterling anglais [6]. L'esterlin fut lui-même subdivisé en 8 *mites* de sorte que 24 mites valaient 1d. gros. Le gros d'argent servait, de plus, de base au « link money » qui liait directement ces monnaies de compte avec les monnaies d'argent courantes ; ainsi par exemple un montant de 5s. 6d. en gros valait toujours 66 gros d'argent courants. Cette corrélation peut être mieux évaluée en calculant la traite du marc en argent : la valeur en monnaie de compte du nombre total de pièces qu'on devait frapper à partir d'un marc d'alliage d'argent selon la formule suivante :

$$\text{Traite} = \frac{\text{Valeur des pièces en deniers} \times \text{taille}}{\text{Titre en deniers argent-le-roy}}$$

Comme on le voit clairement d'après cette formule, tout changement de l'un de ces trois paramètres, ou toute combinaison entre eux, affectait directement la valeur de la traite du marc : une diminution du poids (soit une augmentation de la taille), une réduction du titre (soit une augmentation de l'alliage), une augmentation du taux de change (c'est-à-dire de la valeur de la pièce en monnaie de compte). Chacun de ces changements, et pas seulement les mutations physiques des pièces elles-mêmes, constituait, techniquement parlant, un affaiblissement de la monnaie. Il faut noter qu'une diminution de 50 % de la teneur en argent métal augmentait la traite de 100 % ; une réduction de 25 % l'augmentait d'un tiers, etc. Ce rapport à double sens est exprimable par la formule $\frac{1}{1-x} - 1$, où *x* est le pourcentage (décimal) de réduction de la teneur en argent exprimée en unité de monnaie de compte. A l'inverse un renforcement, défini comme tout changement qui entraîne un accroissement de la teneur en argent de la monnaie de compte induisait pareillement une diminution de la traite [7].

D'après la terminologie employée par le professeur Hans Van Werveke, cette monnaie de compte flamande correspondait au système du type B, basé sur le denier d'argent courant. Depuis au moins 1318-19, cette livre gros était la principale monnaie de compte en usage en Flandre [8] ; et, à partir de cette date, tous les autres systèmes furent rattachés à la livre gros par un taux d'équivalence constant, à savoir : £ 1 gros = £ 12 *parisis* = £ 40 de *paiement* (de manière que 1 gros d'argent valait ls. *parisis* ou 3s. 4d. de *paiement*).

Contrairement au système monétaire uniforme de Flandre, le duché de Brabant présente au cours du XIVe siècle un fouillis de monnaies de compte différentes de types A et B. Les systèmes du type A étaient basés sur des poids fixes d'or ou d'argent ; ils étaient définis en termes d'anciennes pièces très connues, devenues des « monnaies fantômes » (par exemple, vieux écus ou *oude schilden* ; livre de vieux gros ou *pond oude groot*). Les systèmes du type B, toujours au Brabant reposaient sur des pièces d'argent ou d'or à usage courant : florins du Rhin, moutons, pieters, écus, etc.) [9]. La monnaie de compte la plus fréquemment utilisée au Brabant au XIVe siècle était la livre de paiement (*pond payement*) associée à une monnaie d'argent (type B) et qui consistait en 20s. avec 12d. par sou [10].

A l'origine, ce système, anciennement appelé la livre de bonne monnaie, avait été rattaché au gros tournois français — le vieux gros, tel qu'on le frappa entre août 1266 et septembre 1329 (quand il contenait 3,909 gr. d'argent pur) [11]. Cependant, à partir du moment où, en janvier 1337, Philippe VI décide l'affaiblissement de la monnaie française, la livre de paiement fut rattachée aux propres variantes brabançonnes du gros d'argent [12]. Par rapport au gros brabançon, le denier « de paiement » dans cette monnaie de compte valait un *mite*, c'est-à-dire 1/24e d'un gros, de telle sorte que 1 gros brabançon (monnaie effective) valait 24d. ou 2s. de paiement (monnaie de compte). Si l'on consulte les livres de comptes des trésoriers de la ville de Louvain, on trouve, comme Joseph Ghyssens l'a fait remarquer, que le même taux fixe de £1 *oude groot* égal à £24 de paiement est constamment maintenu entre 1345 et 1402 (période pendant laquelle le système de compte repose sur le florin du Rhin) [13]. En conséquence, ce *pond oude groot* de Louvain était aussi devenu une monnaie de compte du type B rattaché à la livre de paiement, par contraste avec le *pond groot* de Malines qui, lui, demeura loyalement une monnaie de compte du type A jusqu'à la réunification monétaire de 1433-34. Enfin, les marchands et corporations drapières du Brabant pendant le XIVe siècle préféraient une autre monnaie de compte, le *groot lakengeld* ou le gros des drapiers. M. Joseph Ghyssens pense qu'il reposait à l'origine sur un monnayage différent du gros des années 1340, mais que plus tard, certainement à partir de 1380, le *groot lakengeld* fut aussi rattaché à la livre de paiement au taux de change fixe de 23/24, de telle sorte que 1 *groot* valait 19s. 2d. ou 230 d. de paiement [14].

Bien que la valeur traditionnelle du gros ait été de 24d. ou 2s. de paiement, il ne reste pas à ce taux. Certes, la caractéristique principale de cette monnaie de compte du type B est de ne pas reposer sur son propre denier d'argent et elle ne fut donc pas aussi bien ancrée aux monnaies courantes que put l'être la livre gros de Flandre, comme des événements postérieurs le démontrèrent avec éclat. Ainsi le « petit gros à quatre lions » d'argent frappé à l'Hôtel de la Monnaie de Vilvorde entre juin 1363 et décembre 1371 valait deux fois plus que le vieux gros de paiement de 4s., de telle sorte que 240 gros valaient £ 48 de paiement. De plus, ce gros de Vilvorde avait été frappé en imitant fidèlement le gros flamand de 1361-62 mentionné plus haut, avec le même titre de 6 deniers *argent-le-roy* mais la moitié du poids, soit une taille de 144, et donc il circula en tant que demi-gros [15]. Le gros d'argent flamand valait donc le double, soit 8s. de paiement,de sorte que 240 gros flamands (1 livre gros) valaient £ 96 de paiement.

Par la suite, les deux gros subirent une perte considérable de leur valeur. Mais alors que le gros flamand perd 28 % de sa teneur en argent entre décembre 1363 et septembre 1369, le gros brabançon perd beaucoup plus, 42,9 %, par l'affaiblissement final de juin 1370 (voir tableau 1) [16]. L'Hôtel de Vilvorde cessa toute activité avant Noël 1371, soit longtemps après la fermeture (probable) des Hôtels flamands [17]. Peu après, en 1372, par une ordonnance non datée, les responsables monétaires du Brabant ordonnèrent qu'une nouvelle pièce, le *bryman*, soit frappée à Maastricht, au tarif de « 4 gros dernièrement frappés à Vilvorde », ou 16s. de paiement [18]. Cependant, si l'on considère la quantité d'argent dans une livre de paiement, cette nouvelle monnaie correspondait à un nouvel affaiblissement de 14,9 % comme l'indique le tableau 1. L'histoire de ces *brymannen* ainsi que celle de l'Hôtel de la Monnaie de Maastricht ne sont pas connues (bien que quelques *brymannen* figurent dans le catalogue numismatique d'Alphonse de Witte). Il se peut que ce monnayage ait avorté puisque les *brymannen* ne sont pas mentionnés dans les ordonnances monétaires ultérieures [19].

Ensuite, peu de temps avant juin 1374, un nouvel Hôtel de la Monnaie fut ouvert à Louvain sous la direction de Nicholas Chavre qui produisit les plus anciens comptes de la Monnaie brabançons qu'il nous reste aujourd'hui (9 séries de comptes pour la période 1er juillet 1375 - 8 mars 1383 (n.st.)) [20] » Il est possible aussi que Chavre ait créé un nouveau gros d'argent, communément appelé le *schuerman* ou *sceurken* parce que le revers de la pièce, représentant la cathédrale St. Pierre de Louvain, ressemblait à une grange (*schuere*, en néerlandais *schuur*) [21]. L'inventeur de ce schuerman-là essaya aussi apparemment d'imposer un renforcement de la monnaie d'argent (exprimée en livre de paiement). Car, comme le montre le tableau 1, la valeur attribuée au *schuerman* de 4s. de paiement correspondait en fait à une réévaluation de 12,9 % par rapport au denier gros de Vilvorde (également fixé à 4s. de paiement), et à un contenu en argent supérieur de 32,6 % à celui du *bryman* supposé précédent.

Si ce renforcement avait réussi, cela aurait dû se traduire par une déflation des prix exprimés en livres de paiement et en groots *lakengeld*. La déflation, qui fait souvent naître une impression de perte de revenu, est, en général, assez impopulaire, en particulier durant les périodes de crise commerciale. C'est précisément ce qui se produisit dans les villes drapières des Pays-Bas au cours des années 1370, ce qui pourrait expliquer l'échec de ce renforcement de la monnaie [22].

Comme s'en plaignirent ensuite les conseillers du duc Wenceslas et de la duchesse, « l'ordonnance fut annulée contre la volonté de nos maître et maîtresse et à leur insu », quand les villes brabançonnes ou les Etats menés par Bruxelles fixèrent un nouveau taux de change de 6s. de paiement pour le *schuerman*, soit de 50 % plus élevé [23] . Au même moment, les taux des autres pièces légales étaient augmentés dans la même proportion. Ainsi le lion d'argent flamand ou *plaque*, un double gros frappé à partir de juin 1373, valait désormais 19s. 6d. de paiement au lieu de 13s. ; le pieter d'or brabançon (de 70 schuerman) valait £ 21 au lieu de £ 14 de paiement. Le duc et la duchesse furent obligés de ratifier ce fait accompli humiliant, qui constituait une nouvelle dévaluation de la monnaie. La livre de paiement correspondait en effet maintenant à un poids d'argent de 24,7 % inférieur à celui de la livre définie par le gros de Vilvorde de 1370, et inférieur de 11,6 % à celui — supposé — de la livre du *bryman* de 1372 (voir le tableau 1) [24].

Ces événements monétaires bizarres inaugurent la soi-disant « crise monétaire brabançonne » des années 1375-82, qui constitue indiscutablement l'épisode le plus fameux de l'histoire des monnaies brabançonnes, comme l'ont décrit Charles Piot, Alphonse de Witte et de nombreux autres auteurs, le plus connu étant Henri Laurent dans *La loi de Gresham au Moyen Age* (Bruxelles, 1933) [25]. Malheureusement, et aussi étrange que cela puisse paraître, Laurent omit de faire usage non seulement des comptes de la Monnaie de Louvain établis par Nicholas Chavre entre 1375 et 1383, mais également des comptes flamands publiés au siècle dernier qui datent de cette période (seul Alphonse de Witte fit référence aux comptes de Louvain mais en commettant de nombreuses erreurs) [26]. Si Laurent s'était servi de ces livres de comptes, il n'aurait pas été si prompt à prendre le parti de Wenceslas dans son conflit avec les Etats brabançons sur le droit de frapper de nouvelles monnaies.

Il y a encore plus surprenant. Laurent ne réussit pas à replacer ce conflit dans le contexte de l'histoire politique récente du Brabant. En effet, c'est précisément à ce moment que la puissance et le prestige du duc Wenceslas de Luxembourg — frère de l'empereur Charles IV et époux de la maîtresse en titre du Brabant, la duchesse Joanna (1355-1406) — s'écroulent, pour demeurer à un très bas niveau jusqu'à sa mort à la fin de 1383. Sa chute commence avec la désastreuse défaite de son armée brabançonne et sa propre capture par les forces des ducs de Guelders et de Jülich à la bataille de Baesweiller (Bästweiler), le 22 août 1371 [27]. Pendant sa captivité, les villes du Brabant se réunissent à Bruxelles, de février à avril 1372, pour réaffirmer les droits et privilèges que leur avaient garantis les Chartes de Cortenberg en 1312 et les chartes wallonnes en 1314. Invoquant les premières, elles établissent un Conseil de Cortenberg chargé de défendre ces droits en l'absence de Wenceslas. Le malheureux duc, délivré grâce aux bons offices de son frère Charles IV en juin 1372, retourne à Bruxelles en disgrâce et lourdement endetté. Le mois suivant (12 juillet), il réunit les villes pour leur demander une aide financière de façon à couvrir les frais de la récente guerre. En contrepartie, les villes exigent l'aval des chartes de Cortenberg et des chartes wallonnes avant d'accepter de lever de nouvelles taxes. Le conflit entre le duc et les Etats devient si rude pendant les 20 mois qui suivent qu'une guerre civile semble alors inévitable. Enfin l'évêque de Liège, Jean d'Archel, intervient et arrange une trêve qui est signée le 30 avril 1374. Bien que s'étant excusées pour leur récente opposition envers le duc, les villes gagnèrent la partie en ce qui concerne l'imposition : en effet le conseil de Cortenberg se vit confier la perception des impôts et leur utilisation [28]. Il est probable que les villes exigèrent également qu'il ne fût procédé à aucune modification de la monnaie sans leur accord ; c'est ce qu'on peut déduire des nombreuses rencontres qui eurent lieu entre les villes et les Etats concernant la « question du nouveau monnayage », de janvier 1374 à décembre 1375. De toute évidence, les villes parvinrent au moins à modifier le taux de change sur le scheurman et sur d'autres pièces, comme on l'a vu précédemment. Au cours de juin et juillet 1376, Wenceslas se plaignit auprès des Etats de ne plus pouvoir frapper beaucoup de pièces d'argent à cause de ces mesures [29].

En dépit des plaintes du duc, l'émission des scheurmans (à son nouveau taux supérieur) fut un franc succès, notamment pendant les premiers trente mois figurant sur les comptes de la Monnaie de Chavre à Louvain (du 1er juillet 1375 au 31 décembre 1377), quand presque 4,5 millions d'entre eux furent frappés, soit une moyenne mensuelle de 148 645 pièces ou 333 marcs *argent-le-roy*. Cependant, comme le montre le tableau A, la production de l'atelier de Louvain fut moins impressionnante que celle des ateliers flamands pendant la même période (jusqu'à juin 1377). L'année suivante, 1378, fut en effet désastreuse pour le scheurman et l'Hôtel de la Monnaie de Louvain. Il ne fut frappé que 57 600 pièces (129,2 marcs), soit une moyenne mensuelle de 4 805 pièces. Le premier janvier 1379 (n. st.) — ou peut-être même avant —la Monnaie de Louvain cessa de frapper des monnaies d'argent tout en continuant à frapper des pièces d'or.

Par la suite, le comte Louis de Mäle de Flandre, engagé dans une guerre civile acharnée contre ses villes depuis 1379, ouvrit le 30 janvier 1380 un nouvel Hôtel de la Monnaie à Malines, enclave flamande à l'intérieur du duché de Brabant, à environ 25 km de Bruxelles et Louvain [30]. Il y frappa un nouveau double gros (ou plaque) affaibli qui contenait 9,3 % d'argent en moins que la plaque précédente (frappée, elle, depuis juin 1373). Comme on le voit sur le tableau A, une énorme quantité de cette nouvelle monnaie flamande fut frappée pendant la période de 15 mois qui suivit, à savoir : 18 495 marcs *argent-le-roy* représentant 2 145 000 pièces. Au Brabant, le duc Wenceslas lui emboîta le pas. Il réussit à faire

Tableau A

Production de monnaies d'argent dans les Hôtels de la Monnaie de Flandre et du Brabant, en marcs argent-le-roy, de janvier 1375 à mai 1386

FLANDRE				BRABANT			
Période de monnayage *	Teneur en argent de Double gros	Marcs argent -le-roy	Moyenne mensuelle en marcs	Période de monnayage	Teneur en argent des pièces	Marcs argent -le-roy-	Moyenne mensuelle en marcs
12.I.75-26.V.75	2,229 g.	6.811,5	1.530,0				
26.V.75-13.X.75	2,229 g.	5.091,7	1.111,6	1.VII.75-1.XI.76	0,525[a] g.	6.450,0	403,1
13.X.75-26.VI.76	2,229 g.	4.780,2	565,9				
6.XI.76-17.I.77	2,229 g.	555,2	236,4	1.XI.76-1.I.78	0,525[a] g.	3.539,6	252,8
17.1.77-27.VI.77	2,229 g.	1.638,5	306,2				
27.VI.77-29.I.80	---	--	--	1.I.78-1.I.79	0,525[a] g.	129,2	10,8
				1.I.79-1.IV.80	--	--	--
30.I.80-7.VIII.80	2,022 g.	10.307,5	1.948,4	I.IV.80-1.IV.81	0,504[b] g.	2.000,0	166,7
7.VIII.80-28.IV.81	2.022 g.	8.187,5	940,3				
28.IV.81-3.V.82	2,022 g.	15.787,5	1.297,9	1.IV.81-1.I.82	0,668[c] g.	[266,7]	[29,6]
22.V.82-11.IX.83	2,022 g.	21.775,0	1.307,3	1.I.82-1.I.83	1,333[d] g.	11.162,5	930,2
				1.I.83-8.III.83	0,333[e] g. 0,166 g.	1.345,0	597,7
12.IX.83-29.II.84	1,938 g.	6.588,5	1.051,4	8.III.83-3.IX.84	--	--	--
29.II.84-11.VI.84	1,938 g.	1.509,4	250,2				
10.IX.84-4.XII.85	2,346 g.	9.187,5	619,6	3.IX.84-16.V.86	2,346[f] g.	7.358,5	360,4

* Puisque les comptes de ces Hôtels brabançons intègrent aussi bien les monnayages en argent qu'en or, les dates n'indiquent que les seules périodes où la frappe des monnaies d'argent eut lieu, et pas nécessairement les dates initiales ou finales des émissions.
a) scheurman original — b) scheurman affaibli — c) gros longue-croix qui ne circula pas — d) double gros (groot) — e) labbayes, comme demi ou quart de gros — f) gros conventionnel (flamand)

Sources :

Flandre

Gand et Malines jusqu'à 29 février 1384 : Victor Gaillard, éd. *Recherches sur les monnaies des comtes de Flandre, II : Sous les règnes de Louis de Crécy et de Louis de Mäle* (Gand, 1856).
Malines, 7 août 1380 - 3 mai 1382 : F. and W.P. Blockmans, « Devaluation, coinage, and seignorage under Louis de Nevers and Louis de Mäle, Counts of Flanders, 1330-84 » dans N. Mayhew, éd. *Coinage in the Low Countries (880-1500): The Third Oxford Symposium on Coinage and Monetary History* (*BAR* International Series 54, Oxford, 1979), pp. 69-94.
Malines, 29 février 1384 - 4 décembre 1385 : Archives générales du royaume, comptes en rouleau, n° 2143a et b.

Brabant : Hôtel de la Monnaie de Louvain

Louvain, 1 juillet 1375 - 8 mars 1383 : Archives générales du royaume, comptes en rouleau n° 2591.

Louvain, 3 septembre 1384 - 16 mai 1386 : Archives générales du royaume, comptes en rouleau n° 2589.

redémarrer la frappe de pièces d'argent de la Monnaie de Louvain en y émettant un scheurman affaibli à partir d'avril 1380 [31], ou peu après. Cependant, cette dévaluation fut curieusement modeste : moins 4,1 % en poids comme le montre le tableau 1. Encore plus surprenante, du moins pour le duc, fut la colère des Etats brabançons. Ils le condamnaient pour avoir émis une nouvelle pièce sans leur consentement, en violation des chartes wallonnes et de son propre serment inaugural à l'occasion de la Joyeuse Entrée (*Blijde Inkomst*) de 1356. Pis encore, ils l'accusèrent d'être un véritable faussaire [32].

A plusieurs reprises entre novembre 1380 et avril 1381, Wenceslas clama son innocence et défendit sa récente dévaluation. Mais il se trouva de nouveau dans une position politique particulièrement difficile. En effet, il fut tout-à-fait incapable de venir à bout d'une rébellion de la ville de Louvain qui durait depuis juin 1378. Il ne fait pas de doute que cette incapacité à imposer l'autorité ducale ne fit qu'accroître le mépris des Etats envers le duc, malgré son plaidoyer éloquent [33]. En gros, Wenceslas affirmait qu'il n'avait fait que protéger les ateliers et la circulation brabançons contre les dévaluations étrangères, surtout celle de la plaque flamande frappée à Malines par le comte Louis de Mäle. Il prétendait que, du fait de la vaste circulation de ces pièces « frauduleuses » au Brabant et ce « au-dessus de leur véritable valeur », les Hôtels de la Monnaie brabançons ne pouvaient plus obtenir du métal blanc ; d'ailleurs, ils n'avaient pas frappé de pièces d'argent depuis « trois ans et quatre mois » (jusqu'à novembre 1380) [34]. Plus précisément, Wenceslas accusait Bruxelles et d'autres villes d'avoir, en violation de leurs propres ordonnances qui fixaient la valeur du scheurman à 6s. et celui de la plaque flamande à 19s. 6d. de paiement, permis aux pièces flamandes de monter jusqu'à 20s., et même, récemment (avril 1381) à 24s. alors que leur teneur en argent avait baissé, « ce qui faisait que 11 des nouvelles plaques ne valaient plus 10 des anciennes » [35]. Enfin, Wenceslas affirmait que les Etats avaient accepté auparavant, apparemment dans une ordonnance de mars 1376 aujourd'hui perdue, que si les rois de France et d'Angleterre ou l'empereur allemand ou le comte de Flandre affaiblissaient leurs monnaies, il devait pouvoir en faire autant [36]. De toute façon, au cours des trois dernières années les Etats n'avaient pas réussi à donner une réponse à ses demandes répétées sur les mutations monétaires. Maintenant (en 1380) il se sentait obligé d'agir pour la défense de la monnaie brabançonne.

Il faut reconnaître que la défense de Wenceslas était assez justifiée sur le plan moral car sa dévaluation, de toute évidence, avait été purement défensive. De plus, elle correspondait à une réduction du poids d'argent bien inférieure à celle de la monnaie flamande.

Néanmoins, les affirmations du duc étaient erronées ou trompeuses, et très discutables sur le plan juridique. Tout d'abord, l'arrêt de la frappe de monnaies d'argent n'avait pas pu durer « plus de trois ans », c'est-à-dire depuis le début ou le milieu de 1377, puisque les comptes de la Monnaie de Louvain dirigés par Chavre font état d'émissions de pièces d'argent au cours de deux périodes postérieures : du 1er novembre 1376 au 1er janvier 1378, et du 1er janvier 1378 au 1er janvier 1379. On peut admettre que les dernières pièces (129 marcs seulement) mentionnées dans ce dernier registre aient pu être frappées quelques mois avant la fermeture des comptes (qui font aussi état de frappes d'or). En second lieu, les ateliers flamands ne pouvaient être tenus responsables de l'arrêt du monnayage au Brabant que pour une période de 2 à 9 mois sur un total de 16 à 23 mois d'inactivité. En effet, on ne connaît pas de comptes de la Monnaie flamands pour la période allant du 27 juin 1377 jusqu'à la date d'ouverture de l'Hôtel de la Monnaie de Malines le 30 janvier 1380, c'est-à-dire peu de temps avant l'affaiblissement décrété par Wenceslas. En l'absence de toute ordonnance ou instruction sur les monnaies flamandes il se peut que les Monnaies aient été fermées pendant ces trente mois [37]. Il faut aussi tenir compte du fait qu'au cours des années 1376 et 1377 les Hôtels de la Monnaie aussi bien anglais que français, qui avaient à frapper, eux, des monnaies stables, ne produisirent que des quantités extrêmement réduites de pièces d'argent [38]. Ainsi, l'Hôtel de la Monnaie brabançon a bien pu être la victime, non pas de mutations étrangères, mais d'une raréfaction générale de métaux précieux vers la fin des années 1370, période de crise commerciale, comme nous l'avons indiqué plus haut [39].

Wenceslas n'avait pas raison non plus d'affirmer que la dernière dévaluation flamande de 1380 avait paralysé la frappe de monnaie au Brabant pour cette même année. La production de monnaies d'argent enregistrée dans les livres de comptes de Chavre pour la période du 1er avril 1380 au 1er avril 1381 n'a sans doute pas été aussi importante que celle de l'atelier de Malines pour cette même période, comme l'indique le tableau A. Il n'en reste pas moins qu'elle représente la somme respectable de 2 000 marcs *argent-le-roy*, soit 931 200 scheurmans. Comme ces mêmes livres de comptes prenaient aussi en considération la production de monnaies d'or (*pieters*), il est possible que la frappe d'argent ait commencé quelque temps après la frappe d'or, peut-être au moment de l'ordonnance du mois de novembre 1380, autorisant l'affaiblissement de l'argent. Dans ce cas, la moyenne mensuelle des émissions brabançonnes d'argent aurait été beaucoup plus grande que celle indiquée dans le tableau A.

Enfin, Wenceslas eut tort de s'en prendre aux Flamands et aux villes brabançonnes en ce qui concerne la réévaluation de la plaque flamande. Celle-ci avait vu sa valeur augmenter sur le « marché libre » précisément parce que Wenceslas d'abord, et ensuite les Etats, l'avaient sous-évaluée par rapport au scheurman. Comme le montrent les tableaux 1 et A, la plaque originelle de Gand de 1373-77 contenait (officiellement) 4,24 fois plus d'argent fin que le scheurman primitif de 1374-5, tandis que sa valeur officielle en sous de paiement n'était que trois fois plus élevée (c'est-à-dire 13 s. contre 4s. ; puis 19s. 6d. contre 6s.) Et même si la dévaluation flamande de janvier 1380 fut plus forte que la dévaluation brabançonne d'avril (ou novembre) 1380, la plaque flamande resta encore sous-évaluée : en effet, elle contenait 4,01 fois plus d'argent que le nouveau « petit scheurman ». En conséquence, si le nouveau scheurman valait 6s. de paiement, alors la plaque flamande aurait dû circuler au taux de 24s. de paiement, précisément le taux dont Wenceslas se plaignait en s'adressant aux Etats en avril 1381 ! Finalement, que les Etats du Brabant aient accepté ou non le principe de sanctionner les affaiblissements défensifs, les articles des chartes wallonnes de 1314, comme ceux de la *Blijde Inkomst,* montrent clairement que l'accord des Etats était nécessaire pour chaque modification de la valeur d'une quelconque monnaie [40].

Le but du dernier discours du duc Wenceslas devant les Etats en avril 1381 fut, de toute évidence, de justifier une nouvelle dévaluation de la monnaie d'argent qu'il promulgua tout d'abord dans une ordonnance monétaire générale en date du 19 mai 1381, et qu'il confirma ensuite le 6 juin suivant, en modifiant aussi certains taux de change [41]. Pour justifier le nouvel affaiblissement, l'ordonnance débute par une formulation presque parfaite de la fameuse loi qui fut, beaucoup plus tard, attribuée au financier anglais Sir Thomas Gresham (1519-1579). Cette justification devint une formule figée de presque toutes les ordonnances monétaires qui suivirent aux Pays-Bas [42].

> Au vu des grands dommages et des pertes que nos bonnes villes, nos terres et notre peuple du Brabant ont subis après avoir accepté quotidiennement toutes sortes de pièces étrangères aussi bien d'or que d'argent, qui ont circulé sur tout notre territoire du Brabant à des taux grandement supérieurs à leur valeur réelle, de telle sorte que nous avons perdu la plus grande part de notre or et de notre argent. Considérant que notre industrie et notre commerce se sont beaucoup amoindris et que notre terre aurait à souffrir encore plus de dommages et de pertes si aucun remède n'était apporté contre pièces étrangères frauduleuses...

Les monnaies étrangères en question n'étaient pas, cette fois, spécifiées. Il est sûr que ni les Flamands, ni les Français, ni les Anglais n'avaient modifié aucune de leurs pièces depuis la dernière dévaluation brabançonne d'avril 1380 [43]. Mais en tout cas, la dévaluation du duc Wenceslas fut, en livre de paiement, remarquablement limitée comme le montre le tableau 1 : moins 0,52 % seulement. Cependant, il se peut que cet affaiblissement ait semblé plus grave qu'il ne l'était en fait parce qu'il prit la forme d'un gros d'argent tout-à-fait nouveau appelé la « longue croix » d'après son empreinte, avec un titre de seulement 4d. *argent-le-roy* et une taille de 234 par marc, mais avec une valeur nominale inférieure proportionnellement de 4s. de paiement (c'est-à-dire l'ancien cours du gros, voir tableau 1). Par l'ordonnance du 6 juin 1381, Wenceslas acceptait maintenant un taux d'échange plus fort pour la plaque flamande, à savoir 22s. de paiement. C'était un taux supérieur à celui qu'il avait condamné peu de temps auparavant ; supérieur aussi au taux de 21s. qu'il avait essayé d'imposer le 19 mai, mais encore inférieur au taux du marché, soit 24s. de paiement. Pour être juste, on doit cependant admettre que ce taux n'était pas très éloigné du taux de marché, et mes recherches sur l'histoire monétaire de la fin du Moyen Age montrent que les princes du nord de l'Europe sous-évaluaient systématiquement toutes les monnaies étrangères (et aussi leurs anciennes pièces) qu'ils acceptaient encore en tant que monnaies légales pour permettre l'alimentation en métaux précieux de leurs propres ateliers [44]. Le taux officiel du pieter d'or brabançon fut désormais fixé à £ 23 de paiement, ce qui revenait à reconnaître implicitement une augmentation de la valeur de l'or (en monnaie d'argent, il passait de 70 vieux scheurmans — encore évalués — en réalité sous-évalués—6s. de paiement, à 76 2/3 scheurmans). En effet, le vrai rapport entre les deux métaux, qui était passé au cours du mois de novembre précédent de 8,74:1 à 9,31:1 fut à nouveau augmenté et passa à 9,52:1. L'ordonnance stipulait plus loin que tous les paiements et comptes devaient être faits en livres de paiement ou en groots lakengeld (au rapport préalablement cité de 23/24). Enfin, dans l'ordonnance de juin 1381, le duc Wenceslas et la duchesse Joanna juraient solennellement que les monnaies d'or et d'argent ne seraient plus modifiées pendant au moins 8 années [45].

Il est regrettable qu'Henri Laurent ait conclu son récit, déjà erroné, sur la « crise monétaire » de 1380-81 à la date de cette ordonnance de juin 1381, négligeant par là de considérer les frappes suivantes telles qu'elles apparaissent dans les trois comptes de la Monnaie de Louvain dirigée par Nicholas Chavre [46]. Le premier d'entre eux qui mentionne la frappe de la nouvelle « longue croix » d'argent du duc Wenceslas, débute le 1er avril 1381 (n.st.). Il suggère que, en fait, la dévaluation a bien pu être mise en vigueur plusieurs semaines avant qu'elle ne soit officiellement promulguée au mois de mai de cette même année [47]. De plus, ces mêmes comptes qui allaient jusqu'au 1er janvier 1382, mentionnaient laconiquement un fait étonnant : les Etats brabançons refusèrent d'accorder leur autorisation à la mise en circulation des 93 600 gros longue croix frappés cette année-là, soit l'équivalent de 266,67 marcs *argent-le-roy*, et obligèrent l'Hôtel de la Monnaie de Louvain à les fondre aux frais du duc [48]. C'est sans doute un cas unique dans les annales de l'histoire monétaire, ou en tout cas dans celles de l'Europe du Nord.

Mais presque aussi surprenants sont les comptes suivants de la Monnaie de Louvain qui couvrent la période du 1er janvier 1382 au 1er janvier 1383 (n.st.). En effet, ils mentionnent encore la frappe d'une nouvelle monnaie d'argent, un gros brabançon de 6 deniers *argent-le-roy* taillé à 88 au marc, que le malheureux Wenceslas tenta d'imposer au public en tant que renforcement. Au début, le duc décréta que le cours de ce nouveau gros devait être de 12s. de paiement ; cependant, comme le rapportent les comptes, ce cours fut « forcé » jusqu'à 16s. de paiement [49]. Par rapport à la valeur du gros de longue croix récemment avorté, le cours de 12s. équivaudrait à une très forte réévaluation de 33 % (ou de 32,3 % par rapport au dernier scheurman). Mais le dernier cours « public », qui prévalut, correspondait en fait à une nouvelle *dé*valuation, très faible toutefois : moins 0,28 % seulement. Il est quand même étonnant que les Etats aient apparemment accepté (au cours le plus élevé) cette nouvelle monnaie dont la valeur était quasiment identique à celle qu'ils avaient rejetée l'année d'avant. Peut-être la forte teneur en argent du nouveau gros lui conférait-elle une apparence plus solide ! En tout cas, cette nouvelle pièce rencontra un large succès, de loin le plus grand jamais enregistré. Presque deux millions de gros, totalisant 11 162,5 marcs *argent-le-roy*, furent frappés au cours de l'année 1382, soit une moyenne mensuelle de 930,2 marcs. Cependant, cette production était encore nettement inférieure à la moyenne mensuelle de 1 307,3 marcs *argent-le-roy* atteinte la même année par l'Hôtel de la Monnaie flamand de Malines (voir tableau A). De plus, comme le révèlent les comptes de l'atelier de Louvain, aucun autre gros brabançon ne fut plus frappé par la suite. A la place, on ne frappa plus que la menue monnaie d'argent appellée *labbayes* (de toute évidence des quarts de gros) et ce pour un montant total de 1 345 marcs *argent-le-roy* seulement, du 1er janvier 1383 au 6 mars 1383 (n.st.) [50]. Puis l'atelier de Louvain fut fermé et ne rouvrit plus avant 18 mois.

Pendant ce temps, comme le montre le tableau A, l'Hôtel de la Monnaie flamand de Malines resta très actif. Le 12 septembre 1383, le comte Louis de Mäle entreprit le dernier affaiblissement de sa monnaie d'argent. Pour lui, ce fut une dévaluation relativement faible puisque limitée à moins 4,16 % grâce à la diminution du titre de son double gros de 6 grains. Cette dévaluation rencontra un certain succès, mais la production mensuelle moyenne de 1 051,4 marcs *argent-le-roy* de la nouvelle monnaie au cours des 6 premiers mois ne représentait que 80 % de la production moyenne de l'année précédente, année où Malines avait encore à supporter la concurrence de Louvain. Après le mois de février 1384, comme on peut le voir sur le tableau A, la production flamande baissa de 76 %. A cette date les deux princes, du Brabant et des Flandres, étaient morts ; le duc Wenceslas le 8 décembre 1383 (la duchesse Joanna lui survécut jusqu'en 1406) et le comte Louis de Mäle le 30 janvier 1384 (n.st.) [51].

Le gendre du comte Louis qui lui succéda fut le duc Philippe le Hardi de Bourgogne. Celui-ci continua de frapper le double gros dévalué de son beau-père pendant un peu plus de 4 mois (jusqu'au 10 juin 1384) ; puis, le 10 septembre 1384, il institua ses propres monnaies, complètement différentes. Aussi bien pour les Flandres que pour le Brabant, ce nouveau monnayage s'avéra être une rupture complète avec la tradition récente. Tout d'abord, le nouveau double gros du duc Philippe, avec une taille de 50 au marc de 6 deniers *argent-le-roy*, contenait 21,1 % d'argent en plus par rapport à la dernière émission du comte Louis ; ceci constitua la toute première réévaluation de la monnaie flamande qui ait été enregistrée (en tout cas au XIVe siècle). Ensuite, le renforcement était encore plus fort que celui de la nouvelle monnaie d'or (plus 29,8 %) modifiant le rapport bimétallique en faveur de l'argent : ce rapport passa de 10,5:1 à 9,89:1. Par là même, Philippe inaugurait une politique pro-argent qui fut la caractéristique monétaire majeure de son règne (1384-1404) [52]. Troisièmement, ce nouveau rapport or/argent que Philippe venait juste d'adopter était en fait pratiquement identique à celui qui prédominait à la Monnaie brabançonne depuis janvier 1382 (9,90:1). Quatrièmement, et le plus important, le duc Philippe signait le 16 juillet 1384 une convention monétaire avec sa tante la duchesse Joanna de Brabant par laquelle les Hôtels de Malines et Louvain frapperaient désormais les mêmes pièces d'or et d'argent pendant une durée de 5 ans [53].

Aux termes de cet accord, Joanna devait aussi instituer un renforcement de la monnaie brabançonne ; renforcement un peu moins important, il est vrai, puisque les pièces d'argent voyaient leur valeur augmenter de 17,3 % en livres de paiement et celles d'or de 17,6 % par rapport aux dernières frappes de Wenceslas. On assigna à ce nouveau gros d'argent renforcé la valeur de 12s. de paiement, soit trois fois celle de l'ancien gros brabançon, ce qui fit que le double gros valut 24s. de paiement, c'est-à-dire la valeur qu'avait l'ancien double gros de Louis de Mäle dans les transactions brabançonnes. Le nouvel écu d'or (le *schild*) d'une taille de 50,5 au marc de 23,5 carats, valut £ 24 de paiement, soit 120 vieux gros brabançons ou 40 nouveaux gros renforcés, comme en Flandre. En conséquence, le rapport bimétallique demeura virtuellement inchangé, comme on l'a déjà signalé. Il est possible que l'adoption par le duc Philippe de ce même rapport « pro-argent » (moins pro-argent toutefois que celui de Louvain en 1380-81) ait été le prix à payer pour obtenir l'accord de Joanna pour la frappe en commun de cette nouvelle monnaie forte [54].

Cette convention monétaire, qui mit un terme à plusieurs décennies de rivalité entre les ateliers monétaires, n'était pas aussi inédite qu'il y paraît. En effet, à deux reprises déjà, en 1299-1300 et en 1339, la Flandre et le Brabant avaient signé des traités par lesquels les deux principautés s'engageaient à frapper une monnaie commune [55]. Il semble que la première tentative avorta à cause de l'occupation de la Flandre par les Français. La seconde ne survécut pas au-delà de 1343, au mieux [56]. Cette troisième tentative ne connut pas réellement un plus grand succès. La frappe d'une monnaie commune ne dura que 15 mois en Flandre et pas plus de 20 en Brabant. Il est certain que les émissions monétaires flamandes, du 10 septembre 1384 au 4 décembre 1385, furent singulièrement faibles comparées à celles du règne de Louis de Mäle ; à peine 950,08 marcs d'or fin et 9 187,5 marcs d'*argent-le-roy* [57]. Par contraste, les émissions brabançonnes du 3 septembre 1384 au 16 mai 1386 furent curieusement plus fortes pour l'or mais beaucoup plus faibles pour l'argent : 1 100,33 marcs d'or et 7 358,50 marcs d'*argent le-roy*. En effet, la production mensuelle moyenne de monnaies d'argent à Louvain ne représentait que 58 % de celle de Malines (comme on le voit dans les tableaux A, 1 et 2). Il est plus que douteux que les anciennes pièces d'argent du comte Louis de Mäle aient été entièrement refondues et remplacées par les nouvelles émissions dans les deux principautés ; et naturellement ces réévaluations ne pouvaient espérer réussir sans des refrappes complètes [58].

La preuve la plus indiscutable de l'échec de ce nouveau monnayage commun est le fait que les deux Hôtels de la Monnaie de Malines et de Louvain furent fermés, et ne furent réactivés ensuite que par une politique entièrement différente, à savoir des affaiblissements. Après avoir permis à son Hôtel de la Monnaie flamande de rester en chômage pendant 5 mois (du 4 décembre 1385 au 2 mai 1386), le duc Philippe le Hardi, à partir de cette dernière date, ordonna une dévaluation de 12,9 % de la monnaie d'argent et de 15,8 % de la monnaie d'or [59]. Par la suite, le duc fut conduit à dévaluer sa monnaie encore trois fois : en octobre 1386, avril 1387 et octobre 1388. Par rapport à 1384, les quatre dévaluations réduisirent la teneur des pièces d'or de 36,8 % et celle des pièces d'argent de 33,4 %, ce qui modifia encore le rapport bimétallique en faveur de l'or [60]. Malheureusement pour les historiens, les comptes des ateliers flamands manquent aujourd'hui pour la période du 2 mai 1386 au 1er octobre 1388. Cependant, les comptes qui nous restent sur la dernière dévaluation révèlent que le succès de l'émission des monnaies d'or, sous forme d'imitations des nobles d'or anglais, fut remarquable. Celui de l'émission des monnaies d'argent fut, par contre, modeste, comme on pouvait s'y attendre au vu du nouveau rapport entre les deux métaux. Du 1er octobre 1388 au 20 décembre 1389, l'Hôtel de Gand frappa 5 360,49 marcs d'or fin, soit une moyenne mensuelle de 365,9 marcs ; entre le 1er octobre 1388 et le 6 août 1389, il frappa 8 802,67 marcs *argent-le-roy*, soit 863,85 marcs par mois, chiffre certainement supérieur à celui du renforcement de 1384-1385 [61].

Au Brabant voisin, la duchesse Joanna avait maintenu son Hôtel de Louvain en activité plus longtemps que Philippe, après le renforcement de 1384. Mais, si les maigres résultats ne conduisirent pas à sa fermeture, il est certain que la dévaluation initiale du duc, d'avril-mai 1386, emporta la décision, puisque l'atelier de Louvain ferma vers le 16 mai 1386. Ce n'est pas avant plusieurs mois, après la troisième dévaluation de Philippe en avril 1387, que Joanna chercha à réactiver l'atelier de Louvain en prenant des mesures identiques. Cependant, l'expérience de son mari aidant, elle consulta d'abord les Etats sur une nouvelle frappe et ensuite, le 26 septembre 1387, elle décréta un affaiblissement de ses monnaies d'or de 29,5 % (par rapport à l'ancienne monnaie de 1384). Ses monnaies d'argent furent, quant à elles, affaiblies de 27,6 %. En fait, les nouveaux anges d'or (£ 36 de paiement) et les doubles gros (encore à 24s. de paiement) contenaient exactement les mêmes quantités de métaux précieux que les pièces flamandes (5,019 gr d'or fin et 1,697 gr d'argent fin). Cependant, les nouveaux doubles gros de Joanna n'avaient pas une apparence identique : leur titre était légèrement supérieur (5 deniers 5 grains contre 5 deniers 4 grains pour les pièces flamandes), tandis que leur poids était légèrement inférieur (une taille de 60 au marc contre une de 59,5 pour les pièces flamandes) [62].

Peut-être que ces différences (bien que se compensant entièrement) conduisirent le duc Philippe à croire que Joanna s'engageait dans une contrefaçon frauduleuse, ou bien ne désirait-il pas tolérer la concurrence monétaire avec le Brabant. Toujours est-il qu'invoquant un affront, il exigea que Joanna cesse immédiatement de frapper ses nouvelles pièces.

Joanna protesta en disant qu'elles étaient tout-à-fait bonnes — des imitations loyales des pièces flamandes — et qu'elles étaient frappées dans le plus complet respect des termes de la convention de 1384. Toutefois, comme elle avait maintenant besoin de l'aide de Philippe dans la guerre de Gueldre, elle capitula rapidement en signant une nouvelle convention monétaire le 5 janvier 1388 (n.st.). Cet accord dura jusqu'au 25 juillet 1389 [63]. Elle acceptait de fermer son atelier de Louvain, de ne plus frapper des pièces au Brabant et d'envoyer tous les stocks de métaux précieux à l'atelier flamand de Gand en échange de la moitié des profits de la frappe monétaire flamande. Ce même mois, l'Hôtel de Louvain fut effectivement fermé, sous le contrôle direct des fonctionnaires flamands [64].

Malheureusement, il ne nous reste aucune trace de l'activité de la Monnaie de Louvain en 1387, et en fait il n'y a pas de comptes sur la frappe de monnaie au Brabant jusqu'en juin 1392. Néanmoins, plusieurs historiens ont affirmé que Joanna avait recommencé à battre monnaie dès le début de 1389, ou avait continué à frapper des pièces durant toute cette période. Ces spécialistes ont tous supposé qu'une lettre non datée de la duchesse Joanna au duc Philippe, dans laquelle elle se défend, elle et ses monnaies, contre les allégations flamandes de contrefaçon (comme il est dit précédemment), fut écrite juste avant une convention monétaire que les deux parties signèrent le 12 juin 1389 [65]. Pourtant, le contenu de cette lettre n'autorise pas à la dater de 1389. En effet, Joanna y parle des « angèles qu'on forge en la monnoie de monseigneur de Bourgogne à Gand » c'est-à-dire des anges d'or frappés par le duc Philippe à partir d'avril 1387 et par Joanna à partir (ou en) septembre 1387 [66]. Les livres de comptes de l'Hôtel de la Monnaie de Gand pour la période du 1er octobre 1388 au 20 décembre 1389 prouvent pourtant que seuls des nobles d'or y furent frappés [67]. Ceci indique que la lettre de Joanna fut écrite non pas en 1389 mais juste avant la première convention du 5 janvier 1388, convention que ces historiens ignoraient puisqu'elle n'a été que récemment mise à jour par M. Pierre Cockshaw [68]. Nous n'avons absolument aucune raison de croire que Joanna rompit cet accord, comme il a été suggéré. La convention monétaire flamando-brabançonne fut renouvelée en juin 1389, juste un mois avant sa date normale d'expiration, et elle fut étendue sur une nouvelle période de 5 ans en des termes quasiment inchangés [69]. La duchesse respecta scrupuleusement ce traité, tout au moins dans la mesure où elle garda ses Hôtels de la Monnaie fermés pendant au moins encore trois autres années sur les cinq stipulées [70].

Dans la mesure où la reconduction de cette convention éliminait la menace d'une concurrence de la monnaie brabançonne pour plusieurs années, la conséquence principale qui en découla fut incontestablement de permettre ou d'encourager le duc Philippe le Hardi, 6 mois plus tard, à entreprendre la réforme monétaire la plus risquée et la plus importante de tout son règne. Le 20 décembre 1389, il décrète un brusque renforcement des deux monnaies (qui entre en application le 31 janvier 1390) : la teneur de la monnaie d'or augmente de 41,7 % et celle d'argent de 31,8 %, modifiant une fois de plus le rapport or/argent en faveur de ce dernier [71]. Pourquoi le duc Philippe décida-t-il à une nouvelle réévaluation, qui cette fois était encore plus forte que celle qui avait échoué en 1384 ? C'est un point qui reste à élucider [72]. Peut-être voulait-il restaurer « l'intégrité » de la monnaie flamande après tant de dévaluations drastiques au cours des cinquante dernières années. Peut-être tenait-il à restaurer par là la dignité de sa propre position qui était non seulement celle d'un comte flamand mais aussi celle d'un duc français, oncle du roi Charles VI. Il est sûr que la réforme monétaire de Philippe était un acte courageux pour ne pas dire téméraire, car son amplitude, qui imposa une baisse sévère des salaires et des autres revenus, entraîna de violents remous et presque une rébellion générale [73]. Néanmoins, contrairement à la tentative de réforme de 1384, le nouveau renforcement, la revalorisation du métal blanc et la refrappe des monnaies d'argent furent un grand succès. Comme je l'ai démontré ailleurs, les Hôtels flamands continuèrent à frapper de grandes quantités de pièces jusqu'au début du xve siècle (la production mensuelle moyenne de monnaies d'argent se monta à 1 778,11 marcs *argent-le-roy* durant la décennie 1390-99), et la Flandre préserva une monnaie d'argent forte et stable pendant presque 27 ans, jusqu'en décembre 1416 [74]. Il faut aussi noter qu'en août 1409 le duc Jean sans Peur, fils du duc Philippe et son successeur, allait encore renforcer la monnaie d'argent de 16,3 % [75].

Au Brabant, cependant, on ne suivit pas cette politique de réévaluation monétaire des années 1389-90, en dépit de la convention que Joanna avait signée au mois de juin 1389, par laquelle elle avait en effet agréé la direction monétaire flamande. Au contraire, Joanna décréta apparemment une nouvelle dévaluation de sa monnaie brabançonne en rehaussant le taux de change du gros flamand renforcé en sous de paiement. Selon le professeur Herman Van der Wee, ces nouveaux gros circulèrent au taux de 18s. de paiement pendant l'année 1390 et cette valeur aurait correspondu à une augmentation de la *traite* du marc d'argent de 23,7 %, soit un affaiblissement de 19,2 % ; c'est-à-dire de £ 165,9 de paiement en 1387 à £ 205,2 en 1390 (voir tableau 1) [76]. Puis, deux ans plus tard, la duchesse Joanna demanda au duc Philippe son accord pour une version de la convention qui lui permettait de reprendre la frappe de monnaie au Brabant sous prétexte de vouloir s'opposer à un afflux croissant de pièces étrangères frauduleuses — prétexte désormais classique pour justifier toute dévaluation au Pays-Bas. Ce n'est qu'avec beaucoup de réticences que le duc Philippe donna son accord à une convention modifiée qui fut signée le 28 avril 1392. On y stipulait que toutes les monnaies frappées au Brabant devaient être complètement différentes de celles frappées en Flandre, et que les profits résultant de la frappe de la monnaie tant en Flandre qu'au Brabant devaient être divisés en parts égales [77]. La duchesse ouvrit une nouvelle Monnaie à Vilvorde le 25 Juin 1392 et, au grand désarroi de Philippe, elle entreprit d'y frapper des pièces appelées double gros (du type Roosebeker) dont les dimensions et l'empreinte ressemblaient beaucoup à celles des doubles gros flamands alors courants (avec une taille de 57,5 au marc de 6 deniers), tout en ne contenant que 82,5 % de leur teneur en argent (puisqu'ils avaient une taille de 60 au marc de 5 deniers 4 grains). La réponse de la duchesse Joanna à la violente protestation de Philippe le Hardi fut de transférer son activité de frappe à Louvain en juillet 1393 et de décréter une dévaluation supplémentaire de sa monnaie d'argent de 3,2 % (soit moins 4 grains), comme on le voit sur les tableaux 1 et 2 [78].

Comme le montre le tableau 2, les ateliers de Vilvorde et de Louvain réussirent à frapper une masse considérable de pièces d'argent entre le 25 juin 1392 et le 28 janvier 1395 : 24 602,1 marcs *argent-le-roy* au total, soit une moyenne mensuelle de 793,6 marcs. Mais, malgré les dévaluations de la monnaie brabançonne, cela ne représente que 65 % de la production flamande pendant à peu près la même période (37 875,4 marcs *argent-le-roy* du 1er juin 1392 au 20 mars 1395) [79]. Beaucoup moins forte fut la production de pièces d'or de ces deux ateliers brabançons. En réalité, Vilvorde n'en frappa pas du tout, en dépit de l'ordonnance de Joanna de juin 1392 qui prescrivait la frappe d'une nouvelle série de pieters d'or [80]. Puis, du 16 août 1393 au 28 janvier 1396 (n.st.) son Hôtel de la Monnaie à Louvain parvint à frapper une monnaie d'or toute nouvelle : la *tour* (*tourelles* ou *toren* en flamand) à une taille de 61 au marc titrant 21 carats et valant £ 35 8s. de paiement [81]. Mais au cours de cette période de dix-sept mois, comme on le voit sur le tableau 2, il ne produisit que 1 044,6 marcs d'or fin, soit une moyenne mensuelle de 60,4 marcs, ce qui ne représentait que 19 % et 12,8 % respectivement de la production de pièces d'or dans les ateliers flamands et anglais pendant la même période. Sans doute, l'explication d'une aussi faible production au Brabant tenait-elle au rapport en vigueur entre les deux métaux précieux, qui était encore plus favorable à l'argent et donc défavorable à l'or que ne l'était celui des Flandres, lui-même moins favorable au métal blanc que celui de l'Angleterre [82]. En tout cas, la Monnaie de Joanna à Louvain se vit rapidement à court de métal précieux. C'est cette raison que donna le responsable de l'atelier pour en justifier la fermeture le 28 janvier 1395 (n.st.) [83].

Les enregistrements comptables des Hôtels de la Monnaie de Vilvorde et de Louvain révèlent encore d'autres paradoxes étranges dans l'évolution de la monnaie de compte brabançonne. Les précédents livres de comptes de Louvain — ceux suivant le traité monétaire de 1384 (septembre 1384 - mai 1386) — enregistraient les recettes de seigneurage en livres gros flamands comme on peut s'y attendre pour une monnaie commune reposant sur la monnaie flamande [84]. Cependant, les comptes ultérieurs (ceux de 1392-95) utilisent, quant à eux, trois monnaies de compte différentes (en plus de la vieille livre de paiement) : les esterlins ou *ingelschen* (sterlings), le gros flamand « faible » et le gros flamand « fort ». Les esterlins étaient, en fait, les vieux gros brabançons de 4 s. de paiement utilisés ici pour évaluer les pièces d'argent : le gros valait 4 esterlins et le double gros valait 8 esterlins, de sorte que le gros simple valait 16s. de paiement (par comparaison au gros de 1387 qui valait 12s. de paiement). Les pièces d'argent qu'on appelait *ingelschen* ou esterlins furent, elles, effectivement frappées à Louvain du 12 août 1393 au 28 janvier 1395 : c'étaient des quarts de gros d'une taille de 336 au marc de 3 deniers *argent-le-roy* [85]. De plus, les soi-disant « gros flamands » n'étaient pas flamands du tout, mais une monnaie de compte brabançonne courante dérivée de la convention flamando-brabançonne de juillet 1384 par laquelle trois vieux gros brabançons valaient un « gros flamand » (de la convention), soit 12s. de paiement. C'est pourquoi le nom esterlin fut donné à la valeur représentée par l'ancien gros brabançon (un tiers de ce « gros flamand »), de la même façon qu'un denier sterling anglais avait valu pendant un temps le tiers d'un gros flamand courant. Ces « gros flamands » furent utilisés pour évaluer la tour d'or au taux de 59d. « gros flamands » = £ 35 8s. de paiement ou 44,5 gros brabançons courants, de même que pour évaluer certains taux de seigneurage. Finalement, le « gros fort » (*groten fors*) fut le vrai gros d'argent courant du Brabant (mais *pas* de Flandre) : il valait 4 esterlins ou 16s. de paiement. Dans les comptes de la Monnaie brabançonne, il était employé pour calculer les recettes du seigneurage ainsi que les dépenses, comme un véritable livre gros avec ses subdivisions traditionnelles, c'est-à-dire 20 sous par livre et 12 deniers par sou. L'évolution touche à sa fin. En effet, il s'agit de la première monnaie de compte indigène appartenant au vrai type B que nous rencontrons dans les comptes brabançons à la fin du Moyen Age. C'est une monnaie de compte totalement indépendante de son homologue flamand, et qui repose directement sur le denier d'argent ou gros courant. Ce n'est pas un système dérivé comme la livre de paiement ou la livre de « gros flamands ». Les relations, toutes fixées, que l'on rencontre entre toutes ces monnaies de compte dans les comptes des Hôtels brabançons se présentent comme suit :

— 1 esterlin ou ingelschen = 4s. de paiement = 1 vieux gros

brabançon ;
- 1 «gros flamand » ou « gros faible » = 3 esterlins (vieux gros brabançon) = 12s. de paiement = 3/4 « gros fort » (monnaie d'argent courante de Brabant) ;
- 1 « gros fort » = 4 esterlins = 16s. de paiement = 1 1/3 « gros flamand » ou « gros faible » ;
- 240 « gros fort » = £ 1 «gros fort » = £ 192 de paiement ;
- 240 « gros flamands » = £ L.1 «gros flamands » = £ 144 de paiement ;
- 240 esterlins = 240 vieux gros brabançons = £ 48 de paiement.

Ces relations expliquent pourquoi les termes « faible » ou « fort » furent employés pour distinguer ces deux gros en dépit d'un autre paradoxe de terminologie. En effet, le soi-disant « gros fort » frappé de juillet 1393 à janvier 1395 (0,8144 gr d'argent) avait une teneur en argent égale à 69,4 % seulement de la teneur du gros « convention » de 1384-86 (1,1728 gr d'argent), qui servit de référence au « gros faible » comme monnaie de compte [86].

L'histoire monétaire du Brabant pendant la période comprise entre la fin de notre série de comptes (le 28 janvier 1395) et la fin du règne de Joanna (le 1er décembre 1406) est moins claire. Mais les événements de cette période conduisaient, en fait, à l'évolution de la monnaie de compte brabançonne vers son état définitif. Malheureusement, nous ne possédons pas de comptes monétaires pour le reste du règne de Joanna. Les recettes générales du Brabant montrent que l'Hôtel de la Monnaie de Louvain rouvrit pendant une très courte période, du 25 décembre 1395 au 20 janvier 1396, et qu'ensuite la frappe de monnaie se fit à Maastricht, peut-être jusqu'au 22 mai 1396 (et même plus tard). Cependant, si cela est vrai, on ne dispose pas de pièces qui y auraient été frappées [87]. Il est clair qu'à la fin de l'été 1396, Joanna avait compris que toute nouvelle tentative pour réactiver ses ateliers serait vouée à l'échec. Aussi, le 1er octobre, elle prit la singulière décision de les céder aux villes pour une durée de 10 ans, contre un loyer annuel de 2 000 tours d'or [88]. De nouveau, nous ne disposons pas pour cette période de livres de comptes ni de pièces brabançonnes pour pouvoir déterminer si les villes utilisaient ou non ces Monnaies [89]. Les comptes municipaux de Malines indiquent cependant qu'une dévaluation de 12,5 % (correspondant à une augmentation de 14,3 % de la monnaie de compte) eut lieu vers la fin de 1396 et qu'ensuite deux autres dévaluations suivirent : une de 5,9 % à la fin de 1398 et une de 5,6 % à la fin de 1399 (voir le tableau B), ce qui correspond à une augmentation globale de la monnaie de compte de 28,6 % [90]. Il se peut que ces dévaluations aient été effectuées non en réduisant la teneur d'argent, mais simplement en augmentant les taux offi-

Tableau B
Valeurs comparées des livres (oude) groot de Malines et des livres gros « flamands » du Brabant avec les gros d'argent flamands et les nobles d'or, telles que notées dans les comptes des trésoriers de Malines (1394-1409)

MONNAIE	Noël 1394 Noël 1396	Noël 1396 Pâques 1398	Noël 1398 Pâques 1399	Noël 1399 Pâques 1409
Valeur de £ 1 (oude groot de Malines en £ gros « flamande » du Brabant)	£ 3 10s. 0d.	£ 4. 0s.0d.	£ 4. 5s. 0d.	£ 4 10s. 0d.
Valeur de £ 1 gros de Flandre en £ gros « flamande » du Brabant	£ 1. 14s. 2d. (1,708)	£ 1. 16s. 8d. (1,833)	£ 1. 18s. 4d. (1,916)	£ 2. 0s. 0d. (2,000)
Valeur du gros d'argent de Flandre en sous de paiement	20s. 0d.	22s. 0d.	23s. 0d.	24s. 0d.
Valeur du noble d'or flamand :				
— en gros de Flandre	72d.	72d.	72d.	72d.
— en « gros flamands » du Brabant	120d.*	132d.	138d.*	144d.*
— en gros de Malines	33d.	33d.	33d.	
— en livres de paiement	£ 72. 0s.*	£ 79. 4s.	£ 82. 16s.*	£ 86. 8s.*

* Valeur extrapolée sur la base de valeurs données pour 1396-1398.
Sources :
Stadsarchief Mechelen, Stadsrekeningen Series I : nos 72-85 ; Herman Van der Wee, *Growth of the Antwerp Market and the European Economy, Fourteenth -Sixteenth Centuries*, I : *Statistics* (La Haye, 1963), 123-27.

ciels des pièces d'argent (en esterlins de paiement) comme cela s'était produit plusieurs fois dans le passé (en France aussi). Aussi ces statistiques monétaires ne traduisent-elles pas nécessairement de nouvelles émissions de pièces.

Finalement, avec la dernière de ces dévaluations en 1399, la duchesse Joanna accepta, une nouvelle fois, la monnaie d'argent flamande alors en circulation, c'est-à-dire le gros lourd frappé depuis la réforme de 1389-90, en tant que monnaie brabançonne officielle, mettant ainsi un terme effectif (ou amendant radicalement) la location de ses Hôtels aux villes. Les relations fixes suivantes prévalurent à l'intérieur du duché du Brabant jusqu'en avril 1409, date à laquelle le successeur de Joanna, Antoine de Bourgogne (le fils cadet de Philippe le Hardi) frappa une nouvelle monnaie brabançonne dévaluée [91] :

— 1 gros lourd d'argent de Flandre = 2 gros flamands « faibles » du Brabant = 6 vieux gros brabançons = 24s. Od. de paiement

— 1 livre gros des Flandres et du Brabant = £ 2 « gros flamand » du Brabant = £ 288 de paiement.

Les livres de comptes de trésoriers de Malines confirment que la monnaie de compte brabançonne demeura parfaitement stable pendant toute cette période de dix ans [92].

Il y eut cependant une petite exception à cette unité et stabilité monétaire flamando-brabançonne, exception en fait plus apparente que réelle. Antoine de Bourgogne avait précédemment reçu le marquisat et la ville d'Anvers, le Limbourg et l'Outre-Meuse à administrer ; de plus, en mai 1404, Joanna l'avait officiellement désigné comme son héritier [93]. En juillet-août 1405, il établit un nouvel Hôtel de la Monnaie à Anvers et pendant la période allant du 5 septembre au 10 octobre 1405, il y frappa de nouveaux *écus d'Anvers* d'or (d'une taille de 48 au marc de 23 1/4 carats) ainsi que des pièces d'argent appelées *plaques d'Anvers* qui devaient circuler à Anvers et dans ses territoires de Limbourg [94]. Avec une taille de 72 au marc de 5 deniers 9 grains *argent-le-roy*, les plaques valaient 5 esterlins, soit 1 2/3d. gros de Flandre, ou encore 40s. de paiement. Par rapport à la monnaie courante « commune », exprimée en double gros flamands (qui cessa d'être frappée en juin 1402), l'émission de ces plaques représentait une dévaluation de 15,3 % (voir le tableau 1). Mais la très faible quantité de pièces frappée — 582,3 marcs *argent-le-roy* représentant 93 600 plaques et 4,12 marcs d'or fin représentant 204 écus (voir tableau 2) — montrerait plutôt que leur circulation eut un très faible impact sur l'économie monétaire brabançonne [95].

Beaucoup plus importantes furent les mutations monétaires imposées au Brabant une fois qu'Antoine fut devenu duc en décembre 1406. Il ouvrit un nouvel Hôtel de la Monnaie à Vilvorde le 28 avril 1409 et y frappa de nouveaux double gros (appelés *botdragers* ou plaques), ayant un titre de 5 deniers 5 grains *argent-le-roy* et une taille de 58,5 au marc. Profitant du déplacement de l'atelier de Vilvorde à Louvain, le 5 janvier 1410, il réduisit le titre de 2 grains [96]. Comme le montre le tableau 1, cette mutation représenta, par rapport au gros flamand commun antérieur un affaiblissement de 16,8 %, faisant monter la *traite* du marc de 19s. 0d. gros à 22s. 10d. gros. Pendant ce temps, dans la Flandre voisine, le duc Jean-sans-Peur avait aussi réactivé la frappe de la monnaie, mais avec un nouveau renforcement. Il frappa un nouveau double gros d'une taille de 49 au marc de 6 deniers *argent-le-roy*, qui contenait ainsi 39,8 % d'argent de plus que le nouveau double gros du duc Antoine [97]. Les monnaies métalliques et les monnaies de compte flamandes et brabançonnes divergèrent encore.

Par la suite, de 1416 à 1433, les monnaies des deux principautés bourguignonnes eurent à subir d'autres affaiblissements, parfois brutaux, qu'il n'est pas possible d'aborder dans cette étude. Il suf-

Tableau 1 Le monnayage d'argent au Brabant, 1363-1409

Période de frappe(a)	Pièce	Valeur en sous paiement	Titre en deniers argent-le-roy	Taille au marc de Troyes	Grammes d'argent pur	Grammes d'argent pur dans 1 livre paiement de Brabant	Traite de marc en livres paiement	Valeur de 1 kg d'argent pur en livres paiement
16.VI.63-16.IX.63	Gros aux 4 lions	4	6 den. 0 gr.	144	0,814	4,072	57,60	245,6
16.IX.63-23.VI.70	Gros aux 4 lions	4	?	?	?	?	?	?
24.VI.70-25.XII.71	Gros aux 4 lions	4	4 den. 0 gr.	168	0,465	2.327	100,80	429,8
1372 (?)	Bryman	16	6 den. 0 gr.	74	1,585	1,981	118,40	504,8
	Demi-Bryman	8	6 den. 0 gr.	148	0,792	1,981	118,40	504,8
1. VI.74 ?	Schuerman(b)	4	5 den. 0 gr.	186	0,525	2,627	89,28	380,6
(1.VII.75-1.IV.80)	Schuerman	6	5 den. 0 gr.	186	0,525	1,751	133,92	571,0
1.IV.80-1.IV.81	Double Schuerman	12	5 den. 0 gr.	97	1,008	1,679	139,68	595,5
	Schuerman	6	5 den. 0 gr.	194	0,504	1,679	139,68	595,5
1.IV.81-1.1.82	Double longue-croix	8	4 den. 0 gr.	117	0,668	1,671	140,40	598,6
	Longue-croix	4	4 den. 0 gr.	234	0,334	1,671	140,40	598,6
1.I.82-1.I.83	Gros(c)	12	6 den. 0 gr.	88	1,333	2,221	105,60	450,2
	Gros	16	6 den. 0 gr.	88	1,333	1,666	140,80	600,3
	Demi-Gros	8	6 den. 0 gr.	176	0,666	1,666	140,80	600,3
1.I.83-8.III.83	Labbaye(d)	4	6 den. 0 gr.	352	0,333	1,666	140,80	600,3
3.IX.84-16.V.86	Double Gros	24	6 den. 0 gr.	50	2,346	1,955	120,00	511,6
	Gros(e)	12	6 den. 0 gr.	100	1.173	1,955	120,00	511,6
26.IX.87-(f)	D. Gros	24	5 den. 5 gr.	60	1,697	1,414	165,89	707,2
30.I.88	Gros	12	5 den. 5 gr.	120	0,848	1,414	165,89	707,2
25.VI.92-22.VI.93	D. Gros	32	5 den. 4 gr.	60	1,683	1,052	222,97	950,6
	Gros	16	5 den. 4 gr.	120	0,842	1,052	222,97	950,6
22.VII.93-28.I.95	D. Gros	32	5 den. 0 gr.	60	1,629	1,018	230,40	982,3
	Gros	16	5 den. 0 gr.	120	0,814	1,018	230,40	982,3
12.VIII.93-28.I.95	Esterlin	4	3 den. 0 gr.	336	0,175	0,873	268,80	1.146,0
1399(g)	D. Gros	48	6 den. 0 gr.	57	2,057	0,857	273,60	1.166,5
	Gros	24	5 den. 0 gr.	96	1,018	0,848	276,48	1.178,7
5.IX.05-10.X.05h	Plaque	40	5 den. 9 gr.	72	1,459	0,730	321,49	1,370,6
	Gros	20	4 den. 4 gr.	112	0,727	0,727	322,56	1.375,2
28.IV.09-24.XII.09	Plaque	48	5 den. 5 gr.	58,5	1,740	0,725	323,48	1,379,1
	Gros	24	4 den. 10 gr.	100	0,863	0,719	326,04	1.390,0
5.1.10-	Plaque	48	5 den. 3 gr.	58,5	1,712	0,713	328,74	1.401,6
25.VI.12i	Gros	24	4 den. 8 gr.	100	0,847	0,706	332,31	1.416,8

NOTES

a. Le monnayage d'argent se faisait entre ces dates, mais ne commençait ni ne se terminait nécessairement aux dates indiquées dans les comptes.
b. Le duc Wenceslas fit frapper le schuerman primitif à ce tarif, à partir peut-être de juin 1374 ; mais les Etats (ou villes) augmentèrent le taux de change de 50 % avant le printemps de 1375. Les premiers comptes de la Monnaie de Louvain que l'on connaît ne commencent que le 1er juillet 1375.
c. Le duc Wenceslas avait fixé la valeur de ce nouveau gros à 12 s. paiement, mais elle fut augmentee (par les villes probablement) à 16s. paiement.
d. Le *labbaye* était vraisemblablement un quart de gros (= 4s. paiement, la valeur de l'ancien gros). Les comptes de la Monnaie de Louvain ne précisent pas son titre ou sa taille qui correspondaient sans doute à ceux du gros.
e. Ce gros était prévu par l'ordonnance monétaire, mais en fait il ne fut pas frappé à Louvain.
f. On ne possède pas de comptes. Les dates correspondent à la proclamation officielle du double gros nouveau et la fermeture de la Monnaie de Louvain après l'accord flamand-brabançon.
g. Il s'agit de la monnaie d'argent flamande de 1389-1402 que la duchesse Joanna acceptait comme monnaie principale de Brabant en liant la livre de paiement au gros flamand (1 gros = 24s. paiement et £ 1 gros = £ 288 paiement)
h. Frappé par Antoine en tant que *ruwaard* de Brabant et destiné à circuler seulement dans ses territoires d'Anvers, Limbourg et les terres Outre-Meuse, à l'intérieur du duché de Brabant.

Tableau 2
Les frappes monétaires au Brabant, 1375-1432

Année (29 sept.)	Or (kgs)	Argent (kgs)	Or (£ paiement)	Argent (£ paiement)	Total (£ paiement)
1375	190,05	283,67	988.706	161.960	1.150.666
1376	760,22	1.134,66	3.954.825	647.838	4.602.663
1377	667,56	746,88	3.472.819	426.432	3.899.251
1378	835,08	200,63	4.344.300	114.550	4.458.850
1379	667,57	7,57	3.472.875	4.325	3.477.200
1380	284,29	234,56	1.509.300	139.680	1.648.980
1381	96,28	276,25	538.425	164.640	703.065
1382	7,27	1.984,51	41.400	1.191.240	1.232.640
1383	---	970,03	---	582.296	582.296
1384	8,03	76,07	40.616	38.918	79.534
1385	160,62	1.022,88	812.312	522.873	1.335.185
1386	100,66	644,49	509.049	329.271	838.320
1387					
1388					
1389					
1390					
1391					
1392	---	329,08	---	312.826	312.826
1393	42,57	1.764,21	391.952	1.701.737	2.093.689
1394	176,03	2.821,70	1.620.553	2.775.502	4.396.055
1395	37,07	855,54	341.241	841.218	1.182.459
1396					
1397					
1398					
1399					
1400					
1401					
1402					
1403			(£ gros)	(£ gros)	(£ gros)
1404					
1405	1,01	136,58	46	650	696
1406					
1407					
1408					
1409	51,50	1.424,84	2.310	6.824	9.134
1410	110,41	3.249,66	4.952	15.758	20.710
1411	67,97	2.048,99	3.049	9.978	13.027
1412					
1413					
1414					
1415					
1416					
1417	11,36	755,75	725	4.795	5.520
1418	2,62	174,40	167	1.107	1.274
1419	53,00	1.246,84	3.949	9.462	13.411
1420	10,15	1.477,44	.604	8.756	9.360
1421	5,47	2.394,47	325	14.288	14.613
1422	---	221,78	---	1.334	1.334
1423					
1424					
1425					
1426					
1427					
1428					
1429	12,13	287,89	1.053	2.101	3.154
1430	793,55	4.244,78	68.446	30.990	99.436
1431	1.025,41	673,52	88.866	4.903	93.769
1432	334,11	84,27	29.151	613	29.764
1433					

fira de remarquer que le Brabant continua à dévaluer beaucoup plus ses monnaies que la Flandre, respectant par là une tradition bien établie. Ainsi, quand l'unification monétaire des Pays-Bas bourguignons fut achevée durant la période d'octobre 1433-décembre 1435, la monnaie de compte du Brabant, la livre gros qui restait fermement ancrée au gros d'argent courant, ne valait que les deux tiers de la livre gros flamande. De l'unification jusqu'à la fin de l'ancien régime, les livres gros brabançonnes et flamandes maintinrent, en tant que monnaies de compte basées sur le gros d'argent flamand courant, les parités fixes et figées suivantes [98] :

— 1 gros flamand = 1d. 12 mites gros brabançon ;
— 1 livre gros flamande = 1 livre 10s. 0d. gros brabançonne = £ 432 de paiement ;
— 1 livre gros brabançonne = 13s. 6d. gros flamand = £ 288 de paiement.

Traduit de l'anglais par Francine Gluckstein et Michel Grimm

NOTES

1. Les principales études sont : Charles Piot, (a) « Ancienne administration monétaire de la Belgique », et (b) « Discussions entre le duc de Wenceslas et les états de Brabant au sujet de ses monnaies », (c) « Documents sur quelques monnaies frappées par Antoine, duc de Brabant », *Revue belge de numismatique [jadis Revue de la numismatique belge]*, I (1842-45), 26-76, 173-200, et 247-60 ; Charles Piot, « Notice sur les monnaies de Jeanne, duchesse de Brabant (1383-1406) », *Ibid.*, II (1846), 116-46, 285-9 ; Renier Chalon, « Nouvelle classification des monnaies de Jeanne, duchesse de Brabant », *Ibid* :, XIV (1858), 353-61 ; P.O. Van der Chijs, *De munten der voormalige hertogdommen Braband en Limburg van de vroegste tijden tot aan de Pacificatie van Gend*, 2 vols. (Haarlem, 1851) ; Alphonse de Witte, *Histoire monétaire des comtes de Louvain, ducs de Brabant, et marquis du Saint-Empire romain*, 2 vols. (Anvers, 1894-96) ; Georges Cumont, « Un officier monétaire au XIVe siècle : Nicolas Chavre (mort en 1397), maître de la monnaie de Louvain », *Gazette numismatique française*, I (1897), 187-232 ; Georges Cumont, « Les monnaies de Jean III et de Wenceslas », *Annales de la Société d'Archéologie de Bruxelles*, XV (1901), 5-54 ; Georges Cumont, « Etude sur le cours des monnaies de Brabant pendant le règne de Jeanne veuve (1383-1406) », *Ibid.*, XVI (1902), 93-159 ; Georges Cumont, « Mélanges numismatiques : règne de Jeanne de Brabant, veuve 1383-1406 », *Tijdschrift van het koninklijk Nederlandsch genootschap voor munt-en penningkunde*, X (1902), 197-246 ; Henri Laurent, *La loi de Gresham au Moyen Age : essai sur la circulation monétaire entre la Flandre et le Brabant à la fin du XIVe siècle* (Bruxelles 1933) ; Pierre Cockshaw, « A propos de la circulation monétaire entre la Flandre et le Brabant de 1384 à 1390 », *Contributions à l'histoire économique et sociale*, VI (1970-71), 107-41 ; Joseph Ghyssens, « Le monnayage d'argent en Flandre, Hainaut, et Brabant au début de la guerre de Cent Ans », *Revue belge de numismatique*, CXX (1974), 109-91 ; Joseph Ghyssens, « Monnaies de Brabant d'après les comptes de la ville de Louvain de 1345 à 1354 », *Ibid.*, CXXIII (1977), 149-57. Pour les sources des statistiques dans les tableaux A, B, 1 et 2, voir Munro, «Bullion Flows and Monetary Contraction » (note 2)

2. Pour l'analyse de la production monétaire et les mouvements des métaux précieux, voir John Munro, *Wool, Cloth and Gold : The Struggle for Bullion in Anglo-Burgundian Trade, 1340-1478* (Bruxelles et Toronto, 1973) (possède une bibliographie détaillée concernant les sources statistiques) ; Munro, « Bullionism and the Bill of Exchange in England, 1272-1663 », dans *The Dawn of Modern Banking* (Center for Medieval and Renaissance Studies, University of California, Los Angeles : New Haven et Londres, 1979), pp.169-240 ; Munrò, « Monetary Contraction and Industrial Change in the Late Medieval Low Countries, 1335-1500 », dans Nicholas Mayhew, éd., *Coinage in the Low Countries (880-1500) : Third Oxford Symposium on Coinage and Monetary History* (British Archeological Reports, International Series 54, Oxford, 1979), pp. 95-162 ; Munro, « Mint Policies, Ratios and Outputs in the Low Countries and England, 1335-1420 : Some Reflections on New Data », *Numismatic Chronicle*, 8e série, I (1981), 71-116 ; Munro, « Bullion Flows and Monetary Contraction in Late Medevial England and the Low Countries », dans John Richards, éd., *Precious Metals in the Later Medieval and Early Modern Worlds* (Durham, North Carolina, 1983), pp. 97-158.

3. Le marc de Troyes utilisé en France se subdivisait à partir de l'once de façon différente : 1 marc = 8 onces = 192 deniers (8 x 24) = 4 608 grains (8 x 24 x 24). Pour le reste, les officiers des Monnaies de Flandre, Brabant, Hollande, Namur et Hainaut croyaient, comme le montrent leurs livres, que leur marc-poids était identique à celui de Paris. Cependant, en 1529, les officiers des Monnaies brabançonnes de Charles V firent peser leur marc-poids à Paris et découvrirent qu'il était de 24 grains (1,274 gr.) plus lourd que le marc-poids français (pour un poids théorique de 246,0273 gr.). Au XVIIIe siècle (1756, 1767) d'autres essais montraient que le marc de Bruxelles pesait à ce moment 21 grains de plus que le marc de Paris. On ne peut pas savoir si ces petites différences — respectivement de 0,52 % et de 0,46 % — existaient déjà aux XIVe-XVe siècles, ou même s'il y avait de telles différences entre les marcs de Troyes utilisés dans les Monnaies flamandes et brabançonnes. Je me suis servi moi-même du poids théorique traditionnel de 244,7529 gr. pour les monnaies des deux principautés. Voir Archives générales du royaume de Belgique [AGR], Chambre de Comptes [CC], n° 1324, f° 31v (XVe siècle) ; n° 580, f° 17r. (1688) ; J.A. Décourdemanche, *Traité pratique des poids du Moyen Age* (Paris, 1915), pp. 5-71, 27 ; A. Dieudonné, *Manuel des poids monétaires* (Paris, 1925), pp. 33-35 ; Louis Blancard, « Sur les poids des anciennes provinces belges », *Revue belge de numismatique*, LIV (1898), 62—85 ; E. Fournial, *Histoire monétaire de l'occident médiéval* (Paris, 1970), pp. 25-27, 161-9 (qui se trompe sur certains points).

4. Voir Adolphe Landry, *Essai économique sur les mutations des monnaies dans l'ancienne France de Philippe-le-Bel à Charles VII* (Paris, 1910), pp. 47-53, 65-71, 126-88, 203-10 ; A. Engel et R. Serrure, *Traité de numismatique du Moyen Age*, 3 vols. (Paris, 1891-1905) ; A. Blanchet et A. Dieudonné, *Manuel de numismatique française*, 2 vols. (Paris, 1916), II, 33-45. Le remède pour le titre était normalement de 2 grains ; pour une taille, par exemple, de 100d., ceci ferait 1d. ou 2d. Voir les extraits des comptes des Monnaies cités-dessous.

5. Hans Van Werveke, *De muntslag in Vlaanderen onder Lodewijk Van Mäle* (Bruxelles, 1949), pp. 20-21. Voir notes 3 et 15.

6. Voir N.J. Mayhew, « The Circulation and Imitations of Sterlings in the Low Countries », dans N.J. Mayhew, éd., *Coinage in the Low Countries (880-1500)*,BAR International Series 54, Oxford, 1979), pp. 54-68. De 1279 à 1335, le denier sterling d'Angleterre contenait 1,332 gr. d'argent pur ; de 1335 à 1344, 1,157 gr. Le gros flamand de 1300 contenait 3,794 gr. d'argent pur (soit 2,85 fois le denier sterling) ; et de 1337 à 1343, 2,908 gr. (2,51 fois le denier sterling courant). A noter que du 25 mai 1337 au 15 fév. 1338 et du 28 août 1350 au 1er janvier 1352 la Monnaie de Gand frappait des « petits blancs qu'on dist esterlins », dont 1 égal au tiers d'un gros (*tierchelets*). Mais ces derniers ne contenaient que 0,652 gr. d'argent pur, par comparaison à 1,079 gr. dans le denier sterling. Victor Gaillard, éd., *Recherches sur les monnaies des comtes de Flandre*, 2 vols. (Gand, 1852-56), II : *Sous les règnes de Louis de Crécy et de Louis de Male*, n° 20, pp. 51-3 ; n° 30, pp. 77-8.

7. Voir les sources citées dans la note 4. ; Munro, *Wool, Cloth, and Gold*, pp.11-34.

8. Hans Van Werveke, « Monnaie de compte et monnaie réelle », *Revue belge de philologie et d'histoire*, XIII (1934), 123-52, et son « Munt en politiek : de Frans-Vlaamse verhoudigen vóór en na 1300 », *Bijdragen voor de geschiedenis der Nederlanden*, VIII (1953-54), 1-19 : tous les deux publiés à nouveau dans son *Miscellanea Mediaevalia* (Gand, 1968), pp. 133-58, 209-26. Voir aussi Herman Van der Wee, *Growth of the Antwerp Market and the European Economy, Fourteenth to Sixteenth Centuries*, 3 vols (La Haye, 1963), I, 107-35 ; et Peter Spufford,

Monetary Problems and Policies in the Burgundian Netherlands, 1433-1496 (Leiden, 1970), pp.13-28.

9. Van Werveke, « Monnaie de compte », pp. 140-4, 153 ; Van der Wee, *Antwerp Market*, I, 107-13.

10. Voir Joseph Ghyssens, « Le monnayage d'argent », pp. 162-6 et son « Monnaies de Brabant », pp. 151-3.

11. Le gros tournois original de Louis IX fut frappé d'août 1266 jusqu'à 1303 à la taille de 58 au marc de 12 deniers argent-le-roy (pour un contenu théorique en argent de 4,044 gr.). Affaibli en 1303 par Philippe IV à 9 deniers argent-le-roy, il fut rétabli en 1305 et jusqu'en mars 1318 lorsque Philippe V augmenta la taille à 59 1/6 au marc (= 3,964 gr. d'argent). Philippe VI l'augmenta encore à 60 en sept. 1329 (= 3,909 g. d'argent). Enfin, en janvier 1337, il fit frapper un gros nouveau, le gros à la couronne, 96 au marc de 10 deniers 16 grains d'aloi (= 2,172 g. d'argent). Blanchet et Dieudonné, *Manuel II,* chapitres v - x ; Fournial, *Histoire Monétaire*, pp.92-103.

12. Au mois de mars 1337, le duc Jean III de Brabant fit frapper un demi gros de 9 deniers d'aloi à la taille de 124 au marc (= 1,149 gr. d'argent, soit 2,837 pour 2 demi), et au tarif de 12 d. ou 1s. de paiement. Au mois de mai suivant, le comte Louis de Nevers affaiblit le gros flamand de 10 deniers 6 grains d'aloi à la taille de 57 1/2 (= 3,484 gr. d'argent) à 9 deniers d'aloi à la taille de 60 1/2 (= 2,908 gr. d'argent). Voir Ghyssens, « Monnayage d'argent », pp. 114-24, 156-64 ; et Frans et Willem Blockmans, « Devaluation, Coinage, and Seignorage under Louis de Nevers and Louis de Male, Counts of Flanders, 1330-84 », dans N.J. Mayhew, éd., *Coinage in the Low Countries (880-1500)* (BAR International Series 54, Oxford, 1979), tableau 2, p. 83.

13. Ghyssens, « Monnaies de Brabant », pp. 151-3. Ma propre analyse des comptes de la ville de Louvain confirme ce rapport fixe, comme je l'ai déjà noté: Archives de la ville de Louvain, registres n° 4986-5007 (1345-1402), pour les « weet ende zieden assises ».

14. Voir l'ordonnance monétaire du duc Wenceslas du 19 mai 1381, dans Piot, « Discussions », n° 3, p. 189. Voir aussi Ghyssens, « Monnaies de Brabant », pp.154-55, et son « Monnayage d'argent », pp. 175-6.

15. De Witte, *Histoire monétaire,* I, 139-40. Voir n. 3 et tableau 1..

16. *Ibid.* ; Gaillard, *Monnaies*, II, 173-91.

17. Bien que la frappe cessât à Noël, la Monnaie de Vilvorde ne fut officiellement fermée que le 11 mars 1372 (avec un important déficit). En Flandre, on ne connaît pas de comptes de la Monnaie entre le 25 mai 1370 et le 18 juin 1373. Voir de Witte, *Histoire monétaire*, I, 140 ; Cumont, « Nicolas Chavre », p. 194 ; Gaillard, *Monnaies*, II, n° 95-97, pp. 192-7 ; Blockmans, « Devaluation », tableau 7, p. 89.

18. Le texte de l'ordonnance est dans Piot, « Discussion », n° 5, pp. 198-200. Piot date ce document de 1381, mais de Witte croit comme moi qu'il devait dater d'environ 1371, peu de temps après la fermeture de la Monnaie de Vilvorde : *Histoire monétaire*, I, 140, 151. Le terme *bryman* signifie fiancé : le portrait du prince comme époux sur la pièce.

19. Voir les ordonnances monétaires du 19 mai et du 6 juin 1381, qui évaluent en effet le précédent gros de Vilvorde à 4s. (Piot, « Discussions », n° 3—4, pp. 189, 193). Cependant, de Witte reproduit certaines pièces *brymannen* : *Histoire monétaire*, I, fig. XIX, n° 408-10 et pp. 162-3. L'aloi, taille et valeur du *bryman* ne s'accordent pas avec ceux d'un nouveau monnayage luxembourgeois décidé par le duc Wenceslas, le 3 fév. 1372 (n.st.), dans Charles Piot, « Monnaie de convention entre Wenceslas, duc de Luxembourg, et l'archevêque de Trèves », *Revue belge de numismatique*, I, (1842-45), 357-60. De même, il ne peut s'agir des pièces frappées par la suite à Maastricht en 1396 lorsque la Monnaie de cette ville était ouverte. Voir notes 87-88.

20. Ces comptes, qui se trouvent aujourd'hui dans AGR, Comptes en rouleau (CR) n° 2591, ont une histoire assez curieuse. Ils furent découverts par de Witte qui en parle abondamment en 1894 dans son *Histoire monétaire*, I, 144—51, mais malheureusement de manière assez confuse. Bien que les comptes de Chavre se composent d'une séquence de 9 comptes partiels, de Witte ne donne que le poids total de l'or frappé pour l'ensemble des comptes (14 485 marcs, ce qui est exact) ; pour une raison obscure, il réunit les trois premiers comptes partiels pour l'argent en un seul (1er juillet 1375-1er jan. 1379) et donne comme poids total d'argent frappé 27 075 marcs argent-le-roy au lieu de 24 285 marcs. Enfin, après avoir fait plusieurs fautes mineures dans le calcul des dépenses, il se trompe sur la date de la fermeture des comptes (mars 1385 au lieu de 1383). Trois ans plus tard, en 1897, Georges Cumont corrigea toutes les fautes de de Witte, calcula toutes les données statistiques dans les comptes de Chavre (avec une seule erreur — la taille du schuerman en

1375-76 n'était pas 15s. 2d., mais 15s. 6d. = 186) et écrivit une longue biographie du maître de la Monnaie de Louvain dans la *Gazette numismatique française* (voir note 1). Depuis, ces documents exceptionnels ont été presque complètement ignorés par les numismates et historiens (Ghyssens y a fait référence dans son « Monnaie de Brabant » (note 1), en se trompant sur la date de l'ouverture des comptes (juillet 1345). Il se peut que la Monnaie de Louvain était déjà réouverte en juin 1374 lorsque les comptes du percepteur brabançon, Godefroid de la Tour, font référence au « lucrum monete nove incepte apud Lovanium ». (Cumont, « Nicolas Chavre », pp. 193-4). De Witte se trompe cependant en supposant que les 6 220 pieters d'or dus à Chavre le 1er juillet 1376 sont en relation avec les frappes antérieures : *Histoire monétaire*, I, 140-43.

21. De Witte, *Histoire monétaire*, I, 144 n. 2 ; Van Werveke, « Monnaie de compte », p. 153.

22. Voir Munro, « Monetary Contraction », pp. 104-12 ; Id., « Mint policies », p. 82.

23. D'après le discours du duc Wenceslas devant les Etats, avant avril 1381, publié par Piot, « Discussions », n° 2, p.183 et par Laurent, *Loi de Gresham*, n° 3, p. 120. Piot aussi bien que Laurent attribuèrent un discours précédent, prononcé avant le 24 nov. 1380, aux Etats. Mais il est clair que ce fut Wenceslas lui-même qui l'a prononcé car ses plaintes sont de la même veine « soo es sonder te sprecken met myn heer oft vrouw die Schuerman gesedt op 6s. ». Piot, « Administration monétaire », n° 1, p. 58 et Laurent, *Loi de Gresham*, n° 1, p.111.

24. Le professeur Herman Van der Wee pense que le schuerman atteignit la valeur de 6s. paiement parce qu'il ne réussit pas à remplacer le plus léger gros à 4 lions de Vilvorde comme « link money » au tarif de 4s. paiement. Les ordonnances monétaires de mai-juin 1381 continuèrent en effet d'évaluer le gros de Vilvorde à 4s. paiement et le schuerman primitif de Louvain à 6 s. Mais le gros de Vilvorde, pesant 88,6 % du schuerman en argent fin, devait valoir 5s. 3d. paiement ; ou inversement, si le gros de Vilvorde devait garder la valeur fixe de 4s., alors le schuerman de 1375 ne valait en fait que 4s. 6d. paiement. En réalité, le gros comme le schuerman fut (en 1381) sous-évalué par rapport au gros longue-croix, évalué lui aussi 4s., mais avec 71,8 % seulement du contenu en argent de l'ancien gros de Vilvorde. L'objet de ces sous-évaluations des anciennes pièces était d'encourager l'afflux du métal à la Monnaie pour la fabrication des nouvelles pièces. Voir Van der Wee, *Antwerp*, I, 123 n. 49 ; Piot, « Discussions », n° 3-4, pp. 188-98 ; tableau 1.

25. Voir les sources citées dans la note 1 ; et dans Laurent, chapitre 2, « La crise monétaire brabançonne en 1380-81 », pp. 19-36.

26. Voir les notes 20, 48-49. Pour être juste, il faut noter cependant que c'est seulement en 1979 que deux comptes de grande importance de la Monnaie de Malines (celui de 7 août 1380 - 28 avril 1381 et celui du 28 avril 1381 - 3 mai 1382) ont été publiés (en précis) par le professeur Willem Blockmans, « Devaluation, Coinage and Seignorage under Louis de Nevers and Louis de Male », tableaux 6-7, pp. 85-89.

27. F. Quicke, *Les Pays-Bas à la veille de la période bourguignonne, 1356-1384* (Paris et Bruxelles, 1947), pp.177-220.

28. *Ibid.*, pp. 215-17. Sur la charte wallonne, voir plus loin, p. 273 et note 32.

29. *Ibid.*, p. 218 n.74.

30. Gaillard, *Monnaies*, II, n° 107, pp. 209-10. Voir tableau A et note 26.

31. AGR, CR n° 2591. Puisque ces comptes concernent aussi bien les frappes d'or que les frappes d'argent pendant la même période, on ne peut pas savoir à quel moment cet affaiblissement commença — peut-être pas avant l'ordonnance de nov. 1380 qui l'autorisa (ou le justifia). Voir la note *a* au tableau 1.

32. Ces accusations peuvent être déduites des réponses données par Wenceslas vers nov. 1380 - avril 1381 (voir note 23) : dans Piot, « Administration monétaire », n° 10-11, pp. 56-58 ; Piot, « Discussions », n° 1-2, pp. 179-88 (et le commentaire de Piot, pp.173-8) ; et Laurent, *Loi de Gresham*, n° 1-4, pp.111-29 (et son commentaire, pp.23-34). L'article 2 de la Charte wallonne octroyée par le duc Jean III en 1314, stipula que : « C'on ne fera ne forgera nul denier dedens Brabant, se ce n'est dedens frances villes et par le conseil desdites villes ou du pays ; et ce dernier on eswardera et tenra en bon point par le conseil desdites villes et du pays ». Dans le *Blijde Inkomst* de 1356, Wenceslas et Joanna firent des promesses encore plus contraignantes : de ne pas frapper des monnaies sans le conseil de « tout le pays » ; de ne pas diminuer le poids des pièces sans l'accord du pays (« ende dat men nemmermeer den pennyng lichten en sal sonder consent van onsen ghemeynen land »). Voir Peter Spufford, « Coinage, Taxation, and the Estates General of the Burgundian Netherlands », *Standen en Landen*, XL (1966), 65-7 ; de Witte, *Histoire monétaire*, I, 109-10.

33. Quicke, *Pays-Bas*, pp. 356-63. La révolte prit fin en janvier 1383 avec une paix parrainée par l'évêque Arnold de Liège.
34. Voir les sources citées dans la note 32, en particulier Laurent, *Loi de Gresham*, n° 3, p.121.
35. *Ibid.*, n° 3, p. 121.
36. *Ibid.*, n° 3, p. 118. Voir aussi de Witte, *Histoire monétaire*, I, 145-6 ; Van Werveke, « Monnaies de compte », p. 153. Laurent se trompe en disant que le schuerman ne fut pas frappé avant 1376. *Loi de Gresham*, pp. 27-28.
37. Voir Gaillard, *Monnaies*, II, n° 106-07, pp. 208—10 ; Blockmans, « Devaluation », tableaux 6-7, pp.87-89 ; Munro, « Mint Policies », pp. 99-100.
38. Voir C.G. Grump et C. Johnson, « Tables of Bullion Coined Under Edward I, II, and III », *Numismatic Chronicle*, 4ᵉ série, XIII (1913), 225 ; G.C. Brooke et E. Stokes, « Tables of Bullion Coined from 1377 to 1550 », *Ibid.*, 5 série IX (1929), 28 ; H.A. Miskimin, *Money, Prices and Foreign Exchange in Fourteenth Century France* (New Haven, 1963), appendice D, pp.159-60.
39. Voir notes 2 et 22.
40. Voir n. 32.
41. Textes publiés par Piot, « Discussions », n° 3-4, pp. 188-98 et (en partie) par Laurent, *Loi de Gresham*, n° 5—6, pp. 130-40.
42. Laurent, *Loi de Gresham*, n° 6 (6 juin 1381), p. 131. Voir aussi son commentaire dans le chapitre V, pp.85-105 ; et aussi John Munro, « An Aspect of Medieval Public Finance : the Profits of Counterfeiting in the Fifteenth Century Low Countries », *Revue belge de numismatique*, CXVIII (1972), 127-48 ; Munro, *Wool, Cloth and Gold*, pp. 25-30, 70-102 (en particulier p. 101 n. 20).
43. Voir les sources citées dans la note 38.
44. Voir notes 24 et 42.
45. Laurent, *Loi de Gresham*, n° 6, p. 138.
46. *Ibid.*, p. 36. Voir note 20.
47. Voir notes 20, 31 et tableau 1.
48. Voir note 20 et de Witte, *Histoire monétaire* I, 145-50 (à la page 150, il a confondu les deux émissions distinctes de 1381-1382) ; Cumont, « Nicolas Chavre », p. 223.
49. AGR, CR n° 2591 ; Cumont, « Nicolas Chavre », pp. 223-4. De Witte assigne incorrectement cette frappe (du gros brabançon) à l'ordonnance de juin 1381 : *Histoire monétaire*, I, 149.
50. Voir Cumont, « Nicolas Chavre », p. 225 ; de Witte, *Histoire monétaire*, I, 151.
51. Voir Quicke, *Pays Bas*, pp. 409-11.
52. Voir Munro, « Mint Policies », pp. 78-95.
53. Textes publiés par John Bartier et Andrée Van Nieuwenhuysen, éds. *Les ordonnances de Philippe-le-Hardi, de Marguerite de Mäle, et Jean-sans-Peur, 1381-1419*, I : *Les ordonnances du 16 octobre 1381 au 31 décembre 1393* (Bruxelles, 1965), 50-3 ; Laurent, *Loi de Gresham*, n° 7, pp. 140-3 (commentaire, pp. 40-8) ; dans AGR, CC, carton 65 : dans une version précédente datée du 5 mai 1384.
54. Voir Munro, « Mint Policies », pp. 78-83 . Voir aussi Cockshaw, « Circulation monétaire », pp. 107-15 : H. Enno Van Gelder « Aantekeningen bij de Vlaamse muntslag, 1384-1434 », *Revue belge de numismatique*, CVII (1961), 138-41.
55. Gaillard, *Monnaie*, I, n° 13, pp. 23-6 (oct. 1299), n° 14, pp. 27-8 (avril 1300) ; I.L.A. Diegerick, éd. *Inventaire analytique et chronologique des chartes et documents appartenant aux archives de la ville d'Ypres*, 5 vols. (Bruges, 1853-60), II, n° 504, p. 109 (décembre 1339). Voir aussi de Witte, *Histoire monétaire*, I, 90-2, 112, 131-2.
56. Ghyssens, « Monnayage d'argent », pp.123-9, 160-67.
57. Les comptes de la Monnaie se trouvent dans AGR, CR, n° 2143 (Malines) et n° 2144 et 2589 (Louvain). Laurent a publié des versions remaniées, avec quelques erreurs, dans *La loi de Gresham*, n° 9-10, pp. 147-50 ; et Piot avait publié, il y a longtemps, les comptes de Louvain dans « Notice », n° 1, pp.132-3. Pour des tableaux des frappes flamandes précédentes, voir Munro, « Mint Policies », pp. 102-08 (tableau 1-6) et appendice B, pp. 99-101 ; Blockmans, « Devaluation », pp. 85-9 (tableaux 6-7). En 1365-9, la production annuelle des ateliers flamands était en moyenne 8 518,3 marcs d'or pur (= 2 084, 9 kgs) et 39 359,8 marcs argent-le-roy (= 9 232,0 kgs).
58. Voir Van der Wee, *Antwerp Market*, I, 123 ; Cockshaw, « Circulation monétaire », pp. 107-16 ; Munro, « Mint Policies », pp. 78-83.
59. Voir en particulier Cockshaw, « Circulation monétaire », pp. 113-14 : c'est le premier à donner une version correcte de l'ordonnance monétaire du 18 avril 1386, en rectifiant

les erreurs de Laurent (*Loi de Gresham*, n° 8, p. 146) et d'autres.

60. Voir Cockshaw, « Circulation monétaire », pp. 113-22 ; Munro, « Mint Policies », pp. 80-3 .

61. Ordonnance dans Bartier et Van Nieuwenhuysen, *Ordonnances*, I, n° 193, pp. 292-4. Comptes de la Monnaie de Gand dans AGR, CR n° 284 ; version remaniée dans Laurent, *Loi de Gresham* n°21, pp. 164-6. Voir aussi Munro, « Mint Policies », pp. 83-5, 102-05 (tableaux 1-3).

62. Textes dans Piot, « Administration monétaire », n° 12, pp. 59-61, et de Witte, *Histoi re monétaire*, I, 167-8. La version publiée par Laurent est passablement confuse ; elle a été corrigée par Cockshaw, « Circulation monétaire », p. 119.

63. Textes des plaintes de Philippe dans Laurent, *Loi de Gresham*, n° 13, pp. 154-5 ; texte de la lettre sans date de Joanna à Philippe dans Piot, « Notice sur les monnaies de Jeanne », n° 2, pp. 133-6, analysée à pp. 120-2. Pierre Cockshaw publia le texte de la convention du 5 Janvier 1388, jusqu'alors ignorée, dans « Circulation monétaire », annexe III, pp. 136-8, analysée à pp. 117-20. Pour la guerre de Gueldre, voir Richard Vaughan, *Philip the Bold : The Formation of the Burgundian State* (Londres 1962), pp. 96-9.

64. Voir les sources citées dans la note 62, et aussi Laurent, *Loi de Gresham*, pp. 54-6, 59, 154-6 (doc. n° 13-14), 158 (n° 16 : 4 -- qui signale la fermeture de la Monnaie de Louvain) ; Cumont, « Mélanges numismatiques », pp.197-9 ; de Witte, *Histoire monétaire*, I, 167-8.

65. Laurent, Piot, Cumont et Cockshaw (voir notes 63-4 et 68).

66. Voir note 63 (Piot).

67. AGR, CR, n° 824.

68. Voir note 63. Malgré son importante découverte, Cockshaw acceptait les opinions des auteurs cités dans les notes 63-5 sur la continuation des frappes de Joanna.

69. Texte complet dans Bartier-Van Nieuwenhuysen, *Ordonnances*, I, n° 217-18, pp. 327-9. Voir aussi de Witte, *Histoire monétaire*, I, 167-9 ; Piot, « Notice », pp. 122-3 et doc. n° 2-3, pp. 133-7 ; Laurent, *Loi de Gresham*, pp. 59-61 ; Cockshaw, « Circulation monétaire », pp. 124-6 ; Cumont, « Mélanges numismatiques », pp. 197-9.

70. Voir notes 77-8. La frappe recommença le 25 Juin 1392. Voir aussi Cumont, « Mélanges numismatiques », p. 203 (à propos des comptes de Renier Goetheere du 12 déc. 1391 au 24 juin 1392 : « vander munten niet ontfaen »).

71. Ordonnance dans Bartier-Van Nieuwenhuysen, *Ordonnances*, I, n° 231, pp. 345-8 ; Comptes de la Monnaie de Gand du 18 nov. 1389 - 7 juillet 1390 dans AGR, CR n° 825 ; Laurent, *Loi de Gresham*, n° 22, pp. 166-8.

72. Voir Munro, « Mint Policies », pp. 83-8 ; Hans Van Werveke, « De Vlaamse munthervorming van 1389-90 », *Nederlandsche historiebladen*, I (1938), 336-47, repris dans son *Miscellanea Mediaevalia* (Gand, 1968), pp.268-80.

73. Hans Van Werveke, « De economische en sociale gevolgen van de muntpoltiek der graven van Vlaanderen (1337-1433) », *Annales de la Société d'Emulation de Bruges*, LXXIV (1931), repris dans son *Miscellanea Mediaevalia*, pp.246-54 ; et son « Vlaamse munthervorming », pp.126-30 ; Raymond de Roover, *Money, Banking, and Credit in Medieval Bruges* (Cambridge, Mass. 1948), pp. 227-9 ; De Roover, *The Bruges Money Market Around 1400* (Bruxelles, 1968), pp. 39-40 ; Munro, « Monetary Contraction », pp. 112, 132. Voir aussi Bartier et Van Nieuwenhuysen, *Ordonnances*, I, n° 231, pp. 345-8, n° 239, pp. 358-61 ; n° 262, pp. 399-400.

74. Excepté un affaiblissement léger et temporaire de 0,87 % en janvier 1391, annulé en juin 1393 : Bartier et Van Nieuwenhuysen, *Ordonnances*, I, n° 266, pp. 403-4. Voir Munro, « Mint Policies », pp. 85-95 ; 102-16 (tableaux 1-10) ; Munro, *Wool, Cloth, and Gold*, pp. 58-83.

75. Voir plus haut, p. 285 et note 97.

76. Voir Van der Wee, *Antwerp Market*, I, 123, Tableau XIII.

77. Textes dans Bartier et Van Nieuwenhuysen, *Ordonnances*, I, n° 306, pp. 467-8 ; Louis Deschamps de Pas, *Essai sur l'histoire monétaire des comtes de Flandre de la maison de Bourgogne* (Paris, 1863), n° 30-1, p. viii ; Laurent, *Loi de Gresham*, n° 26, p. 173.

78. Ordonnances monétaires dans Piot, « Notice », n° 4, pp. 137-9 (25 juin 1392) et Laurent, *Loi de Gresham*, n° 33, pp. 186-90 (15 juillet 1393). Les plaintes flamandes du 30 août et 9 sept. 1392 dans *Ibid.*, n° 29-30, pp.178-83 (commentaire de Laurent, pp.69-71). Pour les comptes de Monnaies : (a) Vilvorde, 25,VI.1392 - 22.VII.1393, dans AGR, CR n° 2590 (flamand) et 2592 (français) et une version remaniée dans Piot, « Notice », n° 5, pp. 142-5 ; (b) Louvain, 22.VII.1393 19.IV.1394, dans AGR, CR n° 2590 (flamand) et 2592 (français), dans une version remaniée dans Piot, « Notice, pp. 145-6 ; (c) Louvain,

15.V.1394 - 28.I.1395, dans AGR, CR n° 2588 (qui n'a pas été éditée). Peut-être à cause de cette compétition de la Monnaie brabançonne, le duc Philippe ferma son atelier de Malines vers la fin d'octobre 1392. AGR, CC n° 48.977. Voir aussi de Witte, *Histoire monétaire*, I, 169-71 ; Cumont « Mélanges numismatiques », pp. 203-14 ; Piot, « Notice », pp. 122-5 ; Chalon, « Nouvelle classification », pp. 356-7 ; et Cockshaw, « Circulation monétaire », pp.130-1.

79. Les comptes des Monnaies de Malines et Bruges dans AGR, CC n° 48.977 et CR n° 2146 (Malines) ; CR n° 776-81 (Bruges). Voir aussi Munro, « Mint Policies », tableaux 1-3, pp. 102-05.

80. Voir note 78. Pieters d'or à la taille de 75 au marc.

81. Voir note 78.

82. Voir Munro, « Mint Policies », p. 89, pp. 110-13 (tableaux 8-9).

83. AGR, CR n° 2588 : « ende niet meer ghemunten en const mids dat tgelt soe op liep ». Voir aussi Cumont, « Mélanges numismatiques », pp. 214-20 . Laurent, *Loi de Gresham*, pp.81-2 ; de Witte, *Histoire monétaire*, I, 172.

84. Voir note 57.

85. Voir note 78 (comptes de la Monnaie de Louvain) ; note 6 (à propos des sterlings anglais et esterlins flamands) ; tableau 1.

86. Voir tableau 1 et Van der Wee, *Antwerp Market*, I, 123.

87. Voir Laurent, *Loi de Gresham*, pp. 81-2 ; Cumont, « Mélanges numismatiques », pp. 214-15, 224-30 ; Piot, « Notice », pp. 126-7 ; de Witte, *Histoire monétaire*, I, 172.

88. Texte dans Laurent, *Loi de Gresham*, n° 38, pp. 197-208. Voir aussi de Witte, *Histoire monétaire*, I, 172-4 ; Piot, « Notice », pp. 126-7 ; Cumont, « Mélanges numismatiques », pp.227-28 (à propos d'un paiement de *Torrenghelde* 1400-06).

89. De Witte, bien que doutant fortement que les villes exerçaient des droits de frappe, signale néanmoins une pièce de billon d'origine incertaine qui aurait pu être frappée à Bruxelles, c.1396-99. *Histoire monétaire*, I, 172-4, fig. XXX : 428. Voir aussi Robert Vogeleer, éd. *Mille ans de monnayage bruxellois, 965 - 1965* (Bruxelles, 1965), p. 24 : « Lelewel a cru lire le nom de la ville [Bruxelles] sur un billon noir, mais la pièce a disparu et son attribution est plus que douteuse ».

90. Les taux de change de Van der Wee pour le gros flamand (la pièce) suggèrent une inflation de la livre de paiement seulement. *Antwerp Market*, I, 124.

91. *Ibid.*, I, 124.

92. Archives de la ville de Malines, comptes de la ville I, n° 74-86.

93. Le duc Philippe-le-Hardi était le neveu de la duchesse Joanna, sans descendance, et en partie pour récompenser son aide dans la guerre de Gueldre, elle lui avait cédé les territoires de Limbourg et donnait son accord pour que ses héritiers accèdent au duché de Brabant. Les Etats de Brabant étaient finalement d'accord pour qu'Antoine, fils cadet de Philippe, succède à Joanna, mais à condition que les territoires de Limbourg et Anvers soient réintégrés dans le duché de Brabant (septembre 1403). Voir Vaughan, *Philip the Bold*, pp.89-92, 100-02 ; de Witte, *Histoire monétaire*, I, 179-82.

94. Ordonnance monétaire du 10 juillet 1405 dans Charles Piot, « Documents sur quelques monnaies frappées par Antoine, duc de Brabant », *Revue belge de numismatique*, I (1842-45), 247-8 ; 251-6 (doc. n° 1) : compte de la Monnaie d'Anvers du 5 sept. au 10 oct. 1405 dans de Witte, *Histoire monétaire*, I, 180-1 (d'après AGR, CR, n° 2504a).

95. Voir aussi Cumont, « Mélanges numismatiques », pp. 238-46.

96. Ordonnances monétaires du 24 janvier 1409 et 20 décembre 1409 dans de Witte, *Histoire monétaire,* I, 184-5, et Piot, « Documents », n° 2, pp. 256-60. Comptes des Monnaies : (a) Vilvorde, 28.IV.1409 - 24.XII.1409, dans Fréderic Verachter, éd. *Documents pour servir à l'histoire monétaire des Pays-Bas* (Anvers, 1841), pp. 107-08 (d'après AGR, CC n° 48.967 -- un compte qui manque dans les archives depuis juin 1940) ; (b) Louvain, 5.I.1410 -11.VII.1410, dans Verachter, *Documents*, pp. 108-10 et de Witte, *Histoire monétaire*, I, 185-6 (d'un manuscrit privé) ; (c) Louvain, 12.VII.1410 - 21.III.1411, AGR, CC, n° 18.064 ; (d) Louvain, 21.III.1411 - 25.VI.1412 : les comptes de la Monnaie manquent, mais les recettes générales de Brabant indiquent un seigneurage global de £ 354 gros pour cette période. (De Witte, *Histoire monétaire*, I, 186). A noter que les comptes de la Monnaie utilisent la livre gros, monnaie de compte basée sur le denier d'argent courant ; mais l'ordonnance monétaire de décembre 1409 utilise « groets Brabants payments » pour évaluer la pièce d'argent : 1 botdrager ou double gros = 12 « groets » ; 1 demi-botdrager ou gros = 6 « groets ». Voir p. 279 et note 91.

97. AGR, CR n° 279-280.

98. Van der Wee, *Antwerp Market*, I, 125.

VIII

Deflation and the Petty Coinage Problem in the Late-Medieval Economy: The Case of Flanders, 1334–1484*

Monetary historians have debated whether too many or too few petty coins, those most needed by the general populace, were struck in medieval Europe. But exactly how many were struck can be determined only for Flanders, where petty coinage usually accounted for 1% or less of the bullion minted. These mint-output statistics are explained in part by the demand for high-denomination coins by most merchants who supplied bullion to the mints; but equally also by the relatively small need to replace stocks of petty coin. Severe petty-coin scarcity was not likely a chronic condition in medieval Flanders, but did occur in the deflationary mid-fifteenth century, instigating innovations in state monetary policy.

One of the least-well-studied aspects of European monetary history is the role of petty coinage, especially in the medieval economy. In the current but scant literature on petty coinage, we find two contradictory views: that either too much or too little was struck. Thus Herman Van der Wee (1969, p. 375) has contended that frequently so many petty coins circulated that "under these circumstances an inflation of what we would call fiduciary currency occurred . . . which resulted in a disappearance of the silver 'link' money from circulation because of actual undervaluation." In terms of the familiar Gresham's Law, therefore, the overabundant and thus "cheap" or "bad" petty coins drove out the good "dear" silver money. Philip Grierson (1976, p. 113), however, drawing upon the work of his former student Peter Spufford (1970), has stated the contrary: that medieval "moneyers preferred to strike high denominations to low ones . . . and were apt to leave the public desperately short of small change." What constituted such a shortage was not, however, specified.

Whether too much or too little petty coinage was struck in this era is

* I am greatly indebted to Peter Spufford, Charles Calomiris, Larry Neal, Alan Stahl, and an anonymous referee for their advice and assistance to me in writing this article, whose errors and omissions remain my own.

indeed a question that cannot be easily resolved for most of Europe. Carlo Cipolla (1956, pp. 32–33), to be sure, has stated that late-medieval Italian minting policies resulted in "a chain of alternate periods of shortages of petty coins and excessive coining" from periodic debasements; and that the latter proved more beneficial than harmful in this era when "the overall supply of precious metals proved to be extremely inelastic." But again conditions of coin scarcity or excess are not really defined; and his thesis cannot be verified because Italian mint account data are too sparse.[1] French mint accounts, commencing in the early 14th century (1308), have survived in far greater abundance, but with many lacunae; they are certainly incomplete for the entire kingdom.[2] Only for Flanders and England do we possess mint accounts in a virtually complete, unbroken series in the late-medieval era. Regrettably the English accounts cease giving information for each coin denomination struck after June 1351.[3] Only the Flemish accounts continue to do so; and only for Flanders, therefore, can we answer the questions: how much petty coinage was struck from year to year, and what proportions of total mint outputs were struck in that form?

To understand properly the significance of this debate and the Flemish mint data, we must also (1) understand the nature of medieval minting; (2) define precisely the term "petty coin"; and (3) acquire some quantitative measure of its purchasing power in the economy of late-medieval Flanders. Virtually everywhere in medieval Europe, certainly in Flanders, minting was undertaken at least partly for profit, potentially derived from two charges imposed on coinage.[4] The first was a feudal tax on minting that went directly to the prince as *seigniorage*. His profit, however, was only

[1] His thesis is too complex to reproduce here: see Cipolla (1956, pp. 27–33; and also 1963, 1982); Spengler (1966, pp. 208–214); Cannan (1926, pp. 25–31); and p. 393 below. Bernocchi (1976, Vol. 3, pp. 252–256) has published summaries of the Florentine mint accounts for silver from 1345, but with many gaps: accounts are missing for the years 1392–1422, 1450–1451, 1453–1463, 1465–1471, 1477–1478, 1495–1502. The Venetian mint accounts are still missing; see Lane and Mueller (1985, Chap. 10, Appendix B); for Genoa, Milan, Florence, and Venice, see Day (1978, pp. 23–35, 40–42, 53–54).

[2] For the French mint accounts, see Miskimim (1963, 1984) and Spooner (1972); they provide mint outputs only in total livres and fine *marcs* struck, not by coin denominations.

[3] For an explanation see below pp. 402–403 and n. 15. The various silver coin denominations had been differentiated in the English mint accounts from the first extant accounts, in 1234, to June 1351.

[4] For the numismatics and economics of the following, see Munro (1973, Chap. 1, "The Economics of Bullionism," pp. 11–36; 1979, pp. 178–187; 1983, pp. 109–126); Feavearyear (1963, pp. 1–45); Grierson (1975, pp. 94–123); De Roover (1948, pp. 220–246); Spufford (1970, pp. 29–54, 130–146); Challis (1978, pp. 1–28, 165–198); Van der Wee (1977, pp. 290–300). Prince and mint-master usually also shared another source of profit on minting: any left-over precious metals, the *remèdes* or "tolerances" in fineness and weight that had to be allowed, because of the mechanical crudity of coin stamping and cutting in medieval minting. See the Appendix.

a residual revenue after paying the salaries of his monetary officials and mint inspectors and the capital costs of the mint buildings. The second fee, known as *brassage,* went to the mint-master, to cover his costs for copper alloys used in the coins, the production of coin dies, the wages of his employees, and any funds expended in leasing ("farming") the mint from the prince; his profit was thus also the residual amount. In return for the bullion supplied to the mint, the money-changer or merchant received payment based on the "mint price": the official monetary equivalent or *traite* value of the bullion coined *less* the deductions for seigniorage and brassage, per pound or *marc* (244.75 g) of precious metal, illustrated in Table 1 and the Appendix.

Merchants would supply bullion only if the coins received enjoyed a "premium" over their bullion contents high enough to cover the seigniorage, brassage, and transactions costs. Coins normally commanded such a premium, to circulate by "tale" or number at face value, because of their recognizability (the coin's "stamp"), portability, divisibility, and general convenience in trade. But they could do so only so long as they remained physically unimpaired, to command public confidence, and their circulating quantity did not grow beyond total public demand for coined money.[5] The state (in Flanders and England) sought to protect that premium by preventing the circulation of most foreign coins and by making the mint, its licenced changers, and a few licenced jewelers the sole purchasers of bullion, banning any other bullion transactions. The mints were not, however, always willing and able to buy bullion: most would remain open only so long as the bullion influx and thus coinage revenues were large enough to cover their variable costs.

Frequently medieval princes sought to induce a greater bullion influx by a coinage debasement: reducing the coin's precious metal content, by weight and/or fineness (alloy), in order to strike a higher *traite* or official value of coinage from a given quantity of precious metal. That increase in the traite thus permitted the mint to increase its bullion price for the merchants, the prince's seigniorage, the mint-masters' brassage—and also necessarily the coinage premium. The relationship between the physical and monetary changes, between debasement and the new traite values, was a reciprocal one, expressed by the formula: ΔT (traite) = $[1/(1 - x)] - 1$, in which x is the percentage reduction in the silver content of the penny or other coin linked to the money-of-account. Such changes can be also be seen in Table 1, for the Flemish debasement of November 1428. Thus an 11.76% reduction in the pure silver content of the 2d. coin (from 1.725 g. to 1.522 g.) resulted in a 13.32% increase in

[5] Compare with the recommendation of the late 17th-century Italian writer Geminiano Montanari that the state "not strike more [petty coins] than [are] sufficient for the use of his people, sooner striking too few than striking too many." Cited in Cipolla (1956, p. 30), Spengler (1966, p. 211), Monroe (1923, p. 98). See also p. 407, n. 23; and p. 417, n. 50 below.

TABLE 1
Flemish Coinage Debasement: The Mint Ordinances of June 1418 and November 1428

Double gros	June 1418			November 1428		
Value[a]	2d. gros			2d. gros		
Fineness[b]	6 deniers AR = 50.0% fine = 47.92% pure			5 deniers 8 grains AR = 44.44% fine = 42.59% pure		
Weight[c]	68 cut per marc =		3.599 g	68.5 cut per marc =		3.573 g
Fine silver content AR			1.800 g			1.588 g
Pure silver content			1.725 g			1.522 g
Traite per marc[d] argent-le-roy	$\frac{68.0 \times 2d.}{6/12} = \frac{136d.}{0.50} =$		22s.8d.	$\frac{68.5 \times 2d.}{5.333/12} = \frac{137d.}{0.444} =$		25s.8d. 6 mites
Division of the traite per marc AR	Value in Flemish gros	Number of coins	Percentage of the traite	Value in Flemish gros	Number of coins	Percentage of the traite
Brassage	1s.2d.	7	5.15	1s.2d.6m.	7 1/8	4.62
Seigniorage	4d.	2	1.47	6d.	3	1.95
Total mint charges	1s.6d.	9	6.62	1s.8d.6m.	10 1/8	6.57
Mint bullion price	21s.2d.	127	93.38	24s.0d.	144	93.43
Traite per marc	22s.8d.	136	100.00	25s.8d.6m.	154 1/8	100.00

Double mite (courte)	June 1418			November 1428[e]		
Value[a]	2 mites = 1/12d. gros			2 mites = 1/12d. gros		
Fineness[b]	9 grains AR = 3.125% fine = 2.995% pure			8 grains AR = 2.777% fine = 2.662% pure		
Weight[c]	180 cut per marc =		1.360 g	180 cut per marc =		1.360 g
Fine silver content AR			0.043 g			0.038 g
Pure silver content			0.041 g			0.036 g
Traite per marc[d] argent-le-roy	$\frac{180 \times 1/12d.}{9/24/12} = \frac{15}{0.03125} =$		40s.0d.	$\frac{180 \times 1/12d.}{8/24/12} = \frac{15}{0.02777} =$		45s.0d.
Division of the traite per marc AR	Value in Flemish gros	Number of coins	Percentage of the traite	Value in Flemish gros	Number of coins	Percentage of the traite
Brassage	18s.6d.	2664	46.25	20s.5d.	2940	45.37
Seignoriage	4d.	48	0.83	7d.	84	1.30
Total mint charges	18s.10d.	2712	47.08	21s.0d.	3024	46.67
Mint bullion price	21s.2d.	3048	52.92	24s.0d.	3456	53.33
Traite	40s.0d.	5760	100.00	45s.0d.	6480	100.00

[a] Face value of the coinage: 1 penny or 1d. gros = 12d. (1s.) parisis = 24 mites; 12d. gros = 1s. (sol, shilling).

[b] Fineness: reckoned out of a total of 12 deniers *argent-le-roy*, with 24 grains per denier; a full 12 deniers *argent-le-roy* was commercially fine silver = 23/24ths or 95.833% pure silver.

[c] Weight: reckoned in terms of the *taille* or number cut per *marc de Troyes* = 8 Paris ounces = 244.753 g.

[d] The traite per marc: official value of the coinage struck per *marc argent-le-roy*, calculated as:

$$T = \frac{\text{taille per marc} \times \text{face value of the coin}}{\text{fineness in deniers and grains out of 12 den. AR}}$$

[e] Period of minting double mites: 9 March 1430 to 27 September 1432.

the traite: from 22.667s. (22s.8d.) to 25.6875s. (25s.8d.6m.) per fine silver *marc argent-le-roy*.

As Table 1 further demonstrates, the principles of debasement, or of any coinage alteration, were the same for both large and small coin denominations. It is imperative to realize, second, that the Flemish petty coinage was an integral part of the silver money system. Fully convertible legal tender, it always contained some silver (until 1543), diminishing with debasements and increasing with *renforcements* (coinage reforms), more or less proportionally with changes in other silver coins, according to officially prescribed monetary ordinances (Tables 1, 3, 5).[6] Thus *not* included in this definition are any token coins: i.e., those base-metal jettons of tin, pewter, lead, or copper, containing no precious metal, issued by the Church, other charitable organizations, or even individuals, as unofficial coins, invalid for taxes or official payments, that served only as private credit instruments.[7]

The values assigned to genuine petty coins were some specified constant fractions of the silver penny or other "link money" that anchored the circulating coinage to the prevailing money-of-account. A modern synonym is thus fractional coinage. In medieval Flanders, the most common and very apt synonym was "black money"—*monnaies noires, zwart geld*—because of the coins' very high base-metal contents.[8] Their more formal names were *mites:* the single mite, worth 1/24 of the silver penny *gros* or *groot*, and the double mite or *courte*, worth 1/12d. *gros*.[9] These were the only petty coins struck in 14-century Flanders; but thereafter we may arbitrarily add the quarter-gros, the *gigot* or *zeskin* of 6 mites, first struck in that form in 1410.[10]

[6] See sources cited in n. 4 above; and also nn. 5, 23, 41, and 50. Medieval canon lawyers were agreed that the amounts of petty coinage that had to be accepted in payment should be limited (Monroe, 1923, pp. 36, 96); but in Flanders no specific legal limitations were imposed.

[7] See Mitchiner and Skinner (1983, 1984); Grierson (1975, pp. 32–33, 162–171); Courtenay (1973); and Chalon (1847), on medieval accounting tokens, "jetons de calcul." See below p. 414; and n. 40.

[8] The modern numismatic term is *billon*, a base coin with under 50% silver (Grierson, 1975, p. 193). But that term can be very misleading, since its original medieval meaning was "bullion" (Munro, 1974); furthermore, many medieval coins with less than 50% silver were not then considered "petty," while the English farthing (1/4d.), with 92.5% silver fineness, certainly was.

[9] In the older *parisis* money-of-account system, fixed in value at 1/12th of the gros system from 1318–1320, the single mite was thus worth 1/2d. and the double mite, 1d.—a penny. See the Appendix; Tables 4–6; and Ghyssens (1970, 1974), Dieudonné (1933).

[10] The quarter-gros struck from 1410 was silver rather than black money, with a fineness of 33.3% (falling to 16.7% by 1477). In December 1416, a 3-mite piece of 25% fineness was prescribed, but evidently not struck. See Deschamps de Pas (1861, pp. 223–225) and Tables 4–5. A quarter-gros ("petit blanc") had been briefly struck much earlier, in 1334–1336 (Gaillard, 1856, pp. 34–42). But, with a much higher silver content (85.4% fine) and

Third, one must realize that small silver and petty coins played a far greater role in medieval society than they do in today's economy. For most people, such coins were then certainly the principal means, for many the only means, of transacting retail trade, in buying and selling daily necessities. As Table 2 demonstrates, furthermore, the purchasing power of such coins was surprisingly high in late-medieval Flanders, because prices and wages were then so low.[11] The expression "a penny for your thoughts" takes on new meaning when we find, ca. 1350, that a penny would then buy over 5 lb of cheese or a gallon (4.8 l) of wheat. Thus even the Flemish *courte* (double mite), with which one could have bought 6–7 oz of cheese in 1350 (or again in 1470), should not be too casually dismissed as "small change."

As Table 2 also demonstrates, the purchasing power of such silver coins changed often drastically over the 150 years that constitute the period chosen for this case study, from 1334—when the Flemish mint accounts commence—to 1484, with the transition to the early-modern Habsburg regime. Those years are particularly significant in encompassing the late-medieval economic contraction, or "Great Depression." For Flanders, the most urbanized, commercialized, industrialized, and monetized region in northern Europe, two particularly relevant, interrelated features of this economic contraction were widespread, chronic warfare—most notably the Hundred Years' War (1336–1453); and a growing scarcity of precious metals, especially from the 1370s. Warfare was significant not only for its considerable economic dislocation but more for its financing by often drastic coinage debasements that in turn spawned veritable *guerres monétaires,* especially from the 1330s, in an international competition for bullion. Both the warfare itself and the accompanying debasements were highly inflationary, temporarily overpowering and reversing the prevailing deflationary forces of this era. The intervening periods of peace generally also resulted, in most continental countries, in coinage *renforcements,* monetary reforms, to remedy the inflationary damages from debasements—especially to the prince's feudal and tax revenues, which were usually fixed in money-of-account terms. Since creditors similarly suffered from debasements, the prince's continued access to credit was ultimately dependent also upon a *renforcement*. These reforms were themselves generally deflationary, by converting the current debased coins necessarily into a smaller quantity of strengthened coins. Flanders' monetary history can thus be portrayed as an oscillating pattern of debasement and reform, perhaps similar to Italy's (Cipolla, 1956): (A) 1334–

---

a much higher purchasing power (Table 2)—then worth 3/4 of an English penny sterling, it did not then really qualify as petty coin.

[11] See also Cipolla (1956, pp. 33–34); Spengler (1966, pp. 205–208); and Munro (1975).

TABLE 2
The Purchasing Power of One Flemish Silver Penny Gros (1d.) in Terms of Selected Foodstuffs and the Price of a Basket of Consumables: in 10-year Intervals, 1350 to 1490

Year	Butter[a] Bruges (lb)	Cheese[b] Bruges (lb)	Wheat[c] Bruges (quarts)	Peas[c] Bruges (quarts)	Eggs Brussels (number)	Herring[d] Antwerp (number)	Rhine wine[e] Ghent (pints)	Basket of consumables[f] Flanders (d. gros)
1350	2.05	5.14	4.34					65.7
1360	0.96	2.39	2.60					124.1
1370	0.88	2.19	1.84					162.8
1380	0.80	2.23	3.06					135.5
1390	0.79	2.15	2.23		13	7.2		166.6
1400	1.10	3.43	3.25	2.52	13	11.8	1.15	112.4
1410	1.07	2.73	2.20	3.25	13	8.3	0.98	134.6
1420	0.74	2.39	5.04	2.50	12	3.4	0.98	125.8
1430	0.63	2.34	2.69	2.69	n.a.	6.3	0.57	163.7
1440	0.85	4.18	2.26	1.86	n.a.	7.2	0.54	162.0
1450	0.94	4.05	3.19	2.79	12	8.7	0.70	128.8
1460	0.92	3.26	2.20	2.44	10	6.2	0.57	145.3
1470	0.85	4.95	3.40	3.25	7	5.9	0.65	118.0
1480	0.79	3.61	2.17	2.37	5	2.9	0.51	141.7
1490	0.38	1.55	1.50	0.84	5	4.8	0.41	307.1

[a] Butter, which was much more expensive than cheese in this era, was priced by the *wage* of 83.5 kg = 184.09 lb.
[b] Cheese priced by the *wage* of 60.6 kg = 133.60 lb.
[c] Wheat and peas priced by the *hoet* of 172 liters = 156.22 quarts (U.S. dry)
[d] Herring priced by the barrel of 833 herrings (fresh salted)
[e] Rhine wine priced by the *stoop* = 2.306 liters = 4.876 pints (U.S. liquid)
[f] "Basket of Consumables" contains 45.46 liters of wheat, 39.37 liters of rye, 18.18 liters of barley, 24.37 liters of peas, 163.67 liters of barley malt, 13.61 kg of butter, 13.61 kg of cheese, and 1.225 meters of cheap quality woolen cloth. It is modeled on the Phelps Brown-Hopkins "basket."

1389: warfare, debasements, with very large mint outputs, and severe inflation; (B) 1390–1416: relative peace, strong coinage, "bullion famine," and sharp deflation; (C) 1416–1433: extensive warfare, debasements, and inflation; (D) 1433–1474: relative peace, strong coinage, followed by "bullion famine," low mint outputs, and severe deflation; (E) 1474–1496: warfare, debasements, and severe inflation—with, as well, silver influxes from new Central European mines.[12]

During the inflationary periods (A, C, and E), the relative demand for petty coins would presumably have diminished with the fall in their purchasing power; and correspondingly such demand would have risen with their higher purchasing power during the intervening deflationary periods (B and D), as suggested by Table 2. The exact causes of these alternating inflations and deflations, the mixes of real (demographic) and monetary factors, are not our present concern. Nor can we establish here the role that such individual factors played in determining the aggregate supply of and demand for money, and the denominational composition of the gold, silver, and petty coinage circulations: all of which are reflected only imperfectly in the Flemish mint accounts.

From those mint accounts, the actual quantities of petty coin struck as mites and quarter-gros in Flanders from 1334 to 1484, and the proportions of both the total silver bullion and total values of silver coinage minted in petty coin have been computed and presented in Table 3. The physical composition and the minting costs of both mites and silver *gros* are compared over this 150-year period in Tables 4 and 5. Note first that the mint accounts record the striking of petty coins for only 61 or 40% of these years, with none struck at all from 1339 to 1375. That particular 36-year lacuna may, however, be misleading. For the previous account of 1334–1338, while noting the coinage of 2637 *marcs* of *noire monnoye,* made no official reckoning of them "because My Lord [Count Louis de Nevers] exacts no seigniorage for them."[13] Since the real purpose of the accounts was to record the count's seigniorage revenues, subsequent mint-masters may have seen no need to list issues of mites so long as they remained seigniorage-free. At the same time, so long as they were seigniorage-free, the count had little financial incentive to require their coinage: especially Louis de Nevers' successor, Louis de Male (1346–1384), ill-famed for his highly profitable coinage debasements. Indeed mites do not appear in any monetary or mint ordinance during this 36-

[12] For elaboration and evidence, see Munro (1973, 1979a, 1979b, 1981, 1983a, 1983b, 1984); Day (1978); Spufford (1970); Miskimin (1963, 1964, 1975, 1983, 1984); Van der Wee (1963, Vol. 2, pp. 3–112, 285–316, 369–410); Mayhew (1974a, 1974b); Nef (1941, 1952); Braunstein (1983); Bordo (1986).

[13] Gaillard (1856, Doc. Nos. 17–21, pp. 31–58, with quote on p. 45).

TABLE 3
The Petty Coinage Issues in Late-Medieval Flanders: The Minting of Mites, Double-Mites, Quarter-Gros, and of Total Silver Coinage in Number of Coins, Values of Output in £ Gros, and Marcs of Fine Silver Struck, in Decennial Totals: from 1334 to 1484

		Petty coinage struck				Petty coinage as percentage of total silver coinage		
Decade	No. months mint activity	Coins issued in millions	Value (£ gros Flemish)	Marcs argent-le-Roy (244.75g)	Total silver coinage (Marcs A. R.)	(coins)	(£ gros)	(marcs A. R.)
				Mites and double mites only				
1334–1343	109	2.444	424.3	1350	116,295	15.5	1.2	1.2
1346–1354	105	—	—	—	203,698	0.0	0.0	0.0
1354–1364	110	—	—	—	254,534	0.0	0.0	0.0
1365–1374	110	—	—	—	277,457	0.0	0.0	0.0
1374–1384	116	1.633	567.2	408	97,464	13.0	0.6	0.4
1384–1394[a]	124	1.963	548.5	343	102,096	12.1	0.6	0.3
1394–1402[b]	96	4.454	1056.8	694	161,947	18.8	0.7	0.4
1410–1415[c]	51	—	—	—	76,541	0.0	0.0	0.0
1417–1424	85	1.549	537.8	260	285,153	3.5	0.2	0.1
1424–1434	119	0.993	344.8	165	247,036	2.5	0.1	0.1
1434–1444	123	0.921	285.3	16	105,294	5.0	0.2	0.2
1445–1447[d]	26	0.456	158.3	88	126	98.8	77.6	69.8
1454–1458[e]	55	3.515	880.4	399	3,503	65.0	18.5	11.4
1466–1474	94	2.619	909.3	450	153,299	8.9	0.4	0.3
1474–1484	113	3.994	1386.7	458	132,655	13.3	0.6	0.4

Quarter-gros and mites								
1410–1415[c]	51	0.656	682.8	792	76,541	7.2	1.0	1.0
1417–1424	85	3.777	2859.3	2118	285,153	8.5	0.9	0.7
1424–1434	119	1.294	657.9	403	247,036	3.3	0.2	0.2
1434–1444	123	3.183	2641.7	1967	105,294	17.3	2.1	1.9
1445–1447[d]	26	0.456	158.3	88	126	98.8	77.6	69.8
1454–1458[e]	55	4.838	2258.6	1455	3,503	89.5	47.5	41.5
1466–1474	94	6.749	5212.0	3283	153,299	22.9	2.4	2.1
1474–1484	113	4.622	1939.7	712	132,655	15.4	0.8	0.5

Note. The petty coinages are considered part of the silver coinages; and gold coinages have been excluded from these tables. When the Flemish mints maintained progold ratios (ca. 1350–1390; 1425–1465), gold accounted for from 67 to 98% of the total values of coinages struck. See Munro (1983, pp. 140–141). Flemish and auxiliary mints included (a) *Ghent*: 16.09.1334–27.06.1337; 01.10.1388–23.10.1390; 17.01.1410–05.04.1447; 02.05.1459–16.03.1462; 18.06.1466–09.06.1467; 18.07.1482–21.05.1484; (b) *Bruges*: 20.08.1350–24.10.1354; 01.06.1392–16.06.1402; 02.03.1454–12.10.1458; 23.01.1468–05.04.1482; (c) *Mechelen*: 08.10.1357–02.02.1364; 30.01.1380–29.10.1392; 16.06.1454–16.01.1460; (d) *Valkenberg*: 01.11.1396–01.11.1399; (e) *Namur*: 23.10.1421–10.10.1433.

[a] The mint accounts are missing for 1386–1387. See Table 4, notes *e* and *d*. Brabant's Leuven mint struck 74.472 marcs AR into 482,670 single mites between 24.03.1385 and 14.04.1386 (ARA, Rolrekening No. 2589). While legal tender in Flanders, these mites are not included in this table.

[b] No minting (or mint data) from 17.06.1402 to 17.01.1410.

[c] Although the coinage of mites and double mites was prescribed in the August 1409 mint ordinance (Tables 2–3), none or virtually none was struck in this period. The one possible exception is the account year July 1412–July 1413, for which the *garde de la monnaie's* account notes under "extra account, bullion received" 8 *marc d'oeuvres* of double mites and 18 *marcs d'oeuvres* (alloyed marcs) of single mites, without specifying that they were struck. Had they been, that would have amounted to: 6096 coins, worth 25s.10d. gros, from 0.833 *marc argent-le-roy*. The mint-master's account for the same year, however, explicitly states that no double or single mites were struck (as do all the accounts from January 1410 to November 1419).

[d] Mites and double mites only; no quarter gros. No silver was struck from 05.04.1447 to 02.03.1454.

[e] No silver was struck from 12.10.1458 to 18.06.1466.

TABLE 4
The Coinage of Double Mites (Courtes) and Silver Gros in Flanders, 1334–1484: Taille (Weight), Fineness, and Pure Silver Contents

Date of ordinance or first minting	Double mite Taille No. cut to marc	Double mite[a] Percentage fineness argent-le-roy	Double mite[a] Grams of pure silver	Double mite Traite per marc A.R. in shillings	Gros[a] Grams of pure silver	Silver content of Double mite as percentage of silver in the gros
01.10.1334[b]	264	14.58	0.130	6.286	3.484	3.73
12.01.1375[c]	250	6.25	0.059	27.778	1.114	5.30
16.07.1384[d]				22.500	1.173	
18.04.1386[e]	210	5.56	0.062	26.250	1.022	6.07
29.10.1386[e]	210	5.56	0.062	26.250	1.006	6.16
03.04.1387[e]	210	4.51	0.050	32.313	0.849	5.89
01.10.1388	240	4.17	0.041	40.000	0.781	5.25
20.12.1389[f]	183	4.17	0.053	30.500	1.018	5.21
30.04.1407[g]	156	4.17	0.063	26.000	1.104	5.71
07.07.1407[g]	184 [sic]	4.17	0.053	30.500	1.018	5.21
17.08.1409[h]	168	4.17	0.058	28.000	1.182	4.91
06.12.1416[i]	—	—	—	—	0.958	
12.06.1418	180	3.13	0.041	40.000	0.850	4.82
07.11.1428[j]	180	2.78	0.036	45.000	0.749	4.81
12.10.1433	216	4.17	0.045	36.000	0.814	5.53
15.10.1456[k]	240	4.17	0.0407	40.000	0.814	5.00
23.05.1466	198	3.47	0.0411	39.601	0.703	5.85
13.10.1467	204	3.47	0.040	40.799	0.677	5.91
27.10.1474[l]	—	—	—	—	0.597	
20.12.1477	216	2.78	0.030	54.000	0.522	5.75
18.07.1482	196	2.08	0.025	65.333	0.466	5.36

[a] Silver contents are given in terms of 100% pure silver, rather than in fine or *argent-le-roy* (95.833% pure).
[b] Evidently struck as single rather than double mites, but, if double mites, then a traite of 12.751s. gros Flemish.

[c] There is no record of minting of mites between 07.11.1338 and 12.01.1375; and the silver gros coinages of this interim period are omitted from this table.

[d] In July 1384, Flanders and Brabant agreed to strike a common coinage, to be legal tender in both principalities. The Flemish monetary ordinance prescribed no mites or other petty coinage; but Brabant's Leuven mint struck single mites from 24.03.1385 to 14.04.1386 (not included in Table 4): 180 per marc of 8 grains AR (silver content of 0.036 g)

[e] The mint accounts for 1386–1387, covered by these three ordinances, are missing. See Tables 3, 5.

[f] The mint ordinance of December 1389 made no mention of double mites (single mites only); but minting of double mites commenced at Mechelen in November 1390. In January 1391, a monetary ordinance, revoked in 1393, reduced slightly the weight of the double gros, but left the single gros untouched.

[g] The proposed monetary ordinances of 1407 were evidently failures.

[h] Very few, if any, mites resulted. See Table 3, note *b*.

[i] No mites were prescribed; instead a new coin of 3 mites was prescribed. But with a fineness of 25%, it was silver rather than black money; and no issue is recorded in the mint accounts.

[j] Coinage of mites did not result until March 1430. Contemporary coinage alterations in Namur are omitted from this table (though Namur's silver outputs are included in Table 3).

[k] The new coinage did not commence until September 1457. A previous change in the taille of the single mite in February 1437, from 252 to 300, was merely a correction of an error in the 1433 ordinance, to make the weight correspond to the decreed traite of 37s.6d. per marc.

[l] Mint officials stated that "ne sera faite icy nulle mention des deniers de demi-gros, quars de gros, ne autre noire monnoie"; and no mites or quarter-gros were struck again until December 1477.

TABLE 5
The Double Mite (Black) and Gros (Silver) Coinages in Flanders, 1334–1484: A Comparison of Their Traites per Marc, Seigniorages, Brassages, and Total Mintage Charges, in Shillings and Pence Gros Flemish

	Double mites (black money)					Gros (silver money)			
Date of ordinance or first minting	Traite per marc argent-le-roy (s. gros)	Seigniorage per marc A.R. (d. gros)	Brassage per marc A.R. (s. gros)	Brassage as percentage of traite	Total mintage as percentage of traite	Traite per marc A.R. (s. gros)	Seigniorage per marc A.R. (d. gros)	Brassage per marc A.R. (s. gros)	Total mintage as percentage of traite
01.10.1334[a]	6.286	nil	n.a.	n.a.	n.a.	5.610	1	n.a.	n.a.
12.01.1375[b]	27.778	12	n.a.	n.a.	n.a.	17.538	2	n.a.	n.a.
06.11.1376	27.778	8	n.a.	n.a.	n.a.	17.538	2	n.a.	n.a.
16.07.1384[c]	22.500	nil	8.167	36.3	36.3	16.667	12	1.333	14.0
18.04.1386[d]	26.250	[8.917]		n.a.	34.0	19.125	[1.792]		9.4
29.10.1386[d,e]	26.250	13	7.500	28.6	32.7	19.125	4	1.125	7.6
						19.431	5	1.181	8.2
03.04.1387[d]	32.313	8	10.896	33.7	35.8	23.035	8d10m	1.583	9.9
01.10.1388	40.000	12	17.000	42.5	45.0	25.132	8	2.465	12.5
10.01.1389	40.000	12	17.000	42.5	45.0	25.132	6	2.465	11.8
20.12.1389[f]	30.500	2	13.333	43.7	44.3	19.201	4	1.868	11.5
20.06.1393[g]	30.500	2	12.833	42.1	42.6	19.201	4	1.368	8.9
30.07.1407[h]	26.000	2	10.083	38.8	39.4	17.708	8	1.292	11.1
07.07.1407[i]	30.500	2	12.833	42.1	42.6	19.201	4	1.368	8.9
17.08.1409[j]	28.000	2	12.667	45.2	45.8	16.535	2	1.201	8.3
06.12.1416[k]	—	—	—			20.417	16	1.833	15.5
12.06.1418	40.000	4	18.500	46.3	47.1	23.000	4	1.500	8.0
07.11.1428[l]	45.000	7	20.417	45.4	46.7	26.111	7	1.528	8.1
12.10.1433	36.000	2	13.083	36.3	36.8	24.000	2	1.083	5.2
15.10.1456[m]	40.000	2	n.a.	n.a.	n.a.	24.000	2	1.083	5.2

23.05.1466	39.601	1d.12m.	13.142	33.2	33.5	27.788	1d.12m.	1.330	5.2
13.10.1467	40.799	1d.12m.	13.757	33.7	34.0	28.889	1d.12m.	1.847	6.8
27.10.1474[n]	—	—	—			32.750	6	1.917	7.4
20.12.1477[o]	54.000	6	19.375	35.9	36.8	37.427	6	2.802	8.8
04.12.1480	54.000	7d.6m.	19.271	35.7	36.8	37.427	7d.6m.	2.698	8.8
18.07.1482	65.333d	3d.6m.	26.667	40.8	41.2	41.917	3d.6m.	3.250	8.4
04.04.1484[p]	65.333d	4d.1.5m.	26.660	40.8	41.3	41.917	4d.1.5m.	3.243	8.5

[a] See Table 4, note *b*.
[b] See Table 4, note *c*.
[c] See Table 4, note *d*.
[d] See Table 4, note *e*.
[e] While the October 1386 ordinance basically confirmed the current coinage, a codicil slightly debased the gros coinages and raised the mint prices.
[f] See Table 4, note *f*.
[g] The double gros was fully restored; the mint prices for all silver coinages were raised 6d. per marc at the expense of the brassages.
[h] See Table 4, note *g*.
[i] While the previous mint ordinances were restored, no coinage resulted at the mints.
[j] See Table 4, note *h*; Table 3, note *c*.
[k] See Table 4, note *i*.
[l] See Table 4, note *j*.
[m] See Table 4, note *k*. Either the brassage was raised to 17s.1d. (so that total mintage accounted for 43.1% of the traite) or the mint price for bullion was raised from 22s.9d. per marc AR—the price that remained for all other silver coinages—to 26s.9d.; or perhaps both were raised by 2s.0d. per marc, to induce both merchants and the mint-master to favor the coinage of mites.
[n] No mites were prescribed or issued. See Table 4, note *l*.
[o] The brassages and mint prices for bullion for December 1477 were estimated from those given in the ordinance of December 1480. No ordinance is extant concerning the debasement of the gros and issue of new, debased mites in December 1477. If the mint price had remained unchanged at 30s.4d. per marc AR (as it evidently did for the two patard coinages), then the brassage for double mites would have been 22s.2d. gros per marc = 41.1% of the traite.
[p] The Ghent mint accounts indicate that this ordinance was not observed, and that the seigniorage continued to be imposed at the former rate of 3d.6m. per marc AR, leaving the brassages and mint prices for bullion also at the former rates.

year period.[14] When next recorded, in January 1375, *mites* certainly were subject to seigniorage, which, thereafter, was always charged for their coinage (Table 5). There still ensued some other significant gaps in their issue: in 1378–1385, 1403–1418 (except possibly 1412–1413), 1448–1453, 1459–1465, and 1472–1477, the third and fourth of which reflect general mint inactivity (Tables 3 and 4).

But even apart from these lacunae, and even during the periods of intense mint activity, the Flemish petty coinage outputs were remarkably small for almost all of this 150-year period. We can see from Table 3 that, in terms of the proportion of total silver bullion minted, and even of the total money-of-account values of coinage output, amounts struck as petty coins were rarely more than 1%, and generally under 1%, until the mid-15th century. Furthermore, if we exclude those quarter-gros struck from 1410, and focus only on the true *monnaies noires,* the mites, then those proportions just specified drop dramatically to about 1/10th of 1% in some decades, with the significant exception again of the 1440s and 1450s, to be analyzed later.

If, however, we consider the outputs of petty coinage in terms of the *number* of coins struck, we see that in four of the decades well over 4 million were struck; and in one (1466–1474), 6.8 million, accounting for 23% of total coins then issued. If the prince and his mint-masters had then been questioned about meeting their public responsibilities in providing adequate amounts of petty coinage, undoubtedly they would have pointed to such statistics, possibly with some justification. But most other observers, then and now, would likely endorse Philip Grierson's charge that their mints left the public desperately short of the very coins that most people required in paying for their daily necessities.

Grierson (1976, p. 113) and Spufford (1970, p. 44) have indeed provided a convincing explanation for that *presumed* scarcity, and one also given by Usher (1943, p. 198), Cipolla (1956, p. 28), and Spengler (1966, p. 209): that the costs of minting petty coins, with the crude technology of this era, were much too high to permit any profits for the mint-masters, who exercised a strong influence in constructing medieval monetary ordinances. Grierson's argument that "twelve times as much labour was involved in making 12 pennies as in making one shilling" has obvious merit. But it really applies in principle only to England's peculiar silver coinages, and only after June 1351, from which time all five coin de-

[14] For the mint policies of Count Louis de Male, see Van Werveke (1949a, 1949b); Blockmans (1979); Munro (1981). For the mint documents: Gaillard (1856, Doc. Nos. 28, 39, 40, 43, 44, 45, 47, 52, 59, 60, 63, 70, 72, 74, pp. 74–156); and De Limburg-Stirum (1898, Doc. Nos. 848, 858–859, 913–916, 918–921, 924, 930, 946, 968, 970–971, pp. 121–218). In the only numismatic literature known to me on Louis' petty coinage, Rouyer (1847, pp. 453–454) and Piot (1855b, p. 200) have both described just one extant, undated mite: evidently the same mite, from the obverse–reverse reproductions. Rouyer's weights for three examples (0.96 to 1.06 g.) indicate that this mite was struck between 1375 and 1377.

nominations were struck of sterling fineness (92.5%, to 1542), with proportionally equal weights. Consequently a Tower Pound of sterling silver produced identical *traites* (Tower Pound's money-of-account value by tale) for each and every coin denomination struck. Thus, so long as the English mint's bullion price remained the same for each, all denominations from farthings to groats (4d.) had to bear identical mintage fees per Tower Pound of sterling silver.[15]

Generally elsewhere in medieval Europe, however, and certainly in Flanders, all petty coins were deliberately struck to contain proportionally less silver than that contained in higher denomination *gros* coins, with some combination of inferior fineness and nonproportional weights, as shown in Tables 1, 3–5. Consequently these petty coins enjoyed a far higher *traite* per *marc* than that for the gros: higher values, with proportionally many more such petty coins struck per fine *marc*. Thus the mint could exact much higher brassage and seigniorage fees on petty coins, to cover fully the higher raw material and labor costs involved, while still allowing the mint-master a fair return. He might, however, have incurred a loss with a sudden rise in copper prices or wages—but only until the next coinage debasement.

We cannot, therefore, assume that the coinage of *monnaies noires* was necessarily everywhere always a losing proposition for the mint authorities. Lane and Mueller (1985, p. 202) have found, for example, that "Venice began to make very large profits on black money before the end of the fourteenth century." The real question to be asked instead is were the authorized brassage fees always sufficiently high to ensure that the mint-master would indeed earn a profit?[16] The complete absence of *monnaies noires* (mites) in the Flemish mint outputs from April 1471 to December 1477 may be related to the very low brassage fees in that period of "strong money": amounting to just 34% of the *traite,* compared to the mean of 44% prevailing from 1388 to 1433.[17] When the coinage of mites

[15] That mint policy with identical brassage and seigniorage charges for all silver coins seems to have been unique in late-medieval Europe. Brooke and Stokes (1929, especially pp. 40–42) indicate that in 1547–1550 the Tower Mint did differentiate mintage fees by coin denomination. See also Blunt and Brand (1970), Crump and Johnson (1913), Challis (1978, pp. 305–325), and Munro (1983a).

[16] Spufford (1970, p. 42) has argued that coinage of mites provided "an insignificant profit margin, or even a loss, if made properly," citing in support the 1489 Ghent mint account and estimates of current copper prices. But the authorized brassage, in fact £37.17.11d. gros per *marc argent-le-roy,* was only 32.7% of the double mite's *traite* of £116.0.5d per *marc:* proportionally the lowest such brassage on petty coinage so far in the 15th century, well below the 40.8% of 1484 (Table 5). See also Usher (1943, pp. 196–205).

[17] Furthermore, the Flemish monetary ordinance of October 1474 had pointedly if inexplicably refrained from prescribing the coinage of either mites or quarter-gros. No quarter-gros were struck either between April 1472 and December 1477. See Table 4, n. *l*; Tables 3, 5–6; Algemeen Rijksarchief (Belgium: hereafter ARA), Rekenkamer, Nos. 580 (fo. 100v),

was resumed in the December 1477 debasement, the brassage was again raised, finally to 41% of the traite by 1482 (Tables 3–6). Occasionally the prince himself exacted too high a seigniorage at the direct expense of the mintmaster's brassage or of the merchants' bullion price, or both: as Tables 3–4 and 6 suggest for 1375–1376, 1386–1389, 1430–1432, and 1477–1482. But otherwise the seigniorage fees were either less than or no more than those imposed on the higher denomination coins (and nil in 1334–1338).

Obviously the monetary authorities had to ensure that they did not set the total of brassage and seigniorage fees so high, at the expense of the mint price for bullion, that they thereby encouraged merchants to deliver their bullion to foreign mints. But merchants would rarely have gone to foreign mints just to obtain petty coins, since their traveling and transactions costs would have been much too high in relation to the coins' value. Presumably, therefore, merchants would have been willing to accept domestic petty coins that had proportionally lower silver contents and higher mintage fees, so long as that higher cost did not exceed the petty coins' greater utility—than that for higher-valued coins—in effecting day to day transactions, in paying wages and in buying food, drink, and other daily necessities.

There is thus no justification for the argument that the cost of minting petty coins was universally too high for the prince, the mint-master, or the merchants. A more important criticism of the Grierson thesis, however, is that it fails to specify what amount of petty coinage constituted a "shortage," and under what circumstances. Admittedly, most historians will scoff, retorting that the figures presented here, with chronically less than 1% of mint outputs issued in petty coin, make such shortages self-evident. We must therefore find alternative explanations for these skewed mint statistics, while asking whether such small outputs of petty coins made them truly scarce in relation to (1) the demand for such coinage, and (2) the quantity that circulated domestically.

Indeed, in analyzing the composition of mint outputs, we must first consider the demand for petty coins on the part of those merchants and money-changers or bankers who supplied bullion to the mints. Insofar as such merchants were engaged in the regional and international commerce and finance of the medieval Low Countries, their demand presumably would have been strongly biased in favor of high-value coins, and would thus not reflect the more general, domestic public demand for coinage.

Consider in particular the different spheres of circulation for the various coinage denominations in the Low Countries. Flemish petty coins normally circulated just within Flanders itself; and, as Peter Spufford (1970, p.

---

and 18,107–18,111; Rouyer (1848, p. 430); Deschamps de Pas (1862, pp. 357–360); Spufford (1970, p. 180).

42) has remarked, Burgundian coinage unification in 1433–1434 "did not extend below the quarter-groat," as each province continued to strike its own separate *monnaies noires*. But the higher-value silver gros, patards, and double patards (1d., 2d., and 4d.) had a much wider circulation: throughout the Low Countries and the Rhineland, and sometimes even further abroad.[18] Indeed, occasionally the Flemish resorted to silver (coin and bullion) in financing international trade, when mint ratios so warranted, as may be demonstrated by the wool trade at England's continental staple of Calais. So long as England's Calais mint had favored gold, the Flemish purchased their English wools there with that metal, which accounted for most of its mint outputs. But when, from 1425, the Burgundian mint ratios were altered to favor gold even more strongly than the English, most wool payments were evidently made in silver at Calais, whose mint now "favored" that metal, indeed coining it almost exclusively from the later 1420s.[19] Thus, in view of the medieval Low Countries' prominent role in the regional and international commerce of northern Europe, we should not be surprised to find that high-denomination silver coins normally accounted for a disproportionately high share of mint outputs in that metal. For the reasons just analyzed in the Calais trade, that proportion should have been higher, *ceteris paribus,* when the domestic Burgundian mints favored gold the most strongly, compared to neighboring mints (ca. 1425–1466).

Questions of the relative demand for various kinds of coinage cannot be divorced from those of coinage supply. Indeed one of the central considerations of medieval mint production was the continual replenishment of coinage stocks, which were far from being imperishable. They diminished from coin wear in circulation, from clipping and "sweating," from hoarding or conversion of precious metals into *objets d'art,* from piracy and shipwrecks, from careless losses, and from precious metal exports in financing international trade, diplomacy, papal taxation, and warfare. Such a listing, to be sure, groups together different types of metal losses: those that were permanent, and those that were temporary, or were offset by dishoarding and bullion imports; the loss of the coins themselves, temporary or permanent, and the loss of precious metal from the circulating coin.[20]

While each type of metal loss played its own role in determining the

[18] See Spufford (1964, 1970, pp. 55–129); Munro (1972, 1973, 1981, 1983a). One exception must be noted: Brabant's Brussels mint struck exact copies of Flemish double mites from 06.10.1435 to 31.10.1437. ARA, Rek., Reg. Nos. 17,987–17,988.

[19] See Munro (1973, pp. 65–126, especially Table 1, p. 95; 1979), and for the later 14th century, Munro (1981, especially pp. 102–107).

[20] "Sweating": removing precious metal from coins by shaking them together in a leather bag. For various and differing views on the extent of medieval metal losses from all these various causes, see Patterson (1972), Mayhew (1974a), Grierson (1963, 1975, 1976); Munro (1979b, pp. 178–190; 1983a, pp. 97–112); Craig (1953, pp. xvi, 60); Miskimin (1964, 1983, 1984, pp. 25–90); Johnson (1956, pp. xi–xii). See also n. 4 above and n. 22 below.

need to replenish coin stocks, the last provides an important explanation for many recoinages, the nature of which in turn explains why petty coins normally constituted such a small share of total minting. Any general deterioration in the average quality of the circulating coinage—from wear, tear, clipping, "sweating," and also from the introduction of foreign debased or underweight coins—inevitably reduced and finally eliminated the premium that coins necessarily commanded over bullion (see p. 392). The same result would occur if foreign mints or industrial markets raised their bullion price. In reaction to that loss of metal and coin premium, merchants would discount the entire silver coinage, good and bad alike, by bidding up bullion prices (even commodity prices), high enough that the domestic mint would no longer receive metal. Merchants would then cull any remaining good, high denomination coins and sell or export them as bullion. If the prince wished to revive his mints and coinage circulation, he had three choices: to restore the coinage to its former standard by a compulsory reminting at the public's expense; to do so at his own expense; or to effect a general debasement that more than matched the current inferior standard, while providing himself, the mint-master, and bullion merchants some profit.[21]

For obvious reasons, medieval princes generally selected the third option. To induce merchants and the public to surrender their silver coins voluntarily, the prince's mint necessarily had to offer a bullion price that exceeded at least the *traite* value per marc on the previous coin issues. Thus, in the Flemish silver debasement of November 1428, shown in Table 1 and discussed on p. 389, Duke Philip the Good increased the mint's bullion price for a *marc argent-le-roy* from 21s.2d. to 24s.0d.: from 127 to 144 double gros. To obtain the equivalent amount of fine silver in full-weight double gros of the previous standard set in June 1418, a merchant would have had to supply only 136 such coins: i.e., 22s.8d., the former *traite* value per marc, for a profit of 8 double gros or 16d. per marc. Thus, so long as such coins had not lost more than 5% of their silver from wear, tear, and clipping in circulation, merchants would have gained by surrendering them as bullion to the mint.[22] But a *marc argent-le-roy* derived solely from double mites struck since 1418

[21] See Feavearyear (1963, pp. 10–20); Munro (1973, pp. 11–42); Bordo (1986).

[22] Full weight double gros of the 1418 standard should have contained, on average, 1.800 g fine silver (or 1.725 g *pure* silver: Table 1). If they had lost 5% of their silver contents, to contain on average only 1.710 g fine silver, then the merchant would have had to supply 143.13 such coins (244.753/1.710), worth 23s.10d.6m. gros by tale in current circulation, to obtain the silver in a *marc argent-le-roy*. If the average silver loss had been 6%, he would have required 144.65 old double gros (244.753/1.692), worth 24s.1d.7m by tale. For medieval England, Craig (1953, pp. xvi, 60) has estimated that circulating coins lost on average 0.2% of their silver per annum, i.e., 1.83% per decade; Patterson (1972, pp. 220–221) has given a much higher estimate of 1.0% loss per annum. See also Grierson (1963), whose calculations are closer to Craig's; and n. 20 above.

would have required 5760 such coins, whose monetary value of 40s. gros by tale (= *traite* per marc) was 66.7% greater than the new mint price for bullion. As can be readily determined from Tables 1, 4–5, no profit-seeking merchant would have ever voluntarily surrendered mites as bullion to the mints during any debasement in late-medieval Flanders, because the mint's bullion price per fine *marc* was always less than the previously assigned *traite* value for such petty coins. For most debasements, merchants delivering other small coin (quarter-gros, demi-gros) as bullion would have rarely broken even, and only if such coins had been full weight, a most unlikely condition in view of their presumably high velocity. Thus one may doubt that even the most rigorously enforced recoinage would have produced much petty coin for reminting.

For that very reason indeed, princes and their mint-masters may have preferred to limit the proportion of scarce bullion minted into such coins: insofar as they anticipated that few petty coins would ever return for subsequent debasements, and thus as a source of mint profit. The mint-masters would hardly have welcomed them for recycling, moreover, with the high cost of extracting so little silver from them. But there is no documentary evidence citing such reasons, nor any such evidence that mints deliberately limited petty coin output to protect the premium and support high mintage fees, as later theorists argued.[23]

If domestic reminting of petty coins was largely precluded by their minuscule silver contents, high brassage fees, and thus high *traites,* then similarly that same combination, and the aforementioned adverse value:weight ratio, usually also prevented the export of petty coins as bullion to foreign metal markets or mints, except in times of unusual scarcity.[24] Consequently, losses from precious-metal exports, for whatever reason (or gains from imports), would necessarily have been largely in the form of high-value coins and bullion.

Only in two minor respects was the need to replenish stocks of petty coins possibly greater than that for high denomination coins: the greater likelihood of careless loss, with a small incentive for retrieval; and greater damage in circulation, so as to render the coins unacceptable in trade or taxes. Presumably petty coins had a much higher circulation velocity, to increase the likelihood of damage or careless losses; and certainly

[23] See Monroe (1923, pp. 96–98); Cipolla (1956, pp. 27–33); Spengler (1966, pp. 208–214) on 17th-century Italian writers. See also Cannan (1926, pp. 25–31), Usher (1943, pp. 193–236), and nn. 5, 50. One may argue that the very high mintage fees for petty coinage, representing real costs for both bullion supplier and the mint, would have sufficiently limited the circulation of petty coins to ensure a high enough premium.

[24] See above pp. 404, 406; pp. 409, 411, and nn. 27, 34 below; and De Roover (1949, p. 82); Feavearyear (1963, p. 22); Munro (1973, pp. 29–30). Bautier (1951, p. 170) recounts a Montpellier report of ca. 1310 concerning the illicit export of 100,000 marcs of *monnaies noires*—but without documentation.

their high copper contents rendered them much more susceptible to chemical erosion (Grierson, 1963, p. vii). At the same time, however, copper was more resistant than either silver or gold to purely physical erosion; and that protection may have outweighed the other disadvantages.

These arguments concerning relative coinage replenishment are put forward not to oppose but to complement the demand-based hypotheses, in explaining the small outputs of petty coin. They also reinforce the view that mint production statistics are a very imperfect reflection of actual coinage circulation. Nevertheless, even if the real need for continuous production of petty coin was much less than would be indicated by such statistics, many historians will undoubtedly still not fully exonerate the monetary authorities from Grierson's charge (p. 387) that they left "the public desperately short of small change."

Indeed not until the mid-15th century did the state show any concern about the petty coinage. But only in that era did a scarcity of petty coin become acute enough, evidently, to provoke public concern. In both England and the Low Countries, moreover, the monetary authorities did in fact respond directly with positive relief measures. So many years had passed since a general recoinage, especially in England (1411–1412), that the circulating coins had undoubtedly suffered considerable deterioration, with the consequences already indicated (pp. 405–406). Furthermore, the period ca. 1440–1470 marked the most severe phase of the late-medieval "bullion famine," of sharp monetary contraction, and of considerable deflation (Table 2).[25] In such circumstances, as stressed earlier, the relative demand for petty coins would have risen with their increased purchasing power. At the same time, however, a bullion famine and a deteriorated coinage standard would have seriously curtailed the mints' ability to produce even petty coinage. Indeed coinage outputs across northern Europe were extremely meager during these years, and many mints, unable to cover their costs, were forced to close: the Flemish, in 1447–1453, and again in 1462–1466.[26] Furthermore, when the Flemish mints were open, they maintained a strongly progold ratio (1425–1465), which would normally have discouraged the production of small silver and petty coins especially. Finally, the domestic Flemish circulation of petty coins may have been considerably reduced with the diversion of such coins to uses normally served by higher-value coins, including foreign trade payments and hoarding; and hoarding may have increased in response to the current conditions of economic depression and uncertainty discussed below (p. 416). Spengler (1966, p. 213) has argued that such diversions might occur during periods of monetary scarcity, if

[25] See Day (1978); Spufford (1970, pp. 118–21); Munro (1979a, 1979b, 1983a, 1983b, 1984); Miskimin (1983, 1984, 1985); Mayhew (1974b); Bordo (1986).

[26] Spufford (1970, pp. 116–121; also on the closure of German mints); Munro (1973, pp. 155–162; 1983a); Miskimin (1984, pp. 30–53, 127–190; 1985, for the French mints).

petty coins could be substituted for high-value coins. In fact for these very years of "bullion famine" we have evidence for both the export of *monnaies noires* (to northern France in 1457–1459) and their deposit in coin hoards (in Liège and Brussels, 1465).[27]

Even in England, *despite* the current prosilver mint ratios there, silver coinage outputs in the 1440s had fallen to their lowest ebb since the beginning of the century, during another bullion famine: with an annual average of just 250.6 kg silver = 1,068.8 fine *marcs*. In the 1445 Parliament, a Commons petitioner complained about the "grete defaute" of silver among the poor. The Crown responded by requiring the Tower Mint to increase by 10% the number of halfpennies and farthings struck from the sterling silver pound, while leaving pennies untouched.[28]

In Flanders, the prince's *official* response was similar but came later, despite an even greater silver shortage. In the 1440s, the Flemish mints were coining an annual average of just 510.8 *marcs* (119.8 kg) of fine silver: less than half the English output, and a very drastic drop from the high silver outputs that had followed the Burgundian monetary unification-reform of 1433–1434.[29] It is thus all the more striking to find that, in the 28 months from January 1445 to April 1447 (after which silver outputs temporarily ceased), *monnaies noires* accounted for 70% of the silver bullion minted and 99% of the total number of coins struck. Then in January 1454, a minor gold debasement succeeded in reactivating the Flemish mints, so that in just over 4 years they struck some 3503 fine silver *marcs* (821.7 kg), along with new gold.[30] Of that, 1455 *marcs* were struck in petty coins: 399 *marcs* in mites, the rest in quarter-gros, accounting for 42% of total silver bullion and 90% of the total number of coins issued. If one objects that such proportions are impressive only because total outputs were then so small, consider and compare the average annual outputs of *monnaies noires* (mites) during years of active minting in the three decades concerned, following the Burgundian monetary reform: (a) in 1434–1444: £27.95 gros—just 0.15% of the bullion coined!; (b) in

[27] See Spengler (1966, pp. 212–213). For the Burgundian mites (and counterfeits thereof), Rouyer (1848, pp. 423–429), Deschamps de Pas (1866, pp. 200–206): reports of French officials on confiscations of mites at Boulogne; for the coin hoards, see Tourneur (1928), and n. 34 below. See also pp. 405, 407 above.

[28] From February 1445 to October 1447 only, the London Tower Mint struck both halfpennies and farthings at 33s. instead of 30s. per Tower Pound of sterling silver (349.91 g): i.e., 792 halfpence or 1584 farthings per lb, instead of 720 halfpence or 1440 farthings, thus reducing these coins' weight by 9.1% = 10.0% increase in their *traite* per Pound (see p. 389). G. B. Parliament (1777, Vol. 6, pp. 108–109, No. 36); Munro (1973, pp. 128–131); Brooke and Stokes (1929).

[29] See Table 3; Munro (1973, pp. 98–103; 1983, pp. 112–146); Van Gelder and Hoc (1960, pp. 9–12); Spufford (1970, pp. 4–6, 180–93).

[30] Munro (1973, pp. 149–150, 210); Spufford (1970, pp. 31–37); Van Gelder and Hoc (1960, pp. 12–16).

1445–1447: £75.23 gros; and (c) in 1454–1458: £190.93 gros—almost seven times as much as in 1434–1444. From the mid-1440s, the Flemish mints had evidently been encouraged if not directly ordered to divert more of the silver bullion into *monnaies noires*.

At that time, Duke Philip the Good was unable to adopt any more effective remedy, because of his promise to the provincial Estates in 1433–1434 not to alter the coinage for at least 20 years. But finally, on 15 October 1456, after his promise had expired, the Flemish monetary authorities issued an ordinance that was almost an exact copy of England's 1445 edict. It instructed the Bruges mint to increase by 11.1% the number of double and single mites struck per fine *marc,* by means of a 10% reduction in their weight, while maintaining the former 1433–1434 standards for all other silver coins. The Bruges mint, however, did not commence issuing the new mites until September 1457, after receiving further instructions on 31 August "to supply the poor people with *monnoye noire*."[31] Then, just over a year later, on 12 October 1458, the Bruges mint closed. No more silver was struck for almost 8 years; a few gold coins were struck at Mechelen and Ghent until March 1462, when all Burgundian mints finally shut down (Table 3).

According to Peter Spufford (1970), significant quantities of counterfeit *monnaies noires,* very base imitations of Burgundian mites, were then circulating in the southern Low Countries. In his view, the offending mints in various petty seigniories along the eastern frontiers found it profitable to strike such *monnaies noires,* while Burgundian mints did not, by reducing the silver contents in their imitations.[32] Given the small amount of silver in Burgundian *monnaies noires,* then just 4.2% fine (Table 4), one wonders whether there was any real difference in profitability. Nevertheless this was still a period governed by the 1433–1434 reform principle of "sound money," which had in fact required a 25% increase in the mites' silver contents, as well as no coinage alterations before 1454. Perhaps the 1457 weight reduction, therefore, was also designed to curb competition from those eastern seigniorial mints.

[31] Ordinance of 15 October 1456 given in the Bruges mint account of September 1457–October 1458: ARA, Rek., No. 18,105. See also Deschamps de Pas (1862, pp. 123–124), Rouyer (1848, pp. 422–423); and also Spufford (1970, p. 42, n. 1 and p. 201), citing other documents, in particular a mint official's statement (1447) that any change in the *monnaies noires* would be a violation of the duke's promise not to alter the coinage; and also noting similar issues of new *monnaies noires* in Brabant and Holland. Whether the mint increased its silver bullion price for the coinage of mites is not certain. See Table 5, note *m;* and also Spufford (1966a), Munro (1973, p. 102); for the October 1433 ordinance, Deschamps de Pas (1861, pp. 473–475).

[32] The mints of Gerdigen, Grote Brogel, Reckheim, Rummen, Elsloo, Kessenich, and Kinroi, in the Limburg-Liège-Rhineland region. See Spufford (1970, pp. 44–46, 200–202, Appendix IV); and also Meert (1970); Rouyer (1848, pp. 423–429); Piot (1842, 1855a, 1855b, 1856a, 1856b); Tourneur (1928).

This black-money influx may have been just a temporary phenomenon explained by the current circumstances. For no such coins, or any coins below the double gros, were listed in a Brabantine mint report of December 1430, which condemned the local circulation of counterfeit coins struck by several of the same seigniories (Rummen, Reckheim, and also Arnhem, Liège).[33] Since their mint accounts have not survived, these seigniorial black-money issues cannot be quantified; their significance can be gleaned only from the analysis of two very rare hoards composed almost entirely of such coins buried in Liège and Brussels ca. 1465. Most medieval hoards contain no *monnaies noires;* indeed for that reason and many others, hoards are an unreliable measure of coin circulation.[34]

In this era of bullion scarcity, the Burgundian mints remained closed again for over 4 years, until reactivated by the general, if minor, debasement and recoinage of both gold and silver in June 1466. The Burgundian monetary ordinance of 23 May 1466 effecting that debasement, and a reversion to a prosilver policy, was the first such decree to recognize a direct public interest in the coinage composition, particularly in terms of the public's need for petty coinage. Perhaps to some considerable extent such concern reflects the fact that Duke Philip the Good, responding to English and other foreign debasements in 1464–1465, had to seek agreement from the town-dominated provincial Estates for his own defensive debasement. Those Estates had long claimed a share in the governance of the Burgundian principalities; and seven meetings were required, from January 1465 to May 1466, before the monetary ordinance could be officially promulgated. In such circumstances, we have no grounds for dismissing its preamble as mere hypocrisy[35]:

> that one of the principal points of all good policies on which public well-being, as much for us as for the people, is founded is to have and maintain good money, sound and durable, in both gold and silver coin.

This ordinance, after determining the fineness, weights, and official values of the new coins, gold and silver, then made some stipulations about the composition of the coinage, "so that everyone may be provided with all denominations of gold and silver coins, according to each one's requirements and necessity." For each gold *marc* minted, the mint-master

[33] ARA, Rek., carton 65:2; Munro (1972, 1973, pp. 212–214). See n. 27.

[34] Spufford (1970, pp. 200–213, with Appendix V on Coin-Hoards); Piot (1842, 1855a); Tourneur (1928); Van Keymeulen (1973). Deschamps de Pas (1866, pp. 200–206) believes, however, that the counterfeit mites confiscated at Boulogne in 1458–1459 (see n. 27) were probably struck by Jeanne de Wesemael of Rummen. On coin hoards generally, see Grierson (1975, pp. 124–139; 1976, pp. 106–109; 1979, essays Nos. xxi and xxii).

[35] ARA, Rek., Reg. No. 133 (fo. 174v–179v); see also Munro (1973, pp. 150–179); Spufford (1970, pp. 44–46). Late-medieval Spain evidently also required a similar proportional striking of the silver coinage: Cipolla (1956, p. 31); Usher (1943, pp. 197–198).

was to strike 100 silver *marcs;* and for every 100 silver *marcs* minted in double gros or patards (2d.), he was to strike 10 *marcs* in double patards (4d.), 2 *marcs* in single gros (1d.), 1 *marc* in demi-gros, and 1/2 *marc* in quarter-gros. But this monetary ordinance is also significant for introducing both a new heavy silver coin, the double patard worth 4d. gros, and, more importantly, a differential in the mint bullion prices favoring that new coin (and subsequently, the patard also): 26s.9d. per *marc argent-le-roy,* vs 26s.4d. per *marc* for all other silver coinages.

Whether or not the Burgundian monetary authorities fully realized that this mint price differential contradicted the policy of promoting the petty coinages, state monetary policies had certainly changed, particularly with the provincial Estates' increasing demands for stronger controls over the Burgundian coinage. Peter Spufford (1966a, 1966b, 1970, pp. 147–163) has argued more generally that, because of the Estates' political successes in the late medieval Low Countries, "the doctrine that coinage belonged to the prince had given way to the doctrine that coinage belonged to the people."[36] Indeed, at the very close of our period, in December 1480 and again in April 1484, the new Habsburg ruler, Archduke Maximilian, issued another coinage ordinance similar to that of 1466, "so that the poor people may find themselves sufficiently supplied with *petite monnoie*." That decree required an even greater proportion of the mint output, if still a small one, to be struck in lower denominations, as shown in Table 6.[37] One might still cavil, however, that Count Louis de Nevers (1322–1346) was far more public-spirited than any of his Burgundian or Habsburg successors, in minting *monnaies noires* free of seigniorage; and that Maximilian, at war with his Flemish towns (1482–1494), was as rapacious as any in exploiting the mints.[38]

Thus one may well doubt to what extent the mint-masters actually observed these public-spirited monetary ordinances, which, in effect, prevented them from fully meeting their own customers' demands for coin denominations. An analysis of the Flemish mint accounts following the ordinances of 1466, 1480, and 1484, presented in Table 6, provides a mixed verdict on the mints' compliance. Following the first, the mints

[36] See also Munro (1973); Blockmans (1973, 1974); Bordo (1986); and the influential 14th-century treatise "De Moneta" by Nicholas Oresme, Chaps. 6 ("Thus money belongs to the community and to individuals") and 22, in Johnson (1956, pp. 10–11, 35–37).

[37] The mints were ordered to strike, for every 100 fine silver *marcs* coined into patards, 50 *marcs* in single gros, 10 *marcs* in demi-gros, and 5 *marcs* in quarter-gros. Texts in the name of Maximilian's wife and son, Duchess Marie (December 1480) and Archduke Philip the Handsome (April 1484), are reproduced in Deschamps de Pas (1862, pp. 465–470; 1869, p. 99; 1874, p. 14), who is obviously incorrect in stating that this is the first ordinance requiring such a proportional striking of coins. See also Spufford (1970, p. 45); Grierson (1975, p. 97).

[38] See in particular Spufford (1970, pp. 141–146, 158–163); Blockmans (1973, pp. 128–133; 1974); Van Uytven (1975).

TABLE 6

The Composition of the Silver Coinage Outputs of the Flemish Mints by Coin Denominations, as Percentages of Total Bullion Minted, in Fine Marcs: 1466–1472, 1480–1484, and 1484–1487

Coin name	Value (d.)	Ghent and Bruges 18.06.1466–14.04.1472 Percentage decreed	Percentage actual	Bruges and Ghent 20.12.1480–27.03.1484 Percentage decreed	Percentage actual	Ghent and Bruges 28.03.1484–01.03.1487 Percentage decreed	Percentage actual
Double patard	4	8.8	52.8	—	53.9	—	50.3
Patard	2	88.1	28.8	60.6	11.9	60.6	12.1
Gros (groot)	1	1.8	12.6	30.3	33.2	30.3	36.0
Demi-gros	1/2	0.9	2.7	6.1	0.2	6.1	0.0
Quarter-gros (zeskin: 6 m.)	1/4	0.4	2.8	3.0[a]	0.1	3.0	0.5
Four mites[a]	1/6	—	0.0	—	0.0	—	0.3
Courte (double mite)	1/12	—	0.4	—	0.7[b]	—	0.8
Total silver bullion in fine marcs AR			102,700.6		34,145.2		23,704.8

[a] The December 1480 ordinance further stipulated that 100 silver *marcs* at least be minted into petty coinage of quarter-gros (zeskins) and under, in the following proportions: 14% for quarter-gros, 29% for 4-mite pieces, and 57% for courtes (2 mites). In this period, December 1480 to March 1484, the Flemish mints struck a total of 31.14 *marcs argent-le-roy* into quarter-gros and 248.56 *marcs* into courtes = 279.69 *marcs*, for an annual average of 86.1 *marcs*. The 4-mite piece, an entirely new coin, was not struck until after April 1484.

[b] Of the 248.56 *marcs* AR struck into courtes in 1480–1484, 222.19 *marcs* or 89.4% were struck after another debasement commencing 18 July 1482, when furthermore the seigniorage was more than halved and the brassage sharply increased, as specified in Tables 4–5.

more than met their obligations, at least for denominations below the double gros: such coins accounted for 18.5% of the bullion coined, instead of the stipulated 3.1%. As noted earlier (p. 402 and Table 3), the decade following 1466 marked by far the largest issue of petty coinage in this entire 150-year period. But far less bullion was struck in those lesser denominations, except for the single gros, in the years following the next two ordinances.[39] Those years were highly inflationary ones of civil war and debasement during which the relative demand for petty coins presumably declined.

Those historians already convinced by all the mint-output and monetary data, and certainly those still convinced by the Grierson thesis, will be impatient with the concluding contention that the case for a *chronic* "scarcity" of petty coins has not been proven. To say that such scarcity or shortage characterized the economy of late-medieval Flanders is equivalent to stating that there persisted an excess demand for petty coins at current prices and incomes. While such conditions may have been temporarily true, especially in the mid-15th century, it is difficult to believe that such excess demand was not finally dissipated or satisfied. We lack the evidence to state precisely how—apart from the aforementioned state intervention to have more petty coins minted; but several hypotheses may be advanced, with qualifications.

First, some of that demand was undoubtedly satisfied by the resort to foreign counterfeits of Burgundian-Flemish *monnaies noires*—the very ones discussed above (p. 410)—and also to token coins, though to a much lesser extent. Mitchiner and Skinner (1983, 1984), in their exhaustive studies of medieval token coins, stress that they "should not really be conceived as a straight monetary substitute," that they "did not compete with authorised coinage either in England or on the Continent," and that their scope was severely restricted.[40] Not until 1543 did the Habsburg authorities in the Low Countries adopt the expedient of issuing their own fiat token coinage, as purely copper double mites.[41]

Second, another, at least partial, resolution of the coinage scarcity problem may have come from an increased resort to credit.[42] Van der

[39] See in particular note *b* in Table 6, concerning the change in mintage fees in 1482. A similar exercise, for 1466–1467 and 1480–1482, with less charitable conclusions, is given in Spufford (1970, pp. 44–45).

[40] And also, the token coin "is better thought of as being a chit-for-service." (Mitchiner and Skinner, 1983, p. 29). Most such coins were issued by the Church for alms-giving and other charitable purposes. See n. 7 above.

[41] See Van Gelder and Hoc (1960, p. 75).

[42] See in particular for the Low Countries, De Roover (1948, especially pp. 48–75, 99–219; 1949, pp. 115–117); Van der Wee (1963, Vol. 2, pp. 337–353; 1977, pp. 300–376); and the classic if outdated Bigwood (1921–1922, 2 vols., especially Vol. 1, pp. 235–255, 507–520). For England, see especially Postan (1928, 1930); Holden (1955, pp. 4–84); Munro (1979b, pp. 213–215).

Wee (1963, 1977) has contended that in the Low Countries pawnbroking became a common expedient "to offset coin shortages" for consumption transactions from the mid-14th century; and that from the 15th century the retail trades came to utilize sales credit in the form of "tallies" (notched sticks) or current-account debits, some involving partial settlements in kind ("barter-clearances").[43] Nevertheless we must not exaggerate the current role of credit, most forms of which still remained tied directly or indirectly to precious metals. Peter Spufford (1986, p. xxx) contends that even in 15th-century Venice and Bruges, Europe's two leading commercial centres, only 10% of adult males had bank accounts, and that "the vast majority of transactions . . . were still carried out with actual metallic coin."

In the 15th century, furthermore, especially from the 1420s, the governments of both England and the Low Countries imposed many severe restrictions on credit—apart from the traditional usury prohibitions—as part of misguided policies to promote bullion influxes and protect their coinages. In the latter, Burgundian officials had accused bankers ("tafletiers") of exporting bullion and importing fraudulent coin; and as part of the 1433–1434 monetary reform, the government prohibited deposit-banking, a ban confirmed in 1467, 1480, and 1489. Pawnbroking was also restricted, in 1451 and more strongly in 1473 and 1477. Even municipal authorities imposed similar restrictions, in Antwerp and Lier: forbidding innkeepers to sell on credit (1442, 1457).[44]

Such credit bans were, to be sure, difficult to enforce, especially in retail transactions. But Van der Wee (1963, 1977) and De Roover (1948) are agreed that deposit-banking had virtually disappeared from the Low Countries by the later 15th century; and Van der Wee contends further that "pawnbroking decayed from the second half of the fifteenth century onwards," while current-account tallies did not become truly widespread until the 16th century. Such credit restrictions may also help explain the high real interest rates of the deflationary mid-15th century: 20% on short-term public loans in Flanders, and 43.3% in pawnbroking (2d. per £ per week). In turn, public protests against high interest rates led to more state restrictions on credit.[45]

[43] Van der Wee (1963, Vol. 2, pp. 333–340; and 1977, pp. 300–304). Also used, but more for commercial and investment purposes, were (a) the letter-obligatory (*cédule obligatoire,* a form of promissory note), for which partial settlements were also made by "barter clearances"; and (b) annuity contracts, especially the *bail à rente,* the sale of real estate for hereditary annual payments. Both were transferable, assignable to third parties.

[44] De Roover (1948, pp. 130, 338–342); Van der Wee (1963, Vol. 2, pp. 333–340, 355–358; and also 1977, pp. 302–303); and Munro (1973, Chaps. 4, 6; 1979b, pp. 194–196, 204–208; Appendices D–E).

[45] De Roover (1948, p. 131–133; 339–341); Van der Wee (1963, Vol. 1, p. 526, Appendix 45-1; Vol. 2, pp. 105–109, 335, 355–358; and 1977, pp. 302, 362, Table 26). The Burgundian Great Charter of 1477 decreed that pawnbroking interest rates be cut in half.

Deflation itself obviously brought some considerable relief to coin shortage in general, especially by the midcentury, in allowing each unit of coinage to effect transactions of greater real value; but the deflation, when achieved, did not fully resolve the problem of excess demand for petty-coins specifically. As argued earlier, the monetary and other economic conditions of this era, particularly the progold mint ratio, periodic mint closures, and the "Spengler effect" (p. 408), may have made petty coins a smaller proportion of the domestic money supply, before the midcentury state interventions, and thus even scarcer in relation to the demand for coinage. Furthermore the relationship between money supplies and prices was only indirect, particularly because of considerable institutional wage and price "stickiness": prices did not fall immediately, nor did they fall proportionally, in unison; some indeed remained stable.[46] Furthermore, as indicated earlier, the mid-15th century was a period of considerable economic depression in the Low Countries, with a fall in production and commercial transactions, especially severe in the textile and agrarian sectors of the economy, which suffered extensive impoverishment.[47] It cannot be determined, however, whether the "bullion famine" (and the accompanying deflation) contributed directly or indirectly to that depression or merely reflected it; nor can it be determined whether any petty coin scarcity restricted the volume of retail transactions.

Undoubtedly the true resolution to any problem of "excess demand" or petty-coin shortage in this era, one of limited scope and duration, came subsequently, from the latter 1460s: from the South German silver influxes, as part of the economic recovery based on the expanding Brabant Fairs, though disturbed by anti-Habsburg revolts and civil wars; and from the inflationary coinage debasements spawned by those wars.[48]

Finally, one must face the limitations of these beguiling mint data and admit that the quantity of petty coin "sufficient" for the economy of the late-medieval Low Countries cannot really be specified,[49] while emphasizing a principal conclusion from this study: that the Flemish mint accounts grossly understate the amounts of petty coin in domestic circulation. At the same time, there is certainly no evidence that the Low

[46] See both the composite weighted price index for Flanders and its component series for farinaceous, drink, dairy, and industrial products in Munro (1984, Table B-5, pp. 104–105); and also Table 2 above. The quinquennial composite price index (1450–1474 = 100) fell from a high of 137.7 in 1435–1439 to 120.6 in 1440–1444, to 101.3 by 1450–1454; then rose to 113.9 in 1455–1459, falling thereafter to its nadir of 93.9 in 1460–1464, and recovering only to 96.0 in 1470–1474.

[47] Van der Wee (1963, Vol. 1, pp. 457–474, for wages; Vol. 2, pp. 61–111; and 1978); Munro (1973, Chaps. 4–5; 1979a, 1983b, 1984).

[48] Van der Wee (1963, Vol. 2, pp. 73–88); Munro (1983a, 1984); Nef (1941); Van Uytven (1975).

[49] Compare with Spengler (1966, p. 201): "It is not possible to define the extent of a coin shortage with precision, since the indicators of both supply and demand are indirect."

Countries were ever plagued by any "inflationary excess" quantities of petty coinage, especially not in the mid-15th century—when it accounted for the bulk of mint outputs. In most periods, the Flemish and subsequently the Burgundian monetary authorities evidently provided, if quite unintentionally, the essential requirements for a sound system of petty coinage, as recommended by later theorists: coins struck with a commodity value much lower than the stipulated face value; convertibility of such coins with higher denomination silver coins; state monopoly on such coinage; and strictly limited issue of such coins.[50]

APPENDIX: COINAGE

1. The Flemish monetary system, its coinage and money-of-account, was originally based on the *parisis* system of northern France: with £1 (livre) = 20s. (sols) = 240d. (deniers), or current silver *parisis* pennies. From about 1318–1320, that was superseded in Flanders by the *gros* system, whose coin was originally based upon the French *gros tournois* (first struck in 1266), which ca. 1315–1320 was worth 15d. *tournois* and 12d. *parisis*. By the 1340s, the French and Flemish monetary systems had parted company fully and forever. The Flemish *parisis* system lost its own coins (except the mites) to become simply a money-of-account, subsidiary to and frozen in a permanent relationship with the *gros* system, whose silver penny had become the "link" money, anchor of the Flemish monetary system:

1 livre *gros* [*pond groot*] = 12 livres *parisis*
1 livre *gros* = 20s. *gros* = 240d. *gros*
1s. (sol, schelling, shilling) *gros* = 12d. (deniers, penningen) *gros*
1d. *gros* = 3 *esterlins* [*ingelschen, sterlings*] = 24 *mites* = 12d. or 1s. *parisis*.

2. *Marc de Troyes* was the mint weight unit of France and the Low Countries, consisting of 8 Paris *onces* (= 1/2 of the Paris *livre*), with a theoretical weight of 244.753 g.

3. *Argent-le-roy* was the official standard of fineness for silver, reckoned in terms of 12 *deniers*, with 24 *grains* per *denier;* it was 23/24ths or 95.833% pure silver, vs. English *sterling* fineness of 92.5%.

4. *Taille* is the number of coins to be cut or struck to the alloyed *marc de Troyes* (with a tolerance or *remède* of some specific number of coins per marc), indicating the theoretical weight of a coin.

5. *Traite*, akin to the French *pied de la monnaie,* is the total money-of-account value, by tale, of the mint weight unit of fine metal (*marc*

[50] See Cipolla (1956, p. 27–29); Cannan (1926, pp. 25–31); Usher (1943, pp. 193–236); Monroe (1923, pp. 96–98); Spengler (1966, pp. 208–213); and nn. 5, 23 above.

argent-le-roy, for silver), as struck into coins of the prescribed value, fineness, and weight (i.e., taille). Its calculation is

$$T = \frac{\text{taille (No. of coins per marc)} \times \text{official face value of coin}}{\text{percentage fineness (in deniers and grains } \textit{argent-le-roy}\text{)}}.$$

SOURCES FOR THE TABLES

Mint and Monetary Statistics: Tables 1, 3–6

(a) Ghent, Bruges, and Mechelen Mints, 1334–1384; Gaillard (1856, Vol. 2); Blockmans (1979, pp. 69–94); Van Werveke (1949a, 1949b); Munro (1981, 1983a).

(b) Ghent, Bruges, Mechelen, Valkenberg (Fauquemont), and Namur, 1384–1484: Algemeen Rijksarchief België, Rekenkamer (Archives Générales du Royaume, Chambre de Comptes), rolrekeningen Nos. 776–787 (Bruges, 1392–1402); Nos. 824–831 (Ghent, 1388–1390, 1410–1419); Nos. 2586–2587 (Valkenberg, 1396–1398); Nos. 2142–2143 and 2145–2146 (Mechelen, 1384–1385, 1390–1392); Registers Nos. 48,876–48,877 (Mechelen, 1390–1392); No. 580 (Ghent, 1419–1420); Nos. 18,195–18,198 (Ghent, 1459–1462, 1466–1467, 1482–1484); Nos. 18,103–18,116 (Bruges, 1455–1482); No. 18,203 (Namur, 1421–1433); Algemeen Rijksarchief, Acquits de Lille, Liasses Nos. 936–937 (Ghent, 1410–1447); No. 1512 (Bruges, 1454–1456, 1466–1467; Mechelen, 1454–1456, 1459–1460); Archives départementales du Nord (Lille), Chambre des Comptes, Série B., Nos. 644/15.939 and 19.960/19.312 (Bruges, 1454–1456); No. 1606 (Ghent, 1441–1442).

(c) Additional mints, in Table 6: ARA, Rekenkamer, Registers Nos. 18,106–18,108 and 18,116–18,118 (Bruges); Nos. 18,196–18,199 (Ghent).

(d) Monetary Ordinances and Statistics: Munro (1981, 1983a, 1984); Spufford (1970); Deschamps de Pas (1861, 1862, 1866, 1869); Rouyer (1847, 1848); Gaillard (1856, Vol. 2); Cockshaw (1971); Bartier and Van Nieuwenhuysen (1965).

Note: in a book review in *Revue du Nord* **69** (1986), 542–543, Alain Derville charged that in my earlier work I had missed mint accounts for Ghent (1422, 1433, 1441–1442), Namur (1432–1433), Valenciennes (1433), and Zevenbergen (1433). He is mistaken: all of these accounts are in fact included in my earlier monetary publications (and those for Ghent and Namur, in this one).

Commodity Prices: Table 2

Verlinden and Scholliers (1965–1969, Vol. 1, pp. 44–45: peas; Vol. 2, pp. 33–35: wheat; pp. 64–66: butter; pp. 67–69: cheese); Van der Wee (1963, Vol. 1, pp. 204–206; eggs; pp. 277–281: herring; pp. 294–298: Rhine wine); and Munro (1984, pp. 62–71, 102–109: Flemish price index).

REFERENCES

Bartier, J., and Van Nieuwenhuysen, A. (Eds.). (1965), *Les ordonnances de Philippe le Hardi, de Marguerite de Mâle, et de Jean Sans Peur, 1381–1419*. Vol. I. Brussels: Palais des Académies.

Bautier, R. H. (1951), ''L'or et l'argent en occident de la fin du XIIIe siècle au début du XIVe siècle.'' *Académie des inscriptions et belles-lettres: Comptes rendus des séances de l'année*. Paris. Pp. 169–174.

Bernocchi, M. (1976), *Le monete della repubblica fiorentina,* 3 vols. Florence: Leo S. Olschki.

Bigwood, G. (1921–1922), *Le régime juridique et économique du commerce de l'argent dans la Belgique du moyen-âge*. 2 vols. Brussels: Académie Royale de Belgique, Classe des Lettres XIV.

Blockmans, W. P. (1973), "La participation des sujets flamands à la politique monétaire des ducs de Bourgogne (1384–1500)." *Revue belge de numismatique et de sigillographie* **119,** 103–134.

Blockmans, W. P. (1974), "Autocratie ou polyarchie? La lutte pour le pouvoir politique en Flandre de 1482 à 1492, d'après des documents inédits." *Bulletin de la commission royale d'histoire* **140,** 257–368.

Blockmans, W. P. (1979), "Devaluation, Coinage, and Seignorage under Louis de Nevers and Louis de Male, Counts of Flanders, 1330–84." In N. J. Mayhew (Ed.), *Coinage in the Low Countries, 880–1500: Third Oxford Symposium on Coinage and Monetary History (British Archeological Reports,* International Series 54). Oxford. Pp. 69–94.

Blunt, C. E., and Brand, J. D. (1970), "The Mint Output of Henry III." *British Numismatic Journal* **39,** 61–66.

Bordo, M. D. (1986), "Money, Deflation, and Seigniorage in the Fifteenth Century." *Journal of Monetary Economics* **18,** 337–346.

Braunstein, P. (1983), "Innovations in Mining and Metal Production in Europe in the Late Middle Ages." *Journal of European Economic History* **12,** 573–591.

Brooke, G. C., and Stokes, E. (1929), "Tables of Bullion Coined from 1337 to 1550." *The Numismatic Chronicle,* 5th ser. **9,** 27–69.

Cannan, E. (1926), *Money: Its Connexion with Rising and Falling Prices*. London: King & Son. 5th ed.

Challis, C. E. (1978), *The Tudor Coinage*. Manchester: University Press.

Chalon, R. (1847), "Trois jetons du XVe siècle." *Revue belge de numismatique* (formerly *Revue de la numismatique belge*) **3,** 67–69.

Cipolla, C. M. (1956), *Money, Prices, and Civilization in the Mediterranean World: Fifth to Seventeenth Century*. Princeton, NJ: Princeton Univ. Press (Reissued New York: Gordian Press, 1967).

Cipolla, C. M. (1963), "Currency Depreciation in Medieval Europe." *Economic History Review,* 2nd ser. **15,** 413–422. Reprinted with a few changes in Sylvia Thrupp (Ed.). (1964), *Change in Medieval Society: Europe North of the Alps*. New York: Appleton–Century. Pp. 227–236.

Cipolla, C. M. (1982), *The Monetary Policy of Fourteenth-Century Florence*. Berkeley/Los Angeles: Univ. of California Press.

Cockshaw, P. (1970–1971), "A propos de la circulation monétaire entre la Flandre et le Brabant de 1384 à 1390." *Contributions à l'histoire économique et sociale* **6,** 107–141.

Courtenay, W. J. (1972–1973), "Token Coinage in the Administration of Poor Relief during the Later Middle Ages." *Journal of Interdisciplinary History* **3,** 175–195.

Craig, J. (1953), *The Mint: A History of the London Mint from A.D. 287 to 1948*. Cambridge: University Press.

Crump, C. G., and Johnson, C. (1913), "Tables of Bullion Coined Under Edward I, II, and III." *The Numismatic Chronicle,* 4th ser. **13,** 200–245.

Day, J. (1978), "The Great Bullion Famine of the Fifteenth Century." *Past and Present* **79,** 3–54.

De Limburg-Stirum, T. (Ed.). (1898), *Cartulaire de Louis de Male, 1348–1358,* Bruges: De Plancke.

De Roover, R. (1948), *Money, Banking, and Credit in Mediaeval Bruges: Italian Merchant-Bankers, Lombards and Money-Changers, A Study in the Origins of Banking*. Cambridge, MA: Mediaeval Academy.

De Roover, R. (1949), *Gresham on Foreign Exchange*. Cambridge, MA: Harvard Univ. Press.

Deschamps de Pas, L. (1861, 1862, 1866), "Essai sur l'histoire monétaire des comtes de

Flandre de la maison de Bourgogne." *Revue numismatique,* 2nd ser. **6,** 106–139, 211–237, 458–478; **7,** 117–143, 351–365, 460–480; **11,** 172–219.

Deschamps de Pas, L. (1863), *Essai sur l'histoire monétaire des comtes de Flandre de la maison de Bourgogne.* Paris.

Deschamps de Pas, L. (1869), "Essai sur l'histoire monétaire des comtes de Flandre de la maison d'Autriche." *Revue numismatique,* 2nd ser. **14,** 86–114.

Deschamps de Pas, L. (1874), *Essai sur l'histoire monétaire des comtes de Flandre de la maison d'Autriche et classement de leurs monnaies (1482–1556).* Paris: Arnous de Rivière.

Dieudonné, A. (1933), "Les doubles cornus de Philippe le Bel et les origines de la mite flamande." *Revue belge de numismatique* **85,** 23–41.

Feavearyear, A. E. (1963), *The Pound Sterling: A History of English Money.* Oxford: Clarendon Press. 2nd revised ed. by E. Victor Morgan.

Gaillard, V. (Ed.). (1856), *Recherches sur les monnaies des comtes de Flandre,* Vol. II: *Sous les règnes de Louis de Crécy et de Louis de Male.* Ghent: H. Hoste.

Ghyssens, J. (1970), "Les débuts de la mite et de la monnaie de compte en Flandre." *Revue belge de numismatique et de sigillographie* **116,** 181–189.

Ghyssens, J. (1974), "Le monnayage d'argent en Flandre, Hainaut, et Brabant au début de la Guerre de Cent Ans." *Revue belge de numismatique et de sigillographie* **120,** 109–191.

Great Britain, Parliament (1777), *Rotuli Parliamentorum ut et petitiones et placita in parliamento,* Vol. VI. London.

Grierson, P. (1963), "Coin Wear and the Frequency Table." *The Numismatic Chronicle,* 7th ser. **3,** 1–16. Reprinted in Grierson (1979), *Later Medieval Numismatics,* No. xix.

Grierson, P. (1975), *Numismatics.* London: Oxford Univ. Press.

Grierson, P. (1976), "Medieval Numismatics." In J. Powell (Ed.), *Medieval Studies: An Introduction.* Syracuse. Pp. 103–136. Reprinted in *Later Medieval Numismatics,* No. i.

Grierson, P. (1979), *Later Medieval Numismatics (11th–16th Centuries): Selected Studies.* London: Variorum Reprints.

Holden, J. (1955), *The History of Negotiable Instruments in English Law.* London: Athlone Press.

Johnson, C. (Ed. and trans.). (1956), *The De Moneta of Nicholas Oresme and English Mint Documents.* London: Nelson.

Lane, F. C., and Mueller, R. (1985), *Money and Banking in Medieval and Renaissance Venice,* Vol. I: *Coins and Moneys of Account.* Baltimore/London: Johns Hopkins Univ. Press.

Mayhew, N. (1974a), "Numismatic Evidence and Falling Prices in the Fourteenth Century." *Economic History Review,* 2nd ser. **27,** 1–15.

Mayhew, N. (1974b), "The Monetary Background to the Yorkist Recoinage of 1464–1471." *British Numismatic Journal* **44,** 62–73.

Meert, C. (1970), "Les ateliers des petites seigneuries belges sous la période bourguignonne et la domination espagnole." *Revue belge de numismatique et de sigillographie* **116,** 209–211.

Miskimin, H. A. (1963), *Money, Prices, and Foreign Exchange in Fourteenth-Century France.* New Haven/London: Yale Univ. Press.

Miskimin, H. A. (1964), "Monetary Movements and Market Structure: Forces for Contraction in Fourteenth- and Fifteenth-Century England." *Journal of Economic History* **24,** 478–490.

Miskimin, H. A. (1975), *The Economy of Early Renaissance Europe, 1300–1460.* Cambridge/New York: Cambridge Univ. Press.

Miskimin, H. A. (1983), "Money and Money Movements in France and England at the

End of the Middle Ages." In J. F. Richards (Ed.), *Precious Metals in the Later Medieval and Early Modern Worlds*. Durham, NC: Carolina Academic Press. Pp. 79–96.

Miskimin, H. A. (1984), *Money and Power in Fifteenth-Century France*. New Haven/London: Yale Univ. Press.

Miskimin, H. A. (1985), "L'or, l'argent, et la guerre dans la France médiévale." *Annales: Economies, sociétés, civilisations* **40,** 171–184.

Mitchiner, M., and Skinner, A. (1983), "English Tokens, c. 1200 to 1425." *British Numismatic Journal* **53,** 29–77.

Mitchiner, M., and Skinner, A. (1984), "English Tokens, c. 1425 to 1672." *British Numismatic Journal* **54,** 86–163.

Monroe, A. E. (1923), *Monetary Theory Before Adam Smith*. Cambridge, MA: Harvard Economic Studies. Vol. 25.

Munro, J. H. (1972), "An Aspect of Medieval Public Finance: The Profits of Counterfeiting in the Fifteenth-Century Low Countries." *Revue belge de numismatique et de sigillographie* **118,** 127–148.

Munro, J. H. (1973), *Wool, Cloth, and Gold: The Struggle for Bullion in Anglo-Burgundian Trade, ca. 1340–1478*. Brussels/Toronto: Editions de l'Université de Bruxelles.

Munro, J. H. (1974), "Billon-Billoen-Billio: From Bullion to Base Coinage." *Revue belge de philologie et d'histoire* **52,** 293–305.

Munro, J. H. (1975), "The Purchasing Power of Coins and of Wages in the Low Countries and England, 1500–1514." In R. Mynors and W. Ferguson (Eds.), *The Correspondence of Erasmus, Vol. I: 1501–1514,* Toronto: Univ. of Toronto Press. Pp. 307–345.

Munro, J. H. (1979a), "Monetary Contraction and Industrial Change in the Late Medieval Low Countries, 1335–1500." In N. Mayhew (Ed.), *Coinage in the Low Countries, 880–1500: Third Oxford Symposium on Coinage and Monetary History* (*British Archeological Reports,* International Series 54). Oxford. Pp. 95–161.

Munro, J. H. (1979b), "Bullionism and the Bill of Exchange in England, 1272–1663." In Center for Medieval and Renaissance Studies, UCLA (Ed.), *The Dawn of Modern Banking*. New Haven/London: Yale Univ. Press. Pp. 169–239.

Munro, J. H. (1981), "Mint Policies, Ratios, and Outputs in England and the Low Countries, 1335–1420." *The Numismatic Chronicle,* 8th ser. **1,** 71–116.

Munro, J. H. (1983a), "Bullion Flows and Monetary Contraction in Late-Medieval England and the Low Countries." In J. F. Richards (Ed.), *Precious Metals in the Later Medieval and Early Modern Worlds*. Durham, NC: Carolina Academic Press. Pp. 97–158.

Munro, J. H. (1983b), "Economic Depression and the Arts in the Fifteenth-Century Low Countries." *Renaissance and Reformation* **19,** 235–250.

Munro, J. H. (1984), "Mint Outputs, Money, and Prices in Late-Medieval England and the Low Countries." In E. Van Cauwenberghe and F. Irsigler (Eds.), *Münzprägung, Geldumlauf und Wechselkurse/Minting, Monetary Circulation and Exchange Rates: Akten des 8th International Economic History Congress (Trierer Historische Forschungen*. Trier. Vol. 7). Pp. 31–122.

Nef, J. U. (1941), "Silver Production in Central Europe, 1450–1618." *Journal of Political Economy* **49,** 575–591.

Nef, J. U. (1952), "Mining and Metallurgy in Medieval Civilisation." In M. Postan and E. Rich (Eds.), *Cambridge Economic History of Europe, Vol. II: Trade and Industry in the Middle Ages*. Cambridge: Univ. Press. Pp. 430–493.

Patterson, C. C. (1972), "Silver Stocks and Losses in Ancient and Medieval Times." *Economic History Review,* 2nd ser. **25,** 205–235.

Piot, C. (1842), "Mélanges." *Revue belge de numismatique (Revue de la numismatique belge)* **1,** 151–154.

Piot, C. (1855a), "Notice sur des monnaies noires de Heusden, Born, Limbricht, Brabant, Hainaut et Malines." *Revue belge de numismatique* **11,** 36–60.

Piot, C. (1855b), "Notice sur des monnaies noires de Flandre, Malines, Namur, Luxembourg et Megen." *Revue belge de numismatique* **11,** 198–221.

Piot, C. (1856a), "Notice sur des monnaies de Kessenich, Hornes, Grave, Randerode, Stevenswerd et Reckheim." *Revue belge de numismatique* **12,** 76–95.

Piot, C. (1856b), "Notice sur des monnaies noires et de billon de Reckheim et de Stein." *Revue belge de numismatique* **12,** 309–323.

Postan, M. M. (1928), "Credit in Medieval Trade." *Economic History Review,* 1st ser. **1,** 234–261. Reprinted in Postan (1973), *Medieval Trade and Finance*. Cambridge Univ. Press. Pp. 1–27.

Postan, M. (1930), "Private Financial Instruments in Medieval England." *Vierteljahrschrift für Sozial- und Wirtschaftsgeschichte* **23.** Reprinted in his *Medieval Trade and Finance*. Pp. 28–64.

Rouyer, J. (1847, 1848), "Recherches sur la numismatique du comté de Flandre considéré dans les monnaies noires durant la suzeraineté française." *Revue numismatique* **12,** 437–462; **13,** 404–434.

Spengler, J. P. (1965–1966), "Coin Shortage: Modern and Pre-Modern." *National Banking Review* **3,** 201–216.

Spooner, F. C. (1972), *The International Economy and Monetary Movements in France, 1493–1725*. Cambridge, MA: Harvard Economic Studies. Vol. 138.

Spufford, P. (1964), "Burgundian Double Patards in Late-Medieval England." *British Numismatic Journal* **33,** 110–117.

Spufford, P. (1966a), "Coinage, Taxation, and the Estates General of the Burgundian Netherlands." *Standen en Landen (Anciens pays et assemblées d'états)* **40,** 63–88.

Spufford, P. (1966b), "Assemblies of Estates, Taxation, and the Control of Coinage in Medieval Europe." *Etudes presentées à la commission internationale pour l'histoire des assemblées d'états (XII Congrès international des sciences historiques)* **31,** 115–130.

Spufford, P. (1970), *Monetary Problems and Policies in the Burgundian Netherlands, 1433–1496*. Leiden: E. J. Brill.

Spufford, P. (1986), *Handbook of Medieval Exchange*. London: Royal Historical Society Handbook No. 13.

Tourneur, V. (1928), "La trouvaille de la Petite rue Ravenstein, à Bruxelles." *Revue belge de numismatique* **80,** 123–125.

Usher, A. P. (1943), *The Early History of Deposit Banking in Mediterranean Europe*. Cambridge, MA: Harvard Univ. Press. Vol. 1.

Van der Wee, H. (1963), *The Growth of the Antwerp Market and the European Economy (14th–16th Centuries),* 3 vols. The Hague: Martinus Nijhoff.

Van der Wee, H. (1969), "International Business Finance and Monetary Policy in Western Europe, 1384–1410." *Business History Review* **43,** 374–376.

Van der Wee, H. (1977), "Monetary, Credit, and Banking Systems." In E. E. Rich and C. H. Wilson (Eds.), *Cambridge Economic History of Europe, Vol. V: The Economic Organization of Early Modern Europe*. Cambridge: Univ. Press. Pp. 290–393.

Van der Wee, H. (1978), "Prices and Wages as Development Variables: A Comparison between England and the Southern Netherlands, 1400–1700." *Acta Historiae Neerlandicae* **10,** 58–78.

Van Keymeulen, A. (1973), *Les trésors monétaires modernes trouvés en Belgique, 1434–1830*. Brussels: Cercle d'Etudes numismatiques.

Van Gelder, H. E., and Hoc, M. (1960), *Les monnaies des Pays-Bas bourguignons et espagnols, 1434–1713: Répertoire générale*. Amsterdam: J. Schulman.

Van Uytven, R. (1975), "Politiek en economie: de crisis der late XVe eeuw in de Nederlanden." *Revue belge de philologie et d'histoire* **53,** 1097–1149.

Van Werveke, H. (1949a), *De muntslag in Vlaanderen onder Lodewijk van Male* (Mededelingen van de koniklijke Vlaamse Academie voor Wetenschappen, Letteren, en Schone Kunsten, Klasse der Letteren, no. X:5). Brussels.

Van Werveke, H. (1949b), "Currency Manipulation in the Middle Ages: The Case of Louis de Male, Count of Flanders." *Transactions of the Royal Historical Society,* 4th ser. **31,** 115–127.

Verlinden, C., Craeybeckx, J., and Scholliers, E. (Eds.). (1959–1965), *Dokumenten voor de geschiedenis van prijzen en lonen in Vlaanderen en Brabant (XVe–XVIIIe eeuw),* 4 vols. Bruges: De Tempel.

INDEX

Note: Mints are included with their place-names in the following index, with the exception of the Calais and Tower mints, which are listed separately from the Calais Staple and London, respectively.